PUBLICATIONS
OF THE
NAVY RECORDS SOCIETY

Vol. IV.

INDEX
TO
JAMES' NAVAL HISTORY

INDEX

TO

James' Naval History

EDITION 1886

PREPARED BY
C. G. TOOGOOD

EDITED BY
T. A. BRASSEY

PRINTED FOR THE NAVY RECORDS SOCIETY
MDCCCXCV

THE COUNCIL

OF THE

NAVY RECORDS SOCIETY

1893-4-5

PATRONS

HIS ROYAL HIGHNESS THE DUKE OF SAXE-COBURG AND GOTHA, K.G., K.T. &c.

HIS ROYAL HIGHNESS THE DUKE OF YORK, K.G. &c.

PRESIDENT
EARL SPENCER, K.G.

VICE-PRESIDENTS
LORD GEORGE HAMILTON.   ADMIRAL SIR R. V. HAMILTON, K.C.B.
MARQUIS OF LOTHIAN, K.T.

COUNCILLORS

H.S.H. PRINCE LOUIS OF BATTENBERG, G.C.B.
WALTER BESANT.
HON. T. A. BRASSEY.
REAR-ADMIRAL BRIDGE.
OSCAR BROWNING.
PROFESSOR MONTAGU BURROWS.
REV. H. MONTAGU BUTLER, D.D.
LIEUT.-GEN. SIR A. CLARKE, G.C.M.G.
VICE-ADMIRAL COLOMB.
ADMIRAL SIR EDWARD FANSHAWE, G.C.B.
C. H. FIRTH.

DR. RICHARD GARNETT.
MAJOR-GEN. GEARY, R.A., C.B.
LORD PROVOST OF GLASGOW.
DAVID HANNAY.
SIDNEY LEE.
REAR-ADMIRAL SIR LAMBTON LORAINE, BART.
SIR ALFRED C. LYALL, K.C.B.
CLEMENTS R. MARKHAM, C.B., F.R.S.
CAPT. S. P. OLIVER, late R.A.
COMM. C. N. ROBINSON, R.N.
J. R. THURSFIELD.
CAPT. WHARTON, R.N., F.R.S.
CAPT. S. EARDLEY WILMOT, R.N.

SECRETARY
PROFESSOR J. K. LAUGHTON, King's College, London, W.C.

TREASURER
H. F. R. YORKE, Admiralty, S.W.

The COUNCIL of the NAVY RECORDS SOCIETY wish it to be distinctly understood that they are not answerable for any opinions or observations that may appear in the Society's publications. For these the responsibility rests entirely with the Editors of the several works.

PREFACE

THIS INDEX has been prepared by Mr. C. G. TOOGOOD under my supervision. Two years ago I wished to analyse all the actions of the Great War, both those between Fleets and those between two or more ships, with the view of arriving at some conclusion as to the influence of size on the results of these actions. Had an index to James' 'Naval History' been in existence much trouble would have been saved. I have great pleasure in presenting this Index to the Navy Records Society, and trust that it will be of service to other labourers in the same field.

T. A. BRASSEY.

PARKGATE, BATTLE:
   May 1895.

CONTENTS

		PAGE
Part I.	British and Foreign Ships	1
Part II.	Naval Officers	51
Part III.	Military Officers (including a few Names of Ambassadors, &c.)	176
Part IV.	Naval Actions	187

INDEX

TO

JAMES' NAVAL HISTORY

LIST OF ABBREVIATIONS

A. ....Admiral.	D.A.G. Deputy-Adjutant-General.	Neap. ...Neapolitan.
act. ......acting.		P.C. ......Post-Captain.
actn. ......action.	des. ......destroys.	Por. ......Portuguese.
Ad. ......Adjutant.	destd. ...destroyed.	Pr. ......Purser.
Ad.G. ...Adjutant-General.	drnd. ...drowned.	priv. ......privateer.
Algrn. ...Algerine.	Du. ......Dutch.	pro. ......promoted.
Amb. ...Ambassador.	E.I.C. ...East India Company.	R.A. ......Rear-Admiral.
App. ......Appendix.	exped. ...expedition.	Rds. ......Roads.
As. ......Assistant.	F. ....French.	recaptd. recaptured.
B. ....Boatswain.	Flt. ......Fleet.	recapts. recaptures.
bldg......building.	fndrd. ...foundered.	rprg......repairing.
blt. ......built.	fndrs. ...founders.	Rus......Russian.
Br. ......British.	F.S. ......fire ship.	S. ....Surgeon.
Brg. ......Brigadier, Brigade.	G. ....General.	Sard. ...Sardinian.
bts. ......boats.	gbts......gunboats.	Sig. ......Signalman.
C. ....Captain.	Gvr. ......Governor.	Sp. ......Spanish.
captd. ...captured.	invas. ...invasion.	Sq. ......Squadron.
capts. ...captures.	Ital. ......Italian.	S.S. ......store ship.
Car. ......Carpenter.	k. ....killed.	Swd.......Swedish.
Ck. ......Clerk.	kntd. ...knighted.	T.S. ......transport or troop ship.
cl. ....class.	L.Com. Lieutenant-Commander.	
Cmde. ...Commodore.	M.C. ...Captain Marines.	Turk. ...Turkish.
Com. ...Commanding.	M.L. ...Lieutenant Marines.	U.S. ......United States.
Cox ......Coxswain.	Mar.......Marshal.	V.A. ...Vice-Admiral.
Cr. ......Commander.	Medn. ...Mediterranean.	Ven. ......Venetian.
crsg......cruising.	Mid. ......Midshipman.	Vol. ......Volunteer.
d. ....died.	Mr. ......Master.	w. ....wounded.
Da. ......Danish.	Mt. ......Mate.	wrkd. ...wrecked.

PART I

BRITISH AND FOREIGN SHIPS

(*Note.*—The name of a captured ship is not repeated, but a fresh line is used to indicate her career under her new flag.)

Aboukir (74) .... VI. 117, Medn. Flt.
Acasta (40)............... VI. 99, crsg.; 247, Sq. Boston Bay; 253-6, in America.
Achates (16) .... VI. 135, crsg. with Dryad (36).
Achates (10) .... V. 445, wrkd. W. Indies.
Acheron (bomb.) ...... IV. 13-6, captd. by Hortense (40).
Achille (74) *F.* .... I. 60, 141, Brest Flt.; 163-8, captd. 1st June.
  ,, ,, *Br.* .... II. 285, Sq. off Brest. III. 384, Trafalgar; 416-7, capts. Berwick (74); 443, casualties. IV. 175, Sq. off Rochefort. V. 208, Medn. Flt. VI. 395, rprg.
Achille (74) *F.* .... III. 386-9, Trafalgar; 441-2, destd.
Acorn (18) .... V. 35-6, bts. cutting out exped.
Actif (10) .... I. 440, fndrd. off Bermuda.
Active (32) .... II. 456, wrkd. in St. Lawrence.

B

Active (38)	III. 175, 335, Nelson's Flt. IV. 215, Malta; 289, crsg. V. 233-44, actn. off Lissa; 263, capture of Pomone (40).
Adamant (50)	II. 75-6, Camperdown; 394, capture of Preneuse (40).
Adams (26) *U.S.*	VI. 386, destd. in Penobscot to avoid capture.
Adder (12)	IV. 461, captd. near Abreval, ashore.
Admiral Pasley (16)	III. 37-8, captd. by Sp. gbts.
Adolph Frederic (74) *Swd.*	IV. 299, Br. and Swd. Flt. Oro Rds.
Æolus (32)	IV. 3, 9, Strachan's actn.; 55-8, chases Didon.
Æolus (46)	VI. 395, bldg.
Affronteur *F.*	II. 5, Ireland exped.
Africa (64)	I. 369-70, actn. Da. gbts. III. 384, 428-32, Trafalgar. IV. 165, crsg.; 298, Baltic Flt.; 369-70, actn. Danish flotilla.
Africaine (40) *F.*	III. 127-9, captd. by Phœbe (36).
„ „ *Br.*	IV. 275, capture of Madeira. V. 173-8, captd. by the F.; 180-1, recaptd.; 203, capture of Isle of France.
Agamemnon (64)	I. 72, Medn. Flt.; 117-8, actn. with F. frigates; 284-90, actn. off Genoa; 343, Sq. off Genoa. III. 46-51, Copenhagen; 357-62, Calder's actn.; 384, 387, 432-43, Trafalgar. IV. 90-95, Duckworth's Sq. V. 441, wrkd. Rio de la Plata.
Agincourt (64)	II. 75, Camperdown. III. 175-8, Medn.
Aigle (38)	I. 305, Medn. II. 469, wrkd. off C. Farina, Spain.
Aigle (36)	III. 275-6, des. Charente (20). IV. 313-4, actn. with F. frigates; 400, Basque Rds.; 438, Scheldt exped. VI. 395, rprg.
Aigle (74) *F.*	III. 342, Medn.; 386, 407-14, Trafalgar; 440, captd.
Aimable (32)	I. 377-8, actn. with Pensée (36). II. 416-8, actn. with F. frigates. V. 2, capts. Iris (22).
Ajax (74) *F.*	IV. 444, Flt. Toulon Rds.
Ajax (74)	II. 285, Sq. off Brest; 301, Basque Rds. III. 81, Malta; 357-62, Calder's actn.; 384, 433-4, 443, Trafalgar. IV. 219, burnt Medn.
Akbar, *E.I.C.*	V. 430, becomes Cornwallis (44), afterwards T.S.
Alaart (16) *Da.*	IV. 209, captd. at Copenhagen. V. 441, recaptd. by Danish gbts. off Fredericksvaern.
Alacrity (18)	V. 248-9, captd. by Abeille (24).
Alarm (24) *Du.*	II. 347, captd. Holland exped.
Alarm (32)	I. 331-2, crsg. W. Indies. II. 110-11, capture of Trinidad.
Albacore (18)	III. 234, actn. invas. flotilla. VI. 7, engages Gloire (40).
Alban (10)	V. 445, captd. by Danish gbts.; 451, wrkd. near Aldborough.
Albanaise (14)	III. 477, captd. by mutiny off Malaga.
Albatross (18)	II. 337, Suez.
Albion (74)	VI. 278, Algiers; 365, Navarino.
Alceste (36) *Sard.*	I. 92, captd. by F. Boudeuse (36).
„ (36) *F.*	I. 282, Toulon. II. 295, captd. by Br. Flt.
Alceste (38), late Minerve (40)	IV. 275, capture of Madeira; 326, off Cadiz. V. 119, crew spike battery at Fréjus; 247-8, in actn. Parenza.
Alceste (46)	VI. 394, wrkd. in China Sea.
Alcide (74)	I. 72, Medn. Flt.; 94, Sq. off Corsica; 207-14, Corsica.
Alcide (74) *F.*	I. 72, 91, Toulon; 282, Toulon; 298, captd. off Hyères; 301, blows up.
Alcmène (32)	II. 215, capts. Légère (gbt.); 381, capts. Courageux (priv.). III. 46, Copenhagen. V. 441, wrkd. off Nantes.
Alcmène (40) *F.*	VI. 123, captd. by Venerable (74) off Madeira; 124, renamed Immortalité (38), q.v.
Alert (16)	I. 439, captd. by F. Unité (36).
Alert (16)	V. 365-6, captd. by U.S. Essex (32).
Alerte (14) *F.*	I. 91, Toulon; 325-6, Genoa. 433, recaptd. at retaking of Toulon. II. 295, captd. by Br. Flt.
Alexander (74)	I. 189, Sq. off Ushant; 203-4, captd. by F. Sq. off Sicily.
Alexander (74)	II. 171-2, 191, Nile.
Alexandre (74) *F.*	I. 274-303, recaptd. by Br. Flt. off L'Orient. [worth's actn.
Aelxandre (80) *F.*	III. 312, Brest Flt. IV. 88, Sq. W. Indies; 95-8, captd. Duck-

INDEX TO SHIPS

Alexandria (32) .... III. 93, late Régénérée. IV. 167, off Rio de la Plata. VI. 70-1, engages U.S. President (44).
Alfred (74) .... I. 65, Channel Flt.; 139, 162, 182, 185, actn. 1st June. II. 453, capts. Renommée (36). IV. 200, Copenhagen.
Alfred (36) *E.I.C.* ...... III. 250-3, actn. with F. Sq. under Linois.
Algerine (10) .... V. 226-8, actn. with Danish brigs. VI. 382, wrkd. W. Indies.
Algésiras (74) *F.* ...... III. 386, Trafalgar; 411, captd. ; 454, recaptd. IV. 295, captd. Cadiz by Spaniards.
Alkmaar (50) *Du.* ...... II. 76-9, captd. Copenhagen.
Alliance (36) *Du.* ...... I. 142, convoy escort ; 324-5, captd. by Br. Sq.
Alliance (74) *F.* .... II. 299, late Sp. San Sebastian (74), q.v. III. 312, Brest Flt.
Alligator (28) .... I. 126, capture of Isle St. Pierre. III. 296, capture of Surinam.
Alligator (28) .... VI. 396, bldg. 1820 ; 309, Burmese War, 1824.
Alphea (10) .... VI. 382, destd. in actn. with F. priv. Renard.
Alphonso Albuquerque (74) *Por.* II. 211, Niza's Sq. Medn.
Amaranthe (14) .... II. 378, capts. Vengeur (6) (priv.) ; 474, wrkd. Florida.
Amaranthe (18) .... IV. 381-2, actn. off St. Pierre.
Amazon (38) .... I. 357, Sq. crsg. off Ushant. II. 17, wrkd. off Isle Bas.
Amazon (38) .... III. 46, 51, Copenhagen ; 236, Medn. IV. 129-31, capts. Belle-Poule (40).
Amazon (46) .... VI. 395, bldg.
Amazone (36) *Du.* ...... I. 221, off Java. [consorts.
Amazone (40) *F.* ...... V. 107-8, actn. off Havre ; 211-2, destd. by Berwick (74) and
Ambuscade (32) *Du.* ... II. 76-9, captd. Camperdown ; 87, recaptd. ; 343, Sq. blockaded in the Texel.
Ambuscade (32) .... II. 273-5, captd. by Baïonnaise (28), renamed Embuscade (32), q.v. III. 176, recaptd. by Victory (100).
Amelia (38) .... I. 370, late Proserpine (40), q.v. II. 140, crsg. off Ireland ; 376-7, with F. frigate Sq. V. 27, off San Andero, Spain. VI. 37-41, actn. with Aréthuse (40).
America (74) *F.* .... I. 60, 105, crsg. W. Indies ; 141, 163, actn. 1st June ; 168, 172, captd.
America (64) *Sp.* ...... III. 342, Fr. Sp. Flt. Medn.
Amethyst (38) .... I. 443, wrkd. at Alderney.
Amethyst (36) .... IV. 91-3, Duckworth's Sq. ; 376-80, capts. Thétis (40); 438, Scheldt exped. V. 13-7, capts. Niemen (40) ; 447, wrkd . Plymouth Sound.
Améthyste (44) *F.* ...... V. 352-3, captd. by Southampton (38) ; 354, restored.
Amfitrite (40) *Sp.* ...... III. 493, captd. by Donegal (74).
Amgatten (74) *Rus.* ... IV. 298, actn. Oro Rds.
Amphion (32) .... II. 456, blows up in Hamoaze.
Amphion (32) .... III. 175, Sq. Medn.; 287, capture of Sp. treasure ships. IV. 344-5, actn. with Baleine (30). V. 9, crsg. Adriatic ; 233-44, actn. off Lissa.
Amphitrite (18) .... I. 439, wrkd. Medn.
Amphitrite (40) *Du.* ... II. 343, Sq. blockaded in the Texel.
Amphitrite (40) *F.* ...... V. 439, destd. at Martinique.
Amstel (40) *Du.* ...... VI. 279, Algiers.
Anacreon (18) .... VI. 387, fndrd. in the Channel.
Andromache (32) ...... II. 90, actn. with Algerine. VI. 14, capts. Trave (40).
Andromaque (36) *F.* ... I. 381-3, destd. by Warren's Sq.
Andromaque (40) *F.* ... V. 319-23, destd. by Northumberland (74) off L'Orient.
Andromeda (32) .... III. 17, Sq. off Dunkerque.
Annibal (74) *F.* .... III. 104, late Hannibal (74), q.v. ; 334, 339, Sq. Toulon. IV. 258, chases Spartan (38) ; 444, Flt. Toulon Rds.
Anson (44) .... I. 278, Sq. Quiberon exped.; 355-6, 381-3, Warren's frig. Sq. II. 106, capts. Daphne (20). IV. 114-5, engages Foudroyant (80) ; 169-70, capture of Sp. Pomona (34) ; 465, wrkd. off Helstone, Mount's Bay.
Antelope (50) .... III. 222-5, Sir Sidney Smith's Sq. off Ostende.

Apollo (38)	II. 474, wrkd. Holland.
Apollo (36)	III. 261-4, wrkd. Portugal.
Apollo (38)	V. 208, Medn. Flt. off Toulon.
Apollon (74) *F.*	I. 72-5, Toulon ; 426, renamed Gasparin (74), q.v.
Aquilon (74) *F.*	I. 60, Brest Flt. II. 178, 185, 188, Nile ; 197, captd. ; 208, broken up.
Aquilon (74) *F.*	III. 312, Brest Flt. IV. 391, Willaumez's Sq.; 401, 409, 414, actn. Basque Rds.; 416-7, destd.
Arab (16)	II. 456, wrkd. off Brest.
Arachne (18)	VI. 309, Burmese War.
Aran (74) *Swd.*	IV. 299, Br. and Swd. Flt. Oro Rds.
Ardent (64)	I. 72, Medn. Flt.; 94-6, Sq. off Corsica ; 439, blows up off Corsica.
Ardent (64)	II. 75, 79, 81, Camperdown ; 344, Holland exped. III. 46, 51, 55, Copenhagen. IV. 279, Sq. off Buenos Ayres.
Arethusa (38)	I. 222-4, frigate actn. ; 233, Warren's Sq. crsg. capture of Volontaire (36) ; 278, Quiberon exped. II. 110, Sq. off Trinidad. III. 142, crsg. IV. 169-70, capture of Sp. Pomona (34); 275, 277-9, capture of Curaçoa. V. 12, crsg. N. Spain.
Aréthuse (40) *F.*	I. 91, 92, 431, captd. at Toulon.
Aréthuse (40) *F.*	VI. 36-43, actn. with Amelia (38).
Argo (36) *Du.*	I. 324-5, escapes from Réunion (36) and consorts ; 363-4, captd. by Phœnix (36) and consorts.
Argo (44)	I. 304, convoy escort ; 357, Pellew's Sq. II. 231, Sq. off the Seine ; 359, capts. Sp. St. Teresa (34).
Argonauta (80) *Sp.*	III. 112, actn. in Gut of Gibraltar ; 342, Toulon Flt.; 374, Medn. ; 386, 388-9, 416-7, Trafalgar ; 457, destd.
Argonaute (74) *F.*	III. 386, 415-16, Trafalgar. IV. 295, captd. by Sp. at Cadiz.
Argus (20) *U.S.*	VI. 78-81, captd. by Pelican (18).
Argus (50) *Rus.*	IV. 298, actn. Oro Rds.
Ariadne (20)	III. 319, off Gravelines watching invas. flotilla.
Arienne (40) *F.*	V. 319-23, destd. by Northumberland (74) off L'Orient.
Armada (74)	VI. 117, Medn. Flt.
Armide (40) *F.*	IV. 48, engages Calcutta (54) ; 79, Sq. at Dominique ; 175-7, captd. by Br. Sq. off Rochefort.
,, (38) *Br.*	VI. 231-2, off Chandeleur Isles ; 365, Navarino.
Arrogant (74)	I. 189, Sq. off Ushant ; 333, Sq. Cape of Good Hope ; 390-3, actn. with F. Sq.
Arrogante (74) *Sp.*	II. 110, destd. to avoid capture, Trinidad.
Arrow (28)	II. 388, Holland exped. IV. 13-7, captd. by Hortense (40) and Incorruptible (38).
Artémise (36) *F.*	I. 282, Sq. at Toulon ; 321-4, frigate actn. II. 178, Nile ; 193, captd. (burnt).
Artémise (40) *F.*	IV. 471, destd. by Br. Sq. off Brest.
Artois (38)	I. 233, Warren's Sq.; 235, capts. with Diamond (38) Révolutionnaire (40) ; 278, Quiberon exped.; 355-6, 381-3, Warren's Sq. crsg. II. 462, wrkd. coast of France.
Arve Prindts (80) *Da.*	IV. 464, captd. at Copenhagen.
Asia (64)	I. 240, capture of Martinique.
Asia (84)	VI. 364, Navarino ; 395-6, bldg. (1820).
Assistance (50)	I. 385, Murray's Sq.. III. 485, wrkd. off Dunkerque.
Astræa (32)	I. 315-6, capts. Gloire (36). IV. 473, wrkd. W. Indies.
Astrea (36)	V. 283-94, late F. Astrée, actn. off Madagascar. VI. 124-7, actn. with Etoile (40).
Astrée (36) *F.*	I. 331, exped. to Guadaloupe. V. 137-8, Isle of France ; 165-205, captd. Port Louis, Isle of France.
Atalante, *F.*	II. 5, brig, corvette, Ireland exped.
Atalante (74) *Sp.*	II. 36, St. Vincent.
Atalante (16)	III. 142, crsg. Quiberon Bay ; 194, off St. Guildas. IV. 175, Hood's Sq. off Rochefort ; 466, wrkd. Rochefort.
Atalante (16) *Du.*	III. 265, captd. by Scorpion (18) and Beaver (14).
Atalante (18)	VI. 381, wrkd. Halifax.

INDEX TO SHIPS

Atalante (36) F..........	I. 227-8, captd. by Swiftsure (74), renamed Espion, q.v.
Atalante (40) F..........	III. 283-4, frigate actn. VI. 145-6, actn. with Majestic (56).
Athénien (64) F.	II. 445, captd. at surrender of Malta.
,, ,, Br.	IV. 123, Sq. at Palermo ; 461, wrkd. near Tunis.
Atlas (74) F.	III. 176, 334, Toulon Flt. IV. 471, captd. by the Sp. at Vigo.
Attack (12)	IV. 287, off Rochefort. V. 451, captd. by Da. gbts. off Foreness.
Audacieux (74) F.......	I. 60, Brest Flt.; 141-8, actn. 28th May. IV. 432, renamed Pulstuck (74), q.v.
Audacious (74)	I. 62, 139, Channel Flt.; 146-7, engages Révolutionnaire (110), 28th May ; 148, Plymouth. II. 171, 183-8, Nile ; 197, casualties. IV. 116, Sq. Barbadoes ; 439, Scheldt exped.
Auguste (80) F.	I. 60, Flt. Quiberon Bay.
Aurora (46)...............	VI. 138, late F. Clorinde (40), q.v.
Aurora (46)...............	VI. 395, bldg.
Aurore (36) F.	I. 432, captd. at Toulon.
Austerlitz (130) F.......	IV. 444, Flt. Toulon Rds.
Autumn (16)	III. 173, crsg. off Calais.
Avenger (14)	III. 490, fndrd. off the Weser.
Avenger (16)	V. 450, wrkd. Newfoundland.
Avon (18)	V. 93-4, engages Néréide (40). VI. 165-6, destd. in actn. with U.S. Wasp (20).
Azof (74) Rus.	VI. 365, Navarino.
Babet (20) F.............	I. 222-6, captd. by Warren's Sq. off Isle Bas. III. 482, fndrd. W. Indies.
Bacchante (18) F.	III. 180, captd. by Endymion (40).
Bacchante (20)	IV. 28, 170, crsg. W. Indies ; 243, crsg., capture of Dauphin (12) ; 342, capts. Griffon (16).
Bacchante (38)	V. 349-50, crsg., bts. off Rovigno. VI. 21-4, Adriatic ; 119, surrender of Cattaro.
Bacchus (10)	IV. 475, captd. Leeward Isles.
Badere-Zaffer(44) Turk.	IV. 350-4, captd. by Seahorse (38).
Badine (28) F.	I. 282, Perrée's Sq.; 305-6, Medn.
Bahama (74) Sp.	II. 36, St. Vincent ; 299, Flt. Cadiz. III 386, 389, 415-6, Trafalgar, captd.
Baïonnaise (28) F.	II. 273-5, capts. Ambuscade (32). III. 489, destd. in actn. with Ardent (64).
Banel (64) F.	II. 288, at Toulon.
Banterer (22)	IV. 473, wrkd. in the St. Lawrence.
Barbadoes (28)	III. 351, convoy escort. V. 216, actn. with gun-brigs off Cherbourg; 450, wrkd. Sable Island.
Barbara (10)	IV. 467, captd. by Général Ernouf (priv.), W. Indies.
Barfleur (98)	I. 139, Channel Flt.; 162, 167, 176-7, 1st June ; 271, 274, Isle Groix. II. 34, 38, 48, St. Vincent ; 289, Flt. off Cadiz. III. 356, 358-62, Calder's actn. VI. 117, Medn. Flt.
Barracouta (18)	V. 195, capture of Banda Neira.
Barras (74) F.	I. 91, 282, Toulon Flt.
Batave (74) F.	II. 286, Brest Flt. III. 312, Brest Flt.
Batavier (50) Du.	II. 76-8, Camperdown ; 343, blockaded in the Texel ; 472, captd.
Bato (64) Du.	IV. 460, destd. by Du. at Cape of Good Hope.
Beagle (18)...............	IV. 400, actn. Basque Rds.
Béarnais (16) F.........	V. 46, captd. by Melampus, renamed Curieux.
Beaulieu (40)	I. 240, capture of Martinique ; 410-11, capture of St. Vincent. II. 75, Camperdown.
Beaver (14)...............	III. 265, cutting out Atalante (16).
Bedford (74)	I. 72, Flt. at Toulon ; 96, Genoa ; 214, Sq. Corsica ; 284-90, actn. off Genoa ; 431, capture of Modeste (36). II. 75-9, Camperdown. IV. 236, Sq. off the Tagus.
Belette (28) F.	I. 432, captd. at Toulon.
Belette (18)...............	V. 450, wrkd. Isle Lessoe.

Belle Antoinette (44) *Du.* — II. 347, captd. in Nieuve Diep, Texel.
Belleisle (74) — I. 277, late F. Formidable (74), q.v. III. 175, 335, Nelson's Flt.; 384, 406-9, Trafalgar. IV. 116-7, W. Indies.
Belle-Poule (40) *F.* — IV. 50-2, actn. with Blenheim (74); 129-31, captd. by Warren's Sq.
„ „ (38) *Br.* — V. 9-10, capts. Var (28); 247-8, actn. at Parenza.
Bellerophon (74) — I. 65, Channel Sq.; 139, 144-6, 28th May; 149-53, 29th May; 162, 168-71, 1st June; 262-9, Cornwallis' Sq. II. 171, 183, 186-9, 195-7, Nile; 292, Medn. III. 384, 393, 413-5, Trafalgar; 443, casualties. V. 40, Sq. crsg. Baltic.
Belliqueux (64) — I. 251, capture of St. Domingo. II. 75, 80-1, Camperdown; 344-7, Holland exped. III. 22, capts. Concorde (40). IV. 180-1, capture of Du. Phœnix (32); 186, at Cape of Good Hope.
Bellona (74) — I. 65, Channel Flt.; 189, Sq. off Ushant; 331-2, W. Indies; 441, capts. Duquesne (36). II. 109-10, capture of Sp. Sq. Trinidad; 293, Medn. Sq. III. 46-54, Copenhagen. IV. 3, Strachan's Sq.; 4, parts company; 89, Strachan's Sq.; 116-7, capture of Impétueux (74); 396, 411, actn. Basque Rds.
Bellona (24) *Du.* — I. 416-7, Sq. captd. at Cape of Good Hope.
Bellona (42) *Swd.* — IV. 299, Br. and Swd. Flt. Oro Rds.
Bellona (32) *Ven.* — V. 122, F. Sq. Adriatic; 233-8, actn. off Lissa, captd.; 245, renamed Dover, q.v.
Bellone (36) *F.* — I. 148, 29th May. II. 5, Ireland exped.; 139, Bompart's Sq.; 144-7, captd. by Ethalion (38); 162, laid up.
Bellone (40) *F.* — V. 53-4, crsg. E. Indies; 65, capts. Victor (18); 66, capts. Por. Minerva (52); 131-7, capture of Indiamen; 157-205, captd. Isle of France.
Belvidera (36) — V. 357-61, actn. with U.S. President (44).
Benbow (74) — VI. 395, rprg.
Bermuda (14) — II. 457, fndrd. Gulf of Florida.
Bermuda (18) — I. 385, Murray's Sq. IV. 473, wrkd. Little Bermuda.
Bermuda (10) — VI. 394, wrkd. Gulf of Mexico.
Berwick (74) — I. 72, Flt. at Toulon; 214, Medn. Flt.; 283, captd. by F. Flt.
„ „ *F.* — III. 176, Toulon Sq.; 334, Villeneuve's Sq.; 386, 417, re-captd. at Trafalgar; 457, wrkd.
Berwick (74) — V. 211-2, des. Amazone (40). VI. 117, Medn. Flt.
Beschermer (50) *Du.* — II. 76-80, Camperdown; 343-8, Sq. captd. in the Texel.
Beyrand (64) *F.* — II. 288, at Ancona.
Bienvenue (28) *F.* — I. 241-5, captd. at Martinique, renamed Undaunted (28), q.v.
Biter (12) — IV. 457, wrkd. near Calais.
Blagodath (120) *Rus.* — IV. 298, actn. in Oro Rds.
Blake (74) — IV. 439, Scheldt exped.
Blanche (32) — I. 308, W. Indies; 309-13, capts. Pique (36); 343, Nelson's Sq. Medn.; 406-8, actn. with Sp. Ceres (40). III. 46-55, Copenhagen; 291, at Curaçoa. IV. 38-9, captd. by Topaze (40) and consorts; 43-4, sinks.
Blanche (38) — IV. 160-2, capts. Guerrière (40); 465, wrkd. off Ushant.
Blanche (T.S.) — II. 475, wrkd. in the Texel.
Blazer (12) — III. 482, captd. in the Baltic, restored.
Blenheim (98) — II. 34, 38-49, St. Vincent.
Blenheim (74) — III. 201, Martinique; 255, St. Pierre. IV. 51, actn. with Marengo (74); 465, fndrd. in E. Indies.
Blonde (28) *F.* — I. 432, captd. by Latona (38) and Phæton (38), 1793.
„ (32) *Br.* — I. 240, capture of Martinique.
Blonde (38) — V. 50-2, Guadaloupe.
Blossom (18) — V. 128, bts. cutting out exped.
Boadicea (38) — II. 139-40, off Brest. IV. 3, chases F. Sq. V. 171-2, Isle of France; 187, capts. Vénus (40); 203, capture of the Isle of France.
Bold (12) — VI. 382, wrkd. Prince Edward's Island.
Bombay (74) — V. 208, Medn. Flt.

INDEX TO SHIPS

Bombay (84) .... VI. 395, bldg.
Bombay Castle (74) ... I. 354, wrkd. in the Tagus.
Bombay Castle (36) *E.I.C.* III. 22-3, assists in capture of Médée (36); 250-4, actn. with Linois' Sq. E. Indies.
Bonetta (18) .... III. 482, wrkd. Cuba.
Bonne-Citoyenne (20) *F.* I. 387, captd. by Br. Sq., added to Br. Navy.
„ „ (18) *Br.* II. 34-7, 44, St. Vincent. V. 23-6, capts. Furieuse (20).
Bonnet Rouge (80) *F.* I. 213, late Couronne (80), q.v.
Bordelais (24) .... III. 124-5, capts. and des. Curieux (18).
Boreas (22) .... IV. 465, wrkd. near Guernsey.
Boreas (74) *Rus.* ...... IV. 298, actn. in Oro Rds.
Borée (74) *F.* .... IV. 444, Flt. in Toulon Rds.
Boscawen (80) .... VI. 395, bldg.
Boston (32) *U.S.* ...... III. 32, capts. F. Berceau (22).
Boston (32) .... I. 110-14, actn. with Embuscade (36).
Bouncer (12) .... IV. 457, wrkd. off Dieppe.
Bourbonnaise (38) ...... V. 173, late F. Caroline (40), q.v.
Boxer (12) .... VI. 75-7, captd. by U.S. Enterprise (14).
Boyne (98) .... I. 240, capture of Martinique; 317, burnt at Spithead.
Boyne (98) .... VI. 117-8, Medn. Flt.
Braak (16) .... II. 469, fndrd. in the Delaware.
Braakel (54) *Du.* ...... I. 307, captd. in Plymouth Sound.
Braave (40) *Du.* ...... I. 416-7, Sq. captd. at Cape of Good Hope.
Brave, rasé (50) *F.* ... I. 56, armament of; 264, Brest Flt.
Brave (74) *F.* .... IV. 88, 94-100, captd. by Duckworth's Sq.
Brave (74) .... IV. 12, late Formidable (80), q.v.; 461, fndrd. off Jamaica.
Bravoure (36) *F.* ...... II. 5, Ireland exped.; 280, W. Indies. III. 69, Sq. Egypt exped.; 98-9, destd. by Sq. off Vado.
Brazen (18) .... III. 477, wrkd. near Brighton.
Breslau (74) *F.* .... IV. 444, Flt. in Toulon Rd. VI. 365, Navarino.
Bretagne (110) *F.* ...... I. 60, Flt. Quiberon Bay.
Brevdrageren (14) *Da.* IV. 209, captd. at Copenhagen.
„ (12) *Br.* V. 227-8, actn. with Da. g. brigs.
Brilliant (28) .... II. 250-1, actn. with Régénérée (36).
Brilliant (74) *F.* .... VI. 119, captd. at surrender of Genoa, renamed Genoa (74), q.v.
Briseis (10) .... V. 103-4, capts. Sans-Souci (10), (priv.); 327, Pillau Rds., Baltic. VI. 394, wrkd. off Point Pedras.
Brisk (10) .... VI. 365, Navarino.
Britannia (100) .... I. 72, Medn. Flt. at Toulon; 213, Corsica; 284, 291, actn. off Genoa. II. 34, 38-48, St. Vincent. III. 384, 433-4, Trafalgar; 443, casualties.
Britomart (10) .... VI. 278, Algiers.
Broderchap (50) *Du.*... II. 347, Sq. captd. in the Texel.
Brune (28) *F.* .... I. 282, Perrée's Sq.; 325-6, Genoa. II. 471, captd. at Corfu.
Brunswick (74) .... I. 72, Channel Flt.; 139, 162, 166, 178-82, 1st June; 262-9, Cornwallis' Sq. IV. 200, Copenhagen; 298, Baltic Flt.
Brutus (74) *Du.* .... II. 76-9, Camperdown; 87-8, actn. with Endymion (40).
Brutus, rasé (50) *F.* ... I. 56, armament of; 230, Sq. in actn. off Guernsey.
Bucentaure (80) *F.* ... III. 334, Villeneuve's Sq.; 386, 427, captd. Trafalgar; 454, wrkd.
Bucephalus (36) .... V. 303-5, capture of Java.
Bulldog (bomb.) ...... III. 482, captd. at Ancona.
Bulwark (74) .... V. 312, Medn. Sq. VI. 200, Penobscot exped.
Bustard (16) .... V. 35-6, bts. cutting out exped.
Bustler (12) .... V. 442, wrkd. France.
Busy (18) .... IV. 465, fndrd. off Halifax.

Ça-Ira (80) *F.* .... I. 282, Toulon Flt.; 286-90, captd. by Hotham's Sq. off Genoa.
„ (80) *Br.* .... II. 456, destd. by fire in San Fiorenzo Bay.
Cæsar (80) .... III. 104, Algesiras; 116, actn. in Gut of Gibraltar.
Calcutta (54) .... IV. 46-9, captd. by Allemand's Sq. off Sicily.

Calcutta, en flûte (50) *F.*	IV. 395, 401, 409–13, recaptd. in actn. Basque Rds.
Caledonia (120)	IV. 395, 403–11, 420–2, actn. Basque Rds. V. 207, Medn. Flt. VI. 117, Medn. Flt.
Calliope (28) *F.*	II. 95, destd. by Warren's Sq.
Calliope (10)	V. 104, capts. Comtesse d'Hambourg (14), (priv.)
Calpé (14)	III. 112, 114, actn. in Gut of Gibraltar.
Calypso (36) *F.*	I. 128, Royalist frigate, Martinique.
Calypso (40) *F.*	IV. 393–4, destd. by Stopford's Sq.
Calypso (16)	III. 14, capts. Diligente (6); 490, fndrd. off Jamaica.
Calypso (18)	V. 325–6, with consorts des. Da. Sq.
Cambrian (40)	IV. 36–7, capts. Matilda (10); 146, crsg. off New York
,, (48)	VI. 365, 373, Navarino.
Cambridge (80)	IV. 212, bldg.
Camel, en flûte (44) ...	II. 390–2, actn. with Preneuse (36).
Cameleon (12)	VI. 274–5, actn. with Algrn. Tripoli (20).
Camilla (20)	IV. 44, capture of Faune (16); 387, Guadaloupe.
Camilla (42) *Swd.*	IV. 299, Br. and Swd. Flt. Oro. Rds.
Canada (74)	I. 203–4, actn. with F. Sq. II. 228–9, Warren's Sq.; 297, Medn. Flt.
Canonnière (40) *F.*, late Minerve (38) q.v.	IV. 143–5, actn. with Tremendous (74); 146, Simon's Bay; 363–5, capts. Laurel (22), renamed Confiance, q.v.
Canopus (80)	II. 209, late Franklin (80), q.v. III. 177, Medn. Flt.; 335, Nelson's Flt. IV. 90–101, Duckworth's actn.; 178, Louis' Sq.; 214–5, Malta; 292, Sq. at Syracuse; 445, off Barcelona.
Captain (74)	I. 72, Flt. at Toulon; 96, Genoa; 214, Medn.; 284–91, actn. off Genoa; 431, capts. Impérieuse (38). II. 34, 38, 42–50, St. Vincent; 293, Medn.; 450–1, capture of Ferrol. III. 36, crsg., Réolaise (20) destd. IV. 200, Copenhagen; 275, capture of Madeira. V. 18, W. Indies. VI. 381, burnt in Hamoaze.
Carmagnole (40) *F.* ...	I. 121, capture of Thames (32). III. 17–8, Dunkerque.
Carmen (32) *Sp.*	III. 13–4, captd. by Leviathan (74).
Carnatic (74)	I. 378, crsg. W. Indies.
Carnatic (74)	VI. 395–6, bldg.
Carnation (18)	IV. 331, captd. by F. Palinure (16).
Carnation (18)	VI. 223–4, actn. with U.S. General Armstrong (7) (priv.).
Caroline (36)	IV. 179–80, capts. Du. Maria-Riggersbergen (36); 282–4, capture of Gressie. V. 66, Persian Gulf; 295, Java exped.
Caroline (40) *F.*	V. 53–5, capts. Indiamen; 59–60, captd. at St. Paul's, Isle Bourbon; 61, renamed Bourbonnaise (38), q.v.
Carrère (38) *F.*	III. 78, captd. by Br. Sq.
Carthagénaise (36) *F.* ...	II. 445, captd. at surrender of Malta.
Carysfort (28)	I. 228–9, recapts. Castor (32).
Cassandra (10)	IV. 467, fndrd. Heligoland.
Cassard (74) *F.*	II. 5, Ireland exped. III. 312, Brest Flt. IV. 88, Sq. W. Indies; 117, Rochefort; 395, 401, 408–20, actn. Basque Rds.
Casthor (40) *Du.*	I. 416–7, captd. at Cape of Good Hope.
Castor (32)	I. 142, captd. by F. Sq.
,, ,, *F.*	I. 228–9, recaptd. by Carysfort (28).
,, ,, *Br.*	V. 21, assists at capture of D'Haupoult (74).
Causse (64) *F.*	II. 288, Alexandria. III. 93, captd. at Alexandria.
Censeur (74) *F.*	I. 73, 90, Toulon; 213, Toulon Flt.; 282, 287–90, captd. in actn. off Genoa.
,, ,, *Br.*	I. 295, Leghorn; 303–4, recaptd. by F. Sq. off St. Vincent.
,, ,, *F.*	II. 286, Brest Flt.; 295, 299, Cadiz.
Centaur (74)	II. 292, Medn.; 294–5, capture of Junon (38); 473, des. Sp. Guadalupe (34). III. 244–7, Diamond Rock occupied, cuts out Curieux (16); 296–7, capture of Surinam. IV. 89, Strachan's Sq.; 157, Sq. off Rochefort; 175–7, capture of F. frigates; 200, Copenhagen; 275, capture of Madeira; 298–302, capts. and des. Rus. Sewolod (74), with Implacable (74). VI. 121, actn. in the Gironde.

Centaure (74) *F.*	I. 72, 92, destd. at Toulon.
Centurion (50)	I. 226, crsg. E. Indies ; 236-8, actn. with Cybèle (40). III. 282-5, actn. with F. Sq.
Cephalus (18)	V. 255, crsg. cutting out exped. Civita-Vecchia.
Cerbère (10)	III. 494, wrkd. off Berry Head.
Cerberus (64) *Du.*	II. 76, 78, Camperdown ; 343, captd. by Br. Sq. in the Texel.
Cerberus (32)	II. 102, capts. Epervier (16) (priv.) ; 404-5, engages Sp. frigates. III. 172-3, invas. flotilla. IV. 387, Guadaloupe. V. 120, crsg. Gulf of Trieste ; 232, crsg. N. Italy.
Cerberus (40)	VI. 395, bldg.
Ceres (40) *Sp.*	I. 407-8, actn. with Blanche (32).
Cérès (40) *F.*	VI. 131-2, captured by Br. frigates.
César (16)	IV. 466, wrkd. on coast of Gironde.
Ceylon (32)	V. 183-90, captd. by F. Vénus (40), but recaptd. same day ; 203, at capture of Isle of France.
Challenger (16)	V. 447, captd. off Isle of France.
Chameleon (10)	VI. 396, bldg.
Champion (22)	III. 324, actn. with invas. flotilla.
Chapman (44) *Swd.*	IV. 299, Br. Swd. Flt. Oro Rds.
Charente (36) *F.*	I. 203, Nielly's Sq. II. 5, Ireland exped.; 228-9, chased by Br. Sq.; 472, wrkd. off L'Orient.
Chasseur(priv.)(14)*U.S.*	VI. 247, capts. St. Lawrence (12).
Chatham (74)	IV. 441, built of timbers brought from Flushing.
Cherub (18)	VI. 150-3, assists in capture of U.S. Essex (32).
Chesapeake (36) *U.S.*	IV. 249, Hampton Rds.; 250-5, actn. with Leopard (50). VI. 50-69, captd. by Shannon (38).
Chevrette (20) *F.*	III. 137-41, captd. by cutting out.
Chichester (S.S.)	V. 448, wrkd. in Madras Rds.
Chichester (60)	VI. 395, bldg.
Chiffonne (36) *F.*	III. 131-2, captd. by Sibylle (38).
,, ,, *Br.*	III. 316-17, actn. with invas. flotilla. V. 66, crsg. in Persian Gulf.
Childers (14)	II. 255-6, crsg. off Isle Bas. IV. 315-7, actn. with Da. Lougen (20). VI. 231, off Chandeleur Isles.
Christian VII. (80) *Da.*	IV. 212, captd. at Copenhagen, model for Cambridge (80).
Cigogne (20) *F.*	I. 356-7, skirmish off Brest.
Circe (28)	II. 75, Camperdown. III. 490, wrkd. in the North Sea.
Circe (32)	IV. 332, capts. Palinure (16) ; 380-1, actn. off St. Pierre.
Circe (46)	VI. 395, bldg.
Cisalpin (74) *F.*	II. 286, Brest Flt.
Citoyenne - Française (32) *F.*	I. 101-3, actn. with Iris (32).
Clara (34) *Sp.*	III. 287-8, captured by Br. Sq.
Claudia (10)	V. 442, wrkd. Norway.
Cléopâtre (36) *F.*	I. 105-8, captd. by Nymphe (36) ; 109, renamed Oiseau, q.v.
Cléopâtre (32)	IV. 20-3, recaptd. by Ville de Milan (40) ; 24-6, recaptd. by Leander (50). V. 3-4, at capture of Topaze (40).
Clinker (12)	III. 316-7, actn. with invas. flotilla. IV. 461, fndrd. off Havre.
Clorinde (40) *F.*	III. 205-6, captd. at St. Domingo.
,, (38) *Br.*	V. 203, capture of the Isle of France.
Clorinde (40) *F.*	V. 47-9, capture of Junon (38); 283-91, actn. off Madagascar ; 293, chased into Brest. VI. 133-8, captd. by Eurotas (38) and Dryad (36), late Aurora, q.v.
Clyde (38)	II. 384-5, capts. Vestale (36). IV. 265, crsg. coast of France.
Clyde (46)	VI. 395, bldg.
Cocarde (36) *F.*	I. 264, Brest Flt. II. 5, Ireland exped. ; 280, L'Orient.
Colibri (18)	V. 368-9, off New York. VI. 381, wrkd. at Port Royal, Jamaica.
Colombe (16) *F.*	III. 9-10, capts. Danaé (20).
Colossus (74)	I. 72, Medn. Flt.; 189, Sq. off Ushant ; 271-5, actn. off Isle Groix; 315, Colpoy's Sq. II. 34-40, 47-8, St. Vincent ; 469, wrkd. Sicily.

Colossus (74)	III. 384-9, 415-6, Trafalgar; 443, casualties. IV. 288, Sq. at Palermo.
Comet (F.S.)	III. 477, destd. Dunkerque Rds.
Comet (18)	IV. 371-2, capts. Sylphe (16).
Commerce de Bordeaux (74) *F*.	I. 72, Toulon Flt.; 91, captd. at Toulon.
Commerce de Marseille (120) *F*.	I. 72, Toulon Flt.; 91, captd. at Toulon; 281, used as S.S.
Commerce de Paris (120) *F*.	IV. 444, Flt. in Toulon Rd.
Comus (22)	IV. 203-4, capts. Da. Frederickscoarn (32); 244-5, cutting out [exped.
Comus (32)	VI. 393, wrkd. Newfoundland.
Concepcion (112) *Sp*....	II. 36, St. Vincent; 299, Fr. Sp. Flt. at Cadiz.
Conception (74) *F*. ...	I. 141, Brest Flt.
Concorde (36)	I. 189, Sq. off Ushant; 222-5, capture of Pomone (40) by Warren's Sq.; 278, Quiberon exped.; 357, Pellew's Sq. III. 69-70, actn. with Bravoure (36).
Concorde, La (40) *F*....	I. 105, capts. Hyæna (24). II. 137-8, Ireland exped. III. 22-3, captd. by Belliqueux (64).
Condé de Henrique (74) *Por*.	I. 202, Br. and Por. Flt. in the Channel.
Conde de Regla (112) *Sp*.	II. 36, St. Vincent; 299, F. Sp. Flt. at Cadiz.
Confiance (18)	IV. 237, Lisbon; 264-5, bts. cut out Reitrada (3) (priv.). V. 73-7, capture of Cayenne.
Confiance (37)	VI. 213-6, in Lake Champlain; 217-20, captd. by U.S. Sq.
Confiance (14) *F*.	V. 97, late Cannonière (40), captd. by Valiant (74).
Confiante (36) *F*.	II. 134-6, destd. by Hydra (38) and consorts.
Conflagration (F.S.) ...	I. 88, destd. at Toulon to prevent capture.
Conflict (12)	III. 400, actn. Basque Rds.; 494, wrkd. off the Isle of Wight.
Conflict (12)	V. 445, fndrd. in Bay of Biscay.
Congress (36) *U.S.*......	V. 356-60, Rogers' Sq.; 407, chases Galatea (36); 408, Boston. VI. 73, laid up at Portsmouth, U.S.
Conquérant (74) *F*. ...	I. 73, rprg. at Toulon; 91-2, left at Toulon; 282, Toulon Flt. II. 178-87, captd. at the Nile; 197-207, broken up at Plymouth.
Conquérant (74) *F*. ...	III. 312, Brest Flt.
Conqueror (74)	III. 335, Nelson's Flt.; 384, 393, 427-9, Trafalgar; 443, casualties. IV. 157-8, Sq. crsg. off Rochefort; 236, Sq. off the Tagus. V. 208, Medn. Flt.
Conquistador (74) *Sp*.	II. 36, St. Vincent; 299, F. Sp. Flt. at Cadiz.
Constance (22) *F*.	II. 91, captd. by San Fiorenzo (36) and Nymphe (36).
,, ,, Br. ...	IV. 172-4, recaptd. in Bay of Erqui, goes ashore.
Constant (12)............	VI. 11, crsg. off Bayonne.
Constantine (50) *Rus*.	VI. 365, Navarino; 373, casualties.
Constellation (36) *U.S.*	II. 363-4, capts. F. Insurgente (36). III. 1-3, actn. with F. Vengeance (40).
Constitutie (44) *Du*. ...	II. 347, captd. in the Nieueve Diep, Texel.
Constitution (74) *F*. ...	II. 5, Ireland exped.; 286, Brest Flt. III. 68-9, Sq. Egypt exped.
Constitution (44) *U.S.*	V. 370-1, chased by Br. Sq.; 372-84, capts. and des. Guerrière (38); 408-19, capts. and des. Java (38); 421, Boston. VI. 197-8, capts. Picton (16); 199, meeting with Pique (36); 200, escapes from Junon (38) and Tenedos (38); 247-50, capts. Cyane (20) and Levant (22); 252-6, escapes from Br. Sq.; 257, Boston.
Contest (14)	II. 474, wrkd. Holland.
Contest (12)	IV. 400, actn. Basque Rds. V. 442, fndrd. America.
Convention (74) *F*. ...	II. 286, Brest. Flt.
Convert (32)	I. 439, wrkd. W. Indies.
Coquille (36) *F*.	I. 356-7 Frigate Sq. crsg. II. 139, Ireland exped.; 144-6, captd. by Warren's Sq.; 148, casualties.
Corceyre (26) *F*.	V. 260-1, armed en flûte, captd. by Eagle (74).
Cordelia (10)	VI. 278, Algiers; 288, casualties.
Cormorant (18)	II. 456, accidentally blows up at St. Domingo.

INDEX TO SHIPS

Cormorant (20)	II. 473, with Centaur des. Sp. Guadalupe (34), Medn. III. 477, wrkd. Egypt.
Cornelia (32)	V. 204, capture of the Isle of France.
Cornélie (40) *F.*	III. 334, Toulon Flt.; 386, Trafalgar. IV. 295, captd. by Sp. at Cadiz.
Cornète (36) *F.*	III. 312, Brest Flt. IV. 88, Leissegues' Sq. crsg. Jamaica.
Cornwallis (74)	VI. 266, chases U.S. Hornet (20).
Cornwallis (74)	VI. 396, bldg. 1820.
Cornwallis (40)	IV. 357-8, Isle of France. V. 203, capture of the Isle of France.
Corona (40) *Ven.*	V. 122, Dubourdieu's Sq. crsg., Adriatic ; 238, captd. in actn. off Lissa; 245, renamed Dædalus (38), q.v.
Corso (18)	III. 136-7, crsg. Gulf of Venice.
Côte d'Or (120) *F.*	I. 60, Flt. in Quiberon Bay.
Courageuse (36) *F.*	I. 91-2, left at Toulon. II. 295, captd. by Br. Sq. Medn.
Courageux (74)	I. 72, 88, Flt. off Toulon ; 94, Sq. at Corsica ; 284, 288-9, actn. off Genoa ; 351, wrkd. in Straits of Gibraltar.
Courageux (74)	II. 450-2, capture of Ferrol. IV. 3-9, Strachan's actn. ; 89, Warren's Sq. crsg.
Courier (14) *F.*	I. 236-8, Sq. actn. with Centurion (50).
Courier (12)	II. 413-4, capts. Guerrier (14) (priv.).
Couronne (80) *F.*	I. 73, rprg. Toulon ; 92, left at Toulon ; 213, Toulon Sq. crsg., renamed Bonnet Rouge (80), q.v.
Crafty (10)	IV. 467, captd. by privs. Straits of Gibraltar.
Crane (18)	VI. 317, fndrd. in W. Indies.
Crash (12)	II. 469, captd. Holland.
Créole (40) *F.*	III. 69, Sq. Egypt exped.; 182, captd. by Br.Sq. St. Domingo.
,, (38) *Br.*	III. 182, fndrd. off Jamaica.
Creole (36)	VI. 124-7, actn. with F. frigates.
Crescent (36)	I. 114-6, capts. Réunion (36) ; 230-1, escapes from F. Sq. II. 412-3, capts. Sp. Galgo (16). IV. 473, wrkd. Jutland.
Crown (64)	I. 131, Madras, E. Indies.
Cruiser (18)	III. 171, chases F. gbts. on shore ; 222-4, actn. off Ostende. IV. 205, Copenhagen ; 369, actn. with Da. flotilla.
Culloden (74)	I. 206, Mutiny at Spithead. II. 34-45, St. Vincent ; 49, casualties ; 63, Santa Cruz ; 171, 183, Nile ; 199-201, ashore. IV. 180, Sq. off Batavia Rd.
Cumberland (74)	I. 62, Channel Flt.; 297-301, actn. off Hyères. III. 182, capture of Créole (40). IV. 288, Sq. at Palermo ; 445, off Barcelona.
Curaçoa (36)	V. 344, Sq. off Languelia.
Curieux (16) *F.*	III. 245-7, cut out by bts. of Centaur (74).
,, (18) *Br.*	III. 354, carries Nelson's despatches. IV. 17-8, capts. Dame. Ernouf (16) (priv.) ; 271-2, actn. with Revanche (24) (priv.). V. 441, wrkd. W. Indies.
Curieux (18) *F.*	III. 124-5, captd. and destd. by Bordelais (24).
Curlew (18)	II. 456, fndrd in the North Sea.
Cyane (18)	IV. 456, captd. by Hortense and Hermione (40), Martinique.
,, (26) *F.*	IV. 75, recaptd. by Princess Charlotte (36).
,, (22) *Br.*	V. 32-5, actn. with Cérès (40). VI. 122-4, capture of Alcmène (40) and Iphigénie (40) ; 248-50, captd. by U.S. Constitution (44).
Cybèle (40) *F.*	I. 132, Mahé Rds. ; 236-8, actn. with Centurion (50). IV. 177-8, L'Hermitte's Sq. ; 393-4, destd. by Br. Sq.
Cyclops (28)	I. 305, off Smyrna.
Cygnet (16)	VI. 391, wrkd. Courantine River.
Cynthia (16)	II. 450, capture of Ferrol.
Dædalus (32)	II. 338, Kosseir Bay ; 357-8, capts. Prudente (36).
Dædalus (38)	V. 245, late Ven. Corona (40). VI. 381, wrkd. Ceylon.
Dædalus (46)	VI. 395, bldg.

Dageraad (30) *Du.* ... VI. 279, Algiers.
Dame Ambert (priv.) (16) *F.* III. 276-7, capts. Lilly (14).
Dame Ernouf (16) *F.*... IV. 17-8, captd. by Curieux (16).
Danaë (36) *F.* .... I. 230, Sq. crsg. off Jersey.
„ (40) *F.* .... V. 30-1, actn. with Topaze (36); 449, accidentally burnt at Trieste.
Danaë (20) .... II. 258, late Vaillante (20), q.v. III. 9-10, captd. at Brest, mutiny of crew.
Dannemark (74) *Da.* ... IV. 209, captd. Copenhagen; 439, Scheldt exped.
Danube (74) *F.* .... IV. 444, Flt. at Toulon Rds.
Daphne (20) .... I. 261-2, captd. by Brest Flt. II. 106, recaptd. by Anson (44). IV. 320, crsg., bts. cut out Da. convoy.
Daring (12)............... VI. 36-7, destd. to prevent capture.
Dart (28).................. I. 456, description of. III. 18-9, capts. Désirée (38); 49, Copenhagen.
Dart (10).................. VI. 388, fndrd.
Dartmouth (42) .... VI. 365-9, Navarino.
Dauntless (18) .... IV. 465, captd. at Dantzic.
Dauphin Royal (120) *F.* I. 72, refitting at Toulon; 213, renamed Sans-Culotte; 426, renamed Orient, q.v.
Décade (36) *F.* .... II. 269, captd. by Naiad (38) and consort.
„ „ *Br.* ...... IV. 116, Sq. Barbadoes.
Decatur (priv.) (6) *F.*... VI. 74, capts. Dominica (12).
Décius (20) *F.* .... I. 401, captd. by Lapwing (28); 402, destd. to prevent capture.
Decoy (10) .... VI. 388, captd. by unknown force.
Dédaigneuse (36) *F.* ... III. 123-4, captd. by Br. Sq., added to Br. Navy.
„ „ *Br.*... III. 209-10, Madras. IV. 357, Isle of France; 358, engages Sémillante (36).
Defence (74) .... I. 65, Channel Flt.; 139, 154, 29th May; 155, casualties; 162-3, 168, 1st June; 175, casualties. II. 171, Medn. Flt.; 183-91, Nile; 197, casualties. III. 47, Copenhagen; 384, 439, Trafalgar; 443, casualties. V. 231, wrkd. Jutland.
Defender (12)............ IV. 261, actn. off Cherbourg. V. 442, wrkd. near Folkestone.
Defiance (74) .... II. 293, Medn. Flt. III. 46, 51-5, Copenhagen; 357, Calder's actn.; 384, 440, Trafalgar; 443, casualties. IV. 393-4, actn. with F. frigates.
Dégo (64) *F.* .... II. 445, captd. at the surrender of Malta.
Delft (50) *Du.* .... II. 76-9, captd. Camperdown; 86-7, fndrs.
Delight (16) .... IV. 474, wrkd. Calabria.
Delphinen (16) *Da.* ... IV. 209, captd. at Copenhagen; 474, wrkd. Holland.
Département des Landes (20) *F.* IV. 38-9, capture of Blanche (36); 374-5, capts. Maria (12).
De Ruyter (64) *Du.* ... II. 343-8, captd. by Br. Sq. Vlieter, Texel.
„ (S.S.) ...... III. 494, wrkd. Antigua.
Desaix (74) *F.* .... III. 68, Sq. Egypt. exped.; 96-102, Algesiras; 112, actn. in Gut of Gibraltar.
Désirée (38) *F.* .... III. 18-20, captd. by Dart (28).
„ (36) .... III. 46, 51, Copenhagen. VI. 6, capture of Gluckstadt.
Despatch (18)............ IV. 178-9, Lewis' Sq. capture of Présidente (40).
Destin (74) *F.* .... I. 72, Toulon Flt.; 90, 431, destd. at Toulon.
Déterminée (22) .... III. 490, wrkd. Jersey.
Deux Amis (14) .... II. 474, wrkd. the Isle of Wight.
Devries (64) *Du.* ...... II. 76-9, captd. Camperdown; 87, unserviceable.
Diadem (64) .... I. 284-90, actn. off Genoa; 297, Hyères; 343, Nelson's Sq. II. 34-44, St. Vincent. IV. 279, Sq. at Buenos Ayres.
Diamond (38)............ I. 233, Warren's Sq., Volontaire (36) destd.; 259-61, Bay of Brest; 318, Strachan's Sq.; 354-5, actn. at Herqui, destd. Etourdie (16). II. 128-9, invas. flotilla.
Diana (40) *Du.* .... VI. 279, Algiers.
Diana (38) .... I. 233, Warren's Sq., Volontaire (36) destd. V. 107-8, bts. des. Eliza (40); 213-4, capts. Teazer (12) in the Gironde.

INDEX TO SHIPS

Diana (46)	VI. 395, bldg.
Diana (10)	V. 43-4, capts. Du. Zephyr (14); 445, wrkd. E. Indies.
Diane (40) *F.*	II. 178, Nile; 444, captd. by Br. Sq. off Malta, renamed Niobe (38), q.v.
Dictateur (74) *F.*	I. 73, rprg. Toulon; 90, destd. at Toulon.
Dictator (64)	IV. 200, Copenhagen; 298, Baltic Flt. V. 325-6, des. with consorts Da. Nayaden (40) and four brigs.
Dido (28)	I. 214, Medn. Flt.; 321-4, with Lowestoffe (32) capts. Minerve (40).
Didon (40) *F.*	III. 350-3, Martinique. IV. 56-64, meets Æolus (32); 65-74, captd. by Phœnix (36).
,, (38) *Br.*	IV. 74, laid up in Hamoaze, broken up 1811.
Diligence (18)	III. 477, wrkd. Havana.
Diligent (16) *F.*	IV. 148, captd. by Renard (16).
Diligent (priv.) (16) *F.*	V. 423-4, capts. Laura (12).
Diligente (18) *F.*	IV. 371-3, actn. with Recruit (18); 374, captd. at Martinique, renamed St. Pierre, q.v.
Diomede (44)	I. 236-9, actn. with F. Sq.; 443, wrkd. Ceylon.
Diomède (74) *F.*	III. 312, Brest Flt. IV. 88, Sq. crsg.; 95-8, actn. with Duckworth's Sq.; 102, destd.
Diomede (50)	IV. 186, Sq. at Cape of Good Hope.
Director (64)	II. 75-81, Camperdown.
Dittsmarschen (64) *Da.*	IV. 209, destd. at Copenhagen.
Dix Aout (74) *F.*	II. 286, Brest Flt. III. 68, Egypt exped.
Dolphin, *Swd.*	IV. 299, Br. and Swd. Flt. Oro Rds.
Dominica (14)	V. 442, fndrd. off Tortola.
Dominica (14) *Schooner*	VI. 74-5, captd. by U.S. Decatur (7) (priv.).
Dominica (14) *Cutter*	VI. 391, wrkd. Bermuda, 1815.
Donawerth (74) *F.*	IV. 444, Flt. in Toulon Rds.
Donegal (74)	II. 162, late Hoche (74), q.v. III. 175, Medn.; 335, Nelson's Flt.; 456, Trafalgar; 493, capts. Sp. Amfitrite (40). IV. 90-7, Duckworth's actn.; 393-4, actn. with F. frigates; 396, actn. Basque Rds.
Dordrecht (66) *Du.*	I. 415-6, captd. at Cape of Good Hope.
Doris (36)	II. 142, Warren's Sq. III. 179-80, capts. Affronteur (14). IV. 456, wrkd. in Quiberon Bay, 1805.
Doris (36)	V. 203, capture of the Isle of France.
Doris (42)	VI. 396, bldg.
Dorsetshire, *E.I.C.*	III. 250, actn. with Linois' Sq. E. Indies.
Doterel (18)	IV. 400, actn. Basque Rds.
Dover (T.S.)	V. 245, late Bellona, q.v.
Dover (38)	V. 447, wrkd. in Madras Rds.
Draak (18) *Du.*	II. 389, captd. by Arrow (28) and destd.
Dragon (74)	II. 285, Sq. off Brest; 297, Medn. III. 357, 361-2, Calder's actn. IV. 55, Calder's Sq. crsg.
Drake (14)	III. 201, bts. at Martinique; 256, des. F. priv.; 494, wrkd. Isle Nevis.
Dreadnought (98)	III. 384, 437-8, Trafalgar; 443, casualties. V. 102, bts. actn.
Driade (36) *F.*	I. 264, Brest Flt.
Dristigheten (74) *Swd.*	IV. 299, Br. and Swd. Flt. Oro Rds.
Driver (18)	IV. 146, crsg. off New York. V. 5-7, capture of Junon (40).
Droits de L'Homme (74) *F.*	I. 203, Nielly's Sq. capts. Alexander (74); 264, Brest Flt. II. 5, Ireland exped.; 12-5, actn. with Indefatigable (44) and Amazon (36); 19-21, wrkd.
Droits du Peuple (36) *F.*	I. 441, wrkd. Norway.
Dromedary (T.S.)	III. 477, wrkd. Trinidad.
Druid (32)	I. 230, Saumarez's Sq. actn. with F. Sq. off Jersey.
Druid (48)	VI. 395, bldg.
Dryad (36)	I. 369, capts. Proserpine (40). IV. 3, crsg. with Boadicea; 135, crsg., capture of Clorinde (40); 438, Scheldt exped.
Dubois (64) *F.*	II. 288, Alexandria. III. 93, destd.
Duguay-Trouin (74) *F.*	I. 72, Toulon Flt.; 92, 431, destd. at Toulon.

Duguay-Trouin (74) F.	III. 186-7, actn. with Elephant (74); 373, F. Sp. Flt.; 386, Trafalgar. IV. 3-8, captd. by Strachan's Sq.; 12, renamed Implacable (74), q.v.
Duguay-Trouin (34) F.	I. 226-7, captd. by Orpheus (32), late E.I.C. Princess Royal, q.v.
Duifze (44) *Du.*	II. 347, captd. in the Nieueve Diep.
Duke (98)	I. 127, Martinique exped.
Duncan (74)	VI. 117, Medn. Flt.
Duquesne (74) F.	I. 213, Toulon Sq.; 282, crsg.; 288-9, actn. off Genoa. II. 286, Brest Flt. III. 186, captd. by Bellerophon (74) and Vanguard (74) off St. Domingo.
Duquesne (36) F.	I. 441, captd. by Bellona (74), W. Indies.
Duras (20) F.	I. 332, captd. by Bellona (74), W. Indies.
Eagle (priv.) (14)	II. 252-3, actn. with F. (ex Ven.) Lodi (18).
Eagle (74)	V. 260-1, capts. Corceyre (26); 351, crsg. off Ancona.
Eagle (20) *U.S.*	VI. 213, in Lake Champlain.
Eagle (74) *Rus.*	IV. 298-9, Rus. Flt. Oro Rds.
Earl Camden (30) *E.I.C.*	III. 250-3, actn. with Linois' Sq. E. Indies.
Earl of Abergavenny (30) *E.I.C.*	III. 250-3, actn. with Linois' Sq. E. Indies.
Echo (18)	II. 400-1, bts. cut out Buonaparte (12) (priv.).
Eclair (12) F.	III. 120-1, captd. by Garland.
,, ,, *Br.*	III. 248-9, actn. with Grand Décidé (22) (priv.).
Edgar (74)	I. 62, Channel Flt.; 100, Gell's Sq. Medn. III. 46, 51, 55, Copenhagen.
Eendragt (18) *Du.*	VI. 279, Algiers.
Egmont (74)	I. 72, Flt. off Toulon; 100, Sq. Medn.; 207-14, Corsica. II. 34-41, 48, St. Vincent.
Egyptien (20) F.	II. 414-5, captd. by Solebay (32).
Egyptienne (44) F.	III. 93-4, captd. at Alexandria.
,, ,, *Br.*	III. 357, Calder's actn. IV. 76-7, capts. Libre (38); 129, bts. cut out Alcide (34) (priv.).
Egyptienne (priv.)(36)F.	III. 257-8, captd. by Osprey (18) and Hippomenes; 259, prison ship.
Elbe (40) F.	IV. 391, Brest Flt.; 401, Basque Rds.
Electra (16)	IV. 372, late F. Espiègle (16), q.v.; 474, wrkd. Sicily.
Elena (48) *Rus.*	VI. 365, 373, Navarino.
Elephant (74)	III. 46, 51-4, Copenhagen; 186-7, actn. with Duguay-Trouin.
Eliza (40) F.	V. 107-8, destd. by bts. of Diana (38).
Elizabet (36) F.	I. 385-6, captd. by Topaze (36) and consorts.
Elizabeth (12)	IV. 467, fndrd. W. Indies.
Elizabeth (10)	VI. 391, capsized.
Elizabeth (74)	IV. 236, Sq. off the Tagus. VI. 29, crsg. Adriatic.
Elven (16) *Da.*	IV. 209, captd. at Copenhagen.
Embuscade (36) F.	I. 110-4, actn. with Boston (32). II. 139-46, captd. by Warren's Sq.; 162, renamed Seine (36), q.v.
Embuscade (32)	II. 273-9, Ambuscade captd. by Baïonnaise (28) and named Embuscade. III. 176, recaptd. by Victory (100).
Emerald (36)	II. 63, Sq. off Teneriffe; 93, capture of Sp. frigates. III. 12-4, capture of Sp. frigates; 255-6, bts. cut out Mozambique (10) (priv.). IV. 311-2, bts. at Vivero; 400, actn. Basque Rds.
Emulous (18)	V. 450, wrkd. Sable Island.
Encounter (12)	IV. 400, actn. Basque Rds. V. 451, wrkd. Spain.
Endymion (40)	II. 87-8, armed with 24 pndrs., actn. with Du. Brutus (74). III. 180, capts. Bacchante (18). V. 319-20, crsg. VI. 237-8, bts. repulsed by U.S. Prince de Neufchatel (18) (priv.); 239-46, capture of U.S. President (40).
Engageante (36) F.	I. 222-5, captd. by Concorde (36); 226, hospital ship.
Enterprise (16) *U.S.*	VI. 75-7, capts. Boxer (12).
Entreprenant (74) F.	I. 72, Toulon Flt.; 141, Brest Flt.; 163, 1st June.

INDEX TO SHIPS

Entreprenante (8)	V. 110-11, actn. with F. privs.
Eole (18) *F.*	II. 414-5, captd. by Solebay (32), renamed Nimrod, q.v.
Eole (74) *F.*	I. 60, W. Indies; 105, crsg.; 141, Brest Flt.; 171-2, 1st June. II. 5, Brest Flt. III. 312, Brest Flt. IV. 88, Willaumez's Sq.; 109, Port Royal Bay; 117, chased into Chesapeake; 247, blockaded in Chesapeake.
Epervier (14) *Brig*......	IV. 94, Duckworth's Sq. W. Indies.
,, (18) *Brig Sloop*	VI. 158, capts. U.S. Alfred (16) (priv.); 159-60, captd. by U.S. Peacock (22).
Ephera (F.S.)............	V. 451, wrkd. off Cadiz.
Erebus (18)..............	IV. 302, blockade of Rogerswick.
Erne (20)..................	VI. 394, wrkd. Cape de Verdes.
Escort (12)	III. 235, actn. with invas. flotilla.
Espana (64) *Sp.*	III. 342, Fr. Sp. Flt. at Toulon.
Espérance (10) *F.*	III. 267, capts. Swift (8).
Espérance (22) *F.*	V. 98, late Laurel (22), q.v., captd. by Unicorn (32), renamed Laurestinus, q.v.
Espiègle (16) *F.*.........	I. 121, in Sq. which capts. Thames (32). IV. 371-2, captd. by Sibylle (38), renamed Electra (16), q.v.
Espiègle (16)	II. 382-3, capture of Crash (12).
Espion (36)..............	I. 228, late F. Atalante (36), q.v.
Espion (T.S.)............	II. 475, wrkd. on Goodwin Sands.
Espoir (14)	II. 256-8, capts. Liguria (16); 364-5, capts. Sp. Africa (14).
,, (18)	V. 32-5, actn. with gbts. near Ischia.
Essex (32) *U.S.*	V. 362, New York; 364-6, capts. Alert (16); 368, Delaware Bay. VI. 150-3, captd. by Phœbe (36) and Cherub (18).
Essex, Junior (20) *U.S.*	VI. 150-4, actn. off Valparaiso.
Ethalion (38)	II. 140, observing Bompart's Flt.; 146-7, capts. Bellone (36); 401-2, capts. Sp. Thetis (34); 474, wrkd. off the Penmarcks.
Ethalion (38)	IV. 110, Sq. crsg. W. Indies; 382, off Port Royal.
Etoile (28) *F.*............	I. 356, captd. by Br. Sq.
Etoile (40) *F.*............	VI. 124-7, actn. with Astrea (36); 128-30, captd. by Hebrus (36); 131, renamed Topaze (38), q.v.
Etourdie (16) *F.*.........	I. 355, destd. at Herqui.
Euridice (46) *Swd.*......	IV. 299, Br. Swd. Flt. Oro Rds.
Europa (50)..............	I. 129-30, capture of Cape Nicolas Mole; 251, St. Domingo.
Europe (20) *E.I.C.* ...	V. 54, actn. with F. frigates.
Eurotas (38)	VI. 133-7, armed with Congreve's 24 pndrs., capture of Clorinde (40); 138, renamed Aurora (38), q.v.
Euryalus (36)	III. 384, 452, 466, Trafalgar. IV. 298, Baltic Flt.; 367, bts. cutting out exped.; 439, Scheldt exped. VI. 18, off Toulon.
Eurydice (24)	I. 230, off Guernsey. II. 129, off St. Marcouf.
Eveillé (16) *F.*	I. 329-30, captd. by Br. Sq.
Excellent (74)............	I. 202, Cornwallis' Sq. II. 34, 42-5, St. Vincent. IV. 123, Palermo. V. 35-6, bts. cutting out exped.
Exertion (12)	V. 451, wrkd. River Elbe.
Exeter (30) *E.I.C.*......	III. 22-3, capture of Médée (36); 250-3, actn. with F. Sq.
Expeditie (44) *Du.* ...	II. 347, captd. in Nieuwe Diep by Br. Sq.
Experiment (10).........	II. 457, captd. by Sp. Sq. Medn.
Explosion (bomb.)......	IV. 466, wrkd. Lundy Isle.
Eyderen (16) *Da.*	IV. 209, captd. at Copenhagen.
Ezekiel (74) *Rus.*	VI. 365, Navarino; 373, casualties.
Faderneslandet(74)*Swd.*	IV. 299, Br. Swd. Flt. Oro Rds.
Fairy (16)	III. 3-7, capture of Pallas (38).
Falcon (F.S.)............	III. 477, destd. in Dunkerque Rds.
Falcon (16)	IV. 321, bts. off Endelau.
Fama (34) *Sp.*	III. 288, captd. with consorts and treasure off Cape Santa Maria by Br. Sq.
Fama (16)	V. 441, wrkd. in Baltic.
Fancy (12)	V. 447, fndrd. in Baltic.

Fantome (18)	VI. 387, wrkd. New Brunswick.
Faune (16) *F.*	IV. 38-9, capture of Blanche (36) ; 44, captd. by Goliath (74).
Favorite (40) *F.*..........	V. 122, Sq. crsg. Adriatic ; 241, destd. in actn. off Lissa.
Favourite (18)	IV. 178, captd. by F. Sq.; 242, recaptd. by Jason (32).
Fearless (12)	III. 494, wrkd. in Cawsand Bay.
Fearless (12)	VI. 382, wrkd. Spain.
Félicité (36) *F.*	I. 230, Sq. crsg. off Jersey ; 253-4, capture of Sierra-Léone. III. 312, Brest Flt. IV. 88-98, Willaumez's Sq. W. Indies, V. 23, armed en flûte (14), captd. by Latona (38), unserviceable.
Felix (12)	IV. 467, wrkd. in Bay of St. Andero.
Ferme (74) *F.*	I. 127-8, late Phocion (74), Royalist, at Martinique.
Ferret (18)	VI. 381, wrkd. near Leith.
Ferreter (12)	IV. 366, captd. by Du. gbts.
Fervent (12)	IV. 400, actn. Basque Rds.
Fidelle (38) *F.*	I. 264, Brest Flt. IV. 441, captd. at surrender of Flushing, renamed Laurel (38), q.v.
Fire Fly (12)	IV. 467, fndrd. Spanish Main.
Firm (12)	V. 447, wrkd. France. [prison ship.
Firme (74) *Sp.*	II. 36, St. Vincent. III. 358-61, captd. in Calder's actn.; 371,
Fisgard (38)	II. 160-1, capts. Immortalité (40). III. 475, capture of Vénus (28). IV. 275, capture of Curaçoa.
Flêche (14)	I. 443, wrkd. in San Fiorenzo Bay.
Flêche (18) *F.*	III. 143-4, destd. by Victor (18).
Flêche (16)	V. 445, wrkd. River Elbe.
Fleur de-la-Mer (10) ...	V. 448, fndrd., crew saved.
Flewende-Fisk (14) *Da.*	IV. 209, captd. Copenhagen.
Flibustier (16) *F.*	VI. 10-11, destd. by Telegraph (12) and consorts.
Flora (36)	I. 222, Warren's Sq. crsg.; 233, Volontaire (36) destd.; 306, Troubridge's Sq. crsg. N. Archipelago. II. 249, bts. cut out Mondovi (18). IV. 473, wrkd. Holland.
Flore (32) *F.*	II. 269, captd. by Phaëton (38) and Anson (44) ; 270, curious history of.
Flore (40) *F.*	V. 30-1, crsg. in Adriatic ; 233-7, captd. actn. off Lissa ; 238, escapes ; 446, wrkd. in Adriatic.
Florentina (34) *Sp.* ...	III. 13-4, captd. by Leviathan (74); 14, added to Br. Navy as (36).
Florida (22)	VI. 158, late U.S. Frolic (18), q.v.
Fly (14)	III. 485, fndrd. Newfoundland.
Fly (16)	IV. 456, wrkd. in Gulf of Florida. V. 451, wrkd. Isle of Anholt.
Formidable (74) *F.* ...	I. 264-73, captd. in actn. off Isle Groix ; 277, renamed Belleisle (74), q.v.
Formidable (98).........	II. 297, Medn. Flt. IV. 288, Sq. in Palermo Bay.
Formidable (84).........	VI. 395, bldg.
Formidable (80) *F.* ...	II. 286, Brest Flt. III. 68, Sq. Egypt. exped.; 96, Algesiras ; 112-5, actn. Gut of Gibraltar ; 176, Toulon ; 334, Toulon Flt.; 386, 434, Trafalgar. IV. 3-7, captd. Strachan's actn.; 12, renamed Brave (74), q.v.
Forsigtigheten(66)*Swd.*	IV. 299, Br. Swd. Flt. Oro Rds.
Forte (44) *F.*	I. 387-94, Sq. crsg., actn. with two Br. 74's ; 395, Batavia. II. 365-72, captd. by Sibylle (40); 373, added to Br. Navy.
,, ,, *Br.*............	III. 481, wrkd. in Jedda Harbour, Red Sea.
Fortitude (74)............	I. 207-9, actn. at Mortella ; 214, Flt. off Bastia ; 284-90, actn. off Genoa ; 297, off Hyères.
Fortune (16)	II. 462, wrkd. near Oporto.
Fortune (10)	II. 378-9, captd. by F. frigates, Syria.
Fortunée (36) *F.*	I. 117-8, F. frigates with Agamemnon (64) ; 210, destd. by the Br. at San Fiorenzo.
Foudroyant (80)	II. 142-7, capture of Hoche (74) ; 289, Flt. off Cadiz ; 440-42, capture of Guillaume Tell (80). IV. 89, Warren's Sq. ; 129-31, capture of Marengo (74) ; 236, Sq. blockading Tagus.

INDEX TO SHIPS

Foudroyant (80) *F.*	IV. 88, 109, Willaumez's Sq. crsg.; 113-4, actn. with Anson (44); 115, Havana; 117, Brest; 391, Willaumez's Sq.; 401, 408-22, actn. Basque Rds.; 430, aground.
Fougueux (74) *F.*	I. 261, Brest; 264, Villaret's Flt.; 413, Cape François. II. 5, Ireland exped.; 286, Brest Flt.; 373, Flt. at Corunna; 386, 396, 407, 424, captd. Trafalgar; 453, wrkd.
Fox (10)	II. 462, destd. at Santa Cruz.
Fox (14)	II. 474, wrkd. in Gulf of Mexico.
Fox (32)	II. 237-9, Manilla; 241-3, Samboangon; 338-9, Kosseir Bay.
Foxhound (18)	IV. 400, actn. Basque Rds. V. 441, fndrd. off Halifax.
Franchise (36) *F.*	II. 137, Ireland exped. III. 22-3, escapes from Belliqueux (64) and E.I.C. ships; 180, captd. by Minotaur (74) and consorts. IV. 127-9, bts. cut out Sp. Raposa (12). V. 208, Flt. off Toulon.
Franklin (80) *F.*	II. 178, 192, 207, captd. Nile; 209, renamed Canopus (80), q.v.
Fraternité (36) *F.*	I. 203, Nielly's Sq.; 264, Brest Flt.; 316, escaped from Colpoy's Sq. II. 5, Ireland exped.
Frederica (40) *Du.*	VI. 279, Algiers; 289, casualties.
Frederickscoarn (32)*Da.*	IV. 293-4, captd. by Comus (22).
Freija (36) *Da.*	IV. 209, captd. at Copenhagen. V. 87-9, bts. cutting out exped. Guadaloupe.
Freya (40) *Da.*	III. 41-2, captd. by Br. Sq. North Sea.
Frolic (18)	V. 389-92, captd. by U.S. Wasp (20).
Frolic (18) *U.S.*	VI. 156-7, captd. by Orpheus (36), renamed Florida (22), q.v.
Fromintin (64) *F.*	II. 288, Toulon Flt.
Furet (18) *F.*	IV. 120, captd. by Hydra (38).
Furie (36) *Du.*	II. 270, captd. by Sirius (36), renamed Wilhelmina (32), q.v.
Furieuse (38) *F.*	IV. 76-7, actn. with Egyptienne (44). V. 23-5, captd. by Bonne Citoyenne (32).
Furieuse (36)	IV. 26, at Portsmouth. VI. 35, bts. cutting out exped.
Fury (bomb.)	VI. 278, Algiers.
Fylla (20) *Da.*	IV. 209, captd. at Copenhagen.
Fyren (74) *Da.*	IV. 209, captd. at Copenhagen.
Gabriel (118) *Rus.*	IV. 298, Rus. Flt. Oro Rds.
Gaieté (20) *F.*	II. 98, captd. by Arethusa (38); 99, added to Br. Navy.
Galatea (32)	I. 278, Quiberon exped.; 355-7, Warren's Sq., capture of Unité (36); 381-3, Warren's Sq., Andromaque (36) destd. III. 279-80, bts. repulsed in cutting out Général Ernouf. IV. 168, bts. des. Sp. priv.; 239-41, bts. cut out Lynx (16); 242, renamed Heureux (16), q.v. V. 283-91, armament (36), actn. off Madagascar; 407, escapes from U.S. Congress (36).
Galathéa (16) *Du.*	II. 343-8, captd. in the Vlieter, Texel.
Galathée (36) *F.*	I. 60, Flt. in Quiberon Bay; 441, wrkd. near the Penmarcks.
Galgo (16) *Sp.*	II. 413, captd. by Crescent (36).
Gallardo (74) *Sp.*	II. 110, destd. at Trinidad to prevent capture.
Gamo (32) *Sp.*	III. 132-3, captd. by Speedy (14).
Ganges (30) *E.I.C.*	III. 250, actn. with Linois' Sq. E. Indies.
Ganges (74)	I. 62, Channel Flt.; 100, capture of Général Dumourier (22) (priv.); 189, Sq. off Ushant. III. 46 and IV. 200, Copenhagen.
Ganges (84)	VI. 395-6, bldg.
Ganymede (34)	V. 3, late Hébé (20), q.v.
Gargonte (74) *Rus.*	VI. 365, Navarino; 373, casualties.
Garland (28)	II. 469, wrkd. Madagascar.
Garland (22)	III. 490, wrkd. St. Domingo.
Gasparin (74) *F.*	I. 141, Brest Flt.; 163, 1st June; 426, late Apollon (74), q.v.
Gaulois (74) *F.*	I. 425, renamed Trajan (74), q.v.
Gaulois (74) *F.*	II. 286, Brest Flt.
Gelykheid (64) *Du.*	II. 76-9, captd. at Camperdown.
Général Dumourier (22) *F.*	I. 100, captd. by Br. Sq.

GénéralErnouf(priv.)*F.*	IV. 462, capts. Tobago (10); 467, capts. Barbara (10), W. Indies.
Généreux (74) *F.*	I. 72, Toulon Flt.; 213, 282, Toulon. II. 178, 193-4, Nile; 260-3, capts. Leander (50); 265, Corfu; 439, captd. by Br. Sq. Medn.
Genoa (74)	VI. 119, late F. Brilliant (74), q.v.; 365, Navarino; 373, casualties.
Génois (74) *F.*	IV. 444, Flt. in Toulon Rd.
Gentille (36) *F.*	I. 203, Nielly's Sq.; 316, captd. by Hannibal (74).
Gibraltar (80)	I. 139, Channel Flt.; 162, 176, 1st June; 351-3, accident to. II. 289, Flt. off Cadiz. III. 175, Medn. Flt. IV. 396, 424, actn. Basque Rds.
Gier (14) *Du.*	II. 388, captd. by Wolverine (12); 389, added to Br. Navy.
Gipsy (10)	IV. 13, actn. with privs.
Giraffe (20) *F.*	V. 246-7, destd. by Br. Sq.
Glasgow (40)	VI. 278, Algiers; 289, casualties.
Glasgow (50)	VI. 365, Navarino; 373, casualties.
Glatton (54)	I. 372-5, actn. with F. frigates. II. 345, Holland exped. III. 46, Copenhagen. IV. 244, bts. cutting out exped.
Glenmore (36)	II. 416-7, capts. Bergère (18).
Gloire (36) *F.*	I. 315-6, captd. by Astræa (32); 317, added to Br. Navy.
Gloire (40) *F.*	IV. 48, Allemand's Sq.; 79, Dominique exped.; 175-6, captd. by Br. Sq. IV. 177, added to Br. Navy.
Gloire (40) *F.*	VI. 6-7, actn. with Albacore (26) and Pickle (14).
Gloire (38)	VI. 124, late Iphigénie (40), q.v.
Glommen (16)	V. 441, wrkd. Barbadoes.
Glorioso (74) *Sp.*	III. 375, off Carthagena.
Glory (98)	I. 139, Channel Flt.; 162, 185-6, 1st June. II. 285, Sq. off Brest; 297, Medn. III. 356-62, Calder's action.
Gloucester (74)	VI. 395, rprg.
Goéland (12) *F.*	V. 344-5, actn. with Swallow (16).
Goldfinch (10)	V. 27, actn. with Mouche (16).
Goliath (74)	II. 34-48, St. Vincent; 171, Flt. off Cadiz; 183-94, Nile; 197, casualties. III. 181, capts. Mignonne (16). IV. 44, capts. Torche (18); 200, Copenhagen; 298, Baltic Flt. V. 427, rasé.
Goliath (84)	VI. 395, bldng.
Goree (18)	IV. 330, actn. with F. brigs.
Goshawk (16)	V. 216, crsg. off Cherbourg. VI. 387, wrkd. in the Medn.
Gracieuse (12)	IV. 29, des. Sp. priv.
Grampus (T.S.)	II. 475, wrkd. near Woolwich.
Grand Décidé (22) *F.*	III. 248, actn. with Eclair (12).
Granicus (36)	VI. 278, Algiers; 289, casualties.
Grappler (12)	III. 490, wrkd. Isles de Chosey.
Grasshopper (18)	IV. 270-1, capts. San Josef (12); 326, actn. with Sp. gbts.; 329-30, capts. Sp. treasure ships. V. 232, captd. in Nieueve Diep, Texel.
Greyhound (32)	IV. 162-4, capture of Du. Pallas (36). V. 441, wrkd. Lucania.
Griffon (16) *F.*	IV. 342, captd. by Bacchante (20).
,, ,, *Br.*	V. 317-8, actn. with invas. flotilla, Dieppe.
Griper (12)	IV. 466, wrkd. off Ostende.
Growler (12)	II. 105, captd. by F. privs.
Growler (12)	IV. 400, actn. Basque Rds.
Guachapin (10)	V. 448, wrkd. at Antigua.
Guadalupe (34) *Sp.*	II. 473, destd. by Centaur (74), Medn.
Guadeloupe (16)	V. 46, late Nisus; 253-4, actn. with F. brigs.
Guelderland (64) *Du.*	II. 343-8, captd. by Br. Sq. in the Vlieter, Texel.
Guelderland (36) *Du.*	IV. 322-3, E. Indies; 324, captd. by Virginie (38); 326, added to Br. Navy.
Guerrero (74) *Sp.*	II. 299, F. Sp. Flt. at Cadiz.
Guerrier (74) *F.*	II. 178, Nile; 187, captd.; 206, destd.
Guerrier (priv.) (14) *F.*	II. 413, captd. by Courier (12).
Guerrière (40) *F.*	III. 186, escapes blockade; 188, actn. with Culloden (74). IV. 159-60, crsg. Iceland; 161, captd. by Blanche (38).

INDEX TO SHIPS

Guerrière (38) *Br.* ...... IV. 162, in Yarmouth Rds. V. 369–79, captd. by U.S. Constitution (44); 384, destd.
Gustav III. (74) *Swd.* ... IV. 298, Br. Swd. Flt. Oro Rds.
Gustav IV. Adolph (78) *Swd.* IV. 298, Br. Swd. Flt. Oro Rds.

Haerlem (64) *Du.* ...... II. 76–9, captd. at Camperdown.
Halcyon (16) .... III. 375, off Cape St. Vincent. IV. 185, capts. Sp. Neptuno (14). VI. 387, wrkd. at Jamaica.
Halstaar (32) *Du.* ...... IV. 277, captd. by Br. Sq. Curaçoa.
Hamadryad (36) .... II. 93, late Sp. Ninfa (34), q.v.
Hamadryad (46) .... VI. 395, bldng.
D'Hambourg Comtesse (14) *F.* V. 104, captd. by Calliope (10).
Hannibal (74) .... III. 98–104, captd. at Algesiras, renamed Annibal (74), q.v.
Hannibal (74) .... VI. 128–30, capts. Sultane (40).
Hardi (priv.) (18) *F.* ... II. 93, captd. by Hazard (18).
Har-Fruen (36) *Da.* ... IV. 209, 464, captd. at Copenhagen.
Harpy (18) .... III. 3–7, capture of Pallas (38); 227–30, actn. with invas. flotilla; 315, Sq. off Boulogne.
Harrier (18) .... IV. 52–4, actn. with Sémillante (36); 162–4, capture of Du. Pallas (36). V. 441, fndrd. E. Indies.
Hasard (14) *F.* .... I. 117, Perrée's Sq. crsg.
Hastings (74) .... VI. 396, blt.
D'Haupoult (74) *F.* ... V. 18–22, captd. by Pompée (74), and consorts, renamed Abercromby (74).
Havannah (42) .... VI. 395, rprg.
Havick (16) .... III. 477, wrkd. Jersey.
Havik (14) *Du.* .... V. 91, captd. by Thistle (10).
Hawk (16) .... V. 215–6, bts. cut out Héron (10).
Hawke (18) .... IV. 456, fndrd. in the Channel.
Hazard (18) .... II. 259, capts. Neptune (10).
Hebe (38) .... I. 410, Christian's Sq. capture of Saint Lucie.
Hebe (32) .... III. 320, Sq. off Boulogne.
Hebe (46) .... VI. 395, bldg.
Hébé (20) *F.* .... V. 2–3, captd. by Loire (38), renamed Ganymede (34), q.v.
Hebrus (36) .... VI. 128–30, capts. Etoile (40); 131, renamed Topaze (38), q.v.; 278, Algiers; 289, casualties.
Hecla (bomb.) .... VI. 278, Algiers.
Hector (44) *Du.* .... II. 347, captd. in Nieueve Diep.
Hector (74) .... I. 127, Sq. Martinique; 189, Sq. off Ushant. II. 289, Flt. off Cadiz.
Heldin (32) *Du.* .... II. 76, Camperdown; 347, captd. in Nieueve Diep.
Helena (14) .... II. 457, fndrd. off Holland.
Héliopolis, *F.* (ex *Turk.*) III. 93, captd. at Alexandria.
Henry Addington (30) *E.I.C.* III. 250, actn. with Linois' Sq. E. Indies.
Herald (18) .... IV. 269, bts. cut out César (4) (priv.).
Hercule, rasé (50) *F.* . I. 56, armament of; 331–2, Guadaloupe.
Hercule (74) *F.* .... II. 121–3, captd. by Mars (74).
„ „ *Br.* ... ... II. 124, Plymouth. III. 181–2, actn. with Poursuivante (44); 291, St. Domingo. IV. 200, Copenhagen.
Hercules (64) *Du.* ...... II. 76–9, captd. Camperdown.
Hermenegildo (112) *Sp.* III. 112–3, destd. in actn. Gut of Gibraltar.
Hermes (14) .... II. 462, fndrd.
Hermes (20) .... VI. 387, destd. at Mobile.
Hermione (36) *F.* ...... II. 113, destd. by Thunderer (74) and Valiant (74).
Hermione (40) *F.* ...... III. 339, Toulon Flt.; 386, Trafalgar. IV. 119–20, Cadiz; 164–5, Meillerie's Sq.; 166, Bordeaux.
Hermione (32) .... I. 252, St. Domingo. II. 115–6, crew mutiny, captd. by the Sp.

Hermione, (44) *Sp.*....... II. 405–11, recaptd. and cut out by bts. of Surprise (28), renamed Retribution (32), q.v.
Hero (50) *Rus.* .... IV. 298, Rus. Flt. Oro. Rds.
Hero (74) .... III. 357, 360–2, Calder's actn. IV. 3, 7, 8, Strachan's actn.; 89, Warren's Sq.; 396, actn. Basque Rds. V. 232, wrkd. off the Texel.
Heroine (32) .... I. 337, capture of Trincomalé. IV. 438, Scheldt exped.
Héron (16) *F.*........... V. 216, cut out by bts. of Hawk (16). VI. 278, Algiers.
Héros (74) *F.* .... I. 72, 92, 431, destd. at Toulon.
Héros (74) *F.* .... III. 373, Villeneuve's Flt.; 386, 434, Trafalgar. IV. 295, 471, captd. by the Sp. at Cadiz.
Heureux (74) *F.*......... I. 72, 90, at Toulon; 213, Martin's Sq.; 282, Toulon. II. 178, Nile; 194, captd.; 206, destd.
Heureux (16) .... IV. 242, late F. Lynx (16), q.v.; 334, bts. cutting out exped.
Heureux (22) .... IV. 461, fndrd. in W. Indies.
Hibernia (120) .... IV. 236, Sq. off the Tagus. V. 207, Flt. off Toulon. VI. 117, Medn. Flt.
Hindostan (S.S.) ...... III. 494, lost by fire in the Medn.
Hindostan (50) .... IV. 143, convoy escort.
Hindostan (80) .... VI. 395–6, bldg.
Hippomenes (14) *Du.* III. 203, captd. at Demerara.
,, ,, *Br.* III. 258, capts. Egyptienne (36) (priv.); 272–5, actn. with Buonaparte (18) (priv.); 296, capture of Surinam.
Hirondelle(priv.)(10)*F.* III. 278, cut out by bts. of Tartar (32). IV. 474, wrkd. off Tunis.
Hoche (74) *F.* .... II. 139, Ireland exped.; 145, captd. by Warren's Sq.; 161–2, renamed Donegal (74), q.v.
Holly (10) .... VI. 388, wrkd. off St. Sebastian.
Hope (30) *E.I.C.* ...... III. 250, actn. with Linois' Sq. E. Indies.
Horatio (38) .... V. 5–7, capture of Junon (40); 97, capts. Nécessité (26); 328, bts. cut out Da. gbts.
Horatio (46) .... VI. 395, rprg.
Hornet (20) *U.S.* ...... VI. 44–5, St. Salvador; 46–8, des. in actn. Peacock (18); 98–9, New London; 261–4, capts. Penguin (16); 266, chased by Cornwallis (74).
Hortense (40) *F.* ...... III. 334, Villeneuve's Flt.; 352, Martinique; 386, Trafalgar. IV. 14–6, capture of Arrow (28); 120, Meillerie's Sq.; 164–6, Bordeaux; 395, blockaded in Basque Rds. VI. 44, Brest.
Hotspur (36) .... V. 216, actn. with F. brigs.
Hound (16).............. I. 439, captd. by F. frigates in W. Indies.
Hound (18).............. III. 477, wrkd. Shetland.
Hunter (18).............. II. 462, wrkd. Virginia.
Hussar (28).............. I. 319–20, capts. Raison (14). II. 456, wrkd. coast of France.
Hussar (38).............. III. 494, wrkd. in the Bay of Biscay.
Hyæna (24) .... I. 105, captd. by Concorde (40). II. 102, recaptd. by Indefatigable (44).
Hydra (38) .... II. 133–5, des. Confiante (36). III. 171, bts. cut out Favori (4). IV. 119–20, capts. Furet (18); 263–4, bts. cutting out exped.
Hyène (priv.) (24) *F.*... II. 102, captd. by Indefatigable (44).

Ignition (F.S.) .... IV. 467, wrkd. off Dieppe.
Illustrious (74) .... I. 72, Flt. off Toulon; 214, Medn.; 284–9, actn. off Genoa; 294, wrkd. and destd.
Illustrious (74) .... IV. 43, 47, convoy escort. V. 203, capture of the Isle of France.
Immortalité (40) *F.* ... II. 5, 139, Ireland exped.; 160–2, captd. by Fisgard (38).
,, (36) *Br.*... III. 142, capture of Invention (26) (priv.); 171, bts. cutting out exped.; 230, actn. with invas. flotilla; 320, actn. off Boulogne.
Immortalité (38)........ IV. 177, late Infatigable (40), q.v.
Immortalité (38)........ VI. 124, late Alcmène (40), q.v.

INDEX TO SHIPS

Imogène (18)	IV. 456, fndrd. Leeward Isles.
Impatiente (40) *F*......	II. 5, Ireland exped.; 22, 453, wrkd. Ireland.
Impérial (120) *F.*	III. 312, Brest Flt. IV. 88, Leissègues' Sq.; 97–8, destd. in Duckworth's actn.
Impérieuse (38) *F.*......	I. 97, captd. by Captain (74), renamed Unité (36), q.v.
Impérieuse (38)	IV. 239, crsg. off the Gironde; 384, off Spain; 400–13, actn. Basque Rds.; 440, Scheldt exped. V. 208, Medn. Flt.; 258, Gulf of Salerno.
Impétueux (74) *F.*	I. 60, Flt. Quiberon Bay; 141, Brest Flt.; 163–8, captd. on the 1st June.
,, ,, *Br.* ...	I. 234, 439, destd. by fire at Portsmouth.
Impétueux (74)	II. 285, Sq. off Brest; 297, Medn. Flt.; 450, Sq. at Ferrol.
Impétueux (74) *F.*	III. 312, Brest Flt. IV. 88, Willaumez's Sq.; 109, Port Royal; 116–7, destd. by Br. Sq.
Implacable (74)	IV. 12, late F. Duguay Trouin (74); 298, Baltic Flt.; 300, capture of Rus. Sewolod (74). V., 208, Medn. Flt.
Impregnable (98)	I. 139, Channel Flt.; 162, 176, 1st June. II. 474, wrkd. off Chichester. VI. 278, Algiers; 289, casualties.
Incendiary (F.S.)	III. 71, 482, captd. in the Medn.
Inconnue (16) *F.*	I. 144, destd. by Br. Flt.
Inconstante (36) *F.* ...	I. 122, captd. by Penelope (32), added to Br. Navy.
,, ,, *Br.* ...	I. 453, capts. Unité (28), q.v.
Incorruptible (38) *F.*...	III. 17–9, actn. Dunkerque Rds.; 334, Toulon Flt.; 15–6, capts. Arrow (28).
Indefatigable (44)	I. 361–2, capts. Virginie (40). II. 12–6, Droits de l'Homme (74) destd.; 102, capts. Hyène (24) (priv.); 248, capts. Vaillante (20), renamed Danaë (20), q.v.; 301, at Plymouth. III. 287, capture of Sp. frigates; 311, crsg. off Brest. IV. 139, Isle of Aix; 158, cutting out César (16); 400–13, actn. Basque Rds.
Indienne (40) *F.*	III. 312, Brest Flt. IV. 109, Cadiz; 391, Flt. crsg.; 401, actn. Basque Rds.; 422, destd.
Indivisible (80) *F.*	II. 303, Brest. III. 68, Sq. Egypt exped.
Indomptable (80) *F.* ...	I. 60, Flt. in Quiberon Bay; 141, Brest Flt.; 151–9, 29th May; 161, sent home. II. 5, Ireland exped.; 286, Brest Flt. III. 68, Sq. Egypt exped.; 96, 99–102, Algesiras; 112, Gut of Gibraltar; 176, 334, Toulon; 386, 437, Trafalgar; 455, wrkd. off Cadiz.
Indus (74)	VI. 117, Medn. Flt.
Indus (80)	VI. 395–6, bldg.
Infatigable (40) *F.*	IV. 79, Martinique exped.; 175–6, captd. by Br. Sq.; 177, renamed Immortalité (38), q.v.
Infernal (bomb.)	VI. 278, Algiers.
Inflexible (64)............	IV. 201, Copenhagen.
Insolent (14)	IV. 400, actn. Basque Rds.
Insurgente (36) *F.*	I. 264, Brest Flt.; 413, Sq. off Cape François. II. 363–4, captd. by U.S. Constellation (36).
Intrepid (64)	I. 72, Flt. off Toulon. IV. 123, Sq. at Palermo; 275, capture of Madeira.
Intrépide (74) *F.*	III. 334, Toulon Flt.; 386, 432, captd. at Trafalgar; 457, destd.
Intrépide (16) *F.*	II. 415, captd. by Racoon (18).
Invention (priv.) (24) *F.*	III. 142, captd. by Arethusa (38).
Inveterate (12)	IV. 466, wrkd. near St. Vallery en Caux.
Invincible (110) *F.* ...	II. 285, Brest Flt. III. 312, Brest Flt.
Invincible (74)	I. 65, 139, Channel Flt.; 149–54, 29th May; 176–7, 1st June. II. 109–10, Sq. Trinidad; 420, capture of Surinam. III. 481, wrkd. off Yarmouth.
Iphigenia (32)............	I. 122, capture of Inconstante (36). III. 483, lost by fire at Alexandria.
Iphigenia (36)............	IV. 56, armament of. V. 137, Sq. Isle of France; 163–6, Grand Port; 167, captd. by F. Sq.
Iphigénie (36) *F.*	I. 91, Toulon; 441, captd. by Sp. Sq. Medn.

Iphigénie (36) *F.*	V. 172, late Iphigenia (36); 173, off Isle Bourbon; 175–8, capture of Africaine (38); 182, 203, Port Louis; 205, retaken at the capture of Isle of France.
Iphigénie (40) *F.*	V. 106, launched at Cherbourg. VI. 122–3, captd. by Venerable (74) and Cyane (22); 124, renamed Gloire (38), q.v.
Iris (32) *F.*	I. 91, 432, destd. at Toulon.
Iris (32)	I. 101, actn. with Citoyenne-Française (32). III. 374, crsg. IV. 157, Sq. off Rochefort.
Iris (36) *Da.*	IV. 209, 464, captd. at Copenhagen.
Iris (22) *F.*	V. 2, captd. by Aimable (32), renamed Rainbow (22), q.v.
Irresistible (74)	I. 240, Sq. capture of Martinique; 251, Sq. at St. Domingo; 271–5, actn. off Isle Groix. II. 34, 44–8, St. Vincent; 93, capts. Sp. Ninfa (34) and des. Sta. Elena (34).
Isis (50)	I. 324, Alm's Sq. crsg. North Sea. II. 75–80, Camperdown; 345, Holland exped. III. 46, Copenhagen.
Italienne (40) *F.*.........	IV. 313–4, actn. with Aigle (36); 393–4, actn. with Br. Sq., destd.
Jackall (12)................	IV. 466, wrkd. near Calais.
Jacobin (80) *F.*	I. 141, Brest Flt.; 165–7, 1st June, renamed Neuf-Thermidor (74), q.v., fndrs.
Jalouse (18)................	III. 171, engages batteries Cape Blanc Nez.
Jamaica (24)	III. 46, Copenhagen; 67, invas. flotilla.
Jason (36) *Du.*	II. 454, crew mutiny, captd. at Greenock.
,, (38) *Br.*	II. 247, capture of Seine (40); 469, wrkd. off Brest.
Jason (36)	III. 482, wrkd off St. Malo.
Jason (32)	IV. 76, capts. Naïade (16); 242, recapts. Favourite (18).
,, (38)	V. 3–4, capture of Topaze (40).
Jason (48)	VI. 395, bldg.
Jasper (10)	VI. 394, wrkd. on Mount Batten.
Java (32)...................	IV. 465, fndrd. in E. Indies.
Java (38)	V. 295, late Renommée (40), q.v.; 409, at Portsmouth; 411–5, captd. by U.S. Constitution (44); 419, destd.
Jean Bart (74) *F.*	I. 60, Flt. in Quiberon Bay; 203–4, capture of Alexander (74); 264, Brest Flt. II. 286, Brest Flt. III. 68, Sq. Egypt. exped.; 312, 391, Brest Flt.; 409, destd. actn. Basque Rds.
Jean Bart (20) *F.*	I. 236–7, Renaud's Sq., actn. with Centurion (50).
Jemmappes (74) *F.* ...	I. 141, Brest Flt.; 163, 181–9, 1st June; 191, Brest. II. 286, Brest Flt. IV. 48, Allemand's Sq.; 79–81, Sq. at Dominique; 395, 401, 415, 421, actn. Basque Rds.
Jéna (18) *F.*	IV. 363, Isle of France; 366, captd. by Modeste (36); 367, renamed Victor (18), q.v.
Joie (10) *F.*................	IV. 276, destd. by Aigle (36).
Julia (16)...................	VI. 394, wrkd. Tristan d'Acunha.
Juno (32)...................	I. 207–14, Sq. at Corsica; 216–8, escapes from Toulon.
Junon (38) *F.*............	II. 295, captd. by Br. Sq., renamed Princess Charlotte (36), q.v.
Junon (40) *F.*............	V. 1–7, captd. by Horatio (38) and consorts. V. 8, at Halifax; 47–8, recaptd. by Renommée (40) and Clorinde (40); 49, destd.
Junon (38)	VI. 90, Chesapeake Bay; 200, crsg. off Marblehead.
Jupiter (74) *Du.*.........	II. 76–9, captd. at Camperdown.
Jupiter (50)	II. 392–4, beaten off by Preneuse (36). IV. 473, wrkd. in Vigo Bay.
Jupiter (74) *F.*	I. 303, Richery's Sq. crsg. III. 312, Brest Flt. IV. 88, Leissègues' Sq.; 97, captd. in Duckworth's actn.; 104, renamed Maida (74), q.v.
Juste (80) *F.*	I. 60, Flt. in Quiberon Bay; 141, Brest Flt.; 168, 176, captd. on 1st June.
Justice (40) *F.*	I. 91, Toulon. II. 178, Nile; 444, Malta. III. 93, 480, captd. at Alexandria, transferred to the Turks.
Justitia (74) *Da.*	IV. 209, 464, captd. at Copenhagen.
Kangaroo (18)	II. 154–9, capture of Loire (40).

INDEX TO SHIPS

Kent (74)	II. 345, Holland exped. III. 81, Egypt exped.; 175, Medn. Flt. IV. 288, Sq. at Palermo; 383, bts. cutting out exped. V. 129, Sq. at Palamos; 208, Medn. Flt.
Kent (26) *E.I.C.*	III. 31, captd. by Confiance (22) (priv.).
Kent (78)	VI. 395, rprg.
Kiel (16) *Da.*	V. 227, Da. brigs in actn. with Brevdrageren (12).
Kildwyn (26) *Rus.*	IV. 234, Sq. at Dardanelles.
Kingfisher (18)	I. 140, Channel Flt.; 262-9, Cornwallis' Sq. II. 225, capts. Betsy (16) (priv.); 467, wrkd. off Lisbon.
Kingfisher (18)	III. 353, crsg. IV. 93, Sq. at Basse Terre Rd.; 140, at the Isle of Aix. VI. 26, crsg. off Corfu.
Kite (16)	VI. 19, actn. off Cassis.
Kron-Princesse (74) *Da.*	IV. 209, 464, captd. at Copenhagen.
Kron-Prindts (74) *Da.*	IV. 209, 464, captd. at Copenhagen.
Lacedemonian (12) ...	II. 462, captd. in the W. Indies.
Lamproie (16) *F.*	IV. 447, destd. in the Bay of Rosas.
Lancaster (64)	II. 75, 81, Camperdown. III. 208, Sq. at Pondicherry. IV. 279, Sq. off Buenos Ayres.
Lancaster (60)	VI. 395, bldg.
Langland (20) *Da.*	V. 227-8, actn. with Brevdrageren (12).
Lapwing (28)	I. 62, Channel Flt.; 401, capts. and des. Décius (20) and Vaillante (12).
Lark (18)	III. 148, bts. cut out Sp. Esperanza (priv.); 174, Sq. off Etaples. IV. 91, Sq. off Cadiz; 243, capts. Sp. gbts. V. 441, fndrd. off Cape Causada.
Larne (20)	VI. 303, Burmese War.
Latona (38)	I. 139, Channel Flt.; 329, crsg. off Isle Groix. II. 345, Holland exped. V. 23, capts. Félicité (36).
Latona (46)	VI. 395, bldg.
Laura (10)	V. 423-4, captd. by Diligent (18) (priv.).
Laurel (38)	IV. 441, late Fidelle (40), q.v. V. 450, wrkd. in the Teigneuse.
Laurel (22)	IV. 363-5, captd. by Canonnière (40). V. 98, recaptd. by Unicorn (32), renamed Laurestinus (22), q.v.
Laurestinus (22)	VI. 91, in Chesapeake Bay; 387, wrkd. Bahama Isles.
Lavinia (40)	IV. 290, off Rochefort; 438, Scheldt exped.
Leander (50)	II. 63, Sq. at Teneriffe; 171, Nelson's Sq.; 183, 191-7, Nile; 259-63, captd. by Généreux (74); 268, actn. with F. Pluton (74); 304, restored at Corfu. IV. 24, recapts. Cleopatra (32), capts. Ville de Milan (40); 146, crsg. off New York. VI. 278, Algiers.
Leda (36)	II. 456, fndrd.
Leda (38)	III. 174, Sq. off Calais; 315, off Boulogne. IV. 186, Cape of Good Hope exped.; 279, Sq. Monte Video exped.; 473, wrkd. at Milford Haven. V. 297-303, capture of Java.
Légère (18) *F.*	I. 365-70, captd. by Br. frigates, added to Br. Navy.
,, ,, *Br.*	III. 482, wrkd. off Carthagena.
Légère (22) *F.*	VI. 227-8, actn. with Pilot (18).
Leoben (32) *F.*	II. 215, Sq. at Alexandria.
Léopard (74) *F.*	I. 431, fndrd. in the Bay of Cagliari.
Leopard (50)	I. 364, capture of Du. Argo (36). IV. 250-4, actn. with U.S. Chesapeake (36).
Leopard (T.S.)	VI. 388, wrkd. in the Gulf of St. Lawrence.
Levant (22)	VI. 248-50, captd. by U.S. Constitution (44).
Leveret (18)	IV. 465, wrkd. on the Galloper Rock.
Leviathan (74)	I. 72, Medn. Flt.; 139, 146-52, 29th May; 162-72, 1st June. II. 292, Medn.; 307, Sq. at Palermo. III. 12, Sq. crsg. off Cadiz; 335, Medn.; 384, 430, Trafalgar; 443, casualties. IV. 445, Martin's Sq. crsg. Medn. V. 208, Medn. Flt.; 342, at Agaye.
Leyden (64) *Du.*	II. 76, Camperdown; 343, 348, captd. in the Texel.
,, ,, *Br.*	IV. 201, Copenhagen.

Liberty (14)	I. 354, off Herqui.
Libre (40) *F*.	III. 109–12, actn. in the Gut of Gibraltar. IV. 76–7, captd. by Br. frigates.
Liffey (50)	VI. 309, Burmese War.
Ligurienne (16) *F*.......	III. 10–11, captd. by Peterel (16).
Lilly (14)	III. 276–7, captd. by Dame Ambert (16), renamed Général Ernouf (16), q.v.
Linnet (14)	IV. 305, capts. F. Courier (18). VI. 8–9, captd. by F. Gloire (40).
Linnet (16)	VI. 212, at Lake Champlain ; 218, captd.
Lion (64)	II. 211, Sq. Medn.; 254, actn. with Sp. frigates ; 306, Palermo ; 438–41, Sq. off Malta. V. 303, capture of Java.
Lion (74) *F*.	IV. 48, Allemand's Sq. ; 79, Dominique exped.; 287, Rochefort ; 444–6, destd. in actn.
Little Belt (20) *Da*. ...	IV. 209, captd. at Copenhagen, added to Br. Navy.
Little Belt (18)	V. 275–7, actn. with U.S. President (44) ; 278, at Halifax.
Lively (32)	I. 306, Medn. Flt. ; 313–5, capts. Tourterelle (28), q.v., added to Br. Navy ; 344, Sq. at San Fiorenzo. II. 34, St. Vincent ; 469, wrkd. near Cadiz.
Lively (38)	III. 287–8, actn. with Sp. frigates. V. 444, wrkd. near Malta.
Lodi (18) *F*.	II. 251–3, actn. with Br. priv. III. 93, at Nice ; 188, captd. by Racoon (18).
Loire (40) *F*.	II. 139, Ireland exped. ; 155–7, actn. with Mermaid (32) ; 158–9, captd. by Anson (44) ; 162, added to Br. Navy.
,, (38) *Br*.	III. 180, crsg. off Isle of Bas ; 282, capts. Blonde (30) (priv.). IV. 32, crsg. off Spain, cutting out exped. ; 76, capture of Libre (40). V. 2–3, capts. Hébé (18). VI. 149, off Sandy Hook.
Loire, en flûte (20) *F*.	V. 47–9, actn. off Guadaloupe ; 439, destd. at Anse le Barque, Guadaloupe.
Loland (18) *Da*..........	V. 229, capture of Manly (12).
London (98)	I. 62, Channel Flt. ; 270–3, actn. off Isle Groix. II. 289, Flt. off Cadiz ; 450, Sq. at Ferrol. III. 47, off Isle of Huën, Copenhagen. IV. 89, Warren's Sq. crsg. ; 129–31, capts. Marengo (74) ; 236, Sq. off the Tagus.
London (110)	VI. 395, bldng.
Lord Keith (12) *E.I.C.*	V. 54–6, actn. with F. frigates.
Lougen (18) *Da*.	IV. 316–7, actn. with Childers (14) ; 318, capts. Seagull (16). V. 227–8, capture of Brevdrageren (12).
Loup Garou (16) *F*. ...	V. 104, captd. by Orestes (16).
Lowestoffe (32)	I. 94, Sq. off Corsica ; 207, Mortella ; 284, actn. off Genoa ; 306, Troubridge's Sq. crsg.; 321–4, capture of Minerve (40), q.v., added to Br. Navy. III. 482, wrkd. W. Indies.
Lutine (36) *F*.	I. 90, 432, captd. at Toulon, added to Br. Navy.
,, ,, *Br*.	II. 474, wrkd. Holland.
Lynx (16) *F*.	IV. 79, Dominique exped.; 175, Soleil's Sq.; 239–42, captd. by Galatea (32), renamed Heureux (16), q.v.
Lynx (18)	V. 42, crsg. off Denmark, cutting out exped.
Lyra (10)	IV. 400, actn. at Basque Rds. V. 335, Sq. off Spain.
Lys (74) *F*...............	I. 72, 92, left at Toulon.
Macedonian (38)	V. 394–400, captd. by United States (44).
,, (36) *U.S.*	V. 403, at New York. VI. 98, Decatur's Sq.; 196, blockaded in New London.
Macedonian (S.S.) *U.S.*	VI. 238, 261, off Sandy Hook.
Madagascar (38).........	V. 295, late Néréide (40), q.v.
Madagascar (48).........	VI. 395–6, bldg.
Madison (24) *U.S.*......	VI. 103, at Sackett's Harbour ; 106, at Lake Ontario.
Madras (54)	I. 410, Martinique exped.
Mægera (F.*S.*)	I. 271, Channel Flt. off Isle Groix.
Maganime (74) *Sp*. ...	II. 240, Sq. at Manilla.

INDEX TO SHIPS

Magicienne (32).........	II. 114, at St. Domingo. III. 36, Sq. crsg. off the Morbihan. IV. 94, Duckworth's Sq. off St. Domingo. V. 65, recapts. E.I.C. Windham (30) ; 137, 141, Isle of France ; 157, 164, destd. in actn. at Grand Port.
Magnanime (44).........	II. 142, Warren's Sq.; 145, capture of Hoche (74) ; 269, crsg.
Magnanime (74) *F*. ...	IV. 48, Allemand's Sq. ; 79, Dominique exped. ; 444, Flt. in Toulon Rd. VI. 3, Toulon Flt.
Magnet (18)	V. 441, wrkd. in the Baltic.
Magnet (16)	V. 451, fndrd. near Halifax.
Magnificent (74)	II. 285, Sq. off Brest. III. 493, wrkd. near Brest.
Magnificent (74)	V. 80, St. Maura exped. Adriatic ; 208, Medn. Flt. ; 333-4, escape of ; 336, off Santander.
Mahonesa (34) *Sp*. ...	I. 399, captd. by Terpsichore (32) ; 400, added to Br. Navy.
Maida (74)	IV. 104, late Jupiter (74), q.v. ; 200, Copenhagen.
Maidstone (32)	III. 275, Sq. in Hyères Bay. VI. 83-4, in Chesapeake Bay ; 196, off Connecticut River.
Maire-Guiton (20) *F*....	I. 142, captd. by Br. Sq.
Majestic (74)	I. 62, 139, Channel Flt.; 151, 29th May ; 162, 185, 1st June. II. 171, 289, Flt. off Cadiz ; 307, Palermo. IV. 213, capture of Heligoland. V. 427, rasé.
,, (56)	VI. 144-6, capts. Terpsichore (40) ; 237, Sq. off New York.
Majestueux (120) *F*. ...	IV. 48, Allemand's Sq. crsg. ; 79, Dominique exped. ; 444, Toulon Flt. V. 85, Toulon Flt.
Malabar (54)	I. 409, capture of Du. settlements exped. II. 456, fndrd. in the W. Indies.
Malabar (54)	IV. 126, crsg. off Cuba.
Malabar (74)	VI. 396, blt.
Malabar, *E.I.C.*	V. 303, capture of Java exped.
Malicieuse (16) *F*.	IV. 138, destd. by Pallas (32).
Mallard (12)	III. 67, actn. off Etaples ; 494, captd. near Calais.
Malta (80)	III. 357-61, Calder's actn. IV. 292, at Syracuse. V. 315, Medn. Flt.
Mamelouk (16) *F*. ...	V. 319, Foretier's Sq.; 323, destd. by Northumberland (74).
Mamelouk (priv.) (16) *F*.	V. 110, captd. by Rosario (10).
Manche (40) *F*.	IV. 260-2, actn. with Uranie (38). V. 53, 62, crsg. in the E. Indies ; 64, engages E.I.C. ships ; 131-7, at Port Louis ; 165, at Grand Port ; 203-5, captd. at Isle of France.
Manilla (36)	V. 450, wrkd. in the Texel.
Manilla (48)	VI. 395, bldg.
Manligheten (74) *Swd*.	IV. 299, Br. Swd. Flt. in Oro Rds.
Manly (12)	IV. 461, captd. by Du. gbts. V. 1-2, recaptd. by Onyx (10) ; 229, captd. by Da. gbts.
Mantone (32) *F*.	II. 215, Sq. at Alexandria.
Marat (74) *F*............	I. 203-4, capture of Alexander (74).
Maraudeur (priv.) (14) *F*.	V. 111-2, captd. by Rinaldo (10).
Marengo (74) *F*.	III. 168, in the E. Indies ; 208, at Pondicherry ; 250-3, actn. with E.I.C. ships ; 283-5, actn. with Centurion (50). IV. 51-2, actn. with E.I.C. ships ; 131, captd. by Br. Sq.
Maria (priv.) (14) *Sp*....	IV. 36, captd. by Cambrian (40), added to Br. Navy.
,, (12) *Br*.	IV. 374, captd. by Département des Landes (22).
Maria (10)	IV. 467, fndrd. in the W. Indies.
Maria-de-la-Cabeya (34) *Sp*.	II. 240, at Manilla.
Maria Primeira (74) *Por*.	I. 202, Br. and Por. Flt. in the Channel.
Maria-Riggersbergen (36) *Du*.	IV. 179-80, captd. by Caroline (36), renamed Java (32), q.v.
Marie Antoinette (10)	II. 462, captd. in the W. Indies through mutiny.
Marlborough (74)	I. 65, 139, Channel Flt. ; 146, 28th May ; 174-5, 1st June. II. 289, Flt. off Cadiz ; 428, wrkd. near Belle Isle.
Marlborough (74)	IV. 236, Sq. off the Tagus. VI. 83, in Chesapeake Bay.
Mars (44) *Du*.	II. 76-9, Camperdown ; 343-8, captd. in the Texel.
Mars (64) *Da*.	IV. 202-5, Copenhagen ; 209, destd. by the Br. Flt.

Mars (74)	I. 262-9, Cornwallis' Sq. II. 121-3, capts. Hercule (74); 285, Sq. off Brest; 301, blockading Rochefort. III. 384, 409, Trafalgar; 443, casualties. IV. 165-6, engages F. frigates; 175-6, actn. with F. Sq.; 201, Copenhagen; 298, Baltic Flt.
Martin (16)...............	II. 75, Camperdown. III. 477, fndrd. in the North Sea.
Martin (16)...............	IV. 461, fndrd. near Barbadoes.
Martin (18)...............	VI. 97-8, actn. in Delaware Bay.
Martino-de-Freitas (64) *Por.*	IV. 237, Sq. at Lisbon.
Mastiff (12)...............	III. 477, wrkd. on Yarmouth Sands.
Matilda (34) *Sp.*.........	II. 292, Sq. at Carthagena.
Medea (40) *Sp.*	III. 287-8, captd. by Br. Sq. off Cape Santa Maria.
Médée (36) *F.*............	I. 396-7, engages Pelican (18). II. 137, Savary's Sq. III. 22-3, captd. by E.I.C. ships.
Mediator (32)............	IV. 243, crsg. off St. Domingo; 400-21, destd. in actn. at Basque Rds.
Medusa (Armed T.S.)	II. 470, wrkd. Portugal.
Medusa (74) *Por.*	IV. 237, Por. Flt. at Lisbon.
Medusa (32)	III. 65, off Boulogne; 287, capture of Sp. treasure ships. IV. 279, Monte Video exped. V. 331, bts. cut out Dorade (14); 335, Sq. crsg. off Spain.
Medusa (46)	VI. 395, bldg.
Méduse (40) *F.*	I. 413, Cape François. II. 460, fndrd. America.
Méduse (40) *F.*	V. 283, at the Isle of France; 305-6, off Java. VI. 147, crsg.
Melampus (36)	I. 222-4, Warren's Sq.; 318, Strachan's Sq.; 329, engages F. frigates. II. 146, capture of Hoche; 153, capts. Résolue (36); 226, capts. Volage (22). IV. 116, Strachan's Sq.; 248, in the Chesapeake. V. 46, capts. Béarnais (16); 92, off Guadaloupe.
Melampus (46)	VI. 395, bldg.
Meleager (32)............	I. 214, Medn. Flt.; 284, actn. off Genoa; 297, off Hyères; 343, Sq. off Vado. III. 482, wrkd. in the Gulf of Mexico.
Meleager (36)............	IV. 306, crsg. off Cuba; 473, wrkd. Jamaica.
Melpomène (40) *F.* ...	I. 117, Perrée's Sq.; 213, captd. at Calvi, Corsica, added to Br. Navy.
,, (38) *Br*....	II. 164, Saumarez's Sq.; 255, bts. cut out Aventurier (14); 345, Holland exped. III. 118, off Sénégal. V. 39, actn. with Da. gbts.
Melpomène (40) *F.* ...	VI. 3, Toulon Sq.; 227, captd. by Rivoli (74).
Menelaus (38)............	V. 203, capture of the Isle of France; 315, in Hyères Bay; 348-50, crsg. VI. 147, off L'Orient, recapts. San Juan.
Mercedes (34) *Sp.*	II. 404, convoy escort. III. 287-8, destd. in actn.
Mercure (74) *F.*	I. 282, Toulon Flt. II. 178, 193-4, captd. at the Nile; 206, destd.
Mercure (16) *F.*	V. 122, Dubourdieu's Sq.; 233-8, actn. off Lissa; 338-9, destd. in actn. with Weasel (18).
Mercurius (16) *Da.* ...	IV. 209, captd. at Copenhagen.
Mercury (26)	III. 120, capts. Sans Pareille (20); 135, in the Adriatic. IV. 326, Sq. off Cadiz. V. 28, crsg. in the Gulf of Venice; 37-8, off Rovigno.
Mercury (46)	VI. 395, bldg. [Barfleur.
Merlin (16)...............	II. 280, at Honduras. III. 196, off Calais; 202, off Cape
Mermaid (32)	I. 328, off Grenada; 379-80, actn. with Vengeance (40). II. 155-8, actn. with Loire (40); 247, capture of Seine (40). III. 10, in Marseille Bay. VI. 33, in the Adriatic.
Mermaid (46)............	VI. 395, bldg. [Alexandria.
Meteor (bomb.)	IV. 219-29, Dardanelles; 386, at Rosas. VI. 181-90, at
Mexicano (112) *Sp.* ...	II. 36, St. Vincent; 292, Sq. at Carthagena.
Mezoura (40) *Algrn.* ...	VI. 277, captd. by U.S. Sq. off Cape de Gatte.
Michael (74) *Rus.*	IV. 298, Flt. in Oro Rds.
Mignonne (28) *F.*	I. 117, Perrée's Sq.; 213, destd. by the British at Calvi.
Mignonne (16) *F.*	III. 181, captd. by Goliath (74), added to Br. Navy.
Mignonne (16)	IV. 135, late Phaëton (16), q.v.

INDEX TO SHIPS

Milan (38) .... IV. 26, late F. Ville de Milan (40), q.v.
Milbrook (16)............ III. 34-5, engages Bellone (30); 196, off Calais. IV. 475, wrkd. on the Burlings.
Milford (74) .... VI. 30-2, in the Adriatic.
Minden (74) .... V. 297-303, capture of Java. VI. 278, Algiers.
Minerva (38) .... I. 131, in the E. Indies; 184, actn. off Genoa.
Minerva (28) *Du.* ...... II. 76, Camperdown; 347, captd. in the Nieueve Diep, Texel, 1799.
Minerva (32) *Br.* ...... IV. 154, Finisterre Bay, 1806.
Minerva, *Neap.* .... IV. 123, Sq. off Gaeta, Italy.
Minerva (52) *Por.* ..... IV. 237, Por. Flt. at Lisbon. V. 66, captd. by F. Bellone.
,, (40) *F.*............. V. 131, renamed Minerve, fitted out at Port Louis; 135, capture of E.I.C. ships; 137, at Grand Port; 151-8, actn. at Grand Port; 203-5, captd. in Port Louis, Isle of France; unfit for service.
Minerve (38) *F.* .... I. 91, left at Toulon; 117, Sq. crsg.; 210, captd. at San Fiorenzo, renamed San Fiorenzo (36), q.v.[1] [to Br. Navy.
Minerve (40) *F.* .... I. 282, Toulon Flt.; 321-3, captd. by Br. frigates; 324, added
,, (38) *Br.* .... I. 324, at Ajaccio; 406, capts. Sp. Sabina (40). II. 34, St. Vincent. III. 79, off Vado; 182, captd. at Cherbourg; 185, restored to F. Navy, renamed Canonnière (40), q.v.
Minerve (40) *F.* .... IV. 139, at the Isle of Aix; 140-1, actn. with Pallas (32); 175-6, captd. by Hood's Sq. off Rochefort; 177, renamed Alceste (38), q.v.
Minorca (16) .... III. 83, Egypt exped.
Minotaur (74)............ I. 189, Sq. off Ushant. II. 171, Medn. Flt.; 305, blockading Naples; 432-3, Siege of Genoa. III. 79, in Barcelona Rds.; 81, Egypt exped.; 180, capts. Franchise (36); 384, 436-7, Trafalgar; 443, casualties. IV. 201, Copenhagen. V. 40, crsg. off Finland; 444, wrkd. off the Texel.
Minstrel (18) .... V. 129, Roger's Sq. off Spain; 346, off Alicant.
Minx (12) .... III. 222-7, crsg. off Calais. V. 442, captd. by Da. gbts.
Mistisloff (66) *Rus.* .. II. 344, Holland exped.
Modeste (36) *F.*........ I. 96-7, captd. at Genoa, added to Br. Navy.
,, ,, *Br.* .... IV. 366, capts. Jéna (18), renamed Victor (18), q.v. V. 303, capture of Java exped.
Mohawk (28) *U.S.* ...... VI. 207, at Sackett's Harbour.
Monarca (74) *Sp.* ...... III. 374, F. Sp. Flt. Medn.; 386, 410-13, Trafalgar; 456, destd. by the British.
Monarch (74) .... I. 127, Martinique exped.; 333, Sq. at Cape of Good Hope; 416, capture of Du. Sq. II. 75-8, Camperdown, III. 42, 46, Copenhagen; 232, Sq. off Boulogne. IV. 157, 175, Sq. off Rochefort; 236, off the Tagus.
Monarch (84) .... VI. 395, bldg.
Mondovi (18) *Ven.* ..... II. 249, cut out by the bts. of Flora (36).
Monkey (12) .... V. 42, crsg. off Denmark; 448, wrkd. at Belleisle.
Monmouth (64) .... II. 75-8, Camperdown; 344, Holland exped. III. 175, Medn. Flt.
Monnikendam (40) *Du.* .. II. 76-9, captd. at Camperdown.
Montagnard (74) *F.* .... I. 141, Brest Flt.; 150, 29th May.
Montagne (120) *F.* ..... I. 141, Brest Flt.; 165, 1st June.
Montagu (74)............. I. 62, 132, Channel Flt.; 162, 185, 1st June. II. 75-81, Camperdown; 289, Flt. off Cadiz. III. 313, Invas. flotilla. IV. 116, Strachan's Sq.; 292, Sq. at Syracuse. V. 80, St. Maura exped.
Mont Blanc (74) *F.* .... I. 141, Brest Flt.; 161, Brest; 295, Toulon Rd.; 349, Carthagena. II. 286, Brest Flt. III. 176, Toulon; 334, Sq. crsg.; 358-61, Calder's actn.; 386, 434, Trafalgar. IV. 3-8, captd. in Strachan's actn.; 12, added to Br. Navy.
Mont St. Bernardo(74)*F.* V. 316, launched at Malamacca, Venice.
Montanez (74) *Sp.* ..... III. 374, F. Sp. Flt. Medn.; 386, 414, Trafalgar.
Montebello (130) *F.* ... V. 316, launched at Toulon. VI. 2, at Toulon.

[1] Renamed Fortunée, *vide Navy List*.

Montenotte (32) *F.* ...	II. 215, Sq. at Alexandria.
Montgomery (11) *U.S.*	VI. 115, Lake Champlain.
Montréal (32) *F.*	I. 91, destd. at Toulon.
Morne-Fortunée (12)...	V. 442, wrkd. Martinique.
Mornington, *E.I.C.* ...	V. 303, capture of Java exped.
Moscow (74) *Rus.*	IV. 234, Flt. in the Dardanelles.
Moselle (18)	I. 325, crsg. off Genoa. IV. 119, crsg. off Cadiz.
Moselle (24)	I. 439, captd. at Toulon.
Mosquito (10)............	VI. 365, Navarino.
Motchnoy (74) *Rus.* ...	IV. 234, Flt. in the Dardanelles.
Mouche (16) *F.*	I. 356, Daugier's Sq. V. 27, actn. with Goldfinch (10).
Moucheron (16)	IV. 466, wrkd. in the Medn.
Mucius (74) *F.*	I. 141, Brest Flt.; 174, 1st June; 264, Brest Flt. II. 5, Ireland exped.
Muiron (38) *F.*	II. 215, Sq. at Alexandria; 336, at Corsica. III. 96, 99–100, Algesiras.
Muros (20)	IV. 473, wrkd. Cuba.
Musette (16)	IV. 135, late Voltigeur (16), q.v.
Mutine (16) *F.*	I. 253, Sq. off Sierra Leone; 387, captd. by Stopford's Sq., added to Br. Navy.
Mutine (16) *F.*	II. 62, captd. at Santa Cruz; 63, added to Br. Navy.
,, ,, *Br.*.........	II. 170, Medn.; 307, Sq. off Naples. IV. 205, Copenhagen. VI. 9, capts. Invincible (16); 278, Algiers.
Mutine (16) *F.*	III. 124, crsg. off Barbadoes; 189, actn. with Racoon (18).
Myrtle (18)	V. 313, crsg. off Ushant.
Naiad (38)	II. 269, capture of Décade (36); 401, capture of Sp. frigates. III. 185, off Brest; 384, Trafalgar. IV. 393, off Brest. V. 218, actn. off Boulogne. VI. 274, Algiers.
Naïade (16) *F.*	IV. 75–6, captd. by Jason (32).
Namur (90)...............	II. 24, at Gibraltar; 34–43, St. Vincent; 289, Flt. off Cadiz.
Namur (74)...............	IV. 3–7, Strachan's actn.; 89, Warren's Sq.
Narcissus (20)............	II. 456, wrkd. New Providence.
Narcissus (32)............	III. 275, Hyères Bay. IV. 186, Sq. at the Cape of Good Hope; 313, Sq. off L'Orient. VI. 90, bts. cut out U.S. Surveyor (6); 169, in Chesapeake Bay.
Nassau (T.S.)............	II. 475, wrkd. Holland.
Nassau (64)...............	IV. 200, Copenhagen; 319, capture of Da. Prindts-Christian-Frederic (74).
Nautilus (18)	I. 127, Martinique exped.; 240, capture of Martinique. IV. 136, crsg. off Carthagena; 215, Sq. in Azire Bay; 465, wrkd. in the Levant.
Nautilus (16)	II. 474, wrkd. off Flamborough Head.
Nautilus (14) *E.I.C.*...	V. 303, capture of Java exped. VI. 266, actn. with U.S. Peacock (20).
Nayaden (40) *Da.*	V. 325–6, destd. by Dictator (64).
Néarque (16) *F.*.........	IV. 159, captd. by Niobe (38).
Nécessité (26) *F.*	V. 97, captd. by Horatio (38).
Nemesis (28)	I. 94, Sq. at Corsica; 305, captd. by Sensible (36); 342, recaptd. by a Br. Sq. near Tunis. III. 17, Sq. off Dunkerque; 41–2, capture of Da. Freya (40). V. 99, crsg. off Norway. VI. 95, in Chesapeake Bay.
Nemesis (48)	VI. 395, bldg.
Neptune (74) *F.*.........	I. 60, Flt. in Quiberon Bay; 141, Brest Flt.; 163, 1st June; 261, wrkd. in Péros Bay.
Neptune (80) *F.*.........	III. 177, launched at Toulon; 334, Villeneuve's Flt.; 358, Calder's actn.; 386, 401, 455, Trafalgar. IV. 295, captd. in Cadiz Harbour.
Neptune (98)	II. 285, Sq. off Brest; 297, Medn. III. 384, 428, Trafalgar; 443, casualties. V. 18, Sq. off the Saintes; 69, capture of Martinique.

INDEX TO SHIPS

Neptune (10) *F.*..........	II. 259, captd. by Hazard (18).
Neptune (30) *E.I.C.* ...	III. 22–3, actn. with F. frigates.
Neptune (80) *Sp.*	II. 36, St. Vincent ; 299, Flt. at Cadiz. III. 374, F. Sp. Flt.; 386, 437, captd. at Trafalgar ; 455, recaptd.
Neptuno (20) *Sp.*	III. 142, cut out by the bts. of a Br. Sq. off Corunna.
Neptuno (14) *Sp.*	IV. 185, captd. by Halcyon (16).
Neptunos (80) *Da.*......	IV. 209, captd. at Copenhagen ; 210, destd.
Néréide (36) *F.*	II. 103, captd. by Phœbe (36) ; 105, added to Br. Navy.
,, ,, *Br.*	III. 8, capts. Vengeance (18) (priv.) ; 38, at Curaçoa. V. 58, Sq. at St. Paul's ; 137, at the Isle of France ; 145, off Grand Port ; 151, at Isle de la Passe ; 160, captd. by Bellone (40) and consorts ; 205, recaptd. and broken up at Grand Port.
Néréide (40) *F.*	V. 91, Guadaloupe ; 93, actn. with Rainbow (22) ; 282–7, actn. off Madagascar ; 292, captd. ; 295, renamed Madagascar (38), q.v.
Néréide (38)	V. 190, late Vénus (40), q.v. ; 203, capture of Isle of France exped.
Nereus (46)...............	VI. 395, bldg.
Nestor (74) *F.*	I. 189, Cornice's Sq. crsg. ; 264, Brest Flt. II. 5–9, Ireland exped.
Netley (14)	III. 351, convoy escort. IV. 466, captd. in the W. Indies.
Netley (12)	IV. 474, wrkd. on the Leeward Isles.
Nettuno (16) *Ital.*	IV. 343, captd. by Unité (36), renamed Cretan (16).
Neuf-Thermidor (74) *F.*	I. 261, late Jacobin (74), q.v., fndrd.
Newcastle (50)	VI. 255, chases U.S. Constitution (44).
Niagara (20) *U.S.*	VI. 208, actn. on Lake Huron.
Niemen (40) *F.*	V. 13–5, captd. by Amethyst (36) ; 16, added to Br. Navy.
Niger (32)	I. 62, 139, Channel Flt.; 318, Strachan's Sq.; 362, off the Penmarcks. II. 34, St. Vincent ; 231, Sq. off the Seine. III. 27, Barcelona Rds. VI. 131, capture of Cérès (40).
Nijaden (36) *Da.*	IV. 209, captd. at Copenhagen, added to Br. Navy.
,, ,, *Br.*.........	V. 314, actn. with a F. Sq.
Nile (12)..................	III. 37, crsg. in Quiberon Bay ; 357, Calder's Flt.
Nimble (10)	V. 451, fndrd. in the Cattegat.
Nimrod (18)	II. 415, late Eole (16), q.v. VI. 197, off Buzzard's Bay, Connecticut.
Ninfa (34) *Sp.*............	II. 34, captd. by a Br. Sq., renamed Hamadryad (36), q.v.
Niobe (38)	II. 444, late Diane (40), q.v. IV. 54, Sq. off Cape Finisterre ; 159, capts. Néarque (16). V. 212, Amazone (40) destd.
Nisus (16) *F.*	V. 45, cut out by the bts. of a Br. Sq. ; 46, renamed Guadaloupe, q.v.
Nisus (38)	V. 203, capture of Isle of France exped. ; 303, capture of Java exped.
Nonsuch (30) *E.I.C.*...	I. 218–9, actn. with F. privs.
Norge (74) *Da.*	IV. 209, captd. at Copenhagen ; 212, added to Br. Navy.
North Star (74) *Rus.*....	IV. 298, Flt. in Oro Rds.
Northumberland (74)*F.*	I. 60, Flt. in Quiberon Bay ; 141, Brest Flt. ; 168, captd. on 1st June.
,, ,, *Br.*	II. 289, Flt. off Cadiz ; 307, at Palermo ; 439, 444, blockade of Malta. III. 81, Egypt exped. IV. 93–7, Duckworth's actn.; 101, casualties. V. 312, 320, off L'Orient ; 321, des. F. frigates.
Nymphe (36)	I. 106–8, capts. Cléopâtre (36) ; 222, action with F. frigates ; 271, Channel Flt. II. 91, off Brest ; 287, off Ushant. IV. 327, crsg. off Lisbon. V. 445, wrkd. off the Frith of Forth.
Nymphe (40) *F.*..........	V. 283, off the Isle of France ; 305, escapes from a Br. Sq.
Nymphe (38)	VI. 198, crsg. off Boston.
Nymphen (36) *Da.* ...	IV. 209, 464, captd. at Copenhagen, added to Br. Navy.
,, ,, *Br.*......	IV. 438, Scheldt exped.
Océan (120) *F.*	II. 285, Brest Flt. III. 215, reprg. IV. 391, Brest Flt.; 401, 408, 419–21, actn. in Basque Rds.; 430, in the Charente River.

Ocean (98)	IV. 292, Sq. at Syracuse. VI. 117, Medn. Flt.
Ocean (30) *E.I.C.*	II. 89, escapes a F. Sq. III. 250, actn. with Linois' Sq.
Oiseau (36)	I. 109, late Cléopâtre (36), q.v. II. 94, engages Sp. frigates. III. 123, capture of Dédaigneuse (36).
Oiseau (18) *F.*	II. 99, captd. by Penguin (16).
Oiseau (10) *F.*	III. 298, F. Sq. at Gorée.
Olympia (10)	V. 448, captd. off Dieppe.
Oncle Thomas (20) *F.*	III. 298, F. Sq. at Gorée.
Oneida (16) *U.S.*	VI. 102-6, Canadian Lakes.
Onyx (10)	V. 1, capts. Du. Manly (16) (late Br.).
Oreste (16) *F.*	V. 86, captd. by Scorpion (18), renamed Wellington (16), q.v.
Orestes (18)	II. 129, at St. Marcouf; 474, fndrd. in the Indian Ocean.
Orestes (14)	IV. 456, wrkd. in Dunkerque Rds.
Orestes (16)	V. 104, capts. Loup Garou (16).
Orient (120) *F.*	II. 168, Medn. Flt.; 178, 191, destd. at the Nile, late Sans Culotte (120), q.v.
Oriente (74) *Sp.*	II. 36, St. Vincent; 292, at Carthagena.
Orion (74)	I. 139, Channel Flt.; 152, 29th May; 183, 1st June; 271-5, Isle Groix; 329, chases Tortue (40). II. 34, 38-40, St. Vincent; 166, 171, Medn.; 184-5, the Nile; 197, casualties. III. 384, 432-3, Trafalgar; 443, casualties. IV. 200, Copenhagen; 298, Baltic Flt.
Orion (74) *F.*	I. 72, at Toulon.
Ornen (12) *Da.*	IV. 209, captd. at Copenhagen.
Orpheus (32)	I. 226, in the E. Indies; 336, Malacca exped. II. 412, capts. Du. ships. IV. 185, crsg.; 465, wrkd. Jamaica.
Orpheus (36)	VI. 156, capts. U.S. Frolic (18).
Orquixo (18)	IV. 456, fndrd. near Jamaica.
Osprey (18)	III. 195, off Trinidad; 257, engages Egyptienne (36); 353, crsg. V. 327, off Heligoland.
Otter (18)	V. 57, crsg. off the Isle of France.
Overyssel (64) *Du.*	I. 442, captd. by Polyphemus (64) in Cork Harbour.
,, ,, *Br.*	II. 345, Holland exped.
Owen Glendower (36)	IV. 431, Scheldt exped.

Palinure (16) *F.*	IV. 48, Allemand's Sq.; 331, capts. Carnation (18).
Pallas (32)	I. 189, 262, Sq. off Ushant. II. 469, wrkd. in Plymouth Sound.
Pallas (32)	IV. 138, off the Gironde; 140, actn. with Minerve (40); 400, actn. in Basque Rds. V. 445, wrkd. off the Frith of Forth.
Pallas (36) *Du.*	IV. 163-4, captd. by Greyhound (32) and Harrier (18).
Pallas (38) *F.*	III. 4-6, captd. by a Br. Sq.; 7, renamed Pique (36), q.v.
Pallas (40) *F.*	IV. 395, Sq. blockaded in Basque Rds.
Pandora (14)	II. 462, fndrd. in the North Sea.
Pandora (18)	V. 447, wrkd. on the Scaw Reef, Cattegat.
Pandour (44)	III. 256, off Martinique; 296, Sq. at the capture of Surinam.
Papillon (priv.) (14) *F.*	II. 226-7, captd. by Speedy (14), added to Br. Navy.
,, ,, *Br.*	IV. 30, at Jamaica; 461, fndrd. off Jamaica.
Papillon (16)	I. 203, Nielly's Sq. IV. 260, off Cherbourg. V. 47, captd. by Rosamond (18), added to Br. Navy.
Pasley (16)	III. 149, actn. with Sp. Zebec (22).
Patriote (74) *F.*	I. 72, Medn. Flt.; 141, Brest Flt.; 163, 183, 1st June. II. 5-9, Ireland exped. III. 312, Brest Flt. IV. 88, Willaumez's Sq.; 109, Duckworth's actn.; 117, in Chesapeake Bay; 247, blockaded; 287, at the Isle of Aix; 395, blockaded in Basque Rds.; 401-11, actn. in Basque Rds; 421, in the Charente River; 430, off Rochefort.
Pauline (40) *F.*	V. 10-11, with Pénélope (40) capts. Proserpine (32); 262-3, actn. with Alceste (38) and Active (38); 315, off Toulon. VI. 3, Toulon Sq.
Paz (22) *Sp.*	III. 27, cut out by the bts. of Minotaur (74).

INDEX TO SHIPS 31

Peacock (20) *U.S.*	V. 434, blt. at New York. VI. 159-60, capts. Epervier (18) 267, engages E.I.C. Nautilus (10).
Peacock (18)	VI. 46-8, captd. and destd. by U.S. Hornet (20).
Peacock (18)	VI. 387, fndrd. off the south coast of the United States.
Pearl (32)	I. 91, late Perle (40), captd. at Toulon, q.v. II. 246, crsg. off Sierra Leone. III. 78, Sq. crsg. off Elba.
Pégase (74) *F.*	II. 4, late Barras (74), q.v.; 5, Ireland exped.; 11, at Brest.
Pegasus (28)	I. 62, 139, Channel Flt.; 364, Sq. off the Texel.
Pegasus (46)	VI. 395, bldg.
Pelayo (74) *Sp.*	II. 36, St. Vincent; 292, Sq. at Carthagena; 299, Flt. off Cadiz.
Pelican (18)	I. 396-7, actn. with Médée (36); 410, at Martinique. II. 100, des. Trompeur (12); 454, capts. Du. Jason (36) at Greenock. VI. 78-80, capts. U.S. Argus (18).
Pelletier (74) *F.*	I. 141, Brest Flt.; 163, 1st June; 203, Nielly's Sq.
Pelorus (18)	V. 45, crsg. off Guadaloupe; 69, capture of Martinique exped.
Pelter (12)	V. 442, fndrd. off Halifax.
Pembroke (74)	VI. 395, rprg.
Penelope (18)	II. 298, Flt. off Gibraltar.
Penelope (32)	I. 122, capture of Inconstante (36); 251, St. Domingo. II. 440-3, capture of Guillaume Tell (80). III. 223, crsg. off Ostende. IV. 112, Sq. off Belleisle. V. 69, capture of Martinique exped. VI. 391, wrkd. Canada.
Pénélope (40) *F.*	IV. 291, at Toulon. V. 10, capture of Proserpine (32). VI. 3, Toulon Sq.
Penelope (46)	VI. 395, bldg.
Penguin (18)	II. 99, capts. Oiseau (18). III. 125, engages F. ships; 257, des. Renommée (12). VI. 261-4, captd. by U.S. Hornet (20).
Pensée (36) *F.*	I. 377-8, actn. with Aimable (32).
Perdrix (22)	II. 272, capts. Armée-d'Italie (18).
Perla (34) *Sp.*	I. 407, crsg. III. 480, destd. in the actn. of Gut of Gibraltar.
Perle (40) *F.*	I. 91, 431, captd. at Toulon, renamed Pearl (32), q.v.
Perlen (38) *Da.*	IV. 209, 464, captd. at Copenhagen; added to Br. Navy.
,, ,, *Br.*	V. 209-10, crsg. off Toulon.
Persanne (26) *F.*	V. 262-5, captd. by Unité (36).
Perseus (bomb.)	II. 307, Sq. off Procida; 320, off Alexandria.
Persian (18)	VI. 381, wrkd. W. Indies.
Pert (14)	IV. 466, wrkd. on the Isle of Santa-Margarita.
Peruvian (18)	VI. 201, Penobscot exped.
Peterel (16)	I. 343, Sq. cff Genoa. II. 220, capture of Minorca exped. III. 10, Sq. crsg. in the Bay of Marseille.
Peuple (120) *F.*	I. 264, Brest Flt.
Peuple Souverain (74) *F.*	I. 282, Medn. Flt. II. 178, 189, 197, captd. at the Nile; 207, renamed Guerrier, guardship, Gibraltar.
Phaëton (38)	I. 62, Channel Flt.; 100, Sq. in the Medn.; 139, Channel Flt.; 176, 1st June; 262-9, Flt. off Ushant. II. 106, crsg.; 228; 248, Stopford's Sq.; 269, capture of Flore (32). IV. 53, actn. with Sémillante (36). V. 303-7, capture of Java exped.
Phaëton (16) *F.*	IV. 135, captd. by Pique (36), renamed Mignonne (16), q.v.
Philadelphia (44) *U.S.*	III. 300-2, destd. off Tripoli.
Philomel (18)	V. 84, actn. off Toulon; 346, off Alicante. VI. 365-73, Navarino.
Phipps (14)	V. 108-9, capts. Barbier-de-Séville (16).
Phocion (74) *F.*	I. 128, Royalist, renamed Ferme (74), q.v.
Phœbe (36)	II. 103-4, capts. Néréide (36). III. 8, capts. Heureux (22); 127-9, capts. Africaine (40); 175, Medn. Sq.; 238, Medn.; 384, Trafalgar. IV. 160, crsg. off the Shetland Isles. V. 203, capture of Isle of France exped.; 283-6, actn. off Madagascar; 303-9, capture of Java exped.
Phœnix (36)	I. 62, Channel Flt.; 131, in the E. Indies; 364, capts. Du. Argo (36). III. 78, capture of Carrère (38). IV. 2-9, Strachan's actn.; 65-9, capts. Didon (40); 287, off Isle of Aix. VI. 393, wrkd. near Smyrna.

Phœnix (36) *Du.*	IV. 179, off Java; 181, captd. by a Br. Sq.
Phosphorus (F.S.)	IV. 167, actn. with F. priv. (12).
Piane (40) *F.*	V. 316, blt. at Venice.
Pickle (10)	IV. 475, wrkd. while entering Cadiz.
Picton (14)	VI. 198, destd. by U.S. Constitution (44).
Piémontaise (40) *F.* ...	IV. 150-2, capts. E.I.C. Warren Hastings (44); 307-9, captd. by San Fiorenzo (36), added to Br. Navy.
,, (38) *Br.*...	V. 195, capture of Banda Neira exped.
Pigmy (14)	I. 433, wrkd. on the Motherbank.
Pigmy (14)	IV. 457, wrkd. in St Aubin's Bay, Jersey.
Pigmy (14)	IV. 466, wrkd. near Rochefort.
Pilade (36)	I. 284, actn. off Genoa.
Pilade (16) *F.*............	IV. 332, captd. by Pompée (74).
Pilot (18)..................	V. 257, off Strongoli; 341, off Policastro. VI. 227, actn. with Légère (22).
Pincher (12)	IV. 205, Copenhagen.
Pique (36) *F.*	I. 309-11, captd. by Blanche (32); 313, added to the Br. Navy.
,, ,, *Br.*	II. 247, engages Seine (40); 248, wrkd. on the coast of France.
Pique (36)	III. 7, late Pallas (36), q.v.; 75, crsg. off Brindisi. IV. 134-5, capts. Voltigeur (16) and Phaëton (16). VI. 198-200, with U.S. Constitution (44).
Pitt (36)	IV. 355, off Port Louis, renamed Salsette (36), q.v.
Pitt (12)	IV. 181-2, capts. Superbe (14) (priv.).
Plantagenet (74).........	IV. 236, Sq. off the Tagus. VI. 223-4, Sq. off the Western Isles, bts. repulsed by U.S. priv. General Armstrong.
Plover (18)	IV. 439, Scheldt exped.
Plumper (12)	III. 317-8, crsg. off Granville. IV. 457, captd. off St. Mâlo. V. 451, wrkd. in the Bay of Fundy.
Pluto (68) *Du.*	IV. 284, destd. at Gressie.
Pluton (74) *F.*	II. 5, Ireland exped.; 11, Brest. III. 349, capture of the Diamond Rock; 358, Calder's actn.; 386, 411, Trafalgar. IV. 295, captd. at Cadiz by the Sp.
Podargus (14)	V. 325, Sq. off Norway, actn. with Da. Sq.
Poictiers (74)	V. 313, chasing a F. Sq.; 393, recapts. Frolic (18) and capts. U.S. Wasp (18).
Pollock (24) *Du.*	II. 347, captd. in the Nieuwe Diep, Texel.
Polyphemus (64)	I. 442, capts. Du. Overyssel (64), q.v. II. 460, capts. Tortue (40), q.v. III. 46, Copenhagen; 384, 438, Trafalgar. IV. 157, Sq. off Rochefort; 281, at Buenos Ayres; 382, off Santo Domingo. V. 18, Sq. off the Saintes; 357, at Jamaica.
Pomona (34) *Sp.*	II. 254, Sq. actn. with Lion (64). IV. 169-70, captd. by Br. frigates, renamed Cuba (32).
Pomone (44) *F.*	I. 223, captd. by Warren's Sq.; 226, added to Br. Navy.
,, (40) *Br.*	I. 278, Quiberon exped.; 330, Warren's Sq.; 381, Andromaque (36) destd. II. 96, Sq. crsg.; 119, ashore. III. 78, capture of Carrère (36). IV. 258, crsg. V. 32, capts. Neap. priv.; 246, des. F. vessels; 447, wrkd. on the Needle Rocks.
Pomone (38)	V. 205, late Astrée (40), q.v. VI. 237, Sq. crsg. off New York; 240, capture of U.S. President (44).
Pomone (40) *F.*	V. 262-4, captd. by Alceste (38) and Active (38); 266, broken up.
Pompée (74) *F.*	I. 72, 91, captd. at Toulon, added to Br. Navy.
,, ,, *Br.*	II. 285, Sq. off Brest; 297, in the Medn. III. 98-104, Algesiras. IV. 123, Sq. at Palermo; 200, Copenhagen; 219, Dardanelles; 332, capts. Pilade (16). V. 18, Sq. off the Saintes; 21, capture of D'Haupoult (74); 69, capture of Martinique exped.; 313, chases Allemand's Sq. VI. 2, Medn. Flt.
Porcupine (22)	IV. 268, crsg. in the Adriatic; 289, off Corfu; 345, bts. cutting out expeds.
Porpoise (S.S.)	III. 490, wrkd. in the Pacific Ocean.

INDEX TO SHIPS

Port d'Espagne (14) ...	IV. 259, capts. Sp. priv. in the Gulf of Paria.
Portland (60)	VI. 395, bldg.
Poursuivante (44) *F.* ...	III. 17, Dunkerque Rds. ; 181, actn. with Hercule (74) ; 182, laid up at Rochefort.
Powerful (74)	II. 75-8, Camperdown ; 292, Medn. Flt.; 307, Nelson's Sq. off Sicily. IV. 90, Louis' Sq.; 156, capts. Bellone (36); 180, Sq. off Batavia ; 283, capture of Gressie.
Powerful (84)	VI. 395, bldg.
Précieuse (36) *F.*	II. 31, Ganteaume's Sq. in Bertheaume Bay.
Preneuse (36) *F.*	II. 244, capts. E.I.C. ships ; 390, engages Camel (44) and Rattlesnake (16) ; 393, beats off Jupiter (50) ; 394, destd. by Tremendous (74) and Adamant (50).
President (44) *U.S.* ...	V. 273, actn. with Little Belt (18) ; 359, engages Belvidera (36) ; 407-8, crsg. off Bermuda. VI. 69-71, crsg. ; 147-9, crsg. ; 239-43, captd. by Endymion (40) and consorts. VI. 246, at Spithead ; 247, added to Br. Navy.
Présidente (40) *F.*	IV. 177-8, captd. by Hood's Sq.; 179, added to Br. Navy.
,, (38) *Br.* ...	V. 303-9, capture of Java exped.
Prévoyante (36) *F.*......	I. 319, captd. by Thetis (36) and Hussar (28) ; 320, added to Br. Navy as S.S.
Primrose (18)	V. 441, wrkd. near Falmouth.
Primrose (18)	VI. 142-3, actn. with Duke of Marlborough (packet).
Prince (98)	I. 65, 271, Channel Flt. II. 120, crsg. off Ireland ; 285, Sq. off Brest ; 297, in the Medn. III. 384, 429, 441, Trafalgar.
Prince de Neufchatel (18) *U.S.*	VI. 237, repulses the bts. of Endymion (40).
Prince Eugene (16) *F.*	IV. 264, cut out by the bts. of Hydra (38).
Prince George (98)......	I. 271, Channel Flt. II. 34-43, St. Vincent ; 289, Flt. off Cadiz.
Prince of Wales (98) ...	I. 270, Channel Flt. II. 109, Flt. off Trinidad ; 420, capture of Surinam exped. III. 357-61, Calder's actn. IV. 157, Sq. off Rochefort ; 200, Copenhagen. VI. 2, 117, Medn. Flt.
Prince Regent (120) ...	VI. 395, bldg.
Prince Regent (58)......	VI. 203, launched at Kingston, Lake Ontario.
Princess Charlotte (42)	VI. 203, launched at Kingston, Lake Ontario.
Princess Charlotte (36)	II. 295, late Junon (36), q.v. IV. 13, crsg. W. Indies ; 75-6, recapts. Cyane (26).
Princess Charlotte (110)	VI. 395, bldg.
Princess Orange (74)...	II. 348, purchased from the Dutch, late Du. Washington (74), q.v.
Princess Royal (30) *E.I.C.*	I. 218, captd. by three F. privs. near Java.
Princess Royal (98) ...	I. 72, Medn. Flt. ; 214, Corsica ; 284-90, actn. off Genoa ; 297, off Hyères. II. 289, Flt. off Cadiz.
Princessa-de-Biera (74) *Por.*	I. 202, Br. and Por. Flt. in the Channel.
Princesse Carolina (74) *Da.*	IV. 209, 464, captd. at Copenhagen ; 212, added to the Br. Navy.
Princesse-Sophia-Frederica (80) *Da.*	IV. 209, 464, captd. at Copenhagen.
Princessen-Louisa-Augusta (64) *Da.*	IV. 202, at Fredrickswaern, Norway.
Principe-de-Asturias (112) *Sp.*	I. 407, Sq. chases Minerve (38). II. 36, 49, St. Vincent ; 299, Flt. at Cadiz. III. 373, Flt. off Ferrol ; 386, 437-40, Trafalgar.
Principe-de-Brazil (74) *Por.*	IV. 237, Sq. at Lisbon.
Principe-Reale (74) *Por.*	II. 211, Sq. in the Medn. ; 306, at Palermo. IV. 237, Sq. at Lisbon.
Prindts-Christian-Frederic (74)	IV. 202, at Christiansand, Norway ; 319, destd. by Stately (64) and Nassau (64).
Procris (18)...............	V. 300-3, capture of Java exped.

D

Prometheus (18)	V. 40, Martin's Sq. crsg. off Finland.
Prosélyte (36) *F.*	I. 91, 432, captd. at Toulon, added to Br. Navy.
,, ,, *Br.*	I. 211, destd. in actn. at Bastia.
Prosélyte (32)	III. 482, wrkd. W. Indies.
Prosélyte (bomb)	V. 442, wrkd. in the Baltic.
Proserpine (40) *F.*	I. 264, Brest. Flt.; 356, Daugier's Sq.; 369, captd. by Dryad (36); 370, renamed Amelia (38), q.v.
Proserpine (28)	II. 354-5, wrkd. River Elbe.
Proserpine (34) *Sp.* ...	II. 254, Sq. actn. with Lion (64).
Proserpine (32) *Du.* ...	III. 298, captd. at Surinam, added to Br. Navy.
,, ,, *Br.* ...	V. 10-11, captd. by Pénélope (40) and Pauline (40).
Proserpine (46)	VI. 395, bldg.
Prospero (bomb.)	IV. 466, fndrd. in the North Sea.
Provernoy (48) *Rus.* ...	VI. 365, Navarino.
Providence (*Despatch Vessel*)	II. 462, wrkd. in the Pacific Ocean.
Prudente (36) *F.*	I. 218, Sq. crsg. in the E. Indies; 236, crsg. off the Isle of France; 392, Sercey's Sq. actn. with two Br. 74's. II. 357-8, captd. by Dædalus (32).
Psyché (36) *F.*	III. 268-70, actn. with Wilhelmina (32); 271, at the Isle of France. IV. 18-9, captd. by San Fiorenzo (36); 20, added to Br. Navy.
,, ,, *Br.*	IV. 282, Pellew's Sq. off Gressie. V. 204, capture of Isle of France exped.; 303, capture of Java exped.
Puissant (74) *F.*	I. 72, refitting; 91, captd. at Toulon, added to Br. Navy.
Pulstuck (74) *F.*	IV. 432, late Audacieux (74), q.v.; 435, Sq. off the Calot, in the Scheldt.
Pultusk (16)	V. 45, Sq. crsg. off Guadaloupe, capture of Nisus (16).
Pylades (16)	I. 439, wrkd. Shetland.
Pylades (16)	II. 382, Sq. crsg. off Holland, recapture of Crash (12).
Pylades (18) *Du.*	III. 298, captd. at Surinam.
Quatorze Juillet (74) *F.*	II. 466, destd. by fire at L'Orient.
Quebec (32)	I. 99, Sq. off Ostende; 240, capture of Martinique exped.; 380, off St. Domingo. II. 113, Sq. at Jean-Rabel. IV. 213, capture of Heligoland. V. 105, bts. cut out Jeune Louise (14); 220, Sq. crsg. off the Texel, bts. cutting out exped.
Queen (98)	I. 127, Sq. at Martinique; 139, Channel Flt.; 150, 29th May; 162, 184, 1st June; 270-3, actn. off Isle Groix. II. 112, Sq. at St. Domingo.
Queen Charlotte (100)	I. 62, 139, Channel Flt.; 151-3, 29th May; 165, 1st June; 270-3, actn. off Isle Groix. II. 26-8, Mutiny at Spithead; 293, Medn.; 429-31, lost by fire.
Queen Charlotte (100)	VI. 278, Algiers.
Racehorse (18)	VI. 283-5, actn. off Madagascar.
Racer (12)	V. 445, wrkd. on the coast of France.
Racer (14)	VI. 388, wrkd. in the Gulf of Florida.
Racoon (18)	II. 415-6, capts. Intrépide (16). III. 188, capts. Lodi (10); 189-90, actn. with Mutine (16) off Cuba.
Rafael (80) *Rus.*	IV. 234, Flt. in the Dardanelles.
Railleur (14)	III. 477, fndrd. in the Channel.
Rainbow (22)	V. 2, late Iris (22), q.v.; 93-4, actn. with Néréide (40).
Rainha - de - Portugal (74) *Por.*	I. 202, Br. and Por. Flt. in the Channel. II. 211, Sq. in the Medn. IV. 237, Sq. at Lisbon.
Raison (18) *F.*	I. 319, captd. by Hussar (28), added to Br. Navy.
,, (20) *Br.*	I. 320, at Halifax; 384, engages Vengeance (40).
Raisonable (64)	III. 47, Sq. off Isle Huën, Copenhagen; 357-8, Calder's actn. IV. 45, engages Topaze (40); 186, Cape of Good Hope exped.; 279, Buenos Ayres exped. V. 58, capture of St. Paul's, Isle Bourbon; 141, becomes unserviceable.

INDEX TO SHIPS

Raleigh (18)	IV. 287, escape of Rochefort Sq.
Rambler (14)	V. 127, bts. cut out F. priv.
Ramillies (74)	I. 62, 139, Channel Flt.; 155, 29th May; 180, 1st June. II. 301, Sq. off Aix. III. 47, Sq. off Isle Huën, Copenhagen. IV. 89, Warren's Sq. VI. 100, 193, off New London.
Ranger (14)	I. 440, captd. by a F. Sq. off Brest.
Ranger (18)	IV. 48, captd. by the Rochefort Sq.
Rapid (50) *Rus.*	IV. 298, Flt. in Oro Rds.
Rapid (14)	IV. 329, capture of Sp. ships; 474, destd. in the Tagus.
Raposa (12) *Sp.*	IV. 128, cut out by the bts. of Franchise (36), added to Br. Navy.
,, (10) *Br.*	IV. 474, destd. near Carthagena to prevent capture.
Rattler (16)	III. 222-4, actn. off Ostende. V. 367, meets U.S. Essex.
Rattlesnake (16)	I. 413, capture of Columbo exped.; 416, Sq. in Simon's Bay. II. 391, actn. with Preneuse (36).
Ratvison (74) *Rus.*	II. 344, Holland exped. IV. 234, Flt. in the Dardanelles.
Raven (18)	II. 34, St. Vincent; 469, wrkd. near Cuxhaven.
Raven (18)	III. 494, wrkd. in the Medn.
Raven (18)	IV. 456, wrkd. in Cadiz Bay.
Raven (16)	IV. 436, Scheldt exped. V. 220, Sq. off the Texel; 324, actn. with F. brigs off Flushing.
Rayo (100) *Sp.*	III. 386, 433, Trafalgar; 456, wrkd.
Real Carlos (112) *Sp.*	II. 450, Sq. at Ferrol. III. 112-3, destd. in the Gut of Gibraltar.
Recovery (10)	II. 229, capts. Revanche (10).
Recruit (18)	IV. 273, off the Isle of Sombrero; 372, actn. with Diligente (18). V. 19-20, actn. with F. frigates; 69, capture of Martinique exped.
Redbridge (12)	III. 490, captd. by a F. Sq. off Toulon. IV. 461, wrkd. on the Providence station.
Redbridge (10)	IV. 457, fndrd. near Jamaica.
Rédoubtable (74) *F.*	I. 264, Brest Flt. II. 5, Ireland exped.; 9, 286, Brest Flt. III. 373, Flt. off Ferrol; 386, 424, Trafalgar; 453, wrkd.
Redpole (10)	IV. 400, actn. in Basque Rds. V. 217, actn. off Boulogne.
Redwing (18)	IV. 337, actn. with Sp. privs. V. 9, crsg. in the Adriatic. VI. 17, cutting out exped. Medn.
Régénérée (36) *F.*	I. 264, Brest Flt.; 387-8, Sq. at the Isle of France; 392, Sq. actn. with two Br. 74's. II. 250, actn. with Brilliant (28). III. 93, captd. at Alexandria, renamed Alexandria (36), q.v.
Régulus (74) *F.*	IV. 178, L'Hermitte's Sq.; 391, Brest Flt.; 401, actn. in Basque Rds.; 430, off Rochefort. VI. 121, destd. in the Gironde to prevent capture.
Regulus, en flûte (44)	II. 114, off St. Domingo; 253, crsg. off Porto Rico.
Reindeer (18)	IV. 133, actn. with F. brigs. V. 357, convoy escort, Jamaica. VI. 161-4, destd. by U.S. Wasp (20).
Renard (18)	IV. 27, des. Général Ernouf (20); 147, capts. Diligent (16).
Renard (16) *F.*	V. 345, actn. with Swallow (18).
Renommée (36) *F.*	II. 453, captd. by Alfred (74) off St. Domingo, added to Br. Navy.
,, ,, *Br.*	III. 323, actn. off Calais. IV. 136, 270, watching off Carthagena.
Renommée (40) *F.*	V. 47, capture of Junon (38); 283-8, captd. in actn. off Madagascar; 295, renamed Java (38), q.v.
Renown (74)	II. 301, Sq. off Aix; 450, Sq. at Ferrol. III. 15, crsg. off the Penmarcks; 73, off Cadiz; 175, off Toulon. IV. 288, Sq. in Palermo Bay; 445, Sq. crsg. off Barcelona.
Réolaise (20) *F.*	III. 37, destd. by the bts. of Magicienne (32).
Républicain (110) *F.*	I. 141, Brest Flt.; 163, 185, 1st June; 437, wrkd. on the Mingan Rock.
Républicain (110) *F.*	II. 285, and III. 312, Brest Flt., late Révolutionnaire (110).
Républicaine (20) *F.*	I. 144, destd. by Howe's Flt.
Républicaine (18) *F.*	I. 328-9, captd. by Mermaid (32).
Républicaine (28) *F.*	II. 387, captd. by Tamar (38).
Repulse (64)	II. 293, Medn. Flt.; 426-7, wrkd. off Ushant.

Repulse (74)	III. 357-62, Calder's actn. IV. 89, Warren's Sq.; 219, Dardanelles; 292, Sq. at Syracuse; 439, Scheldt exped. V. 85, actn. with F. frigates; 208, Medn. Flt. VI. 17, crsg. in the Medn.
Requin (10)	III. 482, wrkd. near Quiberon.
Requin (16)	IV. 338-40, actn. with Wizard (16).
Resistance (44)	I. 226, Sq. in the E. Indies; 336, capture of Malacca exped.; 414, capture of Amboyna exped. II. 245, lost by fire in the Straits of Banca.
Resistance (36)	III. 490, wrkd. on Cape St. Vincent.
Résistance (40)	II. 91, captd. by San Fiorenzo (36) and Nymphe (36), renamed Fisgard (38), q.v.
Résolu (priv.) F.	I. 219, captd. by E.I.C. ships.
Résolue (36) F.	I. 121, capture of Thames (32); 131, actn. with Phœnix (36); 132, at Mahé Rds.; 223, actn. with Br. frigates. II. 5, Ireland exped.; 9-11, Brest; 139, Ireland exped.; 152, captd. by Melampus (36); 162, added to Br. Navy (unserviceable).
Resolution (74)	I. 385, Murray's Sq. IV. 200, Copenhagen; 396, actn. in Basque Rds.
Resolution (14)	II. 462, fndrd.
Retribution (32)	II. 411, late Br. Hermione (32), q.v.
Réunion (36) F.	I. 115, captd. by Crescent (36); 117, added to Br. Navy.
,, ,, Br.	I. 324, actn. with Du. Argo (36). II. 456, wrkd. in the Swin.
Revanche (priv.) (10) F.	II. 229, captd. by Recovery (10).
Revanche (12) F.	I. 364, captd. by Suffisante (14).
Revanche (priv.) (24) F.	IV. 271-2, actn. with Curieux (18).
Revanche (40) F.	IV. 159-62, Leduc's Sq. off Iceland.
Revenge (74)	III. 384, 439, Trafalgar; 443, casualties. IV. 157, 175, Sq. off Rochefort; 396, actn. in Basque Rds. V. 106, Sq. crsg. off Cherbourg. VI. 35, bts. cut out F. priv. in the Adriatic.
Revenge (78)	VI. 395, rprg.
Revolutie (64) Du. ...	I. 415-7, captd. at the Cape of Good Hope.
Revolutie (68) Du. ...	IV. 284, destd. at Gressie, in Java, by a Br. Sq.
Révolution (74) F.	I. 60, Flt. in Quiberon Bay; 295, Sq. at Toulon; 303, Sq. crsg.; 345, Sq. at Cadiz. II. 5, Ireland exped.; 11, at Rochefort; 286, Brest Flt.
Révolutionnaire (110) F.	I. 141, Brest Flt.; 146, 28th May; 147, actn. with Audacious (74). III. 312, renamed Républicain (110), q.v.
Révolutionnaire (40) F.	I. 235, captd. by a Br. Sq. off Brest; 236, added to Br. Navy.
,, (38) Br.	I. 271, Channel Flt.; 357-8, capture of Unité (36). II. 7, crsg. off Brest; 399, capts. Bordelais (24); 400, added to Br. Navy. IV. 4-8, Strachan's actn.
Reyna-Louisa (112) Sp.	II. 299, Flt. at Cadiz.
Rhin (40) F.	III. 334, Toulon Flt.; 386, Trafalgar. IV. 120, Sq. at Cadiz; 165, captd. by Mars (74), added to Br. Navy.
,, (38) Br.	V. 334, Sq. off Spain.
Rhodian (10)	VI. 381, fndrd. near Jamaica.
Richmond (12)	IV. 256, crsg. off Portugal.
Rifleman (18)	VI. 201, Penobscot exped.
Rinaldo (10)	V. 111, capts. Maraudeur (14); 217, actn. off Boulogne; 318, Sq. off Boulogne.
Ringdove (18)	V. 50, Sq. off Guadaloupe.
Rippon (74)	VI. 13, crsg. off the Western Isles; 147, crsg. off L'Orient.
Rivoli (74) F.	V. 316, launched at Venice; 338-40, captd. by Victorious (74); 341, added to Br. Navy.
,, ,, Br.	VI. 227, capts. Melpomène (40).
Robert (74) F.	II. 288, at Toulon.
Robust (74)	I. 72, Medn. Flt.; 278, Quiberon exped. II. 91, crsg. off Brest; 142, Warren's Sq. crsg.; 145, capture of Hoche (74); 301, Sq. off Aix.
Robuste (80)	IV. 444-6, destd. to prevent capture by Br. Flt.
Rodney (74)	V. 208, Medn. Flt.

INDEX TO SHIPS

Romaine (40) *F.* ...... II. 5, Ireland exped.; 11, at Brest; 139, Ireland exped.; 151, Donegal Bay; 163, at Brest; 286, Brest Flt.
Roman (16)............... IV. 343, late Ital. Teulie (16), q.v.
Romney (50) .... I. 231, capts. Sibylle (40). II. 345, Holland exped. III. 91, in the Bay of Kosseïr; 493, wrkd. off the Texel.
Romulus (36) .... I. 214, Flt. at Corsica; 284, actn. off Genoa; 408, at Gibraltar. VI. 95, in Chesapeake Bay.
Romulus (74) *F.* ...... VI. 118, actn. with Boyne (98) off Toulon.
Ronco (16) *Ital.*......... IV. 343, captd. by Unité (36); renamed Tuscan (16), q.v.
Rosamond (18) .... V. 47, capts. Papillon (16) off Sante Cruiz Island.
Rosario (10) .... V. 109, actn. with F. privs.; 317, actn. off Dieppe.
Rosario (F.S.) .... III. 477, destd. in Dunkerque Rds.
Rose (28) .... I. 240, capture of Martinique exped.; 246, capture of the Saintes Isles; 439, wrkd. Jamaica.
Rose (18) .... VI. 465-73, Navarino.
Rota (38) *Da.* .... IV. 209, 464, captd. at Copenhagen, added to Br. Navy.
,, ,, *Br.*............. IV. 438, Scheldt exped. VI. 223, Sq. crsg. off the Western Isles, bts. repulsed by U.S. priv.; 235, in East Florida.
Rousseau (74) *F.* ...... II. 286, Brest Flt.
Rover (16) .... II. 469, wrkd. in the Gulf of St. Lawrence.
Rover (priv.) (14) .. ... III. 29, capts. Sp. Santa Ritta (12).
Royal George (100) ... I. 62, 139, Channel Flt.; 185, 1st June; 270-4, actn. off Isle Groix; 341, at Spithead. II. 285, Flt. off Brest. IV. 217-9, Dardanelles. VI. 2, 117, Medn. Flt.
Royal George (20)...... VI. 101-5, Canadian Lakes.
Royal George (30)*E.I.C.* III. 250, actn. with Linois' Sq. E. Indies.
Royal Oak (74) .... VI. 174, Sq. off the Potomac; 193, Jamaica.
Royal Sovereign (100) I. 62, 139, Channel Flt.; 173, 1st June; 262-6, Sq. crsg. off Ushant. III. 236, 335, Medn.; 384, 395, 405, Trafalgar; 443, casualties. IV. 288, Sq. in Palermo Bay. V. 207, Medn. Flt.
Royalist (18) .... VI. 12, actn. with Weser (40).
Rubis (40) *F.* .... VI. 36-7, wrkd. at Tamara, Isles de Los; 383, App.
Ruby (64) .... I. 189, Sq. off Ushant. IV. 200, Copenhagen.
Russel (74) .... I. 65, 139, Channel Flt.; 145, 28th May; 173, 1st June; 271-5, actn. off Isle Groix. II. 75-81, Camperdown; 285, Sq. off Brest. III. 46, Copenhagen. IV. 180, Sq. off Batavia.

Sabina (40) *Sp.* .... I. 406, captd. by Minerve (38); 407, recaptd. by the Sp. III. 112, actn. in the Gut of Gibraltar.
Sabine (16)............... V. 266, crsg. off Cadiz.
Safeguard (12) .... IV. 205, Copenhagen. V. 448, captd. in the Baltic.
Sagesse (20) *F.* .... II. 385, off Rochefort.
Saint Antoine (74) *F.* III. 110, late Sp. San Antonio (74), q.v.; 113, captd. in the Gut of Gibraltar, added to Br. Navy.
,, ,, ,, *Br.* III. 117, at Portsmouth.
St. Albans (64) .... I. 227, crsg. off Ireland; 354, Jervis' Sq. in the Tagus. II. 33, in the Tagus.
St. Anna (74) *Rus.* ... IV. 298, Flt. in Oro. Rds.
St. Cafael (74) *Rus.* ... IV. 234, Flt. in the Dardanelles.
St. Domingo (74) ...... IV. 439, Scheldt exped. V. 83, in Chesapeake Bay.
St. George (98) .... I. 72, Medn. Flt.; 78, Sq. at Genoa; 100, Sq. in the Medn.; 214, Sq. off Bastia; 284-90, actn. off Genoa; 297, off Hyères. II. 33, Sq. off the Tagus; 68, mutiny; 285, Sq. off Brest; 297, at Minorca. III. 47, Sq. off Isle Huën, Copenhagen. IV. 89, Strachan's Sq. V. 231, wrkd. Jutland.
St. George (120)......... VI. 395, bldg.
St. Helene (74) *Rus.*.... IV. 234, Flt. in the Dardanelles.
St. Lawrence (12) ...... VI. 247, captd. by U.S. priv. Chasseur (14) off Havana.
St. Lucia (14)............ IV. 466, captd. on the Leeward Island station.
St. Petro (66) *Rus.* ... IV. 234, Flt. in the Dardanelles.
St. Pierre (18) .... IV. 374, late F. Diligent (18), q.v.

Salamandre (26) *F.* ...	IV. 173-4, destd. by Br. brigs.
Salamine (18) *F.*	II. 379, capts. Fortune (10); 295, captd. by Keith's Sq., added to Br. Navy.
Saldanha (36)............	V. 447, wrkd. off Lough Swilly, Ireland.
Salisbury (50)............	II. 456, wrkd. on the Isle of Avacle, St. Domingo.
Sally (16)	IV. 197, actn. off Dantzic.
Saloman (10)	V. 442, wrkd. in the Baltic.
Salsette (36)	IV. 87, blt. of teak, 1805.
Salsette (36)	IV. 298, Baltic Flt.; 302, Sq. blockading Rogerswick (late Pitt, 36, q.v.).
Salsette (42)	VI. 396, blt. 1820.
Salvador del Mundo (112) *Sp.*	II. 36-44, captd. at St. Vincent; 59, added to Br. Navy.
Samarang (18)	IV. 283, Sq. at Gressie. V. 191, capture of Amboyna exped.; 303, capture of Java exped.
Samarang (28)	VI. 396, bldg.
Samnito (74) *Por.*	I. 79, at Toulon; 297, actn. off Hyères.
Sampson (64)	I. 62, Channel Flt.
San Antonio (74) *Sp.*...	II. 36, St. Vincent; 450, Sq. at Ferrol. III. 110, renamed Saint Antoine (74), q.v.
San Augustin (74) *Sp.*	II. 450, Sq. at Ferrol. III. 112, actn. in the Gut of Gibraltar; 374, F. Sp. Flt. Medn.; 386, 430, captd. at Trafalgar; 457, destd.
San Damaso (74) *Sp.*	II. 110, destd. at Trinidad to prevent capture.
San Domingo (74) *Sp.*	II. 36, St. Vincent
San Fernando (96) *Sp.*	II. 450, Sq. at Ferrol. III. 112, actn. in the Gut of Gibraltar.
San Fiorenzo (36)	I. 210, late F. Minerve (38), q.v. II. 91, capture of Résistance (40); 248, Stopford's frigate Sq.; 302, Sq. in Basque Rds.; 376, actn. with F. frigates. IV. 19, capts. Psyché (36); 308-9, capts. Piémontaise (40).
San Firmin (74) *Sp.* ...	II. 36, St. Vincent.
San Francisco de Asis (74) *Sp.*	II. 292, Sq. at Carthagena; 299, Flt. at Cadiz. III. F. Sp. Flt. Medn.; 386, 456, wrkd. at Trafalgar.
San Francisco de Paula (74) *Sp.*	II. 36, St. Vincent; 292, Sq. at Carthagena; 299, Flt. at Cadiz.
San Fulgencio (64) *Sp.*	III. 374, F. Sp. Flt. Medn.
San Genaro (74) *Sp.* ...	II. 36, St. Vincent.
San Ildefonso (74) *Sp.*	II. 36, St. Vincent. III. 374, F. Sp. Flt. Medn.; 386, 439, 457, captd. at Trafalgar.
San Joaquin (74) *Sp.*...	II. 292, Sq. at Carthagena; 299, Flt. at Cadiz.
San Josef (112) *Sp.* ...	II. 36-46, captd. at St. Vincent; 59, added to Br. Navy.
,, ,, ,, *Br.* ...	III. 307, Flt. off Ushant. VI. 2, 117, Medn. Flt.
San Juan Nepomuceno (74) *Sp.*	II. 36, St. Vincent. III. 374, F. Sp. Flt. Medn.; 386, 407-11, 437, captd. at Trafalgar.
San Justo (74) *Sp.*	III. 386, 407, Trafalgar.
San Leandro (64) *Sp.*	III. 386, 407, 455, Trafalgar.
San Léon (16)............	II. 307, Sq. off Procida.
San Nicholas (80) *Sp.*	II. 36-45, captd. at St. Vincent; 59, added to Br. Navy.
San Pablo (74) *Sp.*......	II. 36, St. Vincent; 292, Sq. at Carthagena; 299, Flt. at Cadiz.
San Pedro Apostol (74) *Sp.*	II. 240, Sq. at Manilla.
San Rafaël (80) *Sp.* ...	III. 342, F. Sp. Flt. at Toulon; 361-71, captd. in Calder's actn.
San Sebastian (74) *Por.*	II. 211, Sq. in the Medn.; 305, Sq. blockading Naples.
San Sebastian (74) *Sp.*	II. 299, renamed Alliance (74), q.v.
San Telmo (74) *Sp.* ...	II. 292, Sq. at Carthagena; 299, Flt. at Cadiz.
San Vincente (80) *Sp.*	II. 110, destd. at Trinidad to prevent capture.
San Ysidro (74) *Sp.* ...	II. 36-44, captd. at St. Vincent; 59, added to the Br. Navy.
Sandwich (90)	II. 71, at the Nore.
Sans Culotte (120) *F.*	I. 90, left at Toulon (late Dauphin Royal (120), q.v.); 213, 282, Toulon Sq. II. 168, Malta exped., renamed Orient (120), q.v.

INDEX TO SHIPS

Sans Culotte (priv.) (12) F.	I. 98, captd. by Scourge (16).
Sans Pareil (80) F.	I. 140, Brest Flt. ; 163, 168, 186, captd. on 1st June ; 187, added to Br. Navy.
,, ,, ,, Br. ...	I. 271-5, actn. off Isle Groix. II. 24, Channel Sq. ; 284, Sq. off Brest ; 301, Sq. off Aix.
Sans Pareille (20) F. ...	III. 120, captd. by Mercury (26).
Sans Souci (priv.) (14) F.	V. 103, captd. by Briseis (10).
Santa Ana (112) Sp. ...	II. 292, Sq. at Carthagena ; 299, Flt. at Cadiz. III. 386, 405, captd. at Trafalgar ; 455, recaptd.
Santa Brigida (34) Sp.	II. 401-3, captd. by a Br. Sq. near Cape Finisterre.
Santa Cazilda (34) Sp.	II. 254, Sp. frigates with Lion (64).
Santa Cecilia (34) Sp.	II. 110, destd. at Trinidad to prevent capture.
Santa Dorotea (34) Sp.	II. 254, captd. by Lion (64) ; 255, added to Br. Navy.
Santa Elena (34) Sp. ...	II. 93, destd. by Irresistible (74) in Conil Bay, near Cadiz.
Santa Gertruyda (34) Sp.	II. 493, captd. by Polyphemus (64) off Cape Santa Maria.
Santa Margarita (36) ...	I. 233, Warren's Sq. ; 240, capture of Martinique exped. ; 366, capts. Tamise (36) (late Thames (32), q.v.) ; 400, capts. Buonaparte (16), (priv.). IV. 3-9, Strachan's actn.
Santa Ritta (12) Sp. ...	III. 29, captd. by Rover (14) (priv.).
Santa Teresa (34) Sp.	II. 359, captd. by Argo (44), added to Br. Navy.
,, ,, (36) Br.	II. 294, Flt. crsg., capture of F. frigates.
Santissima Trinidad (120) Sp.	II. 36-56, St. Vincent ; 57, at Cadiz. III. 386, 428, captd. at Trafalgar ; 457, destd.
Sappho (18)	IV. 307, capts. Da. Admiral Yawl (28).
Saracen (18)	VI. 29, crsg. in the Adriatic ; 119, capture of Cattaro.
Saratoga (26) U.S. ...	VI. 213, at Lake Champlain ; 218, capts. Confiance (37).
Sardine (16) F.	I. 305, at Smyrna ; 342, cut out by the bts. of Waldegrave's Sq. at Tunis.
Sarpedon (10)............	VI. 381, fndrd.
Sarpen (16) Da.	IV. 209, captd. at Copenhagen.
Satellite (16)	V. 445, fndrd. in the Channel.
Saturn (74)	I. 297, action off Hyères. III. 47, Sq. off Isle Huën, Copenhagen. V. 427-8 (54), rasé.
Scemplome (16) F. ...	V. 260, crsg. in the Adriatic.
Sceptre (64)	I. 62, Channel Flt. ; 251, capture of Port-au-Prince exped. ; 416, Sq. at Simon's Bay. II. 474, wrkd. in Table Bay.
Sceptre (74)	IV. 357, Sq. off the Isle of France. V. 81, Sq. off Toulon. VI. 95, in Chesapeake Bay.
Scévola, rasé (50) F. ...	I. 56, armament of ; 230, Sq. off Guernsey ; 264, Brest Flt. II. 5, Ireland exped. ; 10, fndrd. off Ireland.
Scipio (64)	II. 110, Sq. off Trinidad.
Scipion (80) F.	I. 141, Brest Flt. ; 163, 168, 1st June ; 261, fndrd.
Scipion (74) F.	I. 72, at Toulon ; 91, captd. at Toulon ; 92, lost by fire in Leghorn Rds.
Scipion (74) F.	III. 176, at Toulon ; 334, Villeneuve's Flt. ; 358, Calder's actn. ; 386, 434, Trafalgar. IV. 3-8, captd. in Strachan's actn. ; 12, added to Br. Navy.
,, ,, Br.	V. 303, capture of Java exped. VI. 3, actn. off Toulon.
Scipion (74) F.	VI. 365-73, Navarino.
Scorpion (18)	III. 264, bts. cut out Du. Atalante (16). V. 86, capts. Oreste (16) ; 92, off the Saintes. VI. 208, at Lake Ontario.
Scourge (16)	I. 98, capts. Sans Culotte (12). II. 456, fndrd. off Holland.
Scout (16)	I. 439, captd. by two F. frigates, 1794.
,, ,, F.	I. 325, at Genoa, 1795.
Scout (18)	III. 482, wrkd. on the Shingles, Isle of Wight.
Scout (18)	III. 485, fndrd. off Newfoundland.
Scout (18)	IV. 447, Sq. in Rosas Bay. V. 29, bts. at Carri.
Scylla (18)	V. 212, capts. Canonnier (10). VI. 12, actn. with Weser (40).
Seaflower (14)	III. 3, crsg. off St. Malo. IV. 180, Sq. off Batavia Rds. ; 283, Pellew's Sq. at Gressie.
Seaforth (14)	IV. 461, fndrd. on the Leeward Isle station.

Seagull (18)	III. 191, actn. with Lord Nelson (26), late E.I.C. ship.
Seagull (16)	IV. 372, late Sylphe (16), q.v.
Seahorse (38)	II. 63, Sq. at Teneriffe; 206, 215, Sq. off Alexandria; 234, capts. Sensible (36); 305-7, blockade of Naples. III. 275, in the Bay of Hyères; 333, watching Toulon; 335, Nelson's Flt. IV. 31, crsg. off Cape de Gata; 349-53, capts. Turk. Badere-Zaffer (44). VI. 175-81, Potomac exped.; 232, off the Chandeleur Isles.
Sealark (10)	V. 324, capts. Ville-de-Caen (16).
Séduisant (74) *F.*	II. 5, Ireland exped.; 453, wrkd. near Brest.
Seine (40) *F.*	I. 387, Sq. crsg.; 391-4, Sq. actn. with two Br. 74's. II. 89, Sercey's Sq. off Java; 247-8, captd. by Jason (38) and Pique (36); 249, added to Br. Navy.
,, (38) *Br.*	III. 23-5, capts. Vengeance (40); 490, wrkd. off the Texel.
Seine (36)	II. 162, late Embuscade (36), q.v. IV. 31, crsg. off Porto Rico; 110, Cochrane's Sq.
Seine (40) *F.*	IV. 313-4, actn. off L'Orient; 315, at L'Orient. V. 47 (en flûte), Sq. crsg.; 50-2, destd. at Anse la Barque by Br. Sq.
Sémillante (36) *F.*	I. 60, Flt. in Quiberon Bay; 103, actn. with Venus (32); 121, capture of Thames (32). II. 139, Ireland exped.; 144-51, frigate actn.; 376-7, frigate actn. III. 208, Sq. in the E. Indies; 205, Sq. actn. with E.I.C. ships; 283-4, Sq. actn. with Centurion (50). IV. 53-4, actn. with Phaëton (38) and Harrier (18); 355-6, at Port Louis; 358-61, actn. with Terpsichore (32); 362, returns to France.
Semiramis (36)	V. 213-4, des. Pluvier (16).
Sensible (36) *F.*	I. 305, at Smyrna. II. 234, captd. by Seahorse (38), added to Br. Navy.
Sensible (T.S.)	II. 236, at Spithead.
Sentinel (12)	V. 451, wrkd. Isle of Rugen.
Serapis, en flûte (44) ...	III. 296, capture of Surinam exped.
Sérieuse (36) *F.*	I. 91, left at Toulon; 305, Sq. crsg. II. 178, 185, destd. by Orion (74) at the Nile.
Seringapatam (48)	VI. 396, blt. of teak.
Serpent (16)	IV. 77, crsg. in Honduras Bay; 461, fndrd. on the Jamaica station.
Severn (T.S.)	III. 494, wrkd. Jersey.
Severn (40)	V. 432, bldg. VI. 124, engages Etoile (40); 170-5, i Chesapeake Bay; 278-89, Algiers.
Sewolod (74) *Rus.*	IV. 298, Flt. in Oro Rds.; 300-2, destd. by Centaur (74) and Implacable (74).
Shamrock (10)	V. 448, wrkd. on Cape Santa Maria.
Shamrock (10)	VI. 6, Sq. at Heligoland.
Shannon (36)	III. 202, wrkd. and destd. near Cape la Hogue.
Shannon (38)	II. 345, Holland exped. IV. 275, capture of Madeira exped.; 378, crsg. V. 368, chases U.S. Essex. VI. 51-65, capts. U.S. Chesapeake (36).
Sharpshooter (16)	IV. 172, crsg. off St. Malo.
Shearwater (10)	V. 81, Sq. off Toulon.
Sheerness (44)	IV. 456, wrkd. Ceylon.
Shelburne (12)	VI. 156, capture of U.S. Frolic (18).
Sheldrake (16)	IV. 173, capture of Salamandre (26). V. 224, capture of Anholt exped.
Sibylle (40) *F.*	I. 231, captd. by Romney (50); 232, added to Br. Navy.
,, (38) *Br.*	II. 237, at Manilla; 365-71, capts. Forte (44). III. 131, capts. Chiffonne (36). IV. 201, Sq. off the Great Belt; 372, capts. Espiègle (16), renamed Electra (16), q.v.
Sirena (34) *Neap.*	II. 438, Keith's Sq. off Malta.
Sirène (26) *Du.*	I. 416, captd. at the Cape of Good Hope.
Sirène (16	I. 412, capture of Léogane, St. Domingo. II. 456, wrkd. in Honduras Bay.

INDEX TO SHIPS

Sirène (36) F............	II. 5, Ireland exped. ; 280, at L'Orient; 417, chased by Aimable (32). III. 334, Toulon Flt.; 349, capture of Diamond Rock exped. IV. 159, Sq. off Iceland.
Sirène (60) F............	VI. 365-73, Navarino.
Sir Francis Drake (32)	IV. 180, Pellew's Sq. off Batavia. V. 296, capts. Du. gbts.; 303, capture of Java exped.
Sirius (36)	II. 270, capts. Du. Furie (36) and Waakzaamheid (24). III. 357, Calder's actn.; 384, Trafalgar. IV. 142, capts. Bergère (18). V. 59, capture of St. Paul's ; 141, Sq. off the Isle of France ; 155-64, destd. at Grand Port.
Skiold (74) Da.	IV. 209, 464, captd. at Copenhagen.
Skoroy (60) Rus.	IV. 234, Flt. in the Dardanelles.
Skylark (16)	V. 318, wrkd. near Boulogne.
Slaney (20)	VI. 309, Burmese war.
Snake (18)	III. 186, crsg. in the W. Indies.
Soberano (74) Sp.	II. 36-49, St. Vincent ; 292, Sq. at Carthagena ; 299, Flt. at Cadiz.
Société (16) F.	II. 284, at Brest.
Solebay (32)	I. 240, capture of Martinique exped. II. 414-5, capts. four F. brig corvettes. V. 67-8, capture of Sénégal exped.; 441, wrkd. Africa.
Sophie (18)	VI. 231, Sq. off West Florida ; 309, Burmese War.
Southampton (32)	I. 62, 139, Channel Flt. ; 303, Hotham's Sq.; 325, actn. with Vestale (36); 371, capts. Utile (24) ; 408, at Gibraltar. II. 34, St. Vincent. V. 353, capts. Amethyste (38). VI. 381, wrkd. near Conception Island.
Southampton (60)	VI. 395, bldg.
Souverain (74) F.	I. 73, rprg.; 91, left at Toulon.
Sparkler (12)	IV. 474, wrkd. Holland.
Sparrow (16)	VI. 15, Collier's Sq. off Spain ; 128, crsg. off St. Malo.
Sparrowhawk (18)	V. 129, Roger's Sq. off Palamos.
Spartan (38)	IV. 257, crsg. off Nice ; 290, off Sicily; 447, capture of Cerigo. V. 28, Sq. in the Gulf of Venice ; 115-7, actn. with Cérès (42) and consorts; 372, crsg. North America.
Spartiate (74) F.	II. 178, 186-8, 206, captd. at the Nile ; 208, added to Br. Navy.
,, ,, Br.	III. 346, in Carlisle Bay ; 384, 437, Trafalgar; 443, casualties. IV. 288, Sq. in Palermo Bay.
Speedwell (14)	IV. 466, fndrd. off Dieppe.
Speedy (14)	I. 96, Sq. off Genoa ; 303, Sq. off Italy ; 343, Sq. off Oneglia; 439, captd. by F. Sq. off Nice.
Speedy (14)	II. 227, actn. with Papillon (14) ; 382, actn. with Sp. gbts.; 395, des. Sp. coasters. III. 133-4, capts. Sp. Gamo (32) ; 482, captd. by a F. Sq.
Spencer (74)	III. 98-102, Algesiras ; 112-6, actn. in the Gut of Gibraltar ; 335, Medn. Flt. IV. 90-5, Duckworth's actn.; 200, Copenhagen.
Spencer (14)	I. 363, capts. Volcan (12).
Sphynx (20)	I. 388, chased by Régénérée (36) ; 416, Sq. in Simon's Bay.
Sphynx (10)	VI. 396, blt.
Spider (18)	IV. 137, late Sp. Vigilante (18), q.v.
Spitfire (16)...............	VI. 70, crsg. in the North Sea.
Sprightly (12)............	III. 483, capt. by F. Sq. in the Medn.
Stag (32)	I. 324-5, capture of Du. Alliance (36). II. 300, crsg. off Ushant.
Standard (64)	I. 278, Quiberon exped. IV. 214-9, Dardanelles ; 289, 347, off Corfu ; 431, capture of Anholt exped.
Star (18)	IV. 382, crsg. off Guadaloupe. V. 69, capture of Martinique.
Stately (64)...............	I. 333, capture of Cape of Good Hope exped. ; 416, Sq. in Simon's Bay. III. 80, Sq. off Port Ferrajo. IV. 319, with Nassau (64) des. Da. Prindts-Christian-Frederic (74).
States General (74) Du.	II. 76-8, Camperdown.

Statira (38)	IV. 438, Scheldt exped. VI. 83, Sq. at Lynhaven Bay; 193, Sq. off New London; 391, wrkd. Isle of Cuba.
Statira (48)	VI. 395, bldg.
Staunch (18)	V. 145-9, at the Isle of France; 204, capture of Isle of France exped.
Stengel (74) *F.*	II. 288, 305, captd. at Ancona.
Sterling (12)	III. 494, wrkd. near Calais.
Stork (18)	IV. 27, crsg. Porto Rico.
Streatham (30) *E.I.C.*	V. 54-6, captd. by Caroline (40).
Strenuous (16)............	IV. 172, capture of Salamandre (26).
Strombolo (bomb.)......	II. 61, actn. at Cadiz.
Subtle (10)	VI. 382, fndrd. in the W. Indies.
Success (32)...............	II. 289, Flt. off Cadiz; 380, crsg. in the Medn.; 439, capture of Généreux (74); 444, capture of Diane (40). III. 72, captd. by a F. Sq. in the Medn.; 78, at Leghorn; 79-80, recaptd. by a Br. Sq. in the Medn. IV. 184, crsg. off Cuba; 275, capture of Madeira exped. V. 114, crsg. in the Medn.
Suffisant (74) *F.*.........	I. 72, refitting at Toulon; 92, 431, destd. at Toulon.
Suffisante (14)............	I. 364, capts. Revanche (12). III. 490, wrkd. near Cork.
Suffolk (74)...............	I. 62, Channel Flt.; 336, in the E. Indies; 414, capture of Amboyna exped.
Suffren (74) *F.*	I. 60, Flt. in Quiberon Bay. IV. 48, Allemand's Sq.; 79, Dominique exped.; 287, actn. at the Isle of Aix; 444, Flt. in Toulon Rds. V. 10, at Toulon.
Sulphur (bomb.).........	III. 46, Copenhagen.
Sultan (74)	IV. 445, Sq. in the Medn. V. 208, Medn. Flt.
Sultane (40) *F.*	VI. 124, chases Severn (40); 125-7, Frigate actn.; 129-30, captd. by Hannibal (74); 131, added to Br. Navy.
Superb (74)	II. 285, Sq. off Brest; 297, Medn. Flt. III. 97, Sq. off Cadiz; 112-5, actn. in the Gut of Gibraltar; 175, Sq. off Toulon; 335, Nelson's Flt. IV. 90-5, Duckworth's actn.; 201, Copenhagen; 288, Sq. in Palermo Bay; 298, Baltic Flt. VI. 196, off Buzzard's Bay, U.S.; 278-89, Algiers.
Superbe (74) *F.*	I. 60, Flt. in Quiberon Bay; 261, fndrd.
Superbe (14) *F.*	IV. 182, captd. by Pitt (12).
Superbe (74) *F.*	IV. 432, bldg. at Antwerp.
Superieuse (14)	IV. 171, Sq. at Jamaica. V. 5, Pursues Junon (40).
Superior (62) *U.S.* ...	VI. 204, launched at Sackett's Harbour, Ontario.
Surinam (18)	II. 421, late F. Hussar (20). III. 490, captd. by the Dutch at Curaçoa. IV. 277, retaken at the capture of Curaçoa.
Surprise (28)	II. 405-11, late F. Unité (28), q.v., bts. cut out Hermione (32) (late Br.). VI. 192, at Halifax.
Surveillant (18) *F.*......	IV. 177, Sq. crsg. in the Antilles; 178, capture of Favourite (18).
Surveillante (36) *F.* ...	II. 5, Ireland exped.; 11, wrkd. in Bantry Bay.
Surveillante (40) *F.* ...	III. 205, captd. at Cape François, St. Domingo; 206, added to Br. Navy.
,, (38) *Br.*...	V. 100, crsg. off the Morbihan; 334, Sq. off N. Spain. VI. 15, off N. Spain.
Swallow (18)	V. 345, actn. with Renard (16) and Goéland (14). VI. 33, crsg. in the Adriatic.
Swan (10)	IV. 321, off Bornholm, actn. with Da. brig.
Swan (16) *F.*	V. 100, actn. with Queen Charlotte (8).
Swift (16)	I. 413, capture of Colombo exped. II. 462, fndrd. in the China Sea.
Swift (18)	IV. 75, crsg. in Honduras Bay.
Swiftsure (74)............	I. 227-8, capts. Atalante (36); 412, actn. at Léogane, St. Domingo. II. 171, Flt. off Cadiz; 183-90, the Nile; 206, 215, Sq. off Alexandria; 305, Sq. off Naples. III. 13, Sq. crsg.; 76, captd. by a F. Sq. in the Medn.
,, *F.*	III. 77, 176, at Toulon; 334, Sq. crsg.; 358, Calder's actn.; 386, 415, recaptd. at Trafalgar.

INDEX TO SHIPS 43

Swiftsure (74)............ III. 335, Medn. Flt.; 384, 438, Trafalgar; 443, casualties. VI. 36, crsg. off Corsica, bts. cut out Charlemagne (8) (priv.); 117, Medn. Flt.
Swinger (12) .... V. 69, capture of Martinique exped.
Syeren (64) *Da.* .... IV. 209, 464, captd. at Copenhagen.
Sylph (18) .... I. 363, Sq. crsg. off the Texel; 381-3, Andromaque (36) destd II. 95, with Anson (44) des. Calliope (28); 96, actn. off Sable-d'Olonne; 140, crsg. off Ireland; 302, actn. in Basque Rds. III. 145-6, actn. with F. frigate. VI. 200, Penobscot exped.; 391, wrkd. in N. America.
Sylphe (16) *F.* .... IV. 48, Allemand's Sq.; 139, Sq. at Isle of Aix; 371, captd. by Comet (18); 372, renamed Seagull (16), q.v.
Sylvia (10) .... V. 130, crsg. in the Straits of Sunda.
Syren (32) .... I. 98, Sq. off the Maese, Holland; 318, Sq. in Gourville Bay, Jersey.
Syrène (36) *F.* .... IV. 159-62, Leduc's Sq. off Iceland.

Tactique (18) *F.* ...... II. 286, Brest Flt. V. 253-4, actn. with Guadaloupe (16).
Tagus (36) .... VI. 131, with Niger (38) capts. Cérès (40).
Talbot (28)............... VI. 365-73, Navarino.
Tamar (38)............... II. 112, Sq. at Porto Rico; 387, capts. Républicaine (28).
Tamise (36) .... I. 365, late Br. Thames (32), q.v.; 366, recaptd. by Santa Margarita (36).
Tancredi (74) *Neap.* ... I. 284-9, actn. off Genoa.
Tapageuse (14) *F.*...... IV. 138, cut out by the bts. of Pallas (32) in the Gironde.
Tapperheten (66) *Swd.* IV. 299, Br. and Swd. Flt. in Oro Rds.
Tartar (32) .... I. 231, Sq. convoy escort. III. 278, crsg. in the W. Indies. IV. 298, Baltic Flt.; 323, actn. off Bergen. V. 38, off Felixberg; 224-6, capture of Anholt exped.; 447, wrkd. in the Baltic.
Tartar (28) .... II. 462, wrkd. St. Domingo.
Tartarus (18) .... IV. 320, Sq. off Denmark. VI. 102, at Quebec.
Tartarus (bomb.) ...... III. 494, wrkd. near Margate.
Taunton Castle (26) *E.I.C.*................... II. 89, escapes a F. Sq.
Tay (20) .... VI. 393, wrkd. in the Gulf of Mexico.
Teazer (12)............... III. 317, actn. off Granville. IV. 457, captd. by F. gbts. off St. Malo. V. 213-4, recaptd. by Diana (38).
Telegraph (16) .... II. 375, capts. Hirondelle (16).
Telegraph (12) .... VI. 11, des. Flibustier (16); 394, wrkd. on Mount Batten, Catwater.
Téméraire (98) .... III. 384, 424-5, Trafalgar; 443, casualties. V. 208, Medn. Flt.
Téméraire (74) *F.* ..... I. 60, Flt. in Quiberon Bay; 141, Brest Flt.; 163, 173, 1st June.
Tenedos (38) .... VI. 200, crsg. off Marblehead; 238, off Sandy Hook.
Termagant (20) .... III. 354, Medn. Flt.; V. 337, Sq. off Grenada.
Terpsichore (32)......... I. 398-9, capts. Sp. Mahonesa (34), q.v.; 400, added to Br. Navy; 402-5, actn. with Vestale (36). II. 55, crsg. off St. Vincent; 61, actn. at Cadiz; 166, Nelson's Sq. in the Medn.; 180, the Nile. III. 209, at Pondicherry. IV. 180, Sq. off Batavia; 360-1, actn. with Sémillante (36).
Terpsichore (40) *F.* ... VI. 145-6, captd. by Majestic (56).
Terrible (74) .... I. 72, Medn. Flt.; 214, Flt. off Bastia; 284-90, actn. off Genoa; 297, off Hyères. II. 164, Saumarez's Sq.; 297, Medn. Flt. IV. 89, Strachan's Sq.; 116, Sq. crsg. in the W. Indies.
Terrible (110) *F.* ...... I. 60, Flt. in Quiberon Bay; 141, Brest Flt.; 163, 173, 1st June. II. 285, Brest Flt.
Terrible (64) *Du.* ...... IV. 460, wrkd. E. Indies.
Terrible (74) *Sp.* ...... II. 36, St. Vincent. III. 342, Flt. in Toulon Rds.; 374, F. Sp. Flt. Medn.
Terror (bomb.) .... II. 61, actn. at Cadiz. VI. 190, actn. at Baltimore.

Teulie (16) *Ital.*	IV. 343, captd. by Unité (36), renamed Roman (16), q.v.
Thalia (36)	I. 329, chases F. frigates. II. 24, at Gibraltar. V. 357, convoy escort.
Thames (32)	I. 119–20, actn. with Uranie (40); 121, captd. by F. Sq.; 366, recaptd. by Santa Margarita (36). III. 98, Algesiras; 112, actn. in the Gut of Gibraltar. IV. 160, off the Shetland Isles. V. 125, crsg. off coast of Naples; 256, capture of F. gbts.; 259, at Palinuro; 342, capture of the Port of Sapri. VI. 19, capture of Ponza.
Thémis (36) *F.*	III. 334, Villeneuve's Flt.; 352, off Barbuda; 386, Trafalgar. IV. 120, Meillerie's Sq.; 164, in the W. Indies; 166, at Rochefort; 176, Hood's frigate actn.; 291, at Toulon.
Thémistocle (74) *F.* ...	I. 72, at Toulon; 92, 431, destd. at Toulon.
Thérèse (20) *F.*	III. 16–7, destd. by the bts. of Br. Sq. at Noirmoutier.
Thésée (74) *F.*	IV. 199, bldg. at Antwerp.
Theseus (74)	I. 189, Sq. off Ushant. II. 61, actn. at Cadiz; 63, Sq. at Teneriffe; 171, Flt. off Cadiz; 183–6, 193, 206, the Nile; 321, at Acre; 330, takes fire. III. 291, at Curaçoa. IV. 396, actn. in Basque Rds.
Thetis (24) *Du.*	I. 410, captd. at Demerara.
Thetis (38)	I. 319, capture of Hussar (28); 385, Murray's Sq. V. 45, crsg. off Guadaloupe, Nisus (16) cut out; 92, Watson's Sq.
Thetis (34) *Sp.*	II. 401–2, treasure ship, captd. by Br. Sq. near Ferrol.
Thétis (40) *F.*............	IV. 48, Allemand's Sq.; 376–9, captd. by Amethyst (36); 480, added to Br. Navy, renamed Brune (38).
Thisbe (28)...............	I. 385, Murray's Sq.
Thistle (10)...............	V. 91, capts. Du. Havik (14).
Thorn (16)	I. 320–1, capts. Courier National (18).
Thulen (40) *Du.*.........	I. 307, captd. at Plymouth.
Thunder (bomb.)	II. 61, actn. at Cadiz. IV. 368, actn. with Da. gbts.; 400, 422, actn. in Basque Rds. VI. 14, capts. Neptune (16) (priv.).
Thunderer (74)	I. 139, Channel Flt.; 146, 28th May; 162, 185, 1st June; 278, Quiberon exped.; 330, capts. Eveillé (16). II. 112, Sq. at St. Domingo; 280, at St. Domingo. III. 357–61, Calder's actn.; 384, 439–40, Trafalgar; 443, casualties. IV. 214, 219, Dardanelles; 288, 294, Sq. at Palermo.
Thunder (bomb.) ...	IV. 205, Copenhagen.
Tickler (12)...............	IV. 368, 474, captd. in the Great Belt by Da. gbts.
Tigre (74) *F.*	I. 60, Flt. in Quiberon Bay; 66, Vanstabel's Sq.; 203, Nielly's Sq.; 264, 274, captd. in actn. off Isle Groix; 277, added to Br. Navy.
,, ,, *Br.*............	II. 321–6, at Acre. III. 81, Egypt exped.; 335, Medn. Sq. IV. 232, Sq. at Alexandria; 445, Sq. in the Medn.
Tigress (12)...............	IV. 205, Copenhagen; 368, captd. in the Great Belt by Da. gbts.
Tigris (12)	V. 67, capture of Sénégal exped.
Tilsitt (80) *F.*	IV. 432, bldg. at Antwerp.
Timoléon (74) *F.*	I. 282–6, actn. off Genoa; 295, rprg. at Toulon. II. 178, 194–5, destd. at the Nile.
Tirailleuse (14) *F.*	III. 8, crsg. off the Penmarcks.
Tobago (10)	IV. 462, captd. by Général Ernouf (priv.), near Guadaloupe.
Tonnant (80) *F.*.........	I. 72, at Toulon; 213, Martin's Sq.; 282, Toulon Flt. II. 178, 192–5, captd. at the Nile; 208, added to Br. Navy.
,, ,, *Br.*	III. 384, 410–2, Trafalgar; 443, casualties. V. 312, Sq. off L'Orient. VI. 174, Sq. in Chesapeake Bay; 192, at Halifax.
Tonnerre (74) *F.*	IV. 391, Brest Flt.; 401, 413–4, destd. in actn. at Basque Rds.
Topaze (36)...............	I. 385, Murray's Sq. IV. 447, Sq. in Rosas Bay. V. 30, engages Danaë (46) and Flore (40); 31, bts. des. gun vessels off St. Maura.

INDEX TO SHIPS 45

Topaze (40) *F.*	IV. 38-40, capture of Blanche (36); 45, engages Raisonable (64). V. 3-4, captd. by Cleopatra (32) and Hazard (18), added to Br. Navy, renamed Alcmène (38), q.v.
Topaze (38)	VI. 131, late F. Etoile (40), q.v.
Torche (18) *F.*	IV. 38, Baudin's Sq.; 39, capture of Blanche (36); 44, captd. by Goliath (74).
Torride (10)	II. 321, Sq. at Alexandria.
Tortue (40) *F.*	I. 121, late Uranie (40), q.v.; 329, chased by Br. Sq. II. 5, Ireland exped.; 11, captd. by Polyphemus (64), renamed Urania (38), q.v.
Tourterelle (28) *F.*	I. 314, captd. by Lively (32); 315, added to Br. Navy as S.S.
Tourville (74) *F.*	I. 60, Flt. in Quiberon Bay; 66, Vanstabel's Sq.; 141, Brest Flt.; 163, 176, 1st June. II. 5, Ireland exped.; 11, at Brest; 286, Brest Flt. III. 312, Brest Flt. IV. 391, Brest Sq.; 401, 415-7, actn. in Basque Rds.; 422, in the Charente.
Trajan (74) *F.*, late Gaulois	I. 63, Flt. in Quiberon Bay; 141, Brest Flt.; 163, 172, 176, 1st June. II. 5, Ireland exped.; 11, at Brest.
Trajan, en flûte, *F.*	I. 319, Sq. crsg. off Chesapeake Bay.
Trajan (74) *F.*	IV. 432, bldg. at Antwerp.
Trave (40) *F.*	VI. 13, engaged by Achates (16); 14, captd. by Andromache (36), added to Br. Navy.
Tre-Kronen (74) *Da.*	IV. 209, 464, captd. at Copenhagen.
Tremendous (74)	I. 65, 139, Channel Flt.; 162, 176, 1st June; 416, Sq. in Simon's Bay. II. 394, bts. des. Preneuse (36). III. 208, Sq. at Pondicherry. IV. 143-4, actn. with Canonnière (40). V. 313, crsg. off Ushant.
Trent (36)	II. 376, crsg. off Porto Rico. III. 130, off the Isles of Bréhat.
Trente-et-un-Mai(74)*F.*	I. 161-3, 1st June.
Trial (12)	II. 133, Sq. off Havre; 135, Confiante (36) destd.
Tribune (36) *F.*	I. 365-7, captd. by Unicorn (32); 368, added to Br. Navy.
,, ,, *Br.*	II. 107, wrkd. Halifax.
Tribune (36)	IV. 298, Baltic Flt. V. 98, actn. with Da. gun brigs.
Tricolor (74) *F.*	I. 92, 431, destd. at Toulon.
Trident (64)	I. 416, Sq. in Simon's Bay. III. 208, Sq. at Pondicherry.
Trident (74) *F.*	V. 81, bldg. at Toulon. VI. 365-73, Navarino.
Trincomalé (16)	II. 400, blows up in actn. with Iphigénie (22).
Triomphant (80) *F.*	I. 72, refitting at Toulon; 92, 431, destd. at Toulon.
Tripoli (20) *Algrn.*	VI. 274-5, actn. with Cameleon (12).
Triton (32)	II. 91, crsg. off Brest; 96, Warren's Sq. off La Vendée; 248, Stopford's Sq.; 402, capture of Sp. treasure ships.
Triumph (74)	I. 262-7, Sq. off Ushant. II. 75-9, Camperdown; 297, Medn. Flt. III. 357-8, Calder's actn. IV. 89, Strachan's Sq.; 116, Sq. in the W. Indies; 248, in Chesapeake Bay; 376, capture of Thétis (40).
Trompeuse (16)	II. 457, wrkd. Kinsale.
Trusty (50)	I. 126, at Barbadoes. III. 320, Sq. off Calais.
Turbulent (12)	IV. 474, captd. by Da. gbts. in Malmo Bay.
Tuscan (16)	IV. 343, late Ital. Ronco (16), q.v.
Tweed (18)	VI. 381, wrkd. Newfoundland.
Twerday (74) *Rus.*	IV. 234, Flt. in the Dardanelles.
Tyrannicide (74) *F.*	I. 141, Brest Flt.; 152-3, 29th May; 163, 1st June; 349, Villeneuve's Flt. II. 286, Brest Flt.
Uladislaffe (76) *Swd.*	IV. 299, Br. and Swd. Flt. in Oro Rds.
Ulm (74) *F.*	IV. 444, Flt. in Toulon Rds. V. 208, Toulon Flt. VI. 3, Toulon Flt.
Ulysse (74) *F.*	III. 312, Brest Flt.
Ulysses (T.S.)	II. 221, capture of Minorca exped.
Ulysses (44)	V. 69, capture of Martinique exped.
Undaunted (28)	I. 245, late Bienvenue (28), q.v.

Undaunted (38)	II. 456, late Aréthuse (40), q.v., wrkd. in the W. Indies.
Undaunted (38)	V. 342, bts. des. F. priv. at Agaye. VI. 17, bts. cutting out exped. near Marseille ; 35, off Port Nouvelle ; 121, conveys Napoleon to Elba.
Unicorn (32)	I. 365-7, capts. Tribune (36) ; 368, added to Br. Navy, q.v. II. 10, crsg. Channel. III. 15, Sq. off the Penmarcks ; 142, crsg. in Quiberon Bay. IV. 30, off St. Domingo ; 279, Monte Video exped.; 400, Basque Rds. V. 98, recapts. Laurel (22).
Unicorn (28)	II. 270, capts. Vestale (32), q.v., restored to the F. by the U.S. at Rhode Island.
Unicorn (46)	VI. 395, bldg.
Unie (44) *Du.*	II. 347, 372, captd. in the Nieueve Diep, Texel.
Union (98)	VI. 2, 117, Medn. Flt.
Unique (T.S.)	II. 5, Ireland exped.; 11, fndrs. in Bantry Bay.
Unique (10)	III. 296, capture of Surinam exped. IV. 462, captd. by F. priv. V. 442, burnt at Basse Terre, Guadaloupe.
Unité (36)	I. 97, late Impérieuse (38), q.v.
Unité (36) *F.*	I. 356-8, captd. by Révolutionnaire (38) and consorts.
,, ,, *Br.*	IV. 342, capts. Ital. Ronco (16). V. 246, action in Sagone Bay ; 255, off Port Hercule ; 261, Sq. at Lissa ; 265, capts. Persanne (26).
Unité (28) *F.*	II. 405, captd. by Inconstant (36), renamed Surprise (28), q.v.
United Kingdom (26) *E.I.C.*	V. 205, retaken at the capture of the Isle of France.
United States (44) *U.S.*	V. 267-8, launched at Philadelphia ; 394-7, capts. Macedonian (38). VI. 98, Sq. at New London.
Urania (32) *Por.*	IV. 237, Sq. at Lisbon.
Urania (38)	I. 122, late Tortue (40), q.v.
Uranie (40) *F.*	I. 118-20, actn. with Thames (32) ; 121, renamed Tortue (40), q.v.
Uranie (38)...............	III. 137, Sq. off Brest. IV. 259, off Cherbourg ; 261, chases Manche (40).
Uranie (40) *F.*	V. 260-1, at Brindisi. VI. 386, destd. at Brindisi to prevent capture.
Urgent (12)...............	IV. 205, at Copenhagen.
Utile (24) *F.*	I. 371, captd. by Southampton (32) ; 372, added to Br. Navy.
,, (16) *Br.*............	III. 382, fndrd. near Malta.
Utrecht (64) *Du.*	II. 343-8, captd. in the Vlieter, Texel.
Utrecht (32) *Du.*	IV. 463, wrkd. Orkney Isles.
Vaillante (20) *F.*	II. 258, captd. by Indefatigable (44) ; renamed Danaë (20), q.v.
Valeureuse (36) *F.*......	III. 312, Brest Flt. IV. 88, Willaumez's Sq.; 117, broken up at Philadelphia.
Valiant (74)	I. 139, Channel Flt.; 149, 29th May ; 162, 183, 1st June ; 271-2, actn. off Isle Groix. II. 112, Sq. at St. Domingo. IV. 201, Copenhagen ; 396-413, Basque Rds. actn. V. 97, capts. Confiance (14) (late Canonnière) (40) ; 101, Sq. in Basque Rds. VI. 99, off New London.
Van Tromp (54) *Du.*....	IV. 415-7, captd. at the Cape of Good Hope.
Vanguard (74)	I. 65, Channel Flt. ; 249, Sq. at Guadaloupe. II. 167, 171, Medn. Flt.; 188, the Nile ; 212, capture of Goza exped.; 306, at Palermo. III. 182, capture of Créole (40) ; 186, capture of Duquesne (74). IV. 200, Copenhagen ; 213, crsg. in the Great Belt ; 298, Baltic Flt.
Var (26) *F.*...............	V. 9-10, captd. by Belle Poule (38), renamed Chichester (S.S.), q.v.
Varsovie (80) *F.*	IV. 391, Brest Flt.; 401-13, Basque Rds. actn.; 417, destd.
Vasco-de-Gama(74)*Por.*	I. 202, Br. and Por. Flt. in the Channel. IV. 238, rprg.
Vautour (16) *F.*	II. 5, Ireland exped.

INDEX TO SHIPS

Vautour (16) *Br.*	VI. 387, fndrd.
Venerable (74)	I. 308, Sq. off the Texel. II. 75–9, Camperdown; 301, Sq. off Aix. III. 98–104, Algesiras; 109, off Cadiz; 112–6, actn. in the Gut of Gibraltar; 493, wrkd. in Torbay. IV. 433–9, Scheldt exped. V. 334, Popham's Sq. off N. Spain. VI. 122–3, capture of Alcmène (40) and Iphigénie (40).
Vengeance (74)	I. 240, capture of Martinique exped.; 249, Sq. at Guadaloupe. II. 109, Sq. off Trinidad; 112, Sq. at Porto Rico.
Vengeance (40) *F.*	I. 253, Sq. at Sierra-Leone; 379–80, actn. with Mermaid (32); 384, engaged by Raison (20); 413, Sq. at Cape Francois. II. 90, in Fisgard Bay, Wales. III. 1–2, actn. with U.S. Constellation (36); 3, at Curaçoa; 23–4, captd. by Seine (38); 25, added to Br. Navy; 26, unserviceable.
Vengeance (18) *F.*	III. 8, captd. by Néréide (36) off the Penmarcks.
Vengeance (84)	VI. 395, bldg.
Vengeur (74) *F.*	I. 141, Brest Flt.; 163–8, 1st June; 181–2, sinks.
Vengeur (120) *F.*	I. 193, 258, bldg. at Brest. III. 170, launched at Brest; 311, Brest Flt., renamed Imperial (120), q.v.
Vengeur (priv.) (34) *F.*	I. 219, captd. by E.I.C. Sq. in the Straits of Sunda.
Vengeur (priv.) (10) *F.*	I. 358–60, actn. with the bts. of Diamond (38) in Hâvre Rds.
Vengeur (priv.) (16) *F.*	I. 400, captd. by Santa Margarita (36) in the Channel.
Venteux (10) *F.*	III. 180, cut out by the bts. of Loire (38) at the Isle Bas.
Venus (32)	I. 103–4, actn. with Sémillante (36); 139–42, Channel Flt.; 408, at St. John's, Newfoundland.
Venus (24) *Du.*	II. 347, 472, captd. in the Nieueve Diep, Texel.
Venus (36) *Da.*	IV. 209, 464, captd. at Copenhagen.
Vénus (28) *F.*	II. 137–8, Ireland exped. III. 475, captd. by Indefatigable (44) and Fisgard (38) off Lisbon.
Vénus (40) *F.*	IV. 380, at Cherbourg. V. 62, crsg. in the Bay of Bengal; 64–5, capts. E.I.C. Windham (26); 131, 137, at Port Louis; 166–71, at Isle de la Passe; 184–5, capts. Ceylon (32); 187, captd. by Boadicea (38); 190, renamed Néréide (38), q.v.
Venus (46)	VI. 395, bldg.
Vertu (40) *F.*	I. 387, rprg. at Rochefort; 389, at St. Denis, Isle Bourbon; 391–3, Sq. actn. with two Br. 74's; 395, at Batavia. II. 89–90, at the Isle of France; 250, engages Brilliant (28). III. 205, 489, captd. at Cape François, St. Domingo, by a Br. Sq.
Vervachten (64) *Du.*	II. 347, 472, captd. in the Nieueve Diep, Texel.
Vestal (28)	I. 324, Sq. off Norway. III. 76, off Bengazi, Tripoli; 320, actn. off Calais.
Vestale (36) *F.*	I. 282, Toulon Flt.; 325–6, actn. with Southampton (32); 402–4, captd. by Terpsichore (32); 405, escapes into Cadiz. II. (270, see Unicorn (28)) 384–5, captd. by Clyde (38) off Bordeaux.
Vésuve (20) *F.*	II. 134, actn. with Vesuvius (10) and Trial (12); 136, at Havre.
Vesuvius (bomb.)	II. 133, crsg. off Havre; 134–6, actn. with Vésuve (20). IV. 205, Copenhagen.
Veteran (64)	I. 240, capture of Martinique exped.; 248, off Guadaloupe; 313, crsg. W. Indies. II. 75–81, Camperdown; 345, Holland exped. III. 47, Sq. off Isle Huën, Copenhagen.
Vétéran (74) *F.*	III. 312, Brest Flt. IV. 88, Willaumez's Sq.; 112, 313, at Concarneau. V. 312, Sq. at L'Orient.
Victoire (80) *F.*	I. 90, late Languedoc (80), q.v., left at Toulon; 282, Toulon Flt.; 295, rprg. at Toulon; 345, Sq. at Cadiz; 409, Sq. at St. Pierre, Newfoundland.
Victoire (bomb.) *F.*	IV. 142, flotilla actn. with Sirius (36); 447–9, destd. by the bts. of a Br. Sq. in Rosas Bay.
Victoire (18)	IV. 283, Sq. at Gressie.
Victor (18)	II. 347, Holland exped. III. 143–4, des. Flêche (18); 208, Sq. at Pondicherry. IV. 367, broken up.

Victor (18)	IV. 367, late Jéna (18), q.v. V. 54, convoy escort; 65–6, captd. by Bellone (40).
,, ,, F.............	V. 151-4, at Grand Port; 184-6, capture of Ceylon (32); 203, at Port Louis; 205, recaptd. by a Br. Sq. at Port Louis.
Victorieuse (36) F.......	I. 92, 432, destd. at Toulon.
Victorieuse (14)	II. 230, capts. F. priv. off Guadaloupe. III. 92, capture of Marabon, exped. Alexandria.
Victorious (74)	I. 333, capture of Cape of Good Hope exped.; 390–3, actn. with F. frigate Sq. IV. 439, Scheldt exped. V. 338–41, capts. Rivoli (74).
Victory (100)	I. 72, Medn. Flt.; 81, at Toulon; 207–13, Flt. at Corsica; 297–300, actn. off Hyères; 371, Flt. off Toulon. II. 34, 37–48, St. Vincent. III. 176, Nelson's flagship; 241, off Toulon; 335, Medn. Sq.; 346, Sq. in Carlisle Bay, W. Indies; 355, at Spithead; 379, Medn. Flt.; 384, 397–404, 418–25, Trafalgar; 443, casualties; 462, at Gibraltar. IV. 298, Baltic Flt.
Vigilante (18) Sp.	IV. 136, captd. by Renommée (36); 137, renamed Spider (18), q.v.
Ville d'Aix (12) F......	III. 223, actn. off Calais; 319, actn. off Gravelines.
Ville d'Anvers (12) F.	III. 223, actn. off Calais; 319, actn. off Gravelines.
Ville de Berlin (74) F.	IV. 432, Sq. off Calot, Scheldt.
Ville-de-Caen (priv.)(16) F.	V. 324, captd. by Sealark (10).
Ville de Genève (12) F.	III. 318, actn. off Gravelines.
Ville-de-L'Orient (T.S.) F.	II. 5, Ireland exped.; 10, captd. by Doris (36).
Ville-de-Marseille(74)F.	V. 316, launched at Toulon.
Ville de Milan (40) F.	IV. 21–3, capts. Cleopatra (32); 24, captd. by Leander (50), renamed Milan (38), q.v.
Ville de Paris (110) ...	II. 59, 289, Flt. off Cadiz; 294, Medn. Flt. III. 170, Flt. off Brest; 307, at Spithead; 310, Channel Flt.; 312–3, Flt. off Brest. V. 207, Flt. off Toulon.
Ville Mayence (12) F.	III. 318, actn. off Gravelines.
Vincejo (16)	II. 295, off Genoa. III. 80, Sq. off Porto Ferrajo; 219, captd. by F. gbts. in Quiberon Bay.
Viper (14)	II. 92, capts. Sp. Virgin Maria (10); 420, capts. Furet (14). III. 20, off Port Louis.
Vipère (16)	II. 462, fndrd. off the Shannon.
Virgin Maria (10)	II. 92, captd. by Viper (14).
Virginie (40) F.	I. 261, in Brest Rds.; 264–5, Brest Flt.; 361, captd. by Indefatigable (44); 362, added to Br. Navy.
,, (38) Br.	IV. 324–5, capts. Du. Guelderland (36). V. 53, crsg. near Brest.
Vittoria (16) Du.	IV. 163–4, captd. by Harrier (18) and consort.
Vivo (14) Sp.	II. 298–9, capture of Penelope (16) off Gibraltar.
Vlugheld (16) Du.	I. 324–5, actn. off Egeroe, Norway.
Volador (16)	IV. 474, wrkd. in the Gulf of Coro, W. Indies.
Volage (22) F.	II. 226, captd. by Melampus (36), added to Br. Navy.
,, (20) Br.	IV. 341, capts. Requin (16). V. 233–40, actn. off Lissa.
Volcan (12) F.	I. 363, captd. by Spencer (16).
Volcano (bomb.)	II. 302, Sq. at Aix. III. 46, Copenhagen.
Volontaire (36) F.	I. 233, destd. by Warren's Sq. off the Penmarcks.
Volontaire (40) F.	III. 312, Brest Flt. IV. 88, Willaumez's Sq.; 189, captd. at Table Bay, added to Br. Navy.
,, (38) Br. ...	IV. 445, in the Medn. V. 209, off Toulon; 342, off the Rhone. VI. 17, at Morgion, near Marseille.
Voltigeur (16) F.	II. 5, Ireland exped. IV. 133, actn. with Reindeer (18); 135, captd. by Pique (36), renamed Musette (16), q.v.
Vryheid (74) Du.	II. 76–9, captd. at Camperdown.
Vulcain (14) F.	I. 220, with E.I.C. ships. III. 312, Brest Flt.
Vulcan (F.S.)	I. 86, destd. at Toulon.

INDEX TO SHIPS

Waakzaamheid (24) *Du.*	I. 142, convoy escort. II. 76, Camperdown; 270, captd. by Sirius (36); 271, added to Br. Navy.
Wagram (130) *F.*	V. 81, launched at Toulon. VI. 1–3, Toulon Flt.
Waldemar (80) *Da.*	IV. 209, 464, captd. at Copenhagen.
Wanderer (18)	IV. 388, actn. at Isle St. Martin.
Warley (30) *E.I.C.*	III. 250, actn. with Linois' Sq. E. Indies.
Warren Hastings (44) *E.I.C.*	III. 250, actn. with Linois' Sq. IV. 149–52, captd. by Piémontaise (40).
Warrior (74)	II. 289, Flt. off Cadiz. III. 47, Sq. off Isle Huën, Copenhagen; 357, 362, Calder's actn. V. 32, Sq. off Procida.
Warspite (74)	V. 81, Sq. off Toulon.
Washington (74) *Du.*	II. 343, captd. in the Vlieter, Texel; 348, renamed Princess of Orange (74), q.v.
Washington George (32) *U.S.*	III. 158, at Algiers.
Wasp (F.S.)	III. 477, destd. in Dunkerque Rds.
Wasp (18) *U.S.*	V. 390–1, capts. Frolic (18); 393, captd. by Poictiers (74).
Wasp (20) *U.S.*	V. 434, blt. at New York. VI. 161–3, capts. Reindeer (18); 165–6, capts. Avon (18); 167, fndrd. off Madeira.
Wasp (priv.) (20) *U.S.*	VI. 144–5, chased by Majestic (56).
Wassenaer (64) *Du.*	II. 76–9, captd. at Camperdown.
Wattigny (74) *F.*	I. 264, Brest Flt.; 273, actn. off Isle Groix; 386, Isle of France exped.; 413, Sq. at Cape François. II. 5, Ireland exped.; 11, at Brest; 286, Brest Flt. III. 312, Brest Flt.
Weasel (18)	IV. 265, crsg. off Corfu. V. 125, Sq. off Amanthea; 338–9, des. in actn. Mercure (16). IV. 21, bts. cut out F. gbts.; 24, actn. with F. gbts.; 27–32, bt. expeds. in the Adriatic.
Weazle (14)	II. 474, ashore in Barnstable Bay. III. 494, wrkd. in Gibraltar Bay.
Wellington (16)	V. 87, late Oreste (16), q.v.
Weser (40) *F.*	VI. 12–3, captd. by Scylla (18) and consorts; 14, added to Br. Navy.
Wexford (30) *E.I.C.*	III. 250, actn. with Linois' Sq. E. Indies.
Weymouth (T.S.)	III. 477, wrkd. on the Bar of Lisbon.
Whiting (14)	VI. 394, wrkd. on Dunbar Sand, Padstow Harbour.
Wildboar (10)	V. 445, wrkd. Scilly Isles.
Wilhelmina (32)	II. 271, late Du. Furie (36), q.v. III. 267–70, actn. with Psyché (36).
William Pitt (30) *E.I.C.*	I. 218, capture of F. priv.; 220, at the Zuften Isles.
Winchelsea (32)	I. 240, capture of Martinique exped.; 246–8, Sq. at Guadaloupe.
Winchester (60)	VI. 395, bldg.
Windham (26) *E.I.C.*	V. 63–4, captd. by Vénus (40); recaptd. by Magicienne (32); 132–5, captd. by F. Sq.; 155, recaptd. by the bts. of Sirius (36); 171, at Isle Bourbon.
Windsor Castle (98)	I. 72, Flt. off Toulon; 214–5, Flt. at Corsica; 284–9, actn. off Genoa; 297, off Hyères. III. 356–63, Calder's actn. IV. 175, Sq. off Rochefort; 217–9, Dardanelles; 294, Sq. at Palermo.
Wizard (16)	IV. 232, Sq. Alexandria exped.; 338–40, actn. with Requin (16); 383, bt. exped. at Noli. VI. 32, Sq. off Trieste.
Wolf (18)	IV. 126, capts. F. privs. off Cuba; 461, wrkd. on Heneaga, Bahama Isles.
Wolfe (24)	VI. 104, launched at Kingston; 105, actn. on the Canadian Lakes.
Wolverine (12)	II. 132, actn. off Ostende; 352, actn. with F. luggers; 389, capture of Du. Draak (18) and Gier (14). III. 259–60, destd. in actn. with Blonde (30) (priv.).
Wolverine (18)	IV. 331, crsg. off the Saintes.
Woodlark (12)	IV. 457, wrkd. near St. Valery.
Woodlark (10)	VI. 120, Sq. off the Adour River, Spain.
Woolwich (S.S.)	I. 240–2, capture of Martinique exped. VI. 104, at Quebec; 382, wrkd. off Barbuda.

E

Worcester (60) .... VI. 395, bldg.
Wrangler (12)............ V. 330, actn. with Da. gbts. in the Cattegat.

Yarrowflaul (74) *Rus.* IV. 234, Flt. in the Dardanelles.
Yawl, Admiral (28) *Da.* IV. 307, captd. by Sappho (18).
York (64).................. III. 493, fndrd. in the North Sea.
York (74) .... IV. 275, capture of Madeira exped. V. 18, Sq. off the Saintes; 69, capture of Martinique exped.; 208, Flt. off Toulon.

Zealand (74) *Da.* ...... III. 481, destd. off Copenhagen by a Br. Sq.
Zealous (74)............... II. 33, rprg. at Lisbon; 63, Sq. at Teneriffe; 171, Medn. Flt.; 183-7, the Nile; 215-9, Sq. off Alexandria; 305-6, blockading Naples. III. 380, at Gibraltar.
Zebra (18) .... I. 240-2, capture of Martinique exped. II. 110, Sq. off Trinidad.
Zebra (bomb.) .... III. 46, Copenhagen. IV. 205, Copenhagen.
Zeeland (64) *Du.* ...... I. 307, captd. at Plymouth.
Zeelast (22) *Du.* .... II. 412, captd. by Orpheus (32) off Togolanda.
Zee-Ploeg (14) *Du.* ... IV. 179-81, destd. by bts. of Br. Sq. at Java.
Zeerop (14) *Du.* .... IV. 179, captd. by Caroline (36) off Java.
Zeevraght (22) *Du.*...... II. 412, captd. by Orpheus (31) off Togolanda.
Zélandais (80) *F.* ...... VI. 1, launched at Cherbourg.
Zélé (74) *F.*............... I. 264-5, Brest Flt. II. 286, Brest Flt.
Zenobia (10) .... IV. 462, wrkd. on the coast of Florida.
Zephyr (14)............... II. 110, Sq. off Trinidad; 230-1, capture of Gurupano, Isle Margarita.
Zephyr (14) *Du.*......... V. 43-5, captd. by Diana (10) off Isle Celebes.
Zephyr (36) *Du.*.... ..... II. 454, captd by Andromeda (32) and consorts in the Frith of Forth.

PART II

NAVAL OFFICERS

Aalbers, N. S. (C.) *Du.*	IV. 163, Pallas; 164, k. in actn.
Abbott, Thomas (Pilot)	II. 81, Montagu, w. Camperdown.
Abdy, Anthony (C.) ...	IV. 393, Dotterel; 400, crsg.
Abell, Wm. (M.L.) ...	II. 159, Anson, w. in actn.
A'Court, Edwd. Henry (Mid.)	III. 200, Blanche, crsg.; 292, pro. L. Theseus, crsg.
Acklom, George (L.)	II. 135, Hydra, cutting out exped. III. 443, Neptune, Trafalgar, pro. Cr.
Acland, — (C.) *E.I.C.*	I. 336, Bombay Castle, capture of the Cape of Good Hope.
Acton, Edward (Mid.)	IV. 101, Donegal, w. in actn.
Adair, James (Mid.) ...	IV. 326. V. 120, Alceste, cutting out exped.; 248, crsg.; 266, act. L.
Adair, Wm. (M.C.)...	III. 398, Victory, Trafalgar; 421, k. in actn.
Adair, Wm. (Mr.Mt.)	IV 143, Sirius, k. in actn.
Adam, Charles (C.) ...	II. 337, Albatross, crsg. III. 131, Sibylle capts. F. Chiffonne; 316, engages F. flotilla.
Adam, Charles (Mid.)	IV. 345, Porcupine, cutting out exped. V. 37, Mercury, cutting out exped.
Adams, Abraham (Pr.)	II. 114, Magicienne, cutting out exped.
Adams, Charles (L.) ...	IV. 137, Renommée, cutting out exped.
Adams, Chas. (Mr.Mt.)	III. 171, Jalouse, cutting out exped., w.
Adams, William (A.B.)	VI. 270, Eliza, w. in actn.
Adamson, William (B.)	III. 416, Colossus, w. Trafalgar.
Addington, Thomas (Mid.)	VI. 374, Navarino, w.
Addis, Edward Brown (L.)	V. 297, Sir Francis Drake, cutting out exped.
Adye John Miller (L.)	II. 196, Vanguard, w. at Nile.
Affleck, Thomas (C.)...	I. 252, Fly, crsg. St. Domingo; 443, Amethyst, wrkd.
Affleck, William (C.)...	I. 126, Alligator, capture of Isle St. Pierre.
Agairre, Don Juan de (C.) *Sp.*	II. 59, St. Vincent, dismissed.
Agassiz, James (L.) ...	III. 68, Jamaica, cutting out exped.
Aikenhead, John (Mid.)	III. 406, Royal Sovereign, k. at Trafalgar.
Aimes, George (act.L.)	I. 185, Queen, w. in actn. 1st June.
Airey, John (Mr.Mt.)	II. 81, Ardent, w. Camperdown. IV. 101, Mr., Donegal, St. Domingo Rds., w.
Aitchison, Edw. (Mid.)	VI. 288, Leander, w. Algiers.
Alaba, Don Martin (A.) *Sp.*	II. 239, Isle of Luconia.
Alava, Don Ign. Maria de (V.A.) *Sp.*	III. 386, Santa Ana; 406-9, w. Trafalgar, 455.
Aldham, George (Pr.)	VI. 60, Shannon, k. in actn.
Alexander, James (C.)	I. 389, Carysfort capts. Alerte.

Alexander, John (Mid.)	IV. 229, Royal George, w. Dardanelles ; 347, L. Standard, cutting out exped. V. 448, Cr. Fleur de Mer, fndrd., crew saved.
Alexander, Thomas (act.C.)	IV. 288, Superb, crsg. V. 312, C. Colossus, crsg. VI. 181, Devastation (bomb.) ; 184-5, Potomac exped. ; 190, 235, St. Mary's, U.S. ; 309, C.B. ; 328-37, Burmese War ; 338, d. ; 354, App.
Allary, Joseph (C.) F.	I. 141, Conception, crsg. III. 68, Formidable, Brest Flt.
Allègre, Antoine (L.-Com.) F.	V. 27, Mouche engages Goldfinch.
Allemand, Joseph(C.)F.	IV. 444, Breslau, Toulon Sq.
Allemand, Zacharie Jac. Théo. (C.) F.	I. 121, Carmagnole capts. Thames (disabled) 253-4, crsg. ; 409, Cmde. crsg. II. 286, Tyrannicide, off the Saintes. III. 368, pro. R.A. crsg. ; 373-7, 501, App. IV. 47-9, Majestueux ; 50-5, crsg.; 91, 141, 287, Isle of Aix ; 400, 402, 408-30, Basque Rds. ; 444, pro. V.A. Austerlitz, Toulon Flt. V. 80, Toulon ; 312, Lorient ; 313, crsg. ; 314, Brest.
Allen, Charles (L.) ...	V. 40-1, Bellerophon, cutting out exped.
Allen, John (Mid.) ...	I. 122, Penelope, crsg., w. in actn.
Allen, Samuel (L.) ...	V. 199, capture of Banda Neira.
Allen, Thos. (L.Com.)	VI. 388, Dart fndrd., drnd.
Allen, William (C.Ck.)	III. 412, Tonnant, w. Trafalgar.
Allen, William Henry (L.) U.S.	IV. 252, Chesapeake, crsg. V. 403, Cr. Macedonian (prize). VI. 78, pro. C. Argus ; 79, w. in actn. with Pelican ; 82, d.
Allen, — (L. Com.) E.I.C.	V. 66, E.I.C. Prince of Wales, Persian Gulf.
Alleyn, Richard Israel (L.)	IV. 129, Egyptienne, cutting out exped.
Alms, James (C.)	I. 324, Réunion ; 325, actn. off Norway. II. 293, Repulse, St. Vincent's Flt. crsg.; 426, w.; 427, wrkd. III. 476, App.
Alvear, — (C.) Sp. ...	III. 289, Mercedes, passenger.
Alwyn, John C. (Mr.) U.S.	V. 380, Constitution, w. in actn. ; 417, L., w. in actn.
Anderson, Drummond (L.Com.)	VI. 334, Mercury (gbt.), Burmese War.
Anderson, Geo. (C.Ck.)	IV. 345, Porcupine ; 346, cutting out exped. V. 37, Mercury ; 38, cutting out exped.
Anderson, James (C.)...	V. 111-13, Rinaldo engages F. privs. ; 217-20, actn. with F. flotilla.
Anderson, John (Mid.)	III. 54, Bellona, w. Copenhagen. IV. 117, L. Monarch, w. in actn.
Anderson, Luke (Mid.)	II. 196, Alexander, w. Nile.
Andrew, John Wm.(C.)	V. 338, Weasel des. F. Mercure ; 339-41, pro. P.C.
Andrews, Francis(Mid.)	IV. 320, Tartarus, cutting out exped.
Andrews, George (L.)	I. 212, Agamemnon, w. capture of Bastia, Corsica.
Andrews, George (Mr.)	I. 87, capture of Toulon.
Andrews, Henry (Mr.)	IV. 328, Nymphe, cutting out exped.
Andrews, John (Mid.)	V. 155, Sirius, cutting out exped.
Andrews,Jno.H.(Mid.)	VI. 288, Infernal (bomb.), w. Algiers.
Andrews, Wm. (Mid.)	IV. 141, Pallas, w. in actn.
Angas, Jonathan(As.S.)	V. 37, Amphion, cutting out exped.
Annesley, Francis Chas. (L.)	I. 95, Lowestoffe, cutting out exped. V. 126, Pilot, cutting out exped.
Anson, Hon. William (Cr.)	VI. 365, Brisk ; 373-7, Navarino.
Anthony, Charles (L.)	VI. 105, Cr. gbts. Canadian Lakes ; 204-5, C. Star, in actn. Oswego, Canadian Lakes.
Anthony, — (Mr.)......	II. 356, loss of Proserpine.
Antrim, George (Mid.)	II. 196, Vanguard, w. Nile.
Apodaca, Don Sebas. R. de (R.A.) Sp.	II. 110, San-Vicente, destd. to prevent capture.
Appleton,Thos. (M.L.)	IV. 22, Cleopatra, w. in actn.

INDEX TO NAVAL OFFICERS 53

Apthorp, Charles (L.)	I. 225, Concorde, crsg. III. 83, Druid, crsg.
Arbuthnot, Hon. James (L.)	V. 100, 101, Surveillante, cutting out exped. VI. 16, cutting out exped.; 165, pro. C. Avon, actn. with U.S. Wasp; 166, w.; 387, App.
Archbold, Wm. (L.-Com.)	III. 172, Ealing, actn. off Granville.
Archer, John (L.)	VI. 6, capture of Gluckstadt.
Archer, Wm. (Mid.) ...	VI. 74, Dominica, k. in actn.
Ardennes, Chas. Baudin des (L.Com.) F.	V. 344, Renard engages Swallow; 346, w. in actn.
Aregnaudeau, —(C.)F.	III. 259, Blonde (priv.) capts. Wolverine.
Argles, George (L.) ...	II. 122, Mars, w. in actn. III. 36, L.Cr. Nile, off Morbihan 320, C. Trusty, off Calais. IV. 139, Iris, crsg.
Argumosa, Don Teodoro (C.) Sp.	III. 386, Monarca; 406-14, 456, Trafalgar.
Arias, Don Josef de (C.) Sp.	II. 413, Galgo captd. by Crescent.
Armstead, John (Mid.)	IV. 448, Ville de Paris; 449, w. in actn. Bay of Rosas.
Arnold, James (A.B.)	IV. 253, U.S. Chesapeake, k. in actn, deserter.
Arogonez Cayatano (C.) Cuban	VI. 271-3, Zaragonaza, k. in actn.
Arscott, James (Mr.Mt.)	III. 424, Téméraire, Trafalgar. IV. 326, Alceste, cutting out exped.
Arscott, Thomas (L.)...	III. 287, Indefatigable, crsg. IV. 158, cutting out exped.
Arthur, Richard (C.)...	IV. 205, Vesuvius (bomb.), Copenhagen. V. 86, Cherokee engages F. privs. off Dieppe, pro. P.C.
Ashbridge, Robert S. (M.L.)	V. 340, Victorious, k. in actn.
Ashmore, Sam. (M.L.)	IV. 19, San Fiorenzo, w. in actn.
Ashton, Herbert (Mid.)	V. 101, Surveillante, cutting out exped.
Aslinhurst, — (Mid.)...	II. 226, Babet, cutting out exped., w.
Atcherley, Jas. (M.C.)	III. 427, Conqueror, Trafalgar.
Atchison, Arthur (L.)	III. 443, Britannia, Trafalgar; 464, pro. Cr. V. 212, Scylla capts. Canonnier.
Atherton, Robert (Mid.)	VI. 309, 348-51, Burmese War.
Athill, James (Mid.) ...	IV. 447, Tigre, cutting out exped. Bay of Rosas.
Atkins, Chas. Edward (M.L.)	V. 21, Pompée, w. in actn.
Atkins, David (P.C.)...	IV. 31, Seine, crsg. Porto Rico. V. 96, crsg. Rochelle; 231, loss of Defence, drnd.; 447, App.
Atkins, James (L.Com.)	V. 448, Grouper, wrkd. Guadaloupe.
Atkinson, Thos. (Mr.)	II. 326, Theseus at Acre; 330, w. III. 398, Victory, Trafalgar.
Auckland, — (Mid.)...	III. 125, Bordelais, crsg., capture of Curieux, drnd.
Audibert Pierre (C.) F.	II. 352, Rusé (priv.) engages Wolverine.
Austen, Charles John (P.C.)	VI. 393, Phœnix wrkd. near Smyrna.
Austen, Francis William (C.)	III. 10-12, Peterel capts. F. Ligurienne; 339, Canopus, 458; Medn. Sq. IV. 90, Duckworth's Sq.
Austin, John (Gunner)	IV. 9. Courageux, w. in actn.
Austin, Silvester (Mid.)	III. 104, Venerable, w. Algesiras.
Austin, — (B.)	II. 196, Vanguard, w. Nile.
Ayaldi, Don Tomas (C.) Sp.	I. 399, Mahonesa captd. by Terpsichore.
Aylmer, Hon. Fred. Wm. (P.C.)	VI. 278, Severn; 282-9, Algiers; 291, made C.B.
Aylmer, John (P.C.)...	I. 416, Tremendous, Sq. crsg. III. 73 Dragon; 80, Medn. Sq.
Ayscough, John (C.) ...	II. 475, Blanche (T.S.), wrkd. IV. 184, Success capts. Vengeur (priv.). V. 113, crsg. off Calabria.
Ayton, George Henry (Mr.Mt.)	V. 340, Victorious, w. in actn.
Ayton, Geo. H. (Mid.)	IV. 320, Daphne, cutting out exped.

Babington, J. B. (L.)...	VI. 289, Impregnable, Algiers; 291, pro. Cr.
Badcock, William Stanhope (C.)	VI. 175, cutting out exped. Chesapeake Bay.
Bailey, John P. (Mid.)	III. 432, Africa, w. Trafalgar.
Bailie, Edward (M.L.)	IV. 135, Pique, cutting out exped.; 447, C. Cumberland, cutting out exped. Bay of Rosas.
Baillie, — (C.)	II. 315, Fort St. Elmo.
Bain, Henderson (C.)...	V. 303, Harpy, capture of Java.
Bainbridge, Joseph (C.) U.S.	VI. 156, U.S. Frolic captd. by Orpheus.
Bainbridge, Wm. (L.)	II. 419, Queen Charlotte, crsg.; 430, loss of, drnd.
Bainbridge, Wm. (C.) U.S.	III. 158, George Washington, Algiers Rds.; 300, Philadelphia, crsg. V. 408, Cmde.; 418, Constitution capts. Java. VI. 44, 54, 66, St. Salvador.
Baird, Andrew (L.) ...	VI. 340, Boadicea, Burmese War.
Baird, Daniel (Mid.)...	IV. 312, Emerald, cutting out exped.
Baird, John (Car.)	II. 429, loss of Queen Charlotte.
Baird, Wynne (Mid.)...	VI. 287, Glasgow, w. Algiers.
Baker, Hon. E. R. (P.C.)	IV. 473, Jupiter, wrkd. in Vigo Bay, Spain.
Baker, Francis (1st cl. Vol.)	V. 398, Macedonian, w. in actn.
Baker, Henry (L.)......	III. 56, Alcmène, w. Copenhagen.
Baker, Henry Edward Reg. (L.)	II. 58, Diadem, St. Vincent, pro. Cr.
Baker, Hy. Loraine (L.)	IV. 244, Bacchante, in actn. St. Domingo. V. 225, capture of Anholt. VI. 183, C. Fairy, Alexandria.
Baker, Joseph (C.)......	II. 413, Calypso, convoy escort. III. 14, crsg. V. 38, Tartar, crsg.; 224, capture of Anholt; 447, wrkd. in the Baltic.
Baker, Philip Hy. (L.)	IV. 135-6, Pique, w. in actn.
Baker, Robert Hood (Mid.)	VI. 287, Queen Charlotte, w. Algiers.
Baker, Thomas (C.) ...	III. 17, Nemesis, Sq. off Dunkerque; 41, actn. with Da. Freya; 374, Phœnix, crsg. IV. 2, crsg.; 65, capts. F. Didon; 74, 112, Tribune, Sq. crsg.; 298, Vanguard, Baltic Flt. VI. 70, Cumberland, convoy escort.
Balderson, Charles (C.)	IV. 456, Orquixo, fndrd. near Jamaica, drnd.
Balderston, George (L.)	II. 376, Trent, cutting out exped.
Baldwin, Augustus (L.)	IV. 300-1, Implacable, capture of Rus. Sewolod.
Baldwin, John (L.) ...	III. 430, Leviathan, Trafalgar. V. 289, Astrea, w. in actn.; 295, pro. Cr.
Balfour, William (Mid.)	II. 48, Irresistible, w. St. Vincent. IV. 22, L. Cleopatra, w. in actn.; 26, pro. Cr.
Balgonie, David Lord (L.)	IV. 448, Ville de Paris, cutting out exped. Bay of Rosas.
Ball, Alexander John (P.C.)	II. 171, Alexander, Flt. off Cadiz; 196, w. the Nile; 212, 291, blockade of Malta; 445, Gvr. of Malta. III. 74, Sq. crsg.; 341, Malta.
Ball, Arthur (M.L.) ...	III. 411, Tonnant, Trafalgar.
Ball, Henry Lidgbird (P.C.)	II. 338, Dædalus, Sq. crsg.; 357, capts. F. Prudente. IV. 396, Gibraltar, Basque Rds.
Ball, John (B. Mt.) E.I.C.	IV. 154, Warren Hastings, w. in actn.
Ballantyne, George (C.) E.I.C.	I. 219-20, Pigot, actn. with privs.
Ballard, Edward I. (L.) U.S.	VI. 61, Chesapeake, k. in actn.
Ballard, Samuel James (P.C.)	II. 246, Pearl, crsg. III. 78, crsg. Elba. V. 51, Sceptre, actn. off Anse la Barque; 191, capture of Guadaloupe, Cmde.
Ballard, Volant Vashon (P.C.)	V. 50, Blonde, Sq. actn. at Basse Terre; 86, 92, Sq. off Guadaloupe.
Ballard, — (L.) U.S....	VI. 256, Cr. of Levant (prize).
Ballchild, George E. (M.L.)	IV. 230, Meteor (bomb.), w. Dardanelles.

INDEX TO NAVAL OFFICERS 55

Ballinghall, Charles Hy. (M.L.)	III. 17, Renown, cutting out exped.
Bamborough, John (Mr.)	I. 186, Royal George, w. 1st June.
Bambrill, Edw. (A.B.)	VI. 270, Eliza, w. in actn.
Banks, Francis (L.Com.)	VI. 4-6 Blazer, Heligoland.
Banks, John (L.)	V. 324, Northumberland, in actn. with F. frigates, pro. Cr.
Bannatyne, John (Mr. Mt.)	IV. 448, Volontaire, cutting out exped. Bay of Rosas.
Bannister, Geo. (A.B.)	II. 266, Leander in actn.
Bant, Thomas (Mid.)...	III. 414, Bellerophon, w. Trafalgar.
Barbaud, Jean (L.Com.) F.	V. 219, Ville de Lyon (prame) captd. by Naiad.
Barber, James (Mid.)...	VI. 288, Infernal (bomb.), w. Algiers.
Barclay, Andrew (Mr.)	III. 24, Seine, w. in actn.
Barclay, John (Mid.)...	III. 171, Hydra, cutting out exped.
Barclay, Robert Heriot (C.)	VI. 109-14, w. flotilla actn., Lake Erie.
Bargas, Don Josef (C.) Sp.	III. 386, Sp. San Juan Nepomuceno, Trafalgar.
Bargean, Jean Pierre (C.) F.	II. 139, F. Résolue; 143-52, captd. by Melampus. III. 181, F. Mignonne captd. by Goliath.
Barker, George (C.) ...	II. 211, Incendiary (F.S.), Malta; 289, Barfleur, Flt. off Cadiz.
Barker, James (L.) ...	II. 58, Orion, St. Vincent; 197, the Nile; 210, pro. Cr.
Barker, Scory (P.C.)...	II. 106, Tribune, wrkd. near Halifax, drnd.; 462, App.
Barling, Henry (Sig.)...	I. 322, Dido, in actn.
Barlow, Robert (C.) ...	I. 50, Childers, crsg.; 139, Pegasus, Channel Flt. II. 7, Phœbe, crsg.; 103, capts. Néréide. III. 8, capts.
,, Sir Robert ...	Heureux (priv.); 127, capts. Africaine; 129, kntd.; 177, Triumph, Sq. off Toulon.
Barnard, Jean (C.) F....	II. 381, Courageux (priv.) captd. by Alcmène.
Barnes, John (Mid.) ...	V. 257, Pilot, cutting out exped.
Barnes, John (S.) E.I.C.	IV. 154, E.I.C. Warren Hastings, w. in actn.
Barney, Joshua (Cmde.) U.S.	VI. 168, 170-6, flotilla Chesapeake Bay.
Barolovich, — (C.) F.-Ven.	V. 122, F.-Ven. Bellona, Flt. crsg. Adriatic.
Barré, Jean Baptiste (C.) F.	II. 176, Alexandria; 295, Alceste captd. by Br. Flt. V. 338-41, Cmde., Rivoli captd. by Victorious.
Barré, -- (C.) F.	III. 204, St. Domingo.
Barreaut, Michel Pierre (C.) F.	II. 363-4, Insurgente captd. by U.S. Constellation.
Barrett, John (L.Com.)	I. 333, Experiment (S.S.) Isle of St. Lucie. IV. 298, C. Africa, Baltic Flt.; 369-70, w. in actn. with Da. gbts. V. 40-1, Minotaur, crsg. Baltic Flt.
Barretté, Geo. Wilmot (L.Com.)	VI. 72, Dominica captd. by U.S. Decatur, k. in actn.; 382, App.
Barrie, Robert (L.) ...	III. 124, Bordelais, w. in actn. IV. 258, C. Pomone, crsg.; 444, off Toulon. V. 32, crsg.; 246, actn. Bay of Sagone. VI. 168, Dragon; 200-1, actn. St. Mary's, U.S.
Barron, James (Cmde.) U.S.	IV. 249-51, Chesapeake engages Leopard; 253, w. in actn.
Barry, Edward (Mr. Mt.)	IV. 346, Porcupine, cutting out exped.
Bartholomew, David Ewen (C.)	VI. 181, Erebus (F.S.); 185, American War; 190, w.; 236, w.
Bartholomew, Philip (C.)	III. 477, Havick, wrkd. in St. Alban's Bay, Jersey.
Bartlett, —(Mr.) E.I.C.	VI. 267, E.I.C. Nautilus, in actn.
Barton, John Thos. (Pr.)	VI. 163, Reindeer, k. in actn.
Barton, Robert (C.) ...	I. 401, Lapwing capts. F. Décius. III. 69, Concorde engages Bravoure. IV. 44, Goliath capts. Torche; 275, York, Sq. in Funchal Bay. V. 18, Sq. off the Saintes; 69, Martinique; 208, Flt. off Toulon.

Barton, Robt. Cutts (L.)	IV. 447, Apollo, cutting out exped. Rosas Bay.
Barwell, Nathaniel (Mid.)	V. 256, Active, cutting out exped.
Basden, William Benge (Pr.)	VI. 224, Rota, cutting out exped.
Basham, Wm. (M.L.)	II. 67, Emerald, k. at Santa Cruz.
Bashford, James (L.)...	III. 406, Royal Sovereign, w. Trafalgar. V. 42, Princess Caroline, cutting out exped.
Bassan, Sam. (L.Com.)	IV. 457, Bouncer, wrkd. off Dieppe.
Basset, William (L.)...	III. 66, Medusa, w. cutting out exped.
Bastard, John (C.)......	IV. 156, Rattlesnake, capture of Bellone (priv.). V. 369, Africa, N. American Sq.
Baste, — (R.A.) *F*. ...	V. 218, prame flotilla, Boulogne.
Bastin, Robert (L.) ...	IV. 161, Blanche, w. in actn.
Bastin, Thomas (Pr.)...	IV. 270, 330, Grasshopper, w. cutting out exped.
Bate, William (M.L.)...	V. 146, Sirius, cutting out exped.
Bateman, Samuel (L.)	III. 57, Russel, Copenhagen.
Bates, John James (L.)	VI. 40, Amelia, k. in actn.
Bathurst, Walter (P.C.)	II. 289, Ville de Paris, Flt. off Cadiz. IV. 302, Salsette, Br. Swd. Flt.; 355–6, 433, Scheldt exped. VI. 373, Genoa, k. Navarino.
Batt, Joseph B. (L.Com.)	IV. 400, Conflict, Basque Rds. V. 445, fndrd. in Bay of Biscay, drnd.
Batten, John (Mid.) ...	IV. 317, Childers, w. in actn.
Batten, John (Mr.)......	V. 30, Scout, cutting out exped.
Battersby, Henry Robt. (L.)	V. 29, Scout, cutting out exped.; 30, capture of battery at Port Carri, pro. Cr.
Baubin, — (act. L.) *F*.	IV. 153, Piémontaise in actn.
Baudin, François André (C.) *F*.	IV. 38–40, Topaze capts. Blanche; 443, R.A. Robuste, Toulon Flt. V. 85, Majestueux; 207–315, Toulon.
Baugh, Henry (L.Com.)	IV. 329, Rapid, crsg.; 474, destd. by batteries in the Tagus.
Baumgardt, Wm. Aug. (L.)	V. 28, Spartan, crsg.; 114, cutting out exped.; 118, in actn. with Cérès.
Baxter, George (M.L.)	VI. 288, Leander, k. Algiers.
Bayley, John (P.C.) ...	VI. 266, Cornwallis, crsg., chases U.S. Hornet.
Bayley, — (Mid.)	VI. 377, San Fiorenzo, k. in actn.
Bayne, Wm. Henry (C.)	IV. 473, Bermuda, wrkd. at Little Bermuda.
Baynes, Robt. Lambert (Cr.)	VI. 364, Asia; 373, Navarino.
Bayntum, Henry Wm. (P.C.)	II. 456, Réunion, wrkd. in the Swin. III. 181–2, Cumberland, Sq. crsg.; 237, Leviathan, Channel Flt.; 335, Medn. Flt.; 384, 392, 426, Trafalgar; 489, App.
Bayton, James (Mid.) E.I.C.	IV. 154, E.I.C. Warren Hastings, w. in actn.
Bazeley, Henry (C.) ...	II. 132, Harpy, off Ostende. III. 3, crsg. off St. Malo; 4–6, engages Pallas; 8, pro. P.C.
Bazeley, John (P.C.)...	I. 65, 139, Alfred, Channel Flt.; 270, Prince of Wales, Channel Flt.; 297, Barfleur, Medn. Flt. II. 345, Overyssel, Holland exped.
Bazeley, — (L.).........	VI. 314, Sophie, Burmese War.
Bazire, — (Cmde.) *F*.	I. 141, Montagne, Brest Flt.; 177, 1st June; 178, k. in actn.
Beale, James (Mid.) ...	I. 300, Culloden, k. in actn.
Beasley, Fredk. (Mid.)	IV. 9, Namur, w. in actn.
Beatly, — (L.)	II. 330, Theseus, w. at Acre.
Beatty, Daniel McNeale (Mid.)	VI. 288, Severn, w. Algiers.
Beatty, George (M.L.)	II. 324, Theseus, w. at Acre. III. 201, Blenheim, cutting out exped.
Beatty, William (S.)...	III. 398, Victory, Trafalgar; 502, App.
Beauchène, Camille C. A. G. (C.) *F*.	III. 283, Atalante engages Centurion.

INDEX TO NAVAL OFFICERS

Beauclerk, Lord Amelius (C.) — I. 94, Nemesis, Medn.; 304, Juno, convoy escort; 369, Dryad capts. F. Proserpine. IV. 434, Royal Oak, Scheldt exped.
Beaudouin, Louis Alexis (C.) F. — III. 186, Guerrière, crsg.; 386, Fougueux, Trafalgar; 424, k. in actn.
Beaufort, Francis (L.) — III. 33, Phaëton, w. cutting out exped.
Beaulieu, Claude Pascal Morel (C.) F. — III. 78, Carrère captd. by Pomone.
Beaver, Jas. (act.Mr.) — V. 325, Sealark, crsg. in actn.
Beaver, Philip (P.C.)... — II. 432, siege of Genoa. III. 81, Foudroyant, Malta. V. 19, Acasta, Sq. off the Saintes; 70, W. Indies; 203, Nisus, Isle of France; 303-9, Java exped.
Beazeley, George (Mid.) — IV. 320, Daphne, cutting out exped.
Becher, Alex. (L.Com.) — II. 470, Medusa, wrkd. near Portugal. III. 490, C. Déterminée, wrkd. Jersey.
Beckett, James (Car.).. — V. 126, Thames, cutting out exped.
Beckett, J. (C.) .... — III. 494, De Ruyter, wrkd. at Antigua.
Bedar, Martin (L.-Com.) F. — II. 216, Torride captd. by Goliath, w. in actn.
Bedford, Fredk. (Mid.) — II. 248, Jason, w. in actn. III. 129, L. Phœbe, crsg.
Bedford, John (L.) ... — III. 411, Tonnant, Trafalgar; 464, pro. Cr.
Bedford, William (L.). — I. 200, Queen, 1st June, pro. Cr.
Bedford, Wm. (P.C.).. — I. 270, Queen, Channel Flt. IV. 157, Prince of Wales, Sq. off Rochefort; 395, Caledonia, Basque Rds.
Bedingfield, Thomas William (Mid.) — III. 275, Narcissus, w. cutting out exped.
Bedout, Jacques (C.) F. — I. 274, Tigre, actn. off Isle Groix. II. 5, Cmde. Indomptable, Brest Flt.; 286, pro. R.A. Terrible, Brest.
Beens — (C.) F. ...... — I. 315-16, Gloire captd. by Astræa.
Beever, Arthur (Mid.). — VI. 41, Amelia, w. in actn.
Begbie, James (L.) ... — IV. 447-9, Apollo, w. cutting out exped. Rosas Bay.
Belair, Alain Jos. Le Veyer (Cmde.) F. — IV. 88, Impétueux, Willaumez's Sq. crsg.
Belcher, Peter (Mr. Mt.) — VI. 144, Duke of Marlborough (packet), w. in actn.
Belchier, Nathaniel (L.) — II. 376, Trent, cutting out exped. V. 46, Thetis, cutting out exped.
Belding, — (L.) U.S. . — V. 280, U.S. President and Little Belt.
Belhomme, Pierre Jos. Paul (L.Com.) F. — I. 222-5, Babet captd. by Flora.
Belin, — (L.Com.) F. — V. 344-5, Goéland engages Swallow.
Bell, Christopher (L.). — IV. 135, Pique, cutting out exped. V. 108, C. Phipps, capts. Barbier de Seville (priv.).
Bell, Christopher James (L.Com.) — VI. 222, Murray (gbt.), Lake Champlain, U.S.
Bell, George (L.) ...... — II. 17, narrow escape of Indefatigable.
Bell, George Augustus (M.C.) — VI. 373, k. Navarino.
Bell, Henry (Mr.) ...... — IV. 330, Grasshopper, cutting out exped. V. 119, Alceste, cutting out exped.
Bell, James (Mid.)...... — III. 55, Polyphemus, k. Copenhagen.
Bell, John (Mr.)......... — IV. 22, Cleopatra, w. in actn.
Bellairs, Henry (Mid.). — III. 437, Spartiate, w. Trafalgar.
Bellamy, John (L.) ... — III. 130, Trent, cutting out exped. V. 343, C. Eclair, crsg. VI. 34, Port D'Anzo.
Belleisle, — (L.) F. ... — I. 430, Sémillante, k. in actn.
Bellenger, Jacques François (C.) F. — IV. 391, Elbe, Brest Flt.
Belli, George Lawrence (M.L.) — IV. 229, Royal George, k. Dardanelles.
Bennett, Charles (L.).. — III. 411, Tonnant; 453-4, Trafalgar.
Bennett, H. A. (C.) ... — I. 439, Moselle, captd. by the F. at Toulon.
Bennett, Hon. — (Mid.) — I. 185, Montagu, w. 1st June.

Bennett, Jas. (L.Com.)	IV. 374, Maria captd. by F. Département des Landes, k. in actn. ; 474, App.
Bennett, Martin (L.)...	VI. 29–30, Elizabeth, cutting out exped.
Bennett, Richard H. Alex. (P.C.)	IV. 113, Fame, Sq. crsg. ; 386, Rosas Bay.
Bennett, Thomas (L.) .	IV. 354, Seahorse, crsg.
Bennett, William (L.).	IV. 344, Amphion, Rosas Bay.
Benoît, Jean Felix (C.) F.	I. 290, Ca-Ira captd. in actn. off Genoa.
Benson, John (M.L.) .	III, 416, Colossus, w. Trafalgar.
Bentham, Charles (Mid.)	V. 256, Active, cutting out exped.
Bentham, George (L.).	V. 40, Bellerophon, cutting out exped. ; 103, act.Cr. Briseis, capts. Sans Souci (priv.). VI. 223, C. Carnation, crsg. ; 278, Heron, Algiers.
Bentinck, Wm. (P.C.)	I. 139, Phaëton, Channel Flt. ; 176, engages Impétueux, 1st June.
Benyon, Benjamin George (M. L.)	VI. 187, Menelaus, w. in actn. Baltimore.
Berard, ClaudeRené (C.) F.	IV. 338–41, Requin engages Wizard.
Berard, — (C.) F.......	I. 141, Pelletier, Brest Flt.
Beresford, John Poer (C.)	I. 219, Hussar, Chesapeake Bay ; 384, Raison engages F. Vengeance. IV. 36, Cambrian, crsg. ; 391, L'Orient ; 392-6, 418, Basque Rds. V. 313, Poictiers, crsg. ; 393-6, capts. U.S. Wasp and recapts. Frolic.
Bergeret, Jacques (C.) F.	I. 261, Brest Rds. ; 265, engages Mars; 361, captd. by Indefatigable. II. 286, Dix Août, Brest Flt. III. 68, 271, Brest. IV. 18–20, Psyché, captd. by San Fiorenzo ; 391, Varsovie, Brest Flt. ; 400–13, Basque Rds.
Bergevin, Mathieu Charles (C.) F.	II. 139, Romaine, Brest ; 286, Cisalpin, Brest Flt.
Berkeley, Hon. George Cranfield (P.C.)	I. 65, 139, Marlborough, Channel Flt. ; 175, 1st June ; 200, w. II. 285, R.A. Mars, Sq. off Brest ; 301, Sq. off Rochefort ; 302, w. IV. 250, V.A. Halifax ; 256, recalled.
Berkeley, Velterers Cornewall (P.C.)	II. 55, Emerald, crsg. ; 57, 93, actn. in Conil Bay, Trafalgar.
Berkley, Hon. Frederick (Mid.)	III. 200, Blanche, cutting out exped.
Bernard, Henry Richard (L.)	VI. 30, Elizabeth, crsg. Adriatic.
Bernard, — (Pilot) ...	II. 238, Fox, at Manilla.
Berrenger, Charles (C.) F.	II. 285, Républicain, Brest. III. 334, Scipion, Toulon ; 386, Trafalgar. IV. 9, captd. by Strachan's Sq. w.
Berry, Edward (L.) ... ,, Sir Edward ...	II. 45, Captain, in actn. ; 58, pro. Cr. ; 171, C. Vanguard off Cadiz ; 183, the Nile ; 262, 268, kntd. ; 438, Foudroyant, crsg. off Malta ; 440-1, engages Guillaume Tell. III. 384, Agamemnon ; 387, w. Trafalgar. IV. 90, Duckworth's Sq.
Berry, John (L.)	III. 439, Revenge, w. Trafalgar.
Berry, — (Mid.)	III. 67, w. cutting out exped.
Berthelin, Mathurin Théo. (L.Com.) F.	I. 356, Etoile (S.S.) captd. by Br. Sq.
Bertie, Albermarle (P.C.)	I. 62, Edgar, Channel Flt. ; 100, Medn. ; 139, Channel Flt. ; 271, Thunderer ; 330, capts. Eveillé. II. 301, Renown, Sq. off Aix. V. 190, V.A. ; 203, Isle of France exped.
Bertie, Thomas (P.C.)...	II. 344, Ardent, Holland exped. III. 46, Copenhagen. IV. 89, St. George, Strachan's Sq.
Bertie, Willoughby (C.)	V. 445, Satellite, fndrd. in the Channel, drnd.
Bertram, Charles (L.)..	IV. 312, Emerald, cutting out exped., pro. Cr. 381, C. Persian, wrkd. W. Indies.
Bescond, Pierre Marie (Cmde.) F.	II. 286, Fougueux, Brest Flt.

INDEX TO NAVAL OFFICERS 59

Best, Richard (Mr.Mt.)	III. 104, Cæsar, Algesiras, drnd.
Bettesworth, Geo.Edm. Byron (L.)	III. 246, Centaur, w. cutting out exped.; 310, C. Curieux. IV. 17, capts. Dame Ernouf (priv.); 322, Tartar; 323-4, k. in actn. off Bergen.
Bettson, Nicholas (Mid.)	II. 196, Bellerophon, w. the Nile.
Bevan, Rowland (L.)..	I. 182, Brunswick, w. 1st June.
Bevians, William (L.).	II. 58, Irresistible, St. Vincent, pro. Cr. IV. 400, C. Lyra, Basque Rds.
Beville, Charles (C.) *F.*	VI. 3, Melpomène, actn. off Cape Sepet, Toulon Sq.
Bevis, Thomas (L.) ...	V. 289-95, Astræa, w. in actn.
Beynon — (M.L.) ...	V. 348, Menelaus, capture of batteries.
Bezemer, — (C.) *Du.*	I. 416, Du. Havik, Sq. at the Cape of Good Hope.
Bial, Don Quaj (C.) *Sp.*	II. 254, Sp. Proserpine, actn. off Carthagena.
Bickerton, Sir Richard, Bart. (P.C.)	I. 189, Ruby, 1st June. II. 164, Terrible, Sq. crsg. III. 72, R.A.; 81, Kent, Egypt exped.; 175, 238, Medn. Flt.; 335, Royal Sovereign; 345, 379, Medn.
Biddle, James (L.) *U.S.*	V. 391, U.S. Wasp, in actn. VI. 98, C. U.S. Hornet; 99, 194-5, crsg.; 261-5, capts. Penguin.
Biffin, — (Mid.).........	VI. 328, Burmese War.
Bignell, Geo. (L.Com.)	VI. 112, Hunter, in actn. Canadian Lakes.
Bigot, Armand François Le (C.) *F.*	IV. 395, Pallas, off Isle of Aix.
Bigot, Julien Gabriel (L.Com.) *F.*	I. 387, Seine, Sq. crsg. II. 247-9, captd. by Jason; 286, C. Rousseau, Brest Flt. IV. 88, Impérial, Brest.
Billiet, Simon (C.) *F.*	IV. 14-7, Incorruptible capts. Arrow.
Bingham, Arthur Batt. (C.)	V. 275-7, Little Belt engages U.S. President; 278, Halifax; 282, pro. P.C.
Bingham, Joseph (L.)..	I. 200, Audacious, 1st June, pro. Cr. IV. 357, C. Sceptre, Sq. off the Isle of France.
Binny, W. *E.I.C.*	VI. 322, Good Hope (T.S.), Burmese War.
Birbeck, Michael (Mr.)	III. 279-80, Galatea, k. cutting out exped.
Birch, Joseph (Mr.Mt.)	IV. 170, Bacchante, cutting out exped.
Birchall, William (L.).	I. 400, Santa Margarita, capture of Buonoparte (priv.). III. 46, Cr. Harpy, Copenhagen; 64, pro. P.C.
Bird, John Gibbs (Mid.)	IV. 9, Courageux, w. Strachan's actn.
Bishop, George (L.) ...	VI. 84, Statira, cutting out exped.
Bissell, Austin (C.) ...	III. 182, Creole, fndrd.; 188, Racoon capts. Lodi; 189, crsg. off Cuba; 494, App. IV. 51, Blenheim engages Marengo; 465, fndrd. E. Indies, drnd.
Bissell, William (L.) ...	IV. 404, Basque Rds.
Bissett, Alexander (L.)	IV. 383, Wizard, cutting out exped.
Bissett, James (P.C.)...	II. 112, Janus, St. Domingo. IV. 89, Courageux, St. Helens; 439, Dannemark, Scheldt exped.
Bissett, John James P. (M.L.)	VI. 288, Infernal (bomb.), k. Algiers.
Black, James (L.)	III. 410, Mars, w. Trafalgar. VI. 21, C. Weasel; 24-5, w. in actn. with F. gbts.; 32, Adriatic.
Blackburn, — (Mr.) ...	I. 289, Illustrious, w. actn. off Genoa.
Blacker, Stewart (L.)...	V. 103, Dreadnought, w. cutting out exped.
Blackler, Robert Thos. (L.)	V. 161, Iphigenia, w. in actn.
Blackmore, Annesley (Mid.)	IV. 447, Cumberland, cutting out exped. Rosas Bay.
Blackstone, Thos.(Mid.)	IV. 159, Indefatigable, cutting out exped.
Blackwood, Henry (L.)	I. 177, Invincible, 1st June; 200, pro. Cr. II. 250-1, C. Brilliant, engages Régénérée; 440-3, Penelope, capture of
,, Hon. Henry (C.)	Guillaume Tell. III. 380, Euryalus, off Cadiz; 384, 390-2, 426, 448, 465, Trafalgar. IV. 218-9, Ajax, Dardanelles; 465, Ajax burnt. V. 81, 83, 85, Warspite, Sq. off Toulon.
Blair, Hamilton (Mid.)	V. 248, Belle Poule, actn. at Parenza.

Blake, — (Sub.L.) ...	IV. 172, Batabano, Isle of Pines.
Blakeley, Johnston (C.) U.S.	VI. 161, U.S. Wasp capts. Reindeer; 167, Wasp fndrs.
Blakeney, Richd. (M.L.)	V. 7, Horatio, w. in actn. capture of Junon.
Blakiston, Thomas (L.)	VI. 35, Revenge, cutting out exped.
Blamey, Geo. Wm. (C.)	IV. 435, Harpy, Scheldt exped.
Blanc, George Le (L.-Com.)	IV. 467, Cassandra, fndrs. near Heligoland. V. 442, Minx, captd. off the Scaw.
Blanch, — (M.L.)	II. 135, Hydra, cutting out exped.
Blanckley, Edward (L.)	VI. 335, Alligator, act.Cr. of the Sophie, Burmese War.
Bland, Loftus Otway (L.)	I. 314, Lively, w. in actn. II. 62, cutting out exped.; 256, Cr., Espoir capts. Sp. Liguria; 258, pro. P.C.; 473, Flora wrkd. Holland.
Bland, Thomas (M.L.)	IV. 31, Seine, cutting out exped.
Blankett, John (P.C.)	I. 333, 416, America, Sq. at the Cape of Good Hope. II. 338, R.A. Leopard, Mocha. III. 90–1, capture of Suez.
Blanquet, Armand Sim. Mar. (R.A.) F.	II. 168, Toulon; 178–9, Franklin, the Nile; 199, w. in actn.
Blavet, — (C.) F.	I. 141, Juste, Brest Flt.
Blennerhasset, Goddard (L.)	IV. 380, Amethyst capts. Thétis, pro. Cr. V. 447, C. Challenger, captd. off the Isle of France.
Blessing, — (C.) Swd.	IV. 299, Swd. Faderneslandet, Br. Swd. Flt. Oro Rds.
Bligh, George Miller (L.)	III. 425, Victory, w. Trafalgar. V. 261, pro. Cr. Acorn, Isle Lissa.
Bligh, John (L.)	II. 58, Barfleur, St. Vincent, pro. Cr. III. 186, C. Theseus, crsg.; 291–2, Curaçoa. IV. 200, Alfred, Copenhagen; 238, Sq. off the Tagus; 396, Valiant; 411, 416–8, Basque Rds. V. 97, capts. Confiance.
Bligh, Richard Rodney (P.C.)	I. 189, Alexander, 1st June; 203, captd. by Jean Bart and consorts; 205, R.A. court-martialled; 439, App.
Bligh, William (P.C.)	II. 75, Director, Camperdown. III. 46, Glatton, Copenhagen; 307, Warrior, off Ushant.
Blow, John Aitken (L.)	II. 442, Foudroyant, w. in actn. IV. 368, act.Cr. Charger, Isle of Saltholm. V. 226, C. Algerine, in actn.; 229, dismissed.
Bloye, Henry (Mid.) ...	VI. 16, Surveillante, St. Sebastian.
Bloye, Henry (Mr.Mt.)	VI. 120, Lyra crsg., drnd. River Adour, Spain.
Bloye, Robert (C.) ...	V. 335, Lyra, Sq. off Spain. VI. 15, off Castro D'Urdeales.
Bloys, — (R.A.) Du. ..	II. 76, Du. Brutus, Camperdown; 82, w. in actn.
Blucke, William (M.L.)	VI. 19, capture of Cassis batteries.
Bluett, Buckland Stirling (L.)	III. 265, Beaver, w. cutting out exped.; 266, pro. Cr. IV. 90, C. Wasp, convoy escort.
Blyth, Samuel (L.)	V. 74, Confiance; 75, Trio; 220–1, Quebec, w. cutting out exped.; 222, pro. Cr. VI. 75–6, C. Boxer captd. by U.S. Enterprise; 78, k. in actn.; 382, App.
Blythe, James (Mid.) ...	II. 122, Mars, k. in actn. capture of F. Hercule.
Boardman, Richard Ball (L.)	V. 248, Belle Poule, actn. Parenza.
Boardman, Thomas (Mr.Mt.)	V. 37, Amphion, cutting out exped.
Bock, De — (C.) Du.	II. 343, Du. Mars, captd. in the Texel by Br. Sq.
Bodie, James (Cox.) ...	IV. 257, Spartan, cutting out exped. off Nice.
Boger, Coryndon (L.-Com.)	III. 30, Gipsy, w. in actn.
Boger, Edmond (P.C.)	IV. 461, Brave, fndrd. off Western Isles, crew saved.
Boger, Richard (M.L.)	IV. 320, Daphne, cutting out exped.
Bogue, John (Pr.)	VI. 41, Amelia, k. in actn.
Boileau, Lestock Francis (M.L.)	IV. 221, Standard, Dardanelles.
Boissi, Chevalier Chas. L. P. de (Ad.G.) F.	V. 32, C. of the Neap. Lucien Charles (priv.), captd. by Br. Pomone.
Bolman, Henry (Mid.)	IV. 37, Cambrian, cutting out exped.

INDEX TO NAVAL OFFICERS

Bolton, Henry (Mid.) — V. 340, Victorious, w. in actn.
Bolton, William (Mid.) — I. 312, Blanche, k. in actn.
Bolton, William (C.)... — II. 388, Wolverine, off the Vlieter. III. 46, Arrow, Copenhagen; 223, Aimable, Sq. crsg. IV. 275, Fisgard,
,, Sir William — W. Indies; 433, Scheldt exped. V. 319, Endymion chases F. frigates.
Bompart, Jean Bap. Franc. (C.) *F.* — I. 110-13, Embuscade engages Boston. II. 139, Cmde. Hoche, Brest; 141, Ireland exped.; 143-5, capture of Hoche; 284, Bompart's Sq.
Bonami, Eus. Marie Joseph (C.) *F.* — IV. 444, F. Lion, Toulon Flt.
Bonasa, Don Raphael (C.) *Sp.* — II. 110, Arrogante, Sp. Sq. W. Indies.
Bonavie, Jean Baptiste (L.Com.) *F.* — II. 249, Mondovi captd. by Flora. III. 143-5, Flêche captd. by Victor.
Bond, Francis Godolphin (L.Com.) — III. 36, Netley capts. Sp. San Miguel (priv.).
Bond, John Holmes (Mr.Mt.) — VI. 264, Penguin, w. in actn.
Bond, Robert (Mid.)... — IV. 174, Sheldrake, w. in actn.
Bone, William (L.) ... — V. 21, Pompée, w. in actn.
Bones, Robert (L.Com.) — V. 67, Tigris, capture of Sénégal exped.
Bonnefoux, — (Cmde.) *F.* — I. 60, Terrible, Brest Flt.
Bonnie, Bernard (L.-Com.) *F.* — V. 97, Nécessité captd. by Horatio.
Boorder, James (C.) ... — II. 351, Espiègle, Lemmertown; 382, capture of Crash.
Borja, — (A.) *Sp.* ... ... — I. 432, Sp. Flt. at St. Piétro.
Boscawen, George (Mid.) *E.I.C.* — VI. 318-22, Burmese War.
Boss, John (L.Com.)... — VI. 381, Rhodian, fndrd. near Jamaica, crew saved.
Bougainville, H. Y. P. Baron de (C.) *F.* — VI. 131-2, Cérès captd. by Tagus and consort.
Bouillon, Prince of (C.) *F. Royalist* — III. 494, Severn, wrkd. in Grouville Bay, Jersey.
Bounton, John (L.) ... — IV. 70, Phœnix, k. in actn.
Bourayne, Cèsar Joseph (C.) *F.* — IV. 143-5, Canonnière engages Tremendous; 363, Isle of France; 365, capts. Laurel.
Bourchier, Henry (L.) — IV. 30, Unicorn, cutting out exped. V. 211, Hawk, crsg.; 215, actn. with F. gbts.; 216, pro. P.C.
Bourdé, Guillaume Fr. Joseph (C.) *F.* — II. 70, convoy escort; 234-5, Sensible captd. by Seahorse.
Bourgeois, Eug. Jos. Romain(Qrmaster.)*F.* — IV. 417, Tourville, Basque Rds. actn.
Bourgonnière, —(Mid.) *F.* — III. 248, Curieux, k. in actn.
Bourne, Henry (L.) ... — V. 118, Spartan, in actn.
Bourne, Richard (L.-Com.) — II. 130, Sandfly, St. Marcouf; 131, pro. Cr. IV. 79, C. Felix, watching off Rochefort.
Bouverie, Hon. D. Pleydell (P.C.) — IV. 279, Medusa, S. American Sq. V. 331, 335, Sq. off Spain.
Bouvet, François Joseph (Cmde.) *F.* — I. 60, Audacieux, Brest Flt.; 141, R.A.; 259, Brest. II. 5-8, Droits de l'Homme, Ireland exped.; 12, actn. with Br. frigates; 23, off Ushant.
Bouvet, Louis (C.) *F.* — II. 420, Furet (priv.) captd. by Viper.
Bouvet, Pierre Fr. Hen. Etienne (C.) *F.* — V. 131, Minerve; 152-9, actn. at Grand Port; 172-82, Isle of France. VI. 36, Aréthuse; 37-44, actn. with Amelia.
Bover, Peter Turner (L.) — II. 30, London, Spithead mutiny.
Bowater, Edward (P.C.) — II. 285, Magnificent, Sq. off Brest.
Bowen, George (L.) ... — I. 403, Terpsichore, w. in actn.
Bowen, George (L.) ... — VI. 27, Apollo, crsg.

Bowen, James (Mr.) ...	I. 164, Queen Charlotte, 1st June; 200, pro. L. II. 219 C. Argo; 220, Minorca; 231–2, crsg.; 359–60, capts. Sp. St. Teresa.
Bowen, James (L.)......	III. 180, Loire, cutting out exped.
Bowen, John (C.)	IV. 387, Camilla, Guadaloupe.
Bowen, Richard (L.)...	I. 242, Boyne, West Indies; 245, pro. Cr.; 250, w.; 398, C. Terpsichore, capts. Sp. Mahonesa; 402–6, capts. Vestale. II. 55, engages Sp. Santisima, Trinidad; 57–60, 63, Teneriffe; 65–7, Santa Cruz; 68, k.
Bowen, Robert C. (Mid.)	VI. 287, Superb, k. Algiers.
Bowen, William (P.C.)	II. 289, Prince George, Br. Flt. off Cadiz.
Bowen, William (L.)...	IV. 22, Cleopatra, w. in actn.
Bower, John (C.)	IV. 466, Atalante, wrkd. at Rochefort.
Bowes, Wm. John (Mid.)	III. 55, Monarch, w. Copenhagen.
Bowie, — (Schoolmaster) U.S.	VI. 243, U.S. President, capture of.
Bowler, Wm. Pitt (Mid.)	IV. 75, Swift, cutting out exped.
Bowles, William (C.)...	IV. 205, Ætna (bomb.), Copenhagen.
Bowyer, George (R.A.)	I. 65, Prince, Channel Flt.; 139, Barfleur; 176, 1st June; 199, w. in actn.; 200, created Baronet.
Boxer, Edward (L.) ...	IV. 447, Tigre, cutting out exped. Rosas Bay.
Boxer, James (Mid.)...	II. 321–6, Tigre, at Acre. IV. 232, Alexandria. V. 318, Cr. Castilian, off Boulogne; 451, Skylark, wrkd. near Boulogne.
Boyack, Alex. (L. Com.)	IV. 457, Dove captd. by Rochefort Sq.
Boyce, Chas. (L.) E.I.C.	VI. 266–8, E.I.C. Nautilus captd. by U.S. Peacock; 269, w. in actn.
Boyce, — (Mid.)	I. 186, Royal George, w. in actn.
Boyd, George (Mid.)...	I. 108, Nymphe, k. in actn.
Boyd, Walter S. (M.L.)	III. 201, Blenheim, cutting out exped.
Boyle, Hon. Courtenay (P.C.)	III. 275, Seahorse, off Hyères; 333, off Toulon. IV. 31, crsg. off Cape de Gata, Spain.
Boyle, Courtney (C.)...	III. 477, Cormorant, wrkd. on the coast of Egypt.
Boyle, Thos. (C.) U.S.	VI. 247, U.S. Chasseur (priv.) capts. St. Lawrence.
Boyles, Charles (P.C.)	I. 227, Swiftsure capts. Atalante. III. 356, Windsor Castle, Sq. off Ferrol. IV. 175, Sq. off Rochefort; 217, Dardanelles; 294, Palermo; 452, App.
Boys, Charles Worsley (P.C.)	IV. 438, Statira, Scheldt exped. V. 27, crsg. off San Andero, Spain.
Boys, Thomas (L.)......	I. 225, Concorde, in actn; 297, Cr. Flêche, off Hyères. IV. 313, C. Saturn, crsg. off L'Orient.
Boyter, Alex. (Mr. Mt.)	IV. 448, Topaze, Rosas Bay.
Bozec, Pierre Marie Le (C.) F.	II. 284, convoy escort; 387, Républicaine, off Surinam.
Braam, Van (C.) Du....	II. 343, Du. Leyden captd. by Br. Sq.
Brace, Edward (C.) ...	II. 154, 158–9, Kangaroo engages F. Loire. III. 374, C. Iris, crsg. IV. 324–5, Virginie capts. Du. Guelderland. V. 53, crsg. VI. 18, Berwick, crsg.; 117, Br. Flt. off Toulon; 278, Impregnable, Algiers, made C.B.
Bradford, — (Mid.) ...	VI. 96, Mohawk, cutting out exped.
Bradley, James (C.) ...	II. 133, Ariadne, off Bruges.
Bradley, James (L.) ...	V. 297, Sir Francis Drake, cutting out exped.
Bradley, William (C.)	I. 140, Comet (F.S.), Flt. off Ushant. IV. 236, Plantagenet, Sq. off the Tagus.
Bradley, William (L.)	IV. 447, Cumberland, cutting out exped. Rosas Bay.
Brady, Wm. Hollinshed (Mid.)	IV. 447–9, Cumberland, w. cutting out exped. Rosas Bay. [Wasp.
Braimer, David (C.) ...	V. 219, 318, Castilian, off Boulogne. VI. 166, chases U.S.
Braithwaite, Wm. (L.)	III. 196, Blanche, cutting out exped.; 292, W. Indies.
Brand, Geo. R. (L. Com.)	III. 296–8, Unique, w. capture of Surinam. IV. 462, captd. by F. priv. near Leeward Isles.
Brand, Wm. Alex. (L.)	VI. 84, Chesapeake Bay.

INDEX TO NAVAL OFFICERS 63

Brand, Wm. Hy.(Mid.) VI. 27, Apollo, Isle Augusta.
Brattle, Jeremiah (M.L.) V. 120-1, Cerberus, w. in actn., Groa.
Brattle, Thomas (M.L.) IV. 370, Africa, w. in actn.
Braund, Thomas (Mid.) III. 406, Royal Sovereign, k. Trafalgar.
Bray, James (L.Com.) V. 451, Plumper, wrkd. in Bay of Fundy.
Bray, James (Car.)...... II. 326, Tigre at Acre.
Bray, John (L.) .... III. 84, k. at Alexandria.
Bray, Joseph (L.Com.) IV. 475, Capelin, wrkd. off Brest Harbour.
Bray, Josias (L.)......... III. 417, Achille, w. Trafalgar.
Bray, Samuel (Gunner) V. 88, Freija, cutting out exped.
Bremer, James John Gordon (C.) VI. 12, 15, Royalist, Sq. N. Spain ; 393, made C.B., Comus wrkd. off Cape Pine, Newfoundland.
Brenton, Edward Pelham (C.) III. 196, 202, Merlin, crsg. IV. 381-2, Amaranthe engages Cigne. V. 69, Pompée, Martinique exped. ; 372, Spartan crsg. N. America.
Brenton, Jahleel (C.)... II. 382, Speedy ; 395, engages Sp. gbts. ; 397, pro. P.C. III. 97, Cæsar, off Cadiz ; 108-15, actn. Gut of Gibraltar ; 182, Minerve ; 184-5, captd. off Cherbourg (goes ashore) ;
„ Sir Jahleel ... 490, App. IV. 257, kntd. Spartan, in actn. ; 290, crsg. ; 449, Isle of Cerigo. V. 28, Gulf of Venice ; 114, Terrecino ; 115-16, engages Cérès and consorts ; 117, w. in actn.
Bretèche, J. M. Bertaud la (L.Com.) F. IV. 447, Lamproie (S.S.), Rosas Bay.
Bretel, Jac. Fr. Ignace (C.) F. III. 78-9, Succes, Porto Ferrajo. IV. 189, Volontaire captd. by Br. Sq. in Table Bay.
Breton, François Désiré (C.) F. V. 53, Manche ; 92, Cherbourg ; 131, 137, Astrée, Port Louis. VI. 145-6, Terpsichore captd. by Majestic.
Bretonnière, De la (C.)F. VI. 365, 373, Breslau, Navarino.
Brett, James (act. Mr.) IV. 143, Sirius, w. in actn.
Briarly, Alexander (Mr.) III. 50, 62, Bellona ; Copenhagen.
Brice, Nathaniel (L.-Com.) IV. 336, Jackdaw ; 467, App.
Bridge, Philip (B.)...... II. 442, Foudroyant, w. in actn.
Bridges, George Francis (Mid.) IV. 447, Tigre, cutting out exped. Rosas Bay.
Bridges, Philip Henry (Mid.) III. 180, Loire, cutting out exped. ; 181, pro. L.
Bridport, Lord, K.B.(A.) I. 62, 199, 206, Sir Alexander Hood, K.B., q.v.
Briggs, Joseph (L.) ... II. 273, Ambuscade, w. in actn.
Briggs, Thomas (C.) ... III. 74, Salamine, crsg. IV. 185, Orpheus, crsg. V. 203, Clorinde, capture of Isle of France exped.
Brigstock, JohnR.(Mid.) VI. 136, Eurotas, w. in actn.
Brine, Augustus (P.C.) I. 251, Sceptre, St. Domingo.
Brisac, George (C.) ... I. 98, Scourge capts. Sans Culotte (priv.) ; 388, Sphynx, crsg.
Brisbane, Charles (L.) I. 212, Corsica ; 215, Gourjean Bay ; 294, C. Tarleton, Spezia Bay ; 325, Moselle, Genoa. II. 94, Oiseau, crsg. III. 137, Doris, off St. Mathieu ; 181, Goliath capts. Mignonne. IV. 90, Arethusa, convoy escort ; 169, engages Sp. Pomona and gbts. ; 170, w. in actn ; 275-7, capture of
„ Sir Charles... Curaçoa ; 278, kntd.
Brisbane, Henry (L.)... I. 233, Romney, in actn. pro. Cr.
Brisbane, James (C.)... III. 46, Cruiser, Copenhagen ; 64, pro. P.C. V. 9-10, Belle Poule capts. F. Var ; 80, St. Maura ; 247-8, Parenza. VI. 2, Pembroke, off Toulon ; 279, made C.B., Queen Charlotte,
„ SirJames,C.B. Algiers ; 337, kntd. ; 340-1, Boadicea, Burmese War ; 344, d. ; 357, App.
Brisbane, John S. (Mid.) V. 45, Hazard, cutting out exped.
Bristow, William (Mid.) III. 66, k. cutting out exped.
Brodie, Thos. Chas.(L.) II. 326, gbts. at Acre.
Broke, Philip Bowes Vere (P.C.) IV. 378, Shannon, crsg. V. 368, crsg. ; 371, chases U.S. Constitution. VI. 50, 52-8, capts. U.S. Chesapeake ; 59,
„ Sir Philip B. V., Bart. w. in actn. ; 66, created Baronet.

64 JAMES' NAVAL HISTORY

Brokenshaw, Luke (Mr.)	III. 439, Revenge, w. Trafalgar.
Bromley, Robert Howe (C.)	III. 324, Champion, actn. with F. flotilla. IV. 112, convoy escort.
Brookes, — (Mid.)......	IV. 248, cutting out exped.
Brooks, Edw. F. (Mid.)	III. 439, Revenge, k. Trafalgar.
Brooks, John (B.)	II. 81, Russel, w. Camperdown. III. 426, Téméraire, w. Trafalgar.
Broom, Jas. (Mid.) *U.S.*	IV. 253, U.S. Chesapeake, w. in actn.
Broom, Jas. (M.L.) *U.S.*	V. 61, U.S. Chesapeake, k. in actn.
Brouard, Gabriel Auguste (C.) *F.*	III. 350, Algésiras, crsg.; 386, Trafalgar. IV. 444, Commerce de Paris, Toulon Flt.
Broughton, John (P.C.)	IV. 306, Meleager, crsg. W. Indies.
Broughton, W. H. (L.-Com.)	II. 462, Providence, wrkd. in the Pacific Ocean.
Broughton, Wm. Robert (P.C.)	III. 223, Penelope, crsg. IV. 112, Sq. crsg.; 396, Illustrious, Basque Rds. V. 203, capture of the Isle of France; 296, 303, Cmde., Java exped.
Browell, William (P.C.)	I. 271, Sans Pareil, Channel Flt. II. 302, Basque Rds.
Brown, Andrew (Mid.)	II. 195, Goliath, k. the Nile.
Brown, Chas. (L.Com.)	VI. 382, Subtle, fndrd. in the W. Indies, drnd.
Brown, David (Pr.) ...	VI. 74, Dominica, k. in actn.
Brown, Jeremiah (L.)...	III. 443, Ajax, Trafalgar; 464, pro. Cr.
Brown, John (P.C.) ...	I. 240, Asia; 243-4, capture of Martinique.
Brown, John (B.)	III. 140, Beaulieu, cutting out exped.
Brown, John (L.Com.)	IV. 380, Morne Fortunée, crsg. V. 442, wrkd. near Martinique.
Brown, Peter (Mid.) ...	VI. 374, Dartmouth, k. Navarino.
Brown, Robert Hunter (C.) *E.I.C.*	III. 250, E.I.C. Dorsetshire, actn. with Linois' Sq. E. Indies.
Brown, Samuel (L.) ...	IV. 74, Phœnix, in actn.
Brown, Thomas (C.) ...	IV. 456, Orestes, wrkd. Dunkerque Rds. VI. 149, Loire, crsg.; 169, Chesapeake Bay.
Brown, William (P.C.)	I. 139, Venus, Channel Flt. II. 289, 307, Foudroyant, Flt. off Cadiz. III. 357, 361, Ajax, Calder's actn. 384, Calder's court-martial.
Brown, William (A.B.)	I. 328, Rose, w. in actn.
Brown, William (Mid.)	III. 412, Tonnant, k. Trafalgar.
Brown, Wm. (Mr.Mt.)	V. 417, Java, w. in actn.
Brown, William (C.) ...	II. 132, Kite, crsg. off Ostende.
Brown, — (Mr.).........	II. 275, Ambuscade, k. in actn.
Brown, — (Sub.L.) ...	IV. 172, cutting out exped.
Brown, — (L.)	VI. 207, Canadian Lakes.
Browne, Philip (C.) ...	IV. 439, Plover, Scheldt exped.
Browne, Richard (C.)...	II. 112, Beaver, W. Indies.
Browne, Robt. (Mr.Mt.)	III. 441, Defiance, w. Trafalgar.
Browne, Thomas (P.C.)	V. 312, Bulwark, off L'Orient.
Bruce, Charles (Mid.)...	V. 37, Mercury, cutting out exped.; 120, Amphion, cutting out exped.
Bruce, Charles (Mr.Mt.)	VI. 22, Bacchante, cutting out exped.
Bruce, Charles (Mid.)...	VI. 119, Bacchante, surrender of Cattaro, Adriatic.
Bruce, Wm. Henry (L.)	V. 99, Belvidera des. Da. gbts.; 358, w. in actn.
Brueys, Eustache (R.A.) *F.*	I. 342, Toulon Flt. II. 70, Toulon; 168, V.A. Orient; 169, takes Malta; 176-8, 444, the Nile; 198, k. in actn.
Bruilhac, Alain A. Marie (C.) *F.*	II. 228-9, Charente chased by Canada; 285, Océan, Brest Flt. III. 250, Belle Poule, Linois' Sq. with E.I.C. ships.
Bruix, Eustache (Cmde.) *F.*	I. 60, Indomptable, Brest; 264, R.A.; 276, Isle Groix. II. 123, 131, 207, 276, Minister of Marine; 284-5, pro. V.A. Brest Flt.; 291, 296-8, 300, Medn. III. 10, 217, 229-30, 243, 309, invas. flotilla; 316, d.
Brulton, John (L.)	IV. 447, Tigre, cutting out exped. Rosas Bay.
Brunet, Charles (L.-Com.) *F.*	IV. 38, Faune, Sq. actn. with Blanche.
Brunet, François (L.-Com.)	V. 109, Barbier de Seville (priv.) captd. by Phipps.

INDEX TO NAVAL OFFICERS 65

Bryant, Edward (Mid.)	V. 77, Confiance, Cayenne.
Buchan, Edw. (L.Com.)	VI. 112-13, Lady Prevost, w. in actn., Canadian Lakes.
Buchanan, Archibald (L.Com.)	V. 195, Mandarin (T.S.), capture of Banda Neira exped.
Buchanan, Chas. M. D. (Mid.)	VI. 35, Revenge, cutting out exped.
Buchanan, John (P.C.)	II. 359, Leviathan, capture of Sp. Santa Teresa.
Buchanan, William (L.)	II. 222, Leviathan, Minorca.
Buchanan, William (L.)	V. 327, Dictator, in actn., pro. Cr.
Buckle, Thos. D. (Mid.)	VI. 41, Amelia, w. in actn.
Buckly, William (Mr.)	III. 14, Calypso, cutting out exped.
Buckner, Chas. (V.A.)	II. 71-3, Sandwich, mutiny at the Nore.
Buckoll, Richard (L.)	I. 323, Dido, w. in actn. ; 324, pro. Cr.
Budd, George (L.) *U.S.*	VI. 61, U.S. Chesapeake, w. in actn. with Shannon.
Buddin, William (Mid.)	IV. 177, Monarch, k. in actn.
Buderhof, — (L.Com.) *Da.*	V. 329, Da. cutter, w. in actn.
Buille, — (C.) *F.*	II. 295, Courageuse captd. by Br. Sq. Medn.
Bulford, John (L.)	V. 398, Macedonian, w. in actn. VI. 126, Astrea, in actn.
Bulkeley, Rich. (Mid.)	III. 425, Victory, w. Trafalgar.
Bulkley, Robt. (M.L.)	II. 62, Lively, cutting out exped.
Bull, John (L.)	IV. 243, Lark capts. Sp. coasters.
Bull, John (C.)	VI. 142-3, Duke of Marlborough (packet), actn. with Primrose.
Bull, Thomas (act. Mr.)	VI. 274, Tyne, cutting out exped., pro. Mr.
Bullen, Charles (L) ...	II. 88, Monmouth, Camperdown, pro. Cr. III. 384, C. Britannia, Trafalgar. IV. 445, Volontaire, crsg. V. 342, crsg.
Bullen, Joseph (C.) ...	I. 212, Corsica ; 366, Vol. in actn., pro. P.C.
Bullen, Joseph (Mid.)	IV. 100, Superb, w. in actn.
Buller, Edward (P.C.)	III. 357, Malta, Calder's actn.
Buller, Sir Edw. (R.A.)	V. 173, Com. at. Plymouth.
Buller, William (L.) ...	I. 176, Impregnable, w. in actn.
Bunbury, R. H. (L.)...	VI. 374, w. Navarino.
Bunce, Richard (M.C.)	IV. 124, Eagle, Isle Capri. V. 304, capture of Java.
Buonaparte,Jérôme (C.) *F.*	III. 168, 378, Pomone. IV. 88, Vétéran ; 111-13, 178, Sq. crsg. Concarneau ; 458, App. V. 266, Sq. crsg.
Burdett, George (L) ...	II. 58, Egmont St. Vincent, pro. Cr. VI. 83, C. Maidstone, Chesapeake Bay.
Burdwood, Daniel (L.Com.)	II. 113, Penelope (cutter), off Jean Rabel.
Burgess, Rich. Randell (P.C.)	I. 304, Argo, convoy escort ; 357, Pellew's Sq. crsg. II. 175, Ardent, Camperdown ; 81, k. in actn.
Burgess, Samuel (L.)...	III. 148, Sylph, in actn. VI. 282, Queen Charlotte, Algiers.
Burgess, William (L)...	I. 200, Impregnable, 1st June, pro. Cr.
Burgess, — (A.B.)......	I. 107, Nymphe, in actn.
Burke, Henry (act.L.)	I. 357, Galatea, w. in actn. III. 15-17, Renown, w. cutting out exped. ; 27, w. cutting out exped., pro. Cr. ; 191, C. Seagull recapts. E.I.C. Lord Nelson. IV. 456, Seagull fndrs., drnd.
Burke, Walter (L.) ...	III. 139-40, Doris, k. cutting out exped.
Burlton, George (L.)...	I. 199, Bellerophon, 1st June, pro. Cr.; 313-4, act.C. Lively capts. Tourterelle. II. 306, C. Haerlem, Palermo. III. 73, off Cadiz. IV. 200, Resolution, Copenhagen ; 396, Basque Rds. V. 207, Ville de Paris, Channel Flt. VI. 2,
,, Sir Geo. K.C.B.	117, Boyne, off Toulon ; 266, R.A. K.C.B. Cornwallis.
Burman,Chas.(L.Com.)	IV. 474, Netley, wrkd. on Leeward Island.
Burn, John (P.C.)	III. 83, Blonde, Alexandria.
Burnet, John (A.B.) ...	V. 280, U.S. President and Little Belt.
Burnett, Robert (Car.)	IV. 170, Bacchante, cutting out exped
Burney,Franc.(Mr.Mt.)	III. 66, w. cutting out exped.
Burney, Wm. (Gunner)	IV. 385-6, Impérieuse, Rosas Bay.
Burns, John (Gunner)	II. 268, Leander, in actn.

F

Burns, John (L.)......	V. 57, Otter, cutting out exped.; 138, cutting out exped.; 151, 161, k. at Grand Port.
Burnside, Robert (S.)	IV. 440, w. Scheldt exped.
Burr, Edward (B.)......	III. 55, Polyphemus, w. Copenhagen.
Burroughs, Charles (L.)	II. 88, Russel, Camperdown, pro. Cr.
Burrowes, Alex. Saunderson (C.)	IV. 172-3, Constance engages Salamandre, k. in actn.; 461, App.
Burrows, John (L.)......	I. 351, act.C. Courageux, wrkd. near Straits of Gibraltar, drnd.
Burrows,Wm.(L.Com.) U.S.	VI. 75-8, U.S. Enterprise capts. Boxer, k. in actn.
Burstal, Richard (Mr.)	III. 195, Atalante, cutting out exped.
Burt, Edward (L.Com.)	IV. 461, Redbridge, wrkd. on Providence station.
Burt, George (Mid.) ...	V. 103, Dreadnought, w. cutting out exped.
Burton, Chas. F.(M.L.)	II. 323, Acre. VI. 287, C. Queen Charlotte, w. Algiers.
Burton, Jas. Ryder (C.)	VI. 274, Cameleon engages Algrn. Tripoli; 275, pro. P.C.
Burton, Thos.(L.Com.)	V. 445, Wildboar, wrkd. Scilly Isles.
Burton, William (M.L.)	VI. 17, Volontaire, cutting out exped.
Busey, John (act.L.) ...	II. 410, k. cutting out exped.
Bush, George (Sub.-L.)	IV. 256, Richmond, cutting out exped.
Bush, Wm. S. (M.L.) U.S.	V. 380, U.S. Constitution, w. in actn.
Bushby, John (L.)	II. 62, Lively, cutting out exped.; 322-3, Tigre, at Acre.
Busigny, Simeon (M.L.)	III. 426, Téméraire, k. Trafalgar.
Bustamente, Don Joseph (R.A.) Sp.	III. 287, St. Medea captd. by Br. Sq.
Buthane, Charles (1st class Vol.)	V. 239, Amphion, w. in actn.
Butler, James Edward (M.L.)	I. 112, Boston, k. in actn.
Butler, John O'Brien (Mid.)	IV. 345-6, Porcupine, w. cutting out exped.
Butt, Henry Samuel (C.)	III. 18, Falcon (F.S.), destd. Dunkerque Rds.; 477, App.
Butterfield, Wm. (L.)	II. 124, Mars, in actn. pro. Cr.; 259, C. Hazard capts. F. Neptune.
Buyskes, Armand Adrien (R.A.) Du.	V. 91, Du. Havik captd. by Thistle.
Byam, Wm. Henry (P.C.)	V. 371, Thetis, convoy escort.
Byard, Sir Thos. (P.C.)	I. 72, Windsor Castle, Flt. off Toulon; 214, Corsica. II. 75, Bedford, Camperdown; 142, Foudroyant, crsg. Cawsand Bay.
Byng, George (P.C.)...	IV. 180, 186, Belliqueux, Batavia Rds.; 188, Cape of Good Hope.
Byng, Henry Dilkes (C.)	V. 274, Gorée, off Sandy Hook. VI. 96, Mohawk, Chesapeake Bay.
Byng, Hon. John (A.)	I. 137, libel on.
Byrn, Edward (Mid.)	III. 140, w. cutting out exped.
Byron, Richard (P.C.)	V. 99, Belvidera, crsg.; 357-60, engages U.S. President, w. in actn.; 371, chases U.S. Constitution. VI. 83, Chesapeake Bay.
Cable, Chas. P. (Mid.)	III. 432, Orion, w. Trafalgar.
Cadir, Bey (A.) Turk.	II. 214, Isle of Cerigo.
Cadogan, Hon. Geo. (C.)	IV. 456, Cyane captd. by F. frigates. VI. 26, Havannah capts. F. gbts.
Cagigal, Don Felix Xado (C.) Sp.	III. 386, Sp. San Augustin; 431, w. Trafalgar.
Cahuac, Bertrand (M.L.)	III. 292-5, Theseus, w. at Curaçoa.
Caiger, Herbert (L.)...	IV. 323-4, Tartar, cutting out exped.
Caird, David (Mr.) ...	I. 176, Impregnable, k. 1st June.
Cairnes, J. W. (L.) ...	VI. 289, Queen Charlotte, Algiers; 291, pro. Cr.
Calder, Robert (P.C.)	I. 189, Theseus, 1st June. II. 34, Victory, St. Vincent. III.
,, Sir Robert ...	73, R.A. kntd. W. Indies; 307, V.A. off Ferrol; 310-11, Channel Flt.; 356, off Ferrol; 365-70-5-7, Calder's actn.; 383, returns home; 500-1, App. IV. 54, Finisterre; 58-9, 76, court-martialled; 78, blockading Isle of Aix; 451-2, App.

INDEX TO NAVAL OFFICERS

Caldwell, Benj. (R.A.)	I. 139, Impregnable, Channel Flt.; 250, 312, 409, V.A., Com. Leeward Isles station.
Caldwell, Jas. (Mr.Mt.)	IV. 447-9, Tigre, k. cutting out exped.
Caldwell, John (Mid.)	II. 433, Haerlem, cutting out exped.
Callam, — (Mr.Mt.)...	III. 262, loss of Apollo.
Callenan, John Jas. (L.)	V. 42, Minotaur, k. cutting out exped.
Callie, Josef (C.) *Sp.*...	III. 148-9, Sp. Esperanza (priv.) captd. by Lark, k. in actn.
Calthrop, Richd. (Mid.)	VI. 288, Leander, k. Algiers.
Calton, Alexander (Mid.)	VI. 374, w. Navarino.
Camas, Jean J. Filhol (C.) *F.*	III. 334, Berwick, Toulon Flt.; 386, Trafalgar; 417, k. in actn.
Came, Chas. (L.Com.)	I. 443, Flêche, wrkd. in San Fiorenzo Bay.
Camelleri, Joseph (Mid.)	V. 256, Active, cutting out exped.
Cameron, Hugh (C.)...	V. 3, Hazard, Guadaloupe; 19, off the Saintes; 45, des. F. priv.; 50-2, k. at Basse Terre.
Cameron, John (C.) *E.I.C.*	IV. 189, E.I.C. Duchess of Gordon, Cape of Good Hope.
Campbell, Alexander (L.)	V. 257, Pilot, cutting out exped.; 341, cutting out exped.
Campbell, Colin (L.-Com.)	IV. 305-6, Decouverte, actn. with F. privs., w. in actn. V. 129, Minstrel, crsg.
Campbell, Donald (L.-Com.)	IV. 466, Pert, wrkd. on Isle Santa Margarita.
Campbell, Donald (P.C.)	IV. 200, Dictator, Copenhagen; 298, Baltic Flt.; 439, Audacious, Scheldt exped.
Campbell, Donald (C.)	II. 35, Sp. Carlotta; 211, Sp. Alphonso Albuquerque off Malta. III. 345, R.A., gives information to Nelson.
Campbell, Duncan (M.L.)	III. 33, Phaëton, w. cutting out exped. IV. 448, Volontaire, cutting out exped. Rosas Bay.
Campbell, George (P.C.)	I. 214, Terrible, Flt. at Corsica; 284, off Genoa; 297, Hyères. II. 285, Dragon, Flt. off Brest; 297, Port Mahon. III. 177, R.A. Canopus; 237-8, off Toulon. IV. 425, V.A., Gambier's court martial.
Campbell, Geo. (M.L.)	IV. 244, Comus, w. cutting out exped.
Campbell, Geo. Hy. (L.)	V. 186, Ceylon, in actn.
Campbell, Hon. George Pryce (L.)	V. 358, Belvidera, in actn. with U.S. President.
Campbell, Henry (Mid.)	VI. 287, Queen Charlotte, w. Algiers.
Campbell, Henry (Mid.)	VI. 374, w. Navarino.
Campbell, James (L.)...	VI. 274, Tyne, cutting out exped.
Campbell, Jas. (M.L.)	V. 99, Belvidera, cutting out exped.
Campbell, John (As.-Secretary.)	II. 196, Vanguard, w. the Nile.
Campbell, John (Mid.)	III. 406, Royal Sovereign, w. Trafalgar. IV. 28, L. Bacchante, cutting out exped.
Campbell, John (Mr.Mt.)	VI. 112, Chippeway, Canadian Lakes.
Campbell, John Norman (Cr.)	VI. 365, Albion; 373-4, w. Navarino.
Campbell, Patrick (C.)	III. 18, Dart capts. Désirée; 19, pro. P.C. IV. 342, Unité; 343, actn. with Italian brigs.; 456, Doris, wrkd. in Quiberon Bay. V. 208, Leviathan, Channel Flt.; 342-3, crsg.; 344, Languelia.
Campbell, Peter (C.) *E.I.C.*	V. 54, E.I.C. Lord Keith, actn. with F. frigates.
Campbell, Robert (L.)	II. 58, Blenheim, St. Vincent, pro. Cr. IV. 200, C. Nassau, Copenhagen; 319, capts. Da. Prindts Christian Frederick. V. 313, Tremendous, crsg. off Ushant.
Campling, Henry (Pr.)	V. 216, Hawk, in actn.
Cane, Chas. Du (Mr.Mt.)	IV. 327, Mercury, cutting out exped.
Canes, Edward Jekyl (C.)	III. 482, Utile, fndrd. near Malta, drnd.
Cannadey, Moses (L.-Com.)	IV. 475, Pickle, wrkd. near Cadiz. V. 27, Black Joke, crsg. N. Spain.
Canning, John (C.) *E.I.C.*	I. 218-20, E.I.C. Nonsuch captd. by F. privs.

Cannon, Augustus (L.)	V. 351, Eagle, k. cutting out exped.
Canon, Antoine (C.) *F.*	II. 103–5, Néréide captd. by Phœbe.
Canty, Thomas (Car.)	IV. 448, Topaze, cutting out exped. Rosas Bay.
Capel, Hon. Thomas Bladen (C.)	II. 206–9, 265, Mutine, off Corfu. III. 238, Phœbe; 336, crsg. off Corsica; 384, Trafalgar; 481, Meleager, wrkd. in the Gulf of Mexico. IV. 215, Endymion, Constantinople. VI. 196, Hogue, crsg.
Capelle, Van de (C.)*Du.*	II. 343–7, Du. Washington captd. in the Texel.
Cappellan, Baron T. Van de (V.A.) *Du.*	VI. 279, Du. Melampus; 291, Algiers.
Caraccioji, Chevalier (C.) *Neap.*	I. 284, Neap. Tancredi, Flt. off Genoa.
Caraccioli, Chevalier (C.) *F. Ven.*	V. 126, Ancona; 260, Palinuro.
Carden, John Surman (L.)	II. 162, Fisgard, in actn., pro. Cr. IV. 119, C. Moselle, off Cadiz. V. 394, Macedonian; 397–402–5, captd. by United States; 450, App.
Carden, Paul Kyffin (L.)	V. 343, Leviathan, cutting out exped.
Carew, Thomas (L.) ...	V. 199, capture of Banda Neira. VI. 278, C. Jasper, Algiers; 394, wrkd. on Mount Batten.
Carey, Lionel (Mid.)...	III. 146, Sylph, w. in actn.
Caro, — (C.) *F.*	II. 377, Sémillante, k. in actn.
Carp, — (C.) *Du.*	III. 265–7, Du. Atalante, k. in actn.
Carpenter, Chas. (P.C.)	I. 331, Alarm, crsg. W. Indies.
Carpenter, Hon. Charles (P.C.)	I. 62, Intrepid, Channel Flt.; 72, off Toulon.
Carpenter, Daniel (L.-Com.)	VI. 382, Algerine, wrkd. W. Indies.
Carpenter, James (P.C.)	I. 309, Quebec, crsg. III. 12, Leviathan, crsg. off Cadiz.
Carpentier, Jean M. Michel (L.Com.) *F.*	I. 365, Légère, crsg., escapes Br. frigates.
Carr, Robert (L.Com.)	V. 45, Attentive, cutting out exped.; 86, off Guadaloupe.
Carr, William (L.Com.)	III. 248–9, Eclair engages Grand Décidé (priv.). IV. 466, Netley captd. by F. frigates, W. Indies.
Carra, John (Mid.)......	II. 323, k. at Acre.
Carrage, — (C.) *Du.*....	II. 283, Du. Scipio, k. in actn.
Carrington, Alfred Octavius (M.L.)	V. 40, Bellerophon, cutting out exped.
Carrington, Gordon (Mid.)	V. 42, k. cutting out exped.
Carrington, — (B.)......	II. 49, Captain, w. St. Vincent.
Carroll, George P. (L.)	IV. 124, Bay of Naples.
Carroll, William Fairbrother (L.)	IV. 221, Dardanelles.
Carter, Benjamin (L.)	I. 382, Artois, cutting out exped.
Carter, Edmund (M.L.)	I. 355, Diamond, in actn.
Carter, John (L.)	IV. 221, Thunderer, Dardanelles.
Carter, Thomas (M.C.)	VI. 85, Marlborough, Chesapeake Bay; 202, Dragon, Canadian Lakes.
Carter, Wm. A. (Mid.)	VI. 288, Severn, w. Algiers.
Carteret, Philip (P.C.)	V. 218, Naiad, off Boulogne.
Carthew, James (L.)...	I. 241, capture of Martinique. III. 18, Rosario (F.S.), destd. Dunkerque Rds.; 477, App.
Carthew, Wm. (P.C.)	II. 114, Regulus (en flûte), crsg. W. Indies.
Casa-Bianca (Cmde.) *F.*	II. 127, 178, Orient, Aboukir Bay; 198, w. the Nile; 199, Orient blows up, k.
Case, William (L.) ...	II. 231, Victorieuse, cutting out exped.
Casey, David O'Brien (Mid.)	II. 116, mutiny of Hermione.
Casey, Edward (B.)...	V. 21, Pompée, k. in actn.
Cashman, William (L.)	IV. 383, Kent, cutting out exped.
Cassel, James (M C.)...	II. 81, Belliqueux, w. Camperdown

INDEX TO NAVAL OFFICERS

Cassin, John (Cmde.) U.S.	VI. 90, Norfolk; 91, Chesapeake Bay.
Cassin, Stephen (L.) U.S.	VI. 213, Lake Champlain.
Castagnier, Jean Joseph (Cmde.) F.	I. 147, crsg. III. 19, Dunkerque.
Castle, George (Mid.)	V. 37, Amphion, cutting out exped. VI. 231, L. Chandeleur Isles.
Cathcart, Robert (L.)	II. 197, Bellerophon, the Nile; 210, pro. Cr. IV. 318, Seagull captd. by Da. Lougen; 319, pro. P.C.; 474, App. VI. 70-1, Alexandria engages U.S. President.
Cauchard, Charles Alexandre (L.) F.	III. 442, Achille, k. Trafalgar.
Caulfield, James (C.)	IV. 368, Thunder (bomb.), Saltholm Isle; 400, Basque Rds. V. 203, Cornwallis, Isle of France.
Caulfield, Thos. Gordon (C.)	II. 219, Aurora, Minorca. IV. 180, Russel, off Batavia. VI. 2, 117, Hibernia, Medn. Flt.
Cayley, William (P.C.)	II. 109, Invincible, off Trinidad; 420, capture of Surinam.
Cayme, George (Mr.)	V. 126, Weazle, cutting out exped.
Cecil, William (L.)	IV. 328, Nymphe, cutting out exped.
Cederstrom, Baron (C.) Swd.	IV. 299, Swd. Forsigtigheten, Br. Swd. Flt. Oro Rds.
Cerf, De (C.) Du.	I. 416, Du Sirène, captd. at the Cape of Good Hope.
Chads, Hy. Ducie (L.)	V. 146, Sirius, Isle de la Passe; 162, Grand Port; 414-17-22, Java, w. in actn. VI. 309, C. Arachne; 311-15-21-27, Burmese War; 338, Alligator; 344, made C.B.
,, Hy. Ducie, C.B.	
Chair, Henry William de (Mr. Mt.)	IV. 448, Apollo, cutting out exped. Rosas Bay.
Chalas, Don Raimond de (C.) Sp.	II. 405, Hermione recaptd. by the bts. of Surprise.
Chalmers, Chas. Wm. (Mid.)	IV. 127, Franchise cutting out exped.
Chalmers, John (Mid.)	V. 42, w. cutting out exped.
Chalmers, Wm. (Mr.)	III. 406, Royal Sovereign, k. Trafalgar.
Chamberlayne, Charles (P.C.)	I. 297, Bombay Castle, Flt. off Hyères.
Chamberlayne, Edwin Henry (P.C.)	V. 245, Unité and F. frigates; 255, Italy; 261, Sq. at Lissa.
Chamberlayne, Geo. (L.)	III. 130, Trent, cutting out exped.
Chambers, Geo. (M.L.)	II. 80, Venerable, w. Camperdown.
Chambers, Jas. (Mid.)	VI. 374, w. Navarino.
Chambers, Samuel (C.)	IV. 155, Port Mahon, crsg. Cuba.
Chambers, Thos. (L.)	VI. 163, Reindeer, w. in actn.
Chambon, — (C.) F.	II. 178, Mercure, the Nile; 286, Indomptable, Brest Flt.
Chamier, Fredk. (Mid.)	VI. 146, Menelaus; 186-7, Baltimore.
Champain, William (C.)	II. 230, Zephyr, Trinidad. IV. 76, Jason capts. Naïade.
Champlin, Guy R. (C.) U.S.	VI. 223-4, U.S. General Armstrong (priv.), in actn.
Chapman, Charles Matthew (Mid.)	V. 248, Belle Poule, actn. at Parenza.
Chapman, Edmund Andrew (Mid.)	III. 441, Defiance, w. Trafalgar.
Chapman, John (M.-Sergeant)	IV. 331-3, Carnation, in actn.
Chapman, Patrick (L.)	II. 81, Triumph, w. Camperdown.
Chapman, — (B.)	I. 172, Bellerophon, w. 1st June. II. 196, w. the Nile.
Charbonnier, — (C.) F.	I. 321, Artémise, actn. with Br. frigates.
Charles, Hornsby (Mid.)	I. 275, Queen Charlotte, w. in actn.
Chartres, Edward A. (L.)	V. 248, Belle Poule, actn. at Parenza.
Chassin, — (C.) F.	II. 224, Cheri (priv.) captd. by Pomone, k. in actn.
Chatterton, Jos. (Mid.	III. 104, Spencer, w. Algesiras.

Chauncey, Isaac (Cmde.) U.S. — V. 400, description of U.S. United States. VI. 103, U.S. Madison; 108, 196, 203-8, Canadian Lakes.
Chauvin, Henri (L.-Com.) F. — V. 138, Estafette, Isle of France.
Cheap, Thomas (C.) E.I.C. — I. 218, E.I.C. Britannia, actn. with F. frigates.
Cheeseman, Richard (L.) — III. 104, Pompée, w. Algesiras.
Cheminant, Louis Ange (L.) F. — III. 247-8, Curieux, w. in actn.
Cheshire, Chas. (Mr.) — II. 114, Magicienne, cutting out exped.
Cheshire, John (L. Com.) — VI. 120, Adriatic.
Chesnaye, John Christian (Sub.-L.) — V. 130-1, Sylvia, crsg., capts. prow, Straits of Sunda.
Chesneau, Michel J. André (C.) F. — IV. 164-5, Rhin captd. by Mars.
Chesshire, John (L.) ... — I. 200, Alfred, 1st June, pro. Cr.
Chetham, Edward (L.) — III. 25, Seine, in actn., pro. Cr. IV. 197, C. Sally, off Dantzic.
,, Edward, C.B. — VI. 278, Leander, Algiers, made C.B.
Cheva, Don Joaquin de la (C.) Sp. — IV. 128, St. Raposa captd. by Franchise.
Cheyne, Geo. (L. Com.) — VI. 120, Woodlark, Adriatic.
Chimley, John (Mr. Mt.) — III. 80, Monarch, w. Camperdown.
Christian, Hood Hanway (P.C.) — IV. 438, Heroine, Scheldt exped.
Christian, Sir Hugh Cloberry (P.C.) — I. 62, 281, Queen Charlotte, Channel Flt.; 410, R.A. kntd.; 411-12, capture of St. Vincent, W. Indies.
Christie, — (Mr. Mt.) — III. 224, Aimable, k. in actn.
Christopher, Henry (C.) E.I.C. — IV. 189, E.I.C. Sir William Pulteney, Cape of Good Hope.
Chubb, James (Mr.) ... — II. 106, loss of Tribune.
Church, Charles (B.)... — III. 56, Alcmène, w. Copenhagen.
Church, Steph. G. (P.C.) — I. 385, Topaze capts. Elizabet.
Church, Thomas (L.)... — III. 115, Venerable, w. in actn.
Churruca, Don Cosme (C.) Sp. — III. 386, San Juan Nepomuceno, Trafalgar.
Cisneros, Don B. Hidalgo (R.A.) Sp. — III. 386, Santissima Trinidad, Trafalgar.
Clarges, — (Mid.)...... — I. 175, Marlborough, w. 1st June.
Claridge, Charles (C.) — V. 5, Driver, capture of Junon.
Clariffe, — (C.) .... — I. 416, Du. Casthor captd. at the Cape of Good Hope.
Clark, John (L.) ...... — III. 442, Thunderer, Trafalgar; 464, pro. Cr.
Clark, William (P.C.) — I. 333, Victorious, capt. of Cape of Good Hope exped.; 390-1-4, w. in actn. with F. frigate Sq.
Clark, — (As.S.) ...... — VI. 270, Eliza, in actn.
Clarke, Curtis (L.)...... — VI. 318-22, Burmese War.
Clarke, James (M.L.) — V. 40, Implacable, cutting out exped.
Clarke, John (B.) ...... — III. 437, Minotaur, w. Trafalgar.
Clarke, Richd. Wm. (L.) — III. 37, Marlborough, cutting out exped.
Clarke, Robt. (L. Com.) — IV. 467, Felix, wrkd. in the Bay of St. Andero, drnd.
Clarke, Thomas (L.)... — I. 245, w. capture of Martinique.
Clarke, William (M.L.) — VI. 4, San Josef, w. in actn.
Clarke, William Stanley (C.) E.I.C. — III. 250, E.I.C. Wexford, actn. with Linois' Sq. E. Indies.
Clavell, John (L.) ...... — III. 406, Royal Sovereign, w. Trafalgar.
Clavell, John (L.) ...... — III. 443, Dreadnought, Trafalgar; 464, pro. Cr. IV. 265-6, C. Weasel, actn. with F. T.S.
Clavering, Douglas (Mid.) — VI. 66, Shannon, actn. with Chesapeake.
Clay, Edwd. Sneyd (L.) — II. 80, Venerable, w. Camperdown. V. 445, C. Nymphe, wrkd. in the Firth of Forth.
Clayton, Thos. W. (L.) — I. 200, Tremendous, 1st June, pro. Cr.

INDEX TO NAVAL OFFICERS 71

Clement, Benj. (Mid.) II. 80, Monarch, w. Camperdown. III. 412, L. Tonnant, Trafalgar.
Clément, Louis Marie (C.) *F.* IV. 371, Sylphe captd. by Comet.
Clements, Nicholas Brent (L.) IV. 405, Mediator (F.S.), w. Basque Rds.
Clements, Wm. (M.C.) IV. 9, Namur, w. Strachan's actn.
Clemons, — (Mid.) ... I. 176, Barfleur, w. 1st June.
Clennan, Robert (Mr.) VI. 17, Undaunted, cutting out exped.
Clephane, Robert (L.) IV. 9, Courageux, w. Strachan's actn.; 197, Charles (sloop), off Dantzic. V. 35, C. Acorn, off Trieste; 123, crsg. off Lissa.
Clering, Johanson (Mr.) V. 366, Alert, in actn.
Clifford, Aug. William James (L.) IV. 447, Tigre, cutting out exped. Rosas Bay. V. 255, C. Cephalus, cutting out exped.
Clinch, Chas. (Mr.Mt.) IV. 32-4, Loire, w. cutting out exped.
Clinch, Timothy (C.) III. 353, Osprey, crsg., Barbuda. V. 327, crsg. off Heligoland.
Clyde, Charles (L.) ... III. 37, Captain, cutting out exped.
Coates, George Lewis (Mr.Mt.) V. 113, Success, cutting out exped.
Coates, John (Mid.) ... II. 268, Leander, in actn.
Cobb, Charles (P.C.)... II. 345, Glatton, Holland exped.
Cocault, Raymond (C.) *F.* IV. 106-7, Diligente; 393, Cybèle, actn. with Br. Sq.
Cochet, John (L.) ...... I. 200, Queen Charlotte, 1st June, pro. Cr.
Cochet, — (C.) *F.*...... V. 324, Ville de Caen captd. by Sealark.
Cochrane, Hon. Alexander (R.A.)
,, Sir Alexander, K.B. III. 286, Sq. off Ferrol; 333, Northumberland, off Ferrol; 346, Barbadoes; 356, W. Indies. IV. 89, 93, Basse Terre; 103-4, actn. off St. Domingo, kntd.; 109, Fort Royal Bay; 110, Tortola; 274, Leeward Isles; 279, St. Thomas Island; 333, Martinique; 387, Leeward Isles. V. 18, 22, 69, W. Indies; 190, Guadaloupe. VI. 168, V.A. Bermuda; 174, Tonnant, Chesapeake Bay; 188, Baltimore; 191-2, 231, Chandeleur Isles.
Cochrane, Hon. Alex. Inglis (P.C.) I. 319, Thetis, Chesapeake Bay; 385, Murray's Sq. crsg. II. 285, Ajax, Flt. off Brest; 301, Basque Rds. III. 81-3, 92, Egypt exped.
Cochrane, Hon. Archibald (Mid.) III. 134-5, Speedy, cutting out exped.
Cochrane, Lord (L.) ... II. 419, Queen Charlotte, Gibraltar Bay. III. 97, 108, Speedy captd. by F. Sq.; 133-4, Speedy capts. Sp. Gamo (6th May), pro. P.C.; 482, App.; IV. 138-40, Pallas, crsg.; 239, Impérieuse, crsg.; 384-6, crsg.; 397-400-18-20, Basque Rds. actn.; 425-8, made K.B. V. 428, resigned.
,, Lord, K.B.
Cochrane, Nathaniel Day (C.) IV. 93, Kingfisher; 95, Duckworth's actn.; 104, pro. P.C.
Cochrane, Thos. (P.C.) IV. 242, Jason capts. Favourite; 382, crsg. off Port Royal.
Cock, Wm. Beddeck(L.) V. 343, cutting out exped.
Cockburn, Geo. (P.C.) I. 343, Meleager, Sq. off Vado; 406, Minerve capts. Sp. Sabina. II. 34, Channel Flt.; 35, 55, Lagos Bay; 52-62, Santa Cruz. III. 79, capts. Succès. IV. 332, Pompée capts. Pilade; 434-9, Belleisle, Scheldt exped. V. 69-71-3, Pompée, capture of Martinique. VI. 84, R.A. Marlborough; 88-94-5, Sceptre, Chesapeake Bay; 168-71, Albion; 174-8, Bladensburg, battle of; 189, Baltimore;
,, Sir George (K.C.B.) 192, Bermuda; 227, made K.C.B. Northumberland; 235-6, St. Helena.
Cockerel, Jean Marie (L.Com.) *F.* IV. 330, Pilade, actn. with Gorée; 332, captd. by Pompée.
Cocks, George (C)...... IV. 205, Thunderer (bomb.), Copenhagen.
Cockwell, James (L.) *E.I.C.* IV. 152, E.I.C. Warren Hastings, w. in actn.

Codrington, Edward (P.C.)	III. 384, Orion, Trafalgar. IV. 439, Blake, Scheldt exped.
,, Sir Edw.	VI. 359, V.A. ; kntd. Asia ; 360–7, Navarino.
Codrington, J. H. (L.)	VI. 374, w. Navarino.
Coe, Thomas (C.)	VI. 309, Tees ; 311–25, Burmese War.
Coetnempren, Joseph Marie (C.) *F*.	I. 60, Jean Bart ; 135, executed.
Coffin, John Townshend (L.)	IV. 290, Spartan, crsg. off. Sicily. V. 341, Victorious, in actn.
Coghlan, Jeremiah (act. L.Com.)	III. 20–1, Viper capts. F. brig, w. in actn. IV. 26, C. Renard des. Général Ernouf (priv.) ; 147–8, capts. Diligent. VI. 2, Caledonia, Channel Flt. ; 19, Cassis.
Colachy, — (C.) *F*. ...	II. 272, Armée-d-Italie (priv.) captd. by Perdrix.
Colby, David (L.)	II. 148, Robust, w. in actn. ; 162, pro. Cr.
Colby, Thomas (L.) ...	IV. 221–30, Thunderer, w. Dardanelles.
Cole, Christopher (P.C.)	IV. 180, Culloden, Sq. Batavia Rds. V. 195, Piémontaise ; 198–202, capture of Banda Neira ; 295, Caroline ; 301–3,
,, Sir Christopher	capture of Java. VI. 13, kntd., Rippon, off the Western Isles ; 147, Medn.
Cole, Edward (L.)......	IV. 319, Stately, w. in actn.
Cole, Francis (C.)	I. 61, Eurydice, crsg. ; 230, off Guernsey ; 357, Révolutionnaire capts. Unité. II. 7, Pellew's Sq.
Cole, George Ward (Mid.)	VI. 234, w. cutting out exped.
Cole, Thomas (Mid.)...	II. 442, Foudroyant, w. in actn. III. 201, L. Blenheim, cutting out exped.
Cole, Thos. (Mr.Mt.)	VI. 34, Swallow, cutting out exped.
Cole, William (Mid.)...	VI. 288, Leander, w. Algiers.
Coleman, — (Mid.) ...	I. 289, Courageux, k. in actn.
Collard, Valentine (L.)	II. 58, Britannia, St. Vincent, pro. Cr. III. 315, C. Railleur, crsg. ; 102, Dreadnought, crsg.
Collard, Valentine (C)	II. 462, Fortune, wrkd. near Oporto, drnd.
Collet, Joseph (C.) *F*.	III. 317–8, w. in actn. off Cherbourg. IV. 139, Minerve, Isle of Aix ; 140, actn. with Pallas ; 175–6, Sq. actn. VI. 227, Melpomène captd. by Rivoli
Collett, Isaac Charles Smith (L.Com.)	IV. 467, Woodcock, wrkd. at St. Michael's.
Collier, Edward (L.)...	V. 126–7, Thames, cutting out exped.
Collier, Francis Augustus (L.)	III. 258, Osprey, in actn. IV. 331, C. Wolverine, crsg. ; 380, Circe, actn. off St. Pierre.
Collier, Sir Geo. (P.C.)	I. 449, Canada, App.
Collier, Geo. Ralph (C.)	III. 143–5, Victor, actn. with Flêche. IV. 154–5, Minerva,
,, Sir Geo. Ralph	crsg. ; 210, Surveillante ; 336, kntd. V. 100, crsg. ; 334–6, Sq. off N. Spain ; 429, w. in actn. VI. 15, off N. Spain ;
,, Sir Geo. Ralph (K.C.B.)	252, made K.C.B. Leander ; 258, Isle St. Jago.
Collier, Henry (C.) ...	VI. 204, Magnet, Canadian Lakes.
Collier, John (Mid.) ...	II. 61, Theseus, w. in actn.
Collingwood, Cuthbert (P.C.)	I. 65, Prince, Channel Flt. ; 139, Barfleur, Channel Flt. II. 34, Excellent ; 43, 58, St. Vincent ; 297, R.A. Triumph. III. 354, V.A. Dreadnought ; 375–9, off Cadiz ; 383–4,
,, Lord (V.A.)	394–5, 406, 437, 447–8, Trafalgar ; 463–7, created Baron ; 498, App. IV. 1, Medn. Flt. ; 78, 91, 105–19, Medn ; 121–3, 136, 213, off Cadiz ; 216–90–2, Syracuse ; 293, 341–5–7–8, Isle Tenedos ; 443, Medn. ; 444–7, St. Sebastian ; 469, App. V. 79, Medn., d. ; 439, App.
Collingwood, Francis (C.)	I. 412, Cormorant, Léogane, W. Indies.
Collingwood, Francis E. (Mid.)	III. 422, Victory, Trafalgar.
Collins, Francis (L.) ...	III. 84, w. in actn. Egypt.
Collins, Henry (Mr.Mt.)	V. 255, Unité, cutting out exped.
Collins, James (C.)......	IV. 217, Meteor (bomb.), Dardanelles ; 385, Rosas Bay.

INDEX TO NAVAL OFFICERS 73

Collins, Sir John (P.C.)	I. 72, Berwick, Flt. off Toulon.
Collins, John (L.)	II. 61, Victory, w. in actn.; 196, Alexander, k. the Nile.
Collins, Martin (Mid.)	III. 104, Venerable, w. Algesiras.
Collins, Richard (C.Ck.)	VI. 163, Reindeer, in actn.
Collinson, William S. (L.Com.)	VI. 324, E.I.C. Prince of Wales, Burmese War.
Collis, William (L.) ...	II. 58, Goliath, St. Vincent, pro. Cr.
Collman, John (act.Pr.)	IV. 71, Phœnix, in actn. VI. 41, Amelia, w. in actn.
Collman, William (Pr.)	III. 273, Hippomenes, in actn. IV. 381, Circe, w. in actn.
Colnett, James (C.) ...	II. 456, Hussar, wrkd. on the coast of France.
Colonna, — (C.).........	II. 253, Eagle (priv.), actn. with F. brig.
Colpoys, John (R.A.)..	I. 206, 270, London, Channel Flt.; 277, 315, crsg.; 341, V.A.; 363, off Brest. II. 4, off Brest; 7, 23, Spithead; 28–30, mutiny at.
Colston, Samuel (Secretary's Ck.)	VI. 287, Queen Charlotte, w. Algiers.
Columbine, Edward Henry (P.C.)	V. 67, Solebay, Gorée, Africa; 441, wrkd. on the coast of Africa.
Colville, Hon. John (P.C.)	III. 493, Romney, wrkd. near the Texel. IV. 200, Hercule, Copenhagen.
Colwell, Dennis (Schoolmaster)	V. 398, Macedonian, k. in actn.
Comer, Charles (Mid.)	IV. 100, Northumberland, w. in actn.
Compton, Henry (L.)	I. 343, cutting out exped.
Compton, William (C.)	III. 276, Lilly captd. by F. Dame Ambert; 277, k. in actn.; 494, App.
Comyn, Maurice Keating (Mr.Mt.)	IV. 327, Mercury, cutting out exped.
Conn, Henry (L.)	V. 53, Junon, in actn.
Conn, John (C.).........	III. 65, off Boulogne; 177, Canopus, Medn. Flt.; 335–9, Channel Flt.; 384, Dreadnought, Trafalgar.
Connor, Ross (Mid.)...	III. 282, Loire, w. in actn.
Connor, — (Mid.)......	III. 224, Aimable, w. in actn.
Conseil, — (C.) F. ...	I. 309, Pique captd. by Blanche; 313, k. in actn.
Conway, Hon. Hugh Seymour (P.C.)	I. 72, Leviathan, Medn. Flt.
Conyers, John (Mr.Mt.)	IV. 405, Gibraltar, w. Basque Rds.
Conyers, — (L.Com.)	V. 66, E.I.C. Aurora, Persian Gulf.
Cooban, Robert Baron (L.Com.)	III. 19, Kent (cutter), off Dunkerque.
Coode, John (C.)	VI. 120, Porcupine; 278, Albion; 287, w. Algiers, 291, made C.B.
Cook, Edward (Mid.)	IV. 31, Seine, crsg. Porto Rico.
Cook, Hugh (L.)	III. 443, Agamemnon, Trafalgar; 464, pro. Cr.
Cook, John (C.).........	I. 140, Incendiary (F.S.), Channel Flt.
Cook, John (M.L.) ...	IV. 352, Seahorse, in actn.
Cook, Robert (Mr.Mt.)	V. 220, Quebec, cutting out exped.
Cook, Samuel Edward (L.)	VI. 34, Swallow, cutting out exped.
Cook, Thomas (B.) ...	III. 78, Pomone, k. in actn.
Cook, Thomas (Mr.)...	III. 410, Mars, w. Trafalgar.
Cook, Wm. John (Mid.)	III. 410, Mars, w. Trafalgar.
Cooke, Edward (L.) ...	I. 74–5, Victory, Toulon. II. 237–9, C. Sibylle, Manilla Bay; 365–7, capts. Forte; 375, k. in actn.
Cooke, Francis (A.B.)	II. 46, Captain, in actn.
Cooke, Jervis (M.L.)	V. 46, Thetis, cutting out exped.
Cooke, John (P.C.) ...	I. 380–1, Quebec, W. Indies. II. 91–113, Nymphe, capture of F. frigates. III. 123, Amethyst, off Cape Finisterre; 384, Bellerophon; 413, k. at Trafalgar.
Cookesley, John (L.)...	IV. 405, Gibraltar, Basque Rds.
Coombe, William (L.)	IV. 240, Galatea; 241, w. cutting out exped.; 242, pro. Cr.; 334, Heureux, k, cutting out exped.

Coote, Charles (C.) ...	IV. 48, Ranger captd. by a F. Sq.; 456, App.
Coote, Richard (C.) ...	VI. 7, Borer, crsg.; 196, cutting out exped.; 387, Peacock, fndrd. S. America, drnd.
Corbett, Robert (P.C.)	V. 58-61, Néréide, Port Louis, Isle of France; 173-7, 183, Africaine, k. in actn. with F. frigates.
Corbyn, Edward (Mid.)	III. 410, Mars, k. Trafalgar.
Cordier or Cordelier, J. M. Eman. (C.) *F*.	III. 245-7, Curieux, w., cut out by Br. bts.
Cordova, Don Josef de (A.) *Sp*.	II. 36-47, Santissima Trinidad, St. Vincent; 59, dismissed.
Coréi, Don Josef (C.) *Sp*.	III. 122, Sp. Santa Maria (schooner) captd. by Br. lugger.
Cormack, Richard (L.)	III. 55, Isis, w. Copenhagen.
Cornice, — (R.A.) *F*.	I. 189-90, Majestueux, Bertheaume Bay.
Cornwall, James (P.C.)	II. 68, Marlborough.
Cornwall, Hon. Trefusis (Mid.)	V. 126, Thames, cutting out exped.
Cornwallis, Hon. William (Cmde.)	I. 131-3, Crown, Pondicherry, E. Indies; 206-18, R.A. Spithead; 262, V.A. Royal Sovereign; 264-9, Cornwallis, Sq. off Ushant. III. 137, A.; 141-6, 169, Dreadnought, Channel Flt.; 214, 307, Sq. off Ushant; 310, Ville de Paris; 312-13, actn. Camaret Bay; 368-72, off Ushant. IV. 54-5, Channel Flt.; 87, 117, Flt. off Brest, relieved by Earl St. Vincent; 451-2, App.
Corosin, — (C.) *F*. ...	I. 219, Vengeur (priv.) captd. by E.I.C. ships, k. in actn.
Cosby, Philip (V.A.)...	I. 71-2, Windsor Castle, Medn. Flt.; 214, Flt. in Gourjean Bay.
Cosmao, — (Cmde.) ...	III. 349, Pluton, Fort Royal. V. 207, R.A. Toulon Flt.
Cosnahan, Hugh (Mid.)	VI. 58, Shannon, actn. with Chesapeake; 66, pro. L.
Costerton, Sam. (Mid.)	V. 161, Néréide, w. in actn.
Cotelle, François Auguste (L.) *F*.	II. 146, Bellone, in actn.
Cotes, James (P.C.) ...	I. 118-21, Thames, actn. with Uranie; 205, captd. by F. Sq.; 433, App.
Cotesworth, Charles (Mid.)	IV. 229, Royal George, w. Dardanelles.
Cotgrave, Charles (L.-Com.)	I. 140, Ranger (cutter), Channel Flt.
Cotgrave, Isaac (L.-Com.)	I. 440, Ranger captd. by F. Sq. off Brest. III. 65-6, invas. flotilla off Boulogne.
Cottell, James (M.L.)	V. 146, Iphigenia, Isle de la Passe.
Cotton, Charles (P.C.)	I. 62, 139, Majestic, Channel Flt.
Cotton, Sir Charles, Bart. (P.C.)	I. 262, Mars, Channel Flt. II. 285, R.A. Prince, Sq. off Brest; 297, Medn. III. 307, V.A. San Josef, Channel Flt. IV. 296, A.; 329, Sq. off the Tagus. V. 81-2, Medn. Flt.; 207, 245, Channel Flt.
Cottrell, Frederick (C.)	III. 490, Garland, wrkd. St. Domingo.
Couch, James (L.)	III. 443, Conqueror, Trafalgar; 464, pro. Cr.
Couch, Richard (L.) ...	IV. 101, Superb, Duckworth's actn.; 104, pro. Cr.
Couche, John (M.L.)...	V. 102, cutting out exped.
Coudé, Louis Marie (C.) *F*.	I. 290, Censeur captd. by Hotham's Sq. IV. 88, Cmde. Brave, Brest Flt.
Coudin, Jean Daniel (C.) *F*.	II. 137, Medée, Rochefort Sq. III. 22-3, captd. by E.I.C. ships.
Coulter, John (M.L.)...	V. 102, cutting out exped. Basque Rds.
Couney, — (Mr.)	V. 329-30, Attack, cutting out exped.
Countess, A. G. (Mr. Mt.)	V. 88, Freija, cutting out exped. Calais.
Countess, George (C.)	I. 139, Charon, Channel Flt. II. 91, Robust, off Brest; 140-2, Ethalion, observing Buonaparte's Flt.; 163.
Courand, Jean François (C.) *F*.	I. 140, Sans Pareil, Brest Flt.; 161-3, 186, captd. 1st June; 286, R.A. Brest Flt. III. 325, invas. flotilla, Etaples' division.

INDEX TO NAVAL OFFICERS

Courcy, Hon. Almeira De (Mid.) — IV. 28, Bacchante, cutting out exped.
Courcy, Hon. Michael De (P.C.) — II. 142, Magnanime, Warren's Sq. crsg. ; 269, crsg. ; 297, Canada, Medn. Flt. IV. 38, Cmde., crsg. Jamaica.
Courcy, Hon. Michael De (L.Com.) — IV. 466, St. Lucia captd. on Leeward Isles station.
Courcy, Nevinson De(C.) — VI. 9, Mutine capts. F. Invincible (priv.).
Courdouan, Honore Cyprien (C.) F. — V. 338, Mérinos, actn. with Apollo.
Courtenay, George Wm. Day (P.C.) — I. 110–14, Boston, k. in actn. with Embuscade.
Coutts, David (Mr.Mt.) — I. 275, Queen Charlotte, w. in actn.
Cowan, John Smith (L.) — IV. 146, Leander, off New York.
Cowan, Thomas (Mid.) — I. 87, Toulon.
Cox, Francis (L.) ...... — I. 87, Toulon.
Cox, Richard (L.Com.) — V. 442, Pigeon (cutter), wrkd. near Margate.
Cox, Thomas S. (M.L.) — V. 138, Néréide, cutting out exped. ; 149, Isle de la Passe ; 161, w. at Grand Port. VI. 207, w. Canadian Lakes.
Cox, Wm. L. (L.) U.S. — VI. 61–7, Chesapeake, w. in actn. with Shannon.
Coyde, William (Mid.) — VI. 318, 343, Burmese War.
Crabb, Joseph Wm. (L.) — V. 255–66, Unite, cutting out exped.
Cracknell, James Thos. (M.L.) — V. 40, Implacable, cutting out exped.
Cracraft, Wm. Edward (L.) — I. 180, Brunswick, 1st June ; 200, pro. Cr. ; 443, C. Daphne captd. by Brest Flt.
Craig, Wm. Hy. (M.L.) — III. 293, Pique at Curaçoa. IV. 134, w. in actn.
Craig, — (L.)............ — V. 204, act.Cr. Staunch, capture of the Isle of France.
Craigy, — (M.L.) ...... — I. 235, Artois, k. in actn.
Crandon, Benjamin (Mr.) — V. 41, k. cutting out exped.
Cranley, Alex. (Mid.) — VI. 310, Larne, Burmese War.
Cranstown, Lord (P.C.) — I. 262, Bellerophon, Channel Flt.
Crawford, James (Mr.) — III. 143, Victor, in actn.
Crawford, James Coutts (C.) — II. 289, Childers, Keith's Flt. off Cadiz. V. 303, Hussar, capture of Java exped.
Crawford, John Campbell (L.Com.) — V. 330, Wrangler, actn. with Da. gbts.
Crawford, John Charles (Mid.) — IV. 138, Pallas, cutting out exped.
Crawford, Maurice (Mid.) — VI. 18, Euryalus, cutting out exped.
Crawford, Moses (Mr.) — II. 273, Perdrix, in actn.
Crawford, Richard (L.-Com.) — VI. 391, Dominica, wrkd. Bermuda.
Crawford, Robert (L.-Com.) — VI. 311, Kitty, Burmese War.
Crawley, Edmund (P.C.) — II. 112, Valiant, Sq. at St. Domingo.
Crawley, George (C.)... — IV. 447, Philomel, Rosas Bay ; 449, Isle of Ithaca.
Crawley, James (L.) ... — IV. 124, Eagle, w. in actn.
Crawley, Jeremiah (Car.) — V. 37, Mercury, cutting out exped.
Crawley, P. A. (Mid.) — VI. 129, Hebrus, k. in actn.
Crease, Henry (L.)...... — VI. 186, Menelaus, Chesapeake Bay.
Creighton, John Orde (L.) U.S. — V. 277, U.S. President, in actn. VI. 183, Mr. Cr., ill-treatment of Br. Mid.
Cribb, Richard Wm. (C.) — III. 353, Kingfisher, crsg. Barbuda.
Crickdon, George (L.) — VI. 279, Rhin, cutting out exped.
Cririe, John (L.)......... — VI. 90, Narcissus, cutting out exped.
Crisp, James (Mr.Mt.) — V. 329, cutting out of Da. gbts.
Croft, Richard (L.)...... — III. 443, Orion, Trafalgar ; 464, pro. Cr.
Crofton, Ambrose (L.-Com.) — III. 477, Weymouth (T.S.), wrkd. on Lisbon Bar.
Crofton, Edward (Mid.) — III. 140, w. cutting out exped. IV. 388, C. Wanderer, actn. at Isle St. Martin.

Crofton, Hon. George Alfred (L.)	IV. 36, Cambrian, cutting out exped.
Croke, Wentworth P. (L.Com.)	V. 448, Shamrock, wrkd. on Cape Santa Maria.
Croker, Charles (Mid.)	IV. 326, Alceste, cutting out exped. V. 248, Parenza.
Croker, Walter (L) ...	IV. 221, Active, Dardanelles. VI. Furieuse, cutting out exped.
Cronstadt, — (V.A.) Swd.	III. 62-3, Carlscrona.
Crooke, Chas. Hy. (L.)	IV. 381, Circe, cutting out exped.
Crooke, James (L.) ...	IV. 22, Cleopatra, w. in actn.
Cross, James M. (Mid.)	VI. 288, Infernal (bomb.), w. Algiers.
Crosse, Jean Raimond La (Cmde.) F.	II. 5, Droits de l'Homme, Brest Flt.; 12-17, wrkd. in actn. with Br. Sq.; 127, R.A.; 129-31, Cherbourg. III. 217, invas. flotilla; 232-316-20-32, invas. flotilla.
Crossman, Richard (L.Com.)	IV. 400, Growler, actn. Basque Rds.
Crouch, Edw.Thos.(L.)	IV. 380, Amethyst, in actn.
Crowder, Wm. (Mid.)	V. 101, Surveillante, cutting out exped.
Cull, Richard (L.)......	IV. 347, Standard, cutting out exped.
Cullis, Wm. (L.Com.)	IV. 467, Wagtail (cutter), wrkd. at St. Michael's.
Culverhouse, John (L.)	I. 343, cutting out exped.; 407, Minerve, in actn.
Cumberland, William (P.C.)	IV. 201, Leyden, Copenhagen.
Cumby, Wm.Pryce(L.)	III. 414, Bellerophon, Trafalgar. IV. 382, C. Polyphemus, St. Domingo. V. 18, Sq. off the Saintes. VI. 73, Hyperion, crsg.
Cuming, Wm. (P.C.)	III. 46, Russel, Copenhagen; 356, Prince of Wales, Calder's Sq. V. 208, Bombay, Medn. Flt.
Cummins, Robt. (M.C.)	V. 36, Excellent, cutting out exped.
Cumpson, George (L.)	V. 232, Cerberus, cutting out exped; 240, w. actn. off Lissa.
Cumpston, William(L.)	III. 255, Drake, cutting out exped.
Cunningham, Alex. (C.)	V. 318, Bermuda recapts. Apelles; 319, pro. P.C.
Cunningham, George (Mr.Mt.)	V. 301, Procris, cutting out exped.
Cuppage, Wm. (Mid.)	VI. 4, San Josef, w. in actn.
Curling, Edw. B.(Mid.)	IV. 70, Phœnix, w. in actn.
Currie, Douglas (Mid.)	VI. 374, w. Navarino.
Curry, Richard (C.) ...	III. 83-8-9 Fury (bomb.), Egypt exped.
Curry, Roger Carley(L.)	VI. 96, Contest, w. cutting out exped.
Curry, — (Mr.Mt.) ...	III. 104, Pompée, w. Algesiras.
Curtis, Lucius (P.C.)	V. 65, Magicienne recapts. E.I.C. Windham; 137, Isle of France; 164, Grand Port; 169-70, wrkd.; 445, App.
Curtis, Thomas (Mr.)	III. 271, Wilhelmina, in actn. IV. 354, Seahorse, in actn.
Curzon, Edward (P.C.)	VI. 373, Asia, Navarino.
Curzon,Hon. Hy. (P.C.)	I. 262, Pallas, Channel Sq. II. 301, Indefatigable, off Ferrol; 469, wrkd. Plymouth Sound. IV. 236, Elizabeth, Sq. off the Tagus.
Cutfield,Wm. (Mr.Mt.)	III. 409, Belleisle, w. Trafalgar. IV. 330, L. Grasshopper, in actn.
Cuthbert, Rich. (M.C.)	II. 81, Ardent, w. Camperdown.
Cuthbert, Robert (L.)	II. 190-7, Majestic, the Nile; 210, pro. Cr.; 289, C. Majestic, Medn. Fleet; 365, crsg. Spain.
Cuthbertson,Jas.(M.L.)	IV. 101, Spencer, w. Duckworth's actn.
Dacres, Barrington (C.)	III. 136, Bulldog (bomb.) captd. at Ancona; 188, Culloden, Sq. crsg.; 482, App.
Dacres, James Richard (P.C.)	I. 251, Irresistible, St. Domingo; 271, Barfleur, Channel Flt. II. 34, St. Vincent. III. 346, R.A. Jamaica. IV. 29, Jamaica; 89, pro. V.A.; 128, 171, 184, 275, Jamaica.
Dacres, Jas. Richd. (C.)	IV. 170, Bacchante, W. Indies; 243, capts. Dauphin; 342, capts. Griffon. V. 369-78, Guerrière captd. by U.S. Constitution, w. in actn.; 383-8, 450, App. VI. 248, Tiber, crsg.

INDEX TO NAVAL OFFICERS

Dacres, Richard (P.C.)   I. 62, Sceptre, Channel Flt. ; 251, St. Domingo. IV. 200, Pompée, Copenhagen ; 217, Dardanelles.
Dahlreup, — (L. Com.) Da.   V. 99, Da. gbt. Bolder, off Norway.
Dair, — (M. Sergeant)   II. 262, Leander, k. in actn.
Dalbarade, Etienne (C.) F.   II. 178, Conquérant, w. the Nile.
Dale, James (Mid)......   I. 119, Thames, w. in action.
Dale, John (C) E.I.C.   V. 54–6, 61, E.I.C. Streatham captd. by F. Caroline.
Dale, John L. (L. Com.)   III. 494, Morne-Fortunée, wrkd. in the W. Indies.
Dale, — (Cmde.) U.S.   III. 160, U.S. President, Sq. crsg.
Dalling, John (Mr. Mt.)   V. 37, Amphion, cutting out exped.
Dalrymple, — (Mid.)...   IV. 229, Royal George, w. Dardanelles.
Dalton, Thos. (Mr. Mt.)   I. 182, Brunswick, k. 1st June.
Daly, Cuthbert (Mid.)   IV. 127, Franchise, cutting out exped.
Daly, Cuthbert Featherstone (C.)   IV. 371–2, Comet capts. F. Sylphe.
Daly, Joseph (L.) ......   IV. 382, Polyphemus, cutting out exped.
Daly, Robert (Pr.)......   IV. 334, Heureux, cutting out exped.
Dalzell, — (Mid.) ......   VI. 274, Tyne, cutting out exped.
Damerell, Henry (Mr.)   II. 441, Penelope, k. in actn.
Dance, Nathaniel (Cmde.) E.I.C.   III. 250–4, E.I.C. Earl Camden, actn. with Linois' F. Sq. E. Indies, kntd.
Daniel, Jean J. Léonore (L. Com.) F.   VI. 10–11, Flibustier destd. in actn. by Telegraph.
Daniel, Rob. Savage (L.)   II. 196, Bellerophon, k. the Nile.
Daniel, Wm. Henry (L.)   I. 96, Courageux, w. in actn.
Daniel, Wm. W. (L.) ..   III. 443, Achille, Trafalgar ; 464, pro. Cr.
Darby, Henry D'Esterre (P.C.)   II. 171, Bellerophon, Flt. off Cadiz ; 196, w. the Nile ; 204, 292, Medn. III. 98, Spencer, Algesiras.
D'Arcey, Edward A. (L. Com.)   IV. 337, Barbara captd. by Général Ernouf (priv.) ; 467, App. V. 219, Viper, Boulogne flotilla.
Darley, William (M. L.)   I. 301, Victory, w. in actn.
Darling, Robert (S. Mt.)   III. 119, Melpomène, w. cutting out exped.
Darrac, Don — (C.)Sp.   III. 342, Sp. America F. Sp. Flt. Medn.
Dashwood, Charles (Mid.)   I. 177, Impregnable, 1st June. II. 145, L. Magnanime, in actn. III. 145, C. Sylph ; 146–7, actn. with Artémise ; 148, pro. P.C. IV. 28, Bacchante, crsg. ; 127, Franchise, crsg. ; 201, Sq. off the Great Belt.
Dashwood, William Bateman (L.)   V. 263–4, Alceste, w. in actn. ; 266, pro. Cr. VI. 15, C. Snap, actn. with F. luggers ; 280, Prometheus, Algiers.
Daubenny, Edw. (Mid.)   III. 54, Bellona, w. Copenhagen.
Daugier, François Henri Eugène (Cmde.) F.   I. 356, Proserpine, convoy escort. II. 286, Batave, Brest Flt. III. 229, Boulogne flotilla ; 326, invas. flotilla.
Davers, Charles Sydney (P.C.)   II. 110, Scipio, Sq. off Trinidad.
Davey, Francis Surrage (Mid.)   V. 240, Cerberus, k. in actn.
Davey, John P. (Mid.)   VI. 35, Revenge, cutting out exped.
Davidson, Jas. (C. Ck.)   V. 104, Briseis, k. in actn.
Davidson, — (L. Com.)   V. 66, E.I.C. Fury, Persian Gulf.
Davie, George (Mt.)...   III. 149, Pasley, w. in actn.
Davie, John (Mid.) ...   I. 108, Nymphe, k. in actn.
Davie, John (C.).........   IV. 178, Favourite captd. by F. Sq. ; 461, App.
Davies, Chas. (Mr. Mt.)   V. 301, Procris, cutting out exped.
Davies, David (M.L.)   V. 417, Java, w. in actn.
Davies, Edward (3rd Mt.) E.I.C.   IV. 152, E.I.C. Warren Hastings, w. in actn.
Davies, Hy. Thos. (L.)   IV. 162, Blanche, in actn. pro. Cr. VI. 7, C. Albacore engages Gloire.
Davies, James (L.)......   VI. 289, Severn, Algiers ; 291, pro. Cr.
Davies, Lewis (Cr.) ...   VI. 365–71–3, Rose, Navarino.

Davies, Wm. (Mr.Mt.)	II. 195, Goliath, k. the Nile.
Davis, James (Mr.Mt.)	IV. 319, Stately, w. in actn.
Davis, John (L.)	IV. 326, Virginie, in actn., pro. Cr. VI. 387, C. Anacreon, fndrd. in the Channel, drnd.
Davis, John (Mr.)	IV. 338, Redwing, w. in actn.
Davis, Lewis (L.)	II. 378-9, Com. Fortune captd. by F. Sq.; 474, App. III. 77, C. Swiftsure, w. in actn.; 87, w. in actn.
Davis, Samuel (L.) ...	V. 128, Blossom, k. cutting out exped.
Davis, Thomas J. Jas. Wm. (L.)	V. 126, Weazle, cutting out exped.
Davis, William (M.L.)	VI. Furieuse, cutting out exped.
Davis, — (Mr.Mt.) ...	II. 242, Fox, capture of batteries.
Davison, John (M.L.)	II. 380, Success, cutting out exped.
Davy, John (Mid.) ...	IV. 448, Scout, cutting out exped. Rosas Bay.
Dawes, Richard (L.)...	I. 185, Queen, w. 1st June; 200, pro. Cr.
Daws, Thos. (Mr.Mt.)	IV. 9, Courageux, w. in actn. V. 109, L. Rosario, actn. with F. privs.
Dawson, William (L.)	IV. 19, San Fiorenzo, w. in action; 309, in actn.; 311, pro. Cr.
Dawson, — (Car.)......	IV. 137, Nautilus, cutting out exped.
Dawson, — (Mid.) ...	VI. 274, Tyne, cutting out exped.
Dawson, — (C.)..........	VI. 340, Arachne, Burmese War; 355, d.
Day, Robt.I.W.(M.L.)	III. 105, Audacious, w. Algesiras.
Day, Thomas (Mr.Mt.)	IV. 326, Alceste, cutting out exped. V. 120, cutting out exped.
Deacon,Hy.Collins(L.)	V. 138-40, Néréide, w. cutting out exped; 149, Isle de la Passe; 161, w. at Grand Port.
Dean, William (L.) ...	III. 15-17, Fisgard, cutting out exped.; 185, Naiad, cutting out exped.
Dean, William (Mr.)...	III. 19, Vigilant (lugger) cuts out Désirée.
Dean, William (Mid.)	III. 135, Speedy, cutting out exped.
Debenham, John (L.-Com.)	VI. 120, Lyra, Adriatic.
Debush, William (L.)	II. 216, Goliath, w. cutting out exped.
Decatur, Jas. (L.) U.S.	III. 303, k. in actn. at Tripoli.
Decatur, Stephen (L. Com.) U.S.	III. 301, U.S. Intrepid (ketch), Tripoli; 302, C.; 303, w. in actn. IV. 249, Norfolk, U.S. V. 356, Cmde. United States Sq. crsg.; 395-6, 402, capts. Macedonian. VI. 98, crsg. E. Indies, 193-4; 237, U.S. President; 238-40, captd. by Endymion; 241, w. in actn.; 277, Algiers.
Decrès, Denis (Cmde.) F.	II. 127, invas. flotilla; 168, R.A. Toulon Flt.; 178, Diane, the Nile; 212, Valetta; 439-40, Guillaume Tell. III. 125, V.A., Minister of Marine; 225, 305, Paris; 329-67.
Dedé, Joseph (L.) F....	IV. 379, Thétis, in actn.
Deecker, Samuel Bartlett (L.)	IV. 331, Carnation, w. in actn. V. 48, Jason, in actn.; 53, pro. Cr.
Deferonne,Léonore(C.) F.	II. 139, Ireland exped. III. 334, Intrépide, Toulon Flt.
Degoy, — (P.C.)	I. 433, Scipion burnt in Leghorn Rds.
Dehen, Nicolas Philippe (L.Com.) F.	IV. 38, Torche, Sq. crsg.; 44, captd. by Goliath.
Delafons, John (L.) ...	III. 57, Bellona, Copenhagen.
Delafosse, Edwd. Hollingsworth (L.)	VI. 28, Cerberus, w. in actn.; 289, Hebrus, Algiers; 291, pro. Cr.
Dellamore, John (Mid.)	VI. 374, w. Navarino.
Delmotte, Jean Louis (R.A.) F.	I. 295, Toulon Flt. II. 286, Brest Flt.
Demai, Pi. Ant. Toussaint (L.) F.	II. 295, Alerte captd. by Br. Flt. IV. 120, Furet captd. by Hydra.
Dénian, François A. (C.) F.	I. 115, Réunion captd. by Crescent.
Deniefort, Gabriel (C.) F.	II. 214, Brune, Corfu. III. 350, Achille; 442, w. Trafalgar.

INDEX TO NAVAL OFFICERS 79

Denne, James (M.L.)	IV. 306, Meleager, cutting out exped.
Dennis, Henry (Mid.)	V. 103, Dreadnought, w. cutting out exped.
Dennis, John (Mr.) *U.S.*	IV. 274, U.S. Adams (schooner), Isle Sombrero, W. Indies.
Dennis, J. S. A. (L. Com.)	III. 230, Constitution (cutter), Channel. IV. 474, C. Sparkler, wrkd. on coast of Holland.
Dent, Charles Calmady (Mr. Mt.)	VI. 287, Minden, w. Algiers.
Denton, George (Mid.)	III. 416, Colossus, w. Trafalgar.
Desageneaux, —(C.) *F.*	II. 226, Volage captd. by Melampus.
Desauney, — (C.) *F.* ...	II. 91, Constance captd. by Br. frigates.
Desbrisay, Thos. Hen. Wm. (M.L.)	V. 138, Néréide, cutting out exped.
Descorches, Henri (C.) *F.*	IV. 77, Libre captd. by Br. frigates.
Desgareaux, —(Cmde.) *F.*	I. 222-4, Engageante captd. by Concorde.
Desmartis, — (C.) *F.*	I. 141, Jemmappes, Brest Flt.
Desmontils, René Jac. Henri (L.Com.) *F.*	IV. 38, Département des Landes, capture of Blanche.
Desrostours, Jules (C.) *F.*	VI. 44, Elbe, crsg. Sierra Leone.
D'Esterre, Wm. Parker (C.) *E.I.C.*	V. 63, E.I.C. United Kingdom captd. by F. frigates; 205, recaptd.
Devon, Frederick (Mid.)	VI. 5, Brevdrageren, off Heligoland.
Devon, Thomas Barker (L.Com.)	V. 227, Brevdrageren, off Norway. VI. 4-6, off Heligoland, capts. Da. gbts.
Devonshire, John Ferris (L.Com.)	III. 46, Dart, Copenhagen; 64, pro. P.C. VI. 147, Albion, crsg. Rhode Island.
Dick, Thomas (L.) ...	III. 119, Melpomène, cutting out exped.
Dickens, Francis Geo. (C.)	IV. 474, Voladoz, wrkd. in the W. Indies.
Dickens, George (C.)...	VI. 200, Sylph, Penobscot exped.; 391, wrkd. N. America.
Dickenson, Francis (L.)	III. 66, w. in actn. with invas. flotilla.
Dickenson, Richd. (Cr.)	VI. 365-73, Genoa, Navarino.
Dickinson, Chas. (L.)	VI. 185, Fairy, k. in actn.
Dickinson, James (L.)	V. 120, Cerberus; 232, cutting out exped.; 241, actn. off Lissa; 245, pro. Cr. VI. 261-2, Penguin captd. by U.S. Hornet; 263, k. in actn.
Dickinson, Thos. (L.)	VI. 14, Andromache, w. in actn.
Dickson, Archibald (P.C.)	I. 72, 100, Egmont, Medn. Flt.; 207, Corsica; 214, R.A. Medn. Flt. III. 42, V.A. Monarch, Denmark.
Dickson, Archibald Collingwood (P.C.)	II. 345, Veteran, Holland exped. III. 47, Copenhagen.
,, Sir A. Collingwood	IV. 200, kntd. Orion, Copenhagen; 298, Baltic Flt.
Dickson, Edw. Stirling (C.)	II. 230, Victorieuse capts. Brutus and Couleuvre. III. 299, Inconstant, Gorée. IV. 425. VI. 36, Swiftsure, crsg. Medn.; 117, Medn. Flt.; 227, Rivoli capts. Melpomène.
Digby, Henry (P.C.)...	II. 219, Leviathan, Medn.; 292, 307, Flt. off Sicily.
Digby, Henry (P.C.)...	II. 232, Aurora, crsg., des. F. priv.; 381, Alcmène capts. Courageux (priv.); 402, crsg. III. 384, 428, Africa, Trafalgar.
Digby, Steph. Thos. (C.)	III. 320, Vestal, actn. off Calais.
Dilkes, Charles (C.) ...	IV. 139, Hazard, crsg. Isle of Aix. V. 18, Neptune, Sq. off the Saintes; 69, capture of Martinique exped.
Dilkes, John (P.C.) ...	I. 410, Madras, W. Indies. III. 47, Raisonable, Copenhagen.
Dillon, James (L.Com.)	III. 235, Griffin, invas. flotilla.
Dillon, Wm. Henry (C.)	IV. 315-16, Childers, actn. with Da. Lougen; 317, pro. P.C. V. 319, Leopard, convoy escort.
Diron, Dominique (C.) *F.*	IV. 182, Superbe (priv.) captd. by Pitt. VI. 74, Decatur (priv.) capts. Dominica.
Dix, Edward (C.)	V. 50, 86, Cygnet, crsg. Guadaloupe. VI. 174, Royal Oak, Chesapeake Bay.
Dixon, George (Mid.)	VI. 288, Leander, w. Algiers.

Dixon, John Stewart (L.)	VI. 288, Leander, w. Algiers.
Dixon, John W. Taylor (L.)	I. 241, capture of Martinique. II. 289, C. Princess Royal, Medn. Flt.; 469, Raven, wrkd. near Cuxhaven. III. 47, Ramillies, Copenhagen; 261-2, Apollo, wrkd. on the coast of Portugal, drnd.; 494, App.
Dixon, Manley (P.C.)	II. 211, Lion, Medn. Flt.; 218, Alexandria; 254, capts. Sp. Santa Dorotea; 306, Sq. off Palermo; 438, Malta; 440-1, actn. with Guillaume Tell; 443-4, Généreux, off Malta. III. 73, Medn. Flt. VI. 46, R.A. Montagu, off St. Salvador.
Dixon, Manley Hall (L.)	V. 5, Horatio, w. in actn. VI. 45, C. Montagu, off St. Salvador.
Dixon, Wm. Henry (L.)	V. 327-8, Britomart, w. cutting out exped.
Dobbs, Alexander (L.)	V. 342-44, Undaunted, cutting out exped. VI. 204-11, C. Charwell, Canadian Lakes.
Dobson, Charles (Mid.)	II. 330, Theseus, w. in actn.
Dobson, Man (P.C.)...	II. 112, Queen, Jamaica station.
Dobson, William Burdett (Mid.)	VI. 209, Canadian Lakes; 308, L. Arachne; 312-17, Burmese War; 351, App.
Dodd, Michael (C.) ...	III. 227, Galgo, invas. flotilla.
Domett, Geo. (L.Com.)	VI. 394, Briseis, wrkd. on Point Pedras.
Domett, Wm. (P.C.)	I. 62, 139, 270, Royal George, Channel Flt. II. 285, Flt. off Brest. III. 45-7, London, Copenhagen.
Domett, Wm. (Mid.)	III. 55, Edgar, w. Copenhagen.
Donalan, Geo. (Mr. Mt.)	IV. 70, Phœnix, k. in actn.
Donellan, John (Mid.).	III. 84, w. in actn.
Donnelly, Ross (L.) ...	I. 200, Montagu, pro. Cr. II. 179, C. Narcissus, Medn.; 275, crsg. IV. 186, Cape of Good Hope; 279-80, Ardent, S. America.
Donovan, Thomas (Schoolmaster)	IV. 438, Aigle, w. in actn.
Donovan, William (Mr.)	IV. 366, Modeste, k. in actn.
Dordelin, Alain Joseph (C.) F.	I. 141, Tyrannicide, Brest. Flt. II. 268, R.A. Brest. Flt.
Dordelin, Louis, Auguste (C.) F.	III. 69-70, Bravoure engages Concorde, w. in actn.; 78, Porto Ferrajo.
Doré, Yves François (C.) F.	I. 60, Téméraire, Brest Flt.
Doudet,—(L.Com.)Du.	III. 194, Du. Wraak engages Princess Augusta (cutter).
Douglas, Andrew Snape (P.C.)	I. 100, Phaëton capts. Général Dumourier (priv.); 139, kntd. Queen Charlotte, Channel Flt.; 177, 270, w. 1st June; 277, Channel Flt.
,, Sir Andrew S.	
Douglas, Archibald (L.)	II. 111, Hermione, cutting out exped.
Douglas, Billy (P.C.)..	I. 333, Stately, Sq. at the Cape of Good Hope; 416, Simons Bay. IV. 425, V.A., Gambier's court-martial.
Douglas, Chas. (M.L.)	III. 78, Pomone, w. in actn.
Douglas, Cuthbert (B.)	I. 323, Dido, k. in actn.
Douglas, Hon. George (L.)	V. 6, Horatio, in actn. VI. 248-50-6, C. Levant captd. by U.S. Constitution; 391, App.
Douglas, Hood (B.) ...	V. 256, Cephalus, w. in actn.
Douglas, James (P.C.).	I. 297, Saturn, actn. off Hyères.
Douglas, James (Mr.)..	II. 374, Sibylle, in actn. IV. 365, Laurel, w. in actn.
Douglas, John (M.Maj.)	II. 324-9, Tigre at Acre; 342-6, Alexandria.
Douglas, John (L.) ...	II. 67, w. at Santa Cruz.
Douglas, John B. (S.)	III. 249, Eclair, cutting out exped.
Douglas, John Erskine (P.C.)	IV. 89, Bellona, St. Helena; 116, Barbadoes; 247, Chesapeake Bay. VI. 2, 117, Prince of Wales, Medn. Flt.
Douglas, Joseph (M.L.)	IV. 33, Loire, cutting out exped.
Douglas, Joseph (Mid.)	VI. 36, Swiftsure, k. in actn.
Douglas, Peter John (L.)	IV. 127, Franchise, cutting out exped.; 129, pro. Cr.
Douglas, Stair (P.C.)..	IV. 396, Bellona, Basque Rds. actn.
Douglas, Wm. Henry (L.)	II. 80, Venerable, w. Camperdown. III. 324, C. Cracker, invas. flotilla.

INDEX TO NAVAL OFFICERS 81

Douville, — (C.) *F*. ...	I. 141, Impétueux, Brest Flt.
Dover, James (Mid.)...	V. 220, Naiad, w. in actn.
Dowers, Wm. (L.Com.)	IV. 467, Subtle, wrkd. Bermuda ; 380, Express, crsg. V. 50, Ringdove, crsg. Basse Terre.
Down, Edwd. Augustus (Mr. Mt.)	II. 49, Excellent, w. St. Vincent. V. 9, C. Redwing, crsg. Adriatic.
Downes, John (L.Com.) *U.S.*	VI. 150–3, U.S. Essex Junior captd. by Phœbe.
Downey, George (Mr.)	V. 220, Redbreast, cutting out exped.
Downie, George (L.)...	IV. 31, Seahorse, cutting out exped. ; 352, capture of Turk. Badere Zaffer ; 354, pro. Cr. VI. 213–15, C. Confiance, Lake Champlain.
Downman, Hugh (C.).	II. 226, Speedy engages Papillon (priv.) ; 432, Santa Dorotea, blockade of Savona. IV. 186–9, Diadem, Cape of Good Hope exped.
Downs, Peter (Mid.)...	II. 262, Leander, k. in actn.
Draper, John (L.)	I. 200, Royal George, 1st June, pro. Cr. IV. 200, C. Ruby, Copenhagen ; 238, blockade of the Tagus.
Draveman, George Henri (L.Com.) *F*.	I. 364, Revanche captd. by Suffisante.
Drew, James (C.)	II. 469, Braak, fndrd. in the Delaware, drnd.
Drew, John (P.C.)......	I. 126, Trusty, Barbadoes. II. 102, Cerberus capts. Renard and Epervier (priv.).
Drew, Nicholas (C.Ck.)	IV. 300, Implacable, w. in actn.
Droop, — (C.) *Du*. ...	II. 343, Du. Galathéa, blockaded in the Texel.
Drummond, Adam (C.)	II. 320, Bulldog (bomb.), Alexandria. IV. 3, Dryad, crsg. Ferrol.
Drummond, Peter (Mid.)	VI. 234, w. cutting out exped.
Drury, Augustus Vere (L.Com.)	V. 130, Sylvia capts. prows. ; 131, pro. Cr.
Drury, Edward O'Brien (L.)	IV. 263–4, Hydra, cutting out exped. pro. Cr.
Drury, Henry (P.C.)...	V. 303, Akbar, capture of Java exped.
Drury, John (M.L.) ...	V. 288, Astrea, in actn.
Drury, Joseph (C.) ...	V. 303, Samarang, capture of Java exped. VI. 266, Volage, crsg. E. Indies.
Drury, Wm. O'Brien (P.C.)	II. 75, Powerful, Camperdown ; 292, Medn. V. 141, V.A. ; 191–5, Cape of Good Hope ; 295, d.
Dubedat, — (C.) *F*. ...	I. 101–2, Citoyenne Française engages Iris, k. in actn.
Dubourdieu, Bernard (C.) *F*.	V. 10, Pénélope, Toulon ; 122, Cmde. Favorite, Sq in the Adriatic ; 125, Port Ancona ; 233–5, actn. off Lissa ; 240, k. in actn.
Dubourg, Michael Augustin (C.) *F*.	V. 213, Pluvier captd. off the Gironde.
Duchesne, — (C.) *F*....	II. 105, Espiègle (priv.) capts. Growler.
Duckworth, John Thos. (P.C.)	I. 139, Orion, Channel Flt. ; 200, 1st June ; 412 Leviathan, W. Indies. II. 219–22, Cmde. capture of Minorca ; 291–3, R.A. Palermo. III. 12, Medn. ; 150, W. Indies, capture of Swd. and Da. isles. III. 290, Jamaica.
,, Sir J. T., K.G.	IV. 90, V.A., made K.G. ; 95–9, 101–8, Sq. actn. with Leissegues ; 216–7, Dardanelles ; 223, 233, Alexandria ; 348, 395, Sq. crsg. ; 425, Gambier's court-martial ; 459–63, App.
Duclos, Chas. Jac. César Chaunay (Cmde.) *F*.	IV. 142, Bergere, crsg.; 444, Ulm, Toulon Flt. VI. 3, Toulon.
Dudgeon, Wm. (Mid.)	III. 105, Hannibal, w. Algesiras.
Dufay, — (C.) *F*.	II. 5, Cassard, Ireland exped.
Duff, Alex. (Mr. Mt.)...	III. 410, Mars, k. Trafalgar.
Duff, Archibald (C.) ...	IV. 473, Muros, wrkd. Bay of Honda, Cuba.
Duff, George (P.C.) ...	II. 416–18, Glenmore recapts. Calcutta. III. 375, Mars off Cadiz ; 384–9, k. Trafalgar.
Duff, Norwich (Mid.)...	V. 256, Active, cutting out exped.
Duffell, John (Mid.) ...	VI. 288, Glasgow, w. Algiers.

G

Duffill, John (Mr.Mt.)	VI. 309–10, Larne, Burmese War ; 348, App.
Duffy, Peter (B.)	IV. 177, Monarch, w. in actn.
Dufossey, — (C.) *F.* ...	II. 5, Séduisant, Ireland exped.
Dufoy, — (Cmde.)*F.*...	II. 286, Zélé, Brest Flt.
Duke, William (L.) ...	IV. 184, Success, k. in actn.
Dukkert, — (L.Com.) *Du.*	V. 194, Du. San Pan captd. by Br. Sq.
Dumaresk, Philip (Mid.)	VI. 373, k. Navarino.
Dumaresq, Peter (P.C.)	IV. 298, Victory, Baltic Flt.
Dumaresq, Philip (L.)	III. 116, Cæsar, in actn., pro. Cr.; 172, C. Charwell, invas. flotilla.
Dumourier, — (C.) *F.*	I. 141, Trajan, Rochefort Sq.
Dun, Michael (Mr.) ...	II. 81, Ardent, k. Camperdown.
Dunbar, William (Mr.)	VI. 5, Blazer, cutting out exped.
Duncan, Adam (V.A.) ,, Lord	I. 307, Venerable, Sq. off the Texel ; 342–63–72, A. off the Texel. II. 72–8, Camperdown, created Baron ; 223, North Sea Flt. ; 345, Kent, Holland exped. ; 460, App.
Duncan, Andrew (L.)...	V. 366, Alert, in actn.
Duncan, Andrew (L.-Com.)	V. 442, Saloman (cutter), wrkd. in the Baltic.
Duncan, Crawfurd (P.C.)	III. 112, Por. Carlotta, actn. in the Gut of Gibraltar.
Duncan, Gilbert (C.Ck.)	V. 105, Quebec, cutting out exped.
Duncan, Henry (C.) ...	III. 485, Scout, fndrd. off Newfoundland, drnd.
Duncan, Hon. Henry (C.)	IV. 268, 289–345, Porcupine, crsg. V. 28, Mercury, Sq. crsg.; 37, off Istria ; 258, Impérieuse, Gulf of Salerno ; 344, Languelia. VI. 34, Sq. in the Adriatic.
Duncan, Jas. (L.Com.)	IV. 434, Idas (cutter), Scheldt exped.
Duncan, Robert (Mr.)	V. 209, Téméraire, w. in actn.
Duncan, — (C.)	II. 211, Por. Falcao (brig), Sq. crsg.
Dundas, George (P.C.)	III. 186, Elephant, Sq. off Brest. IV. 109, Fort Royal Bay.
Dundas, Hon. Geo. H. L. (L.)	II. 429–30, loss of Queen Charlotte. III. 97–8, C. Calpé ; 104–12, actn. Gut of Gibraltar. IV. 367, Euryalus, crsg. ; 438, Scheldt exped. V. 81, Medn. VI. 34, Edinburgh, Port D'Anzo.
Dundas, Thomas (P.C.)	III. 374, Naiad crsg. ; 384, Trafalgar. IV. 393, Sq. off Brest.
Dunderdale, Jas. (Mid.)	IV. 448, Apollo, cutting out exped.
Dunford, George (M.L.)	III. 105, Hannibal, w. Algesiras.
Dunlap, Robert (A.B.)	II. 108, loss of Tribune.
Dunlop, Robert Graham (Mr.Mt.)	V. 304, w. capture of Java. VI. 16, L., w. St. Sebastian ; 121, Porcupine, cutting out exped. ; 259, Leander, in actn.
Dunlop, Robert Walter (L.)	III. 57, Alcmène, Copenhagen.
Dunn, David (L.)	V. 239, Amphion, w. in actn. off Lissa, pro. Cr. VI. 33, C. Mermaid, crsg. Adriatic.
Dunn, James (L.)	IV. 448, Topaze, cutting out exped.
Dunn, James (Pr.)......	V. 118, Spartan, in actn.
Dunn, John (C.Ck.) ...	VI. 60–6, Shannon, k. in actn. with Chesapeake.
Dunn, Pasco (L.)	IV. 448, Tuscan, cutting out exped. Rosas Bay.
Dunn, Richard Dalling (C.)	III. 71, Incendiary (F.S.) captd. by F. Sq. ; 291–3, Hercule, Curaçoa ; 482, App. IV. 91, Acasta, Sq. crsg. ; 102, Duckworth's actn. ; 216, Royal George ; 425, Gambier's court-martial. V. 101, Armide, Basque Rds.
Duodo, — (C.) *F.*	V. 240, Bellona, w. in actn. off Lissa.
Dupan, — (C.) *F.*	III. 27, Guêpe (priv.) captd. by Renown.
Duperré, Victor Guy (C.) *F.*	V. 53, Bellone ; 65, capts. Victor ; 66, capts. Por. Minerva ; 131–2, crsg. ; 134, capts. E.I.C. ships ; 135–7, Isle of France ; 151–7, Grand Port ; 159–65, w. in actn. with Br. Sq. ; 315, R.A. Toulon ; 316, Mont St. Bernardo, Venice.
Duplantos, — (Mid.)*F.*	IV. 145, Canonnière, w. in actn.
Duplanty, Louis A. Defredot (L.) *F.*	V. 289, Rénommée, w. in actn.
Dupotet, Jean Henri Joseph (C) *F.*	V. 13–15, Niemen captd. by Amethyst.

Duranteau, Romain (C.) F.	IV. 444, Majestueux, Toulon Flt.
Durban, J. G. (L.) ...	VI. 374, w. Navarino.
Durban, Wm. (P.C.)...	III. 339, Ambuscade, off St. Pietro.
Durell, James (Mid.)	IV. 320, Tartarus, cutting out exped.
Durham, Philip Charles (P.C.)	I. 355–6, 381, Anson, Warren's Sq. II. 106, capts. Daphne; 140–2, crsg.; 147–8–58, capts. Loire; 228, Sq. crsg.; 269, capts. Flore. III. 10, crsg.; 357, Defiance, Calder's actn.; 384, 440–1, w. Trafalgar. IV. 445, Renown, Sq. crsq.;
,, Sir Philip C., K.C.B.	VI. 122, R.A. Venerable; 229, Leeward Isles; made K.C.B.
Dutaillis, André (L.) F.	III. 223, Ville D'Anvers (prame), invas. flotilla.
Dutoya, Morce André, (L.Com.) F.	III. 179, Affronteur captd. by Doris, k. in actn.
Dutton, Richard (L.)...	II. 227, Speedy, k. in actn.
Dutton, Thos. (L.Com.)	III. 494, Demerara captd. by Grand Décidé (priv.).
Duval, Thomas (L.) ...	II. 206, Zealous, the Nile. III. 485, C. Fly, fndrd. off Newfoundland, drnd.
Dwyer, Michl. (Mr.Mt.)	V. 255, Unité, cutting out exped.; 347, L. Minstrel, crsg.
Dyason, Joseph (Mr.)	IV. 374, Maria, in actn.
Dyer, Henry S. (Mid.)	VI. 374, w. Navarino.
Dyer, John Widdicomb (Mid.)	V. 318, Rosario, w. in actn., pro. L. VI. 391, C. Elizabeth, fndrd., drnd.
Dyer, Robert Turtliff (M.L.)	VI. 19, capture of Ponza exped.
Eagar, John (L.)	V. 342, Undaunted, cutting out exped.
Eales, John (Mid.) ...	I. 87, Toulon.
Earle, —(Cmde.) Canadian	VI. 102, Canadian Lakes.
Earnshaw, William (L.)	II. 67, Leander, k. Santa Cruz.
Eastman, Jas. Edw.(L.)	IV. 198, Sally, w. in actn.
Eastman, John (Mid.)	III. 426, Téméraire, w. Trafalgar.
Edevearn, John (Gunner)	V. 72, Pompée, w. in action.
Edfall, Samuel (Mid.)	I. 108, Nymphe, k. in actn.
Edgar, John (Mid.) ...	II. 62, Minerve, w. cutting out exped.
Edgcumbe, John (P.C.)	V. 204, Psyché, capture of the Isle of France; 303, capture of Java exped.
Edge, William (C.) ...	I. 87, Toulon; 271, Prince George, Channel Fleet.
Edgell, Henry Folkes (P.C.)	V. 204, Cornelia, capture of the Isle of France; 303, capture of Java exped.
Edmeades, William (C.) E.I.C.	IV. 189, E.I.C. William Pitt, Cape of Good Hope.
Edmonds, Joseph (L.-Com.)	II. 132, Asp, Ostende. IV. 186, C. Diomede, Sq. at the Cape of Good Hope.
Edmondson, Arthur (C.-Ck.)	VI. 190, k. in action at Baltimore.
Edmunds, Thomas (L.)	IV. 317, Childers, in action.
Edwards, John (L.) ...	I. 112, Boston, w. in action; 114, pro. Cr., d.
Edwards, John (C.) ...	III. 18, Wasp (F.S.), Dunkerque Rds.; 477, destd.
Edwards, Sampson (P.C.)	II. 285, St. George, Medn. Flt.; 297, Channel Flt.
Edwards, Thomas (B.)	IV. 9, Santa Margarita, k. in actn.
Edwards, V. (P.C.) ...	II. 474, Sceptre, wrkd. in Table Bay.
Edwick, John (Pr.) E.I.C.	IV. 152, E.I.C. Warren Hastings, k. in actn.
Eilbracht, — (C.) Du.	II. 343, Du. Beschermer, Sq. captd. in the Texel.
Ekins, Charles (P.C.)	IV. 201–3, Defence, Copenhagen; 238, Sq. off the Tagus. VI. 278, Superb. 287, w. Algiers; 291, made C.B.
Elder, James (Mr.) ...	I. 404, Terpsichore, in actn.
Ellerton, James (Mr.)	IV. 321, Falcon, cutting out exped.

Ellery, William (Mid.)	VI. 108, Wolfe, k. in actn.
Ellicot, Edward (C.)...	IV. 466, Explosion (bomb.), wrkd. on Lundy Isle.
Ellicott, Edward (C.)	IV. 205, Hebe, Copenhagen.
Elliot, Hon. George (P.C.)	III. 275, Maidstone, crsg. IV. 366, Modeste capts. Jéna. V. 302-3, capture of Java exped.
Elliot, Henry (M.L.)...	V. 304, w. capture of Java exped.
Elliot, Jesse D.(L.)*U.S.*	VI. 103, Canadian Lakes.
Elliot, J. (Mr.Mt.) ...	I. 175, Phaëton, w. 1st June.
Elliot, Robert (C.) ...	IV. 217, Lucifer (bomb.), Dardanelles.
Elliot, — (C.)	VI. 120, Martial, Adriatic.
Elliott, Geo. (L.Com.)	IV. 475, Widgeon, wrkd. Scotland.
Elliott, John (Pr.)......	V. 13, Arethusa, crsg. N. Spain.
Elliott, Thomas (Mid.)	IV. 320, Daphne, cutting out exped.
Elliott, William (L.)...	IV. 320-1, Daphne, w. cutting out exped. V. 45-6, C. Pultusk, cutting out exped.
Ellis, George (Ck.)......	III. 224, Cruiser, w. in action.
Ellis, John (L.)	III. 443, Royal Sovereign, Trafalgar ; 464, pro. Cr. VI. 70, C. Spitfire, crsg. North Sea.
Ellis, Samuel Burdon (M.L.)	VI. 19, capture of Ponza exped.
Ellison, Joseph (P.C.)	I. 271-80, Standard, Quiberon exped.
Ellison, Thos. (Mr.Mt.)	II. 196, Bellerophon, k. the Nile.
Elliston, Joseph (P.C.)	I. 230, Druid, Saumarez's Sq., actn. with F. Sq. off Jersey.
Elmhurst, Philip J. (Mid.)	III. 432, Africa, w. Trafalgar.
Elphinstone, Chas. (L.)	II. 241, Sibylle, at Manilla.
Elphinstone, Hon. Charles (C.)	II. 462, Tartar, wrkd. at St. Domingo. III. 357, Egyptienne, Calder's actn.
Elphinstone, Edward (P.C.)	IV. 162-4, Greyhound capts Du. Pallas.
Elphinstone, Hon. Geo. Keith (P.C.) ,, Sir George Keith, K.B.	I. 40, 72, Robust, Medn. Flt.; 76-9, 88, Gvr. of Fort Lamalgue, Toulon ; 333, V.A. K.B. Monarch ; 416-7, capture of Du. Sq. II. 287-9, Barfleur, Com. Flt. off Cadiz ; 291-5, Medn. ; 300, 342, Gibraltar ; 386, 419, Queen Charlotte ; 429, loss of Queen Charlotte ; 432-5, Minotaur ; 436, capture of Genoa ; 438-9, blockade of Malta ; 447-8, El Arich Treaty ; 451-2, Cadiz exped. III. 34, 72-6, Com. Medn. Flt.; 81, A. Foudroyant, Com. Egypt exped. ; 94, created Peer ; 218-20, Com. Downs station ; 232, Boulogne invas. flotilla ; 476, App. V. 320, Com. Channel Flt.
Elphinstone, John (P.C.)	I. 139, Glory, Channel Flt.; 162-85-200, 1st June; 333, capture of the Cape of Good Hope ; 416-7, Simon's Bay. II. 289, Hector, Flt. off Cadiz. III. 73, Medn.
Elphinstone, Thos. (C.)	I. 343, Speedy, crsg. off Oneglia. II. 469, Hamadryad, wrkd. on coast of Portugal. VI. 133, gun trials of Eurotas.
Elton, Henry (L.)	V. 103, Dreadnought, w. cutting out exped.
Elvey, George (Mid.)	V. 42, w. cutting out exped.
Elwin, John (L.)	VI. 264, Penguin, w. in actn.
Emeriau, Maurice Julian (C.) *F.* ,, The Comte ...	II. 178, Spartiate; 188, w. the Nile. V. 207, V.A.; 208-11, 315, Toulon Flt. VI. 1, Toulon Flt.
Emeric, Jean Léon (L.) *F.*	V. 8, Junon, in actn. VI. 122, C. Iphigénie, captd. by Venerable and consort off Madeira.
Emmerton, Jas. (Mr.Mt.)	III. 54, Bellona, w. Copenhagen.
Emparran, Don J.(C.)*Sp.*	III. 112, Sp. Hermenegildo destd. by Br. Sq. in the Straits of Gibraltar.
England, Robert (L.)	II. 81, Belliqueux, w. Camperdown ; 88, pro. Cr.
England, Thomas (L.)	II. 330, Theseus, at Acre. V. 325, L.Com. Flamer off Norway ; 448, C. Safeguard, captd. by the Danes in the Baltic.
Ennis, Edward Michael (M.C.)	VI. 18, Repulse, cutting out exped.
Enslie, James (Mid.) ..	V. 380, Guerrière, w. in actn.

INDEX TO NAVAL OFFICERS 85

Epron, Jaques (C.) *F.* — III. 4–7, Pallas captd. by Loire; 386, 415, Argonaute, Trafalgar. IV. 12, 150–2, Piémontaise capts. E.I.C. Warren Hastings; 154, Isle of France; 309, captd. by San Fiorenzo.
Epworth, Farmery Predam (P.C.) — V. 314, Nijaden, crsg.; 394, Nymphe, crsg. VI. 198, Boston; 200, Bulwark, Penobscot exped.
Errara, Don D. (C.) *Sp.* — II. 254, Sp. Santa Cazilda, Sq. crsg.
Erving, John (A.B.) ... — V. 363, ill-treatment of, by the U.S.
Escano, Don Antonio (R.A.) *Sp.* — III. 342, Sp. Argonauta, Toulon Flt.; 386, 437, Principe de Asturias, Trafalgar.
Esch, Van (C.) *Du.* ... — II. 389, Du. Draak captd. by Arrow and Wolverine.
Escoffier, — (C.) *F.* — III. 267, Espérance (priv.) capts. Swift.
Esquerra, Don J. (C.) *Sp.* — III. 112–13, Sp. Real Carlos, actn. in the Gut of Gibraltar.
Essington, Wm. (P.C.) — I. 416, Sceptre, Sq. at Simon's Bay. II. 75, Triumph; 81, w. Camperdown. IV. 201–4–9, Minotaur, Copenhagen.
Esther, Thos. (act. Mr.) — IV. 167, Phosphorus (F.S.), w. in actn.
Etienne, François Pierre (C.) *F.* — I. 141, Northumberland, Brest Flt.
Etienne, Jean Pierre (C.) *F.* — II. 178, Heureux; 190–3, the Nile.
Etough, Henry Gladwell (act. Mr.) — VI. 66, Shannon, in actn. pro. L.; 234, w. cutting out exped.
Evans, Andrew Fitzherbert (L.) — I. 225, Concorde, in actn.; 363, C. Spencer, capts. F. Volcan. III. 186, Æolus, Loring's Sq. Cape François.
Evans, Henry (C.) — II. 112, Fury, W. Indies.
Evans, Saml. (C.) *U.S.* — VI. 50, U.S. Chesapeake; 52–63, captd. by Shannon.
Evans, — (Mid.) ...... — I. 356, Galatea, k. in actn.
Eveleigh, John (Mid.) — IV. 135, Pique, cutting out exped.
Eveleigh, John (P.C.) — VI. 124–5, Astrea engages Etoile; 126, k. in actn.
Evelyn, Wm. (L. Com.) — V. 442, Pelter, fndrd. off Halifax, drnd.
Everard, Thomas (C.) — V. 451, Ephera (F.S.), wrkd. near Cadiz. VI. 115, Canadian Lakes.
Everingham, Jas. (Mid.) — VI. 236, w. cutting out exped.
Evertz, Cornelius J. (C.) *Du.* — IV. 277, Du. Halstaar; 278, k. at the capture of Curaçoa.
Eves, Francis W. (Mid.) — III. 6, Loire, w. in actn.
Exmouth, Viscount, G.C.B. (A.) — *See* Edward Pellew.
Eyles, Joseph (L.) ...... — I. 200, Ramillies, 1st June, pro. Cr.
Eyles, Thomas (P.C.) — II. 119, Pomone; 450, Renown, Sq. off Spain. III. 15, Warren's Sq. crsg.
Eyre, George (C.) ...... — I. 439, Speedy captd. by F. Sq. off Nice. II. 253, Regulus, crsg. Porto Rico. V. 80, Magnificent, Isle St. Maura exped.; 208, Flt. off Toulon; 240, Adriatic.

Facey, Philip (L.) ...... — II. 380, Success, cutting out exped., pro. Cr.
Faddy, William (M.C.) — II. 196, Vanguard, k. the Nile.
Faddy, William (L.) — IV. 131, London, w. in actn.
Fahie, William Charles (C.) — II. 272, Perdrix capts. Armée-d'Italie (priv.). V. 18–19, Pompée capts. D'Haupoult; 21, w. in actn.; 69–70, Belleisle, capture of Martinique exped.; 190, Cmde. Abercrombie, Sq. at Guadaloupe.
Fair, Robert (Mr.) ...... — IV. 380, Amethyst, in actn.
Fairfax, Edward (Mr.) — IV. 403–6, Caledonia, Basque Rds. actn.
Fairfax, William George (P.C.) — II. 75–9, Venerable, Camperdown; 88, kntd.; 301, Venerable, Sq. blockading Basque Rds.
Falcon, Gordon Thos. (L.) — IV. 252, Leopard, in actn. VI. 248, C. Cyane; 249–56, captd. by U.S. Constitution; 391, App.
Falkiner Charles Leslie (L.) — VI. 58, Shannon capts. Chesapeake; 66, pro. Cr.
Falkland, Lord (P.C.) — IV. 213, Quebec, off Heligoland.
Fama, Clemento (C.) *Sicilian* — V. 244, Sicilian priv. captd. by Ven. schooner.

Fancourt, Robert Devereux (P.C.)	III. 46–50, Agamemnon, Copenhagen.
Fane, Francis William (Mid.)	II. 216, Emerald, Alexandria. IV. 345, C. Hind, crsg. off Spain. V. 129, Cambrian; 139, at Palamos.
Fanshawe, Henry (C.)	V. 232, Grasshopper captd. by the Du. off Texel Isle.
Fanshawe, Robert (C.)	III. 261–4, Carysfort, Barbadoes.
Farewell, Francis George (1st cl. Vol.)	V. 37, Amphion, cutting out exped.; 239, Mid., w. in actn.; VI. 23, Bacchante, cutting out exped.
Fargenel, Jean Mathieu (L.Com.) *F*.	IV. 239, F. Lynx; 240, cut out by the bts. of Galatea; 241 w. in actn.
Fargue, La (C.) *F*. ...	II. 5, Patriote, Ireland exped.
Farmer, Thos. (C.Ck.)	V. 327, Dictator, w. in actn.
Farquhar, Arthur (C.)	IV. 13, Acheron (bomb.) captd. by F. Hortense; 456, fndrd., drnd.
Farquhar, Arthur (P.C.)	VI. 6, Desirée, capture of Gluckstadt exped.
Farquharson, James (C.) *E.I.C.*	III. 250–2, E.I.C. Alfred, actn. with Linois' F. Sq. E. Indies
Farrand,— (C.) *F. Royalist*.	I. 92, Puissant, Toulon.
Farrant, John (Mid.)...	III. 406, Royal Sovereign, w. Trafalgar. V. 30, L. Scout, cutting out exped.
Farrenden, Geo. (Mid.)	V. 120, Cerberus, crsg. Gulf of Trieste.
Farrer, William Wood (C.) *E.I.C.*	III. 250; E.I.C. Cumberland, actn. with Linois' F. Sq. E. Indies. IV. 51–2, actn. with F. frigates.
Faulknor, Jonathan (P.C.)	I. 103–4, Venus, actn. with Sémillante; 233, Diana, Warren's Sq. II. 297, Terrible, Channel Flt.; 474, Impregnable, wrkd. near Chichester.
Faulknor, Robert (C.)	I. 242–5–6, Zebra, capture of Martinique; 308, Blanche capts. Pique; 310, k. in actn.
Faure, Gilbert Amable (C.) *F*.	III. 68, Constitution, Brest. IV. 88, Cmde. Cassard, Sq. W. Indies; 395, Basque Rds. actn.
Faussett, Robert (L.)...	VI. 223, Plantagenet, cutting out exped.
Fauveau, Joseph (C.)*F*.	IV. 395, Jemmappes, Basque Rds. actn.
Fawcett, Henry (Mid.)	IV. 447, Tigre, cutting out exped. Rosas Bay.
Faye, Ant. Jean Baptiste (C.) *F*.	II. 286, Censeur, Brest Flt.
Fayerman, Francis (P.C.)	II. 75, Beaulieu, Camperdown. IV. 288, Formidable, Sq. Palermo Bay
Fearney, Wm. (Cox.)...	II. 46, Captain, St. Vincent.
Featherstone, Barry John (Mid.)	IV. 345, Porcupine, cutting out exped.
Fegan, Charles (M.L.)	V. 118, Spartan, in actn.
Fellowes, Edward (P.C.)	IV. 232, Apollo, Alexandria; 289, off Toulon. V. 81, Conqueror; 208, Flt. off Toulon.
Fellowes, Thomas (C.)	V. 442, Unique, destd. at Guadaloupe. VI. 365, Dartmouth; C.B.; 370–3, Navarino.
Fennel, John (M.L.) ..	IV. 170, Arethusa, w. in actn. V. 13, crsg. N. Spain.
Fennell, John (L.Com.)	III. 357, Nile (lugger), Calder's actn.
Fenning, Tristram (2nd Mt.) *E.I.C.*	V. 134, E.I.C. Ceylon, in actn.
Fenwick, Robert Bisset (Mr.Mt.)	V. 31, Topaze, cutting out exped.
Feretier, Jean Bap. Henri (L.Com.) *F*.	V. 54–6, F. Caroline engages E.I.C. ships; 57–62, pro. C.
Ferguson, John (C.) ...	V. 447, Pandora, wrkd. on Scaw reef, Cattegat.
Fergusson, William (B.)	V. 45, Hazard, w. in actn.
Fergusson, — (L.)......	III. 52, Elephant, Copenhagen.
Ferrett, Francis (L.) ...	II. 81, Veteran, k. Camperdown.
Ferrie, William (L.) ...	III. 409, Belleisle, w. Trafalgar. V. 4–8, C. Supérieure, engages Junon.
Ferrier, John (L.)	V. 35, Cyane, w. in actn.
Ferris, Abel (C.).........	IV. 338–42, Wizard engages Requin.

INDEX TO NAVAL OFFICERS 87

Ferris, John D. (Mr.)	VI. 232, Chandeleur Isles.
Ferris, Solomon (P.C.)	III. 98, Hannibal; 101-9, Algesiras; 182, Jamaica; 481, captd. by F. Sq.
Ferris, William (C) ...	III. 201, Drake, Martinique; 296, Isle of Surinam; 494, wrkd. off Isle of Nevis. IV. 383, Wizard, off Noli, Italy. V. 99, Nemesis, crsg. off Norway; 213, Diana, Basque Rds.; 313, watching Allemand's Sq.
Ferris, William (P.C.)	III. 255, Blenheim, crsg. off St. Pierre.
Ferror, William (Mid.)	VI. 288, Severn, w. Algiers.
Festing, Benjamin Morton (L.)	V. 351, Eagle, cutting out exped. off Cape Maistro, Ancona.
Festing, Robert Worgan George (P.C.)	V. 303-4, Illustrious, capture of Java.
Feteris, William (C.) *Du.*	IV. 163, Du. William, Sq. crsg.
Few, James Leonard (Mid.)	V. 349, Bacchante, cutting out exped. VI. 21, cutting out exped.
Few, James Leonard (Schoolmaster)	V. 120, Amphion, cutting out exped.
Ficerstroud,—(C.) *Swd.*	IV. 299, Swd. Tapperheten, Br. Swd. Flt. Oro Rds.
Field, Francis Ventris (L.)	I. 233, Romney, in actn. II. 456, C. Curlew, fndrd. in the North Sea, drnd.
Field, — (Mid.)	VI. 36, Swiftsure, w. in actn.
Fielding, Charles (C.)	III. 490, Circe, wrkd. in the North Sea.
Fife, Thomas (L.)	III. 443, Belleisle, Trafalgar; 464, pro. Cr.
Figg, William (Mid.)	III. 54, Bellona, w. Copenhagen. VI. 7, L.Com. Pickle, crsg. off the Lizard.
Finch, Chas. (L.Com.)	V. 51, Elizabeth, Basse Terre.
Finch, Thos. (Mr.Mt.)	II. 253-4, Regulus, k. cutting out exped.
Finch, Wm. (L.Com.)	VI. 212, Finch (cutter), Lake Champlain.
Finchley, John (Mid.)	III. 84, w. in actn. Egypt.
Finlay, Edward (Mid.)	V. 248, Belle Poule, Parenza.
Finlay, Moyle (Mid.)	II. 80, Monarch, k. Camperdown.
Finlayson, James (Mr.)	IV. 19, San Fiorenzo, w. in actn.
Finlayson, John (Mid.)	IV. 263, Hydra, cutting out exped.
Finmore, Wm. (M.L.)	IV. 221-30, Standard, w. Dardanelles.
Finn, George (Mr.) ...	II. 427, Repulse, wrkd., dismissed.
Finnimore, Thomas (L.)	V. 42, Prometheus, cutting out exped.
Finnis, Robert (Mid.)	III. 140, w. cutting out exped. VI. 112-13, C. Queen Charlotte (schooner), k. in actn. Canadian Lakes.
Finucane, Henry (Mid.)	VI. 186, Menelaus, Chesapeake Bay.
Finucane, Patrick (L.)	V. 266, Sabine, cutting out exped.
Fiott, Wm. Edwd. (L.)	VI. 259, Leander and U.S. frigates.
Fischer, Olfert (Cmde.) *Da.*	III. 49, Da. Dannebrog; 57-8, Copenhagen.
Fisher, Henry (Mr.Mt.)	VI. 35, Revenge, cutting out exped.
Fitton, Michael (act.L.)	II. 398, Ferret (schooner), actn. with Sp. priv. III. 38, L.Com. Active (schooner), off Amsterdam; 39, engages F. privs.; 121, Port Royal; 122-3, capts. Sp. Santa Maria; 290, Gipsy; 291, Curaçoa; 296, pro. L. IV. 13, engages privs.; 181-4; Pitt capts. F. Superbe (priv.).
Fitzburgh, Henry (Mid.)	IV. 324, Tartar, k. in actn.
Fitzgerald, Lord Charles (P.C.)	I. 262, Brunswick, Sq. crsg. off Ushant.
Fitzgerald, Robert Lewis (C.)	II. 133, Vesuvius (bomb.), off Havre.
Fitzgerald, Thos. (Mid.)	I. 175, Marlborough, w. 1st June V. 42, L.Com. Monkey, engages Da. luggers; 448, wrkd. Belleisle, France.
Fitzgibbon, Philip (L.)	V. 187, Ceylon, in actn.
Fitzgibbon, — (Mid.)	I. 308, Blanche, k. in actn.
Fitzmaurice, Geo. (L.)	IV. 158, Conqueror, cutting out. exped.
Fitzmaurice, James (L.)	IV. 331, Carnation, w. in actn.
Fitzpatrick, John (B.)	I. 175, Defence, k. 1st June.

Fitzroy, G. W. H. (L.)	VI. 369-74, Dartmouth, k. Navarino.
Fitzroy, Lord William (P.C.)	IV. 3-9, Æolus, Strachan's actn. ; 54-9, engages Didon ; 451-2, App. V. 71, capture of Martinique.
Flaxman, James (B.)...	V. 251-2, Alacrity, w. in actn.
Fleeming, Hon. Charles Elphinstone (P.C.)	IV. 76-7, Egyptienne capts. Libre.
Fleming, John (Mr. Mt.)	III. 16, Renown, cutting out exped.
Fleming, John (L.) ...	IV. 127-9, Franchise, cutting out exped.
Fleming, Richard Howell (L.)	VI. 280-6, Queen Charlotte, Algiers ; 291, pro. Cr.
Fletcher, Thomas (Mr.)	III. 35, Milbrook, w. in actn.
Fletcher, William (L.)	V. 323, Northumberland, w. in actn.
Flight, Frederick Hill (M.Maj.)	I. 301, Victory, w. in actn.
Flinn, Edward (L.)...	V. 45, Pelorus, w. in actn.
Flint, William Richard (M.L.)	VI. 84, w. in actn. Chesapeake Bay.
Flintoft, Wm. (act.L.)	IV. 405, Cæsar, w. in actn.
Flores, Don Luis de (C.) *Sp.*	III. 386, Sp. St. Francisco-de-Asis ; 433-4, Trafalgar.
Fogo, — (Mid.).........	I. 176, Barfleur, w. 1st June.
Foley, Thomas (P.C.)	I. 72, St. George, Flt. off Toulon ; 100, Medn. Sq. ; 214, Flt at Corsica ; 284, Medn. ; 297, actn. off Hyères. II. 34, Britannia ; 47-8, St. Vincent ; 60, Goliath ; 171, Flt. off Cadiz ; 184, the Nile ; 216, cutting out exped. III. 46, Elephant, 50-4, Copenhagen.
Folkes, William David (Mid.)	VI. 27, Apollo, capture of Isle Augusta, Adriatic.
Foord, Henry (M.L.)	VI. 136, Eurotas, w. in actn.
Foote, Charles (C.) ...	V. 195, Barracouta ; 202, capture of Banda Neira.
Foote, Edward James (P.C.)	I. 318, Niger, crsg. off France ; 362, crsg. II. 34, St. Vincent ; 56-180, Seahorse, the Nile ; 234-6, capts. Sensible ; 307-14, Bay of Naples. VI. 114, R.A. Barclay's court-martial.
Forbes, Charles (Mid.)	IV. 137, Renommée, w. cutting out exped.
Forbes, James Morrison Biggs (Mid.)	II. 324-30, Theseus, k. at Acre.
Forbes, John (L)	IV. 229, Royal George, w. Dardanelles.
Forbes, Robt. (L.Com.)	III. 37, Lurcher (cutter), crsg. off Morbihan.
Forbes, Hon. Robert (P.C.)	I. 139, Southampton, Channel Flt.
Forbishly, James (Mid.)	II. 81, Montague, w. Camperdown.
Ford, Geo. Arnold (L.)	II. 122, Mars, w. in action.
Ford, John (Cmde.) ...	I. 128, Europa, Jamaica ; 129-30, Cape Nicolas Mole ; 250-1, St. Domingo.
Ford, Zebedee (Mid.)	II. 196, Majestic, k. the Nile.
Forder, George (Mid.)	IV. 264, Confiance, cutting out exped. V. 74, capture of Cayenne.
Forder, Robert (L.) ...	V. 174-77, Africaine, w. in actn.
Foreman, John (L.) ...	VI. 288-91, Infernal (bomb.), w. Algiers, pro. Cr.
Foreman, Walter (L.)...	IV. 269, Herald, cutting out exped.
Foretier, Martin Le (Cmde.) *F.*	V. 319, Arienne destd. by Northumberland.
Forrest, Thomas (L.)...	III. 256, 'Fort Diamond,' in actn. Martinique. V. 40, C. Prometheus, crsg. Baltic ; 41-2, cutting out exped., w., pro. P.C. VI. 122, Cyane engages F. frigates.
Forster, Edwd. R. (Mid.)	VI. 374, w. Navarino.
Forster, Gawen (L.) ...	V. 42, Prometheus, cutting out exped.
Forster, Geo. Wm. (B.)	III. 104, Cæsar, w. Algesiras.
Forster, John (L.)	IV. 447-9, Apollo, w. cutting out exped.
Forster, Matthew (C.)	III. 322, Calypso, actn. off Boulogne.
Forster, Thomas (Mr.)	II. 196, Minotaur, w. the Nile.
Forster, William (L.)...	III. 416, Colossus, w. Trafalgar.

INDEX TO NAVAL OFFICERS 89

Forster, William (B.)...	III. 441, Defiance, k. Trafalgar.
Forteguerri, — (A.) Neap.	I. 79–80, Neap. Guiscardo at Toulon.
Forvell, Saml. (L.Com.)	III. 482, Requin, wrkd. near Quiberon, France.
Foster, James (Mid.)...	VI. 113, Queen Charlotte (sloop), w. Canadian Lakes.
Foster, James (Mid.)...	VI. 288, Severn, w. Algiers.
Fothergill, William (L.)	II. 390-2, Rattlesnake engages Preneuse. III. 208, C. Lancaster, E. Indies. IV. 279, capture of Monte Video.
Fotheringham, Thomas (Mr.)	IV. 126, Malabar, off Isle of Cuba.
Fottrell, Chris. (M.L.)	V. 118, Seahorse, in actn.
Foulerton, Thomas (L.)	III. 135, Kangaroo, w. cutting out exped.
Fourmentin, Denis (C.) F.	II. 105, Rusé (priv.) capts Growler; 352, engages Wolverine.
Fourré, Louis François Hector (L.Com.) F.	IV. 158, César cut out by the bts. of Indefatigable, w.
Fowke, George (P.C.)	III. 482, Prosélyte, wrkd. W. Indies.
Fowler, George (Mid.)	V. 120, Cerberus, cutting out exped.
Fowler, Rob. (L.Com.)	III. 250, passenger on board Earl Camden in actn. with Linois' Sq.; 490, Porpoise (S.S.), wrkd. Pacific Ocean.
Fowler, Thomas (Mid.)	V. 329, w. in actn.
Fradin, Jean Bap. Alexis (C.) F.	I. 356, Tamise, crsg.; 365-6, captd. by Santa Margarita. III. 176, Embuscade captd. by Victory.
Franc, Le (C.) F.	I. 141, Entreprenant, Brest Flt.
Francis, John (L.)......	IV. 158, Prince of Wales, cutting out exped.
Franklin, James (B.)...	V. 277, Little Belt, w. in actn.
Franklin, John (L.) ...	VI. 234, w. in actn. with U.S. gbts.
Franks, Charles Henry (Mid.)	V. 299, Minden, capture of Java.
Fraser, Alex. (P.C.) ...	IV. 143, Hindostan, convoy escort; 200, Vanguard, Copenhagen.
Fraser, George (Mid.)	VI. 35, Revenge, cutting out exped.
Fraser, Henry Tillieux (C.)	V. 93–5, Avon engages Néréide.
Fraser, John (M.L.)...	VI. 236, w. in actn. St. Mary's, U.S.
Fraser, John Went. (Mid.)	VI. 182, Euryalus, Alexandria.
Fraser, Percy (C.)	II. 287, Nymphe, off Ushant. 456, Narcissus, wrkd. near New Providence.
Fraser, Thomas (L.) ...	VI. 309–10; 347–51, Larne, Burmese War.
Frazer, George (M.L.)	II. 114, Regulus, St. Domingo.
Frazer, Simon (Mid.)..	III. 55, Isis, w. Copenhagen.
Frederick, Thomas Lennox (P.C.)	I. 72, Illustrious, Flt. off Toulon; 214, off Corsica; 284–94, actn. off Genoa; 443, wrkd. near Avenga. II. 34, Blenheim; 38–48, St. Vincent; 291, R.A. Edgar, Gibraltar.
Freeman, Edward (Mr.Mt.)	V. 52, Blonde, k. in actn.
Freemantle, Thomas Francis (P.C.)	I. 286, Inconstant engages Ça-Ira; 344, Leghorn Rds. II. 61, w. at Cadiz; 63, Seahorse; 65–7, w. Santa Cruz. III. 46–51–5, Ganges, Copenhagen; 384, Neptune; 401, 408–27, Trafalgar. V. 208, R.A. Rodney, Channel Flt. VI. 27, Adriatic; 30, Fiume; 119, Adriatic.
French, George (Mid.)	III. 171, Hydra, cutting out exped.
French, John Oliver (C.Ck.)	IV. 448, Apollo, cutting out exped.
Freycinet, — (L.) F. ..	IV. 135, Phaëton, w. in actn.
Friend, Chas. (Mr.Mt.)	V. 256, Active, cutting out exped.
Frost, — (Mid.).........	II. 255, w. cutting out exped.
Fuller, Rose Henry (L.)	VI. 36, Swiftsure, cutting out exped.
Fulton, Robert (Mr.)..	VI. 288, Glasgow, w. Algiers.
Funk, John Musser (L.) U.S.	V. 398, U.S. United States, k. in actn.

Furber, Thomas (L.)...	III. 201, 255, Blenheim, cutting out exped.
Furlonger, — (Mr.) ...	III. 276, Aigle, cutting out exped.
Furneaux, John (Mid.)	IV. 229, Royal George, w. Dardanelles.
Fyffe, John (C.).........	IV. 133, Reindeer, actn. with F. brigs.
Gabriel, James Wallace (L.)	IV. 259, Pomone, cutting out exped.
Gabriel, Vere (L.)......	V. 86, Cherokee, cutting out exped.
Gadobert, Benjamin (L.Com.) F.	III. 276, Joie, destd. by Aigle.
Gage, George Henry (P.C.)	III. 137, Uranie, off St. Mathieu, Brest.
Gage, Wm. Hall (L.)..	II. 62, Minerve, cutting out exped. VI. 117, C. Indus, Flt. off Toulon.
Gage, William Henry (P.C.)	IV. 348, Thetis, Constantinople.
Gage, — (P.C.)	II. 180, Terpsichore, Aboukir Bay.
Gahagan, Thos. (Mid.)	III. 55, Edgar, w. Copenhagen.
Gaillard, — (C.) F. ...	I. 103, Sémillante engages Venus; 430, App.
Galiano, Don Dionisio (C.) Sp.	III. 386, Sp. Bahama; 415–16, k. Trafalgar.
Gallaway, James (Mid.)	III. 55, Defiance, w. Copenhagen.
Galleano, Patrizio (C.) Sp.	II. 434, Sp. Prima (galley) at Genoa.
Galles, Morard de (V.A.) F.	I. 60–9, Terrible, Brest Flt.; 135–6, Belleisle Rds. II. 3–6, Brest Flt.; 124, Indomptable. III. 309, Brest; 495, App.
Galloway, Alex. (Mid.)	III. 440, Thunderer, w. Trafalgar.
Galvin, — (Mr.Mt.) ...	II. 107, loss of Tribune.
Galwey, Edward (L.)...	II. 197, Vanguard, the Nile; 210, pro. Cr. IV. 438, C. Dryad, Scheldt exped. VI. 135, capture of Clorinde.
Gambier, James (P.C.)	I. 65, Defence, Flt. off Scilly; 139, Channel Flt.; 155–63–74–5, 200, 1st June. IV. 200, A. Prince of Wales;
,, Lord James	203–9, Copenhagen; 210, created Peer; 286, Channel Flt.; 296–7, Baltic; 390, off Ushant; 395–6–8, 421, Caledonia, Basque Rds. actn.; 425–8, court-martialled; 464, App. V. 439, App.
Ganteaume, Honoré(C.) F.	I. 161–3, Trente-et-un Mai, 1st June; 295, Mont Blanc, Toulon; 305, Cmde., crsg. Medn.; 306, Toulon. II. 31, 127, Brest; 168, Malta exped.; 178, Orient; 179–91, 198–207, blows up at the Nile; 215, R.A.; 332–7, Alexandria. III. 68–75, Indivisible, Egypt exped.; 76, capture of Swiftsure; 77, Toulon; 164, St. Domingo; 170, 215, Brest; 216, 243, 308–14, Imperial, Brest; 348, Brest; 495, App. IV. 47, V.A. Brest Flt.; 286, Toulon; 289–93, Corfu; 443, Toulon; 444, A. Majestueux. V. 10, 80, Toulon.
Gape, Joseph (Mid.) ...	V. 37, 120, Amphion, cutting out expeds.
Gardner, Alan (R.A.)	I. 127–8, Queen, Martinique; 139, Channel Flt.; 150–5, 167,
,, Sir Alan ...	200, 1st June; 270, kntd., V.A. Channel Flt.; 274–7, actn. off Isle Groix. II. 28, Spithead mutiny; 297, A.; 301, Royal Sovereign; 426–7, Channel Flt. crsg. off Brest.
Gardner, Alan Hyde (P.C.)	I. 337, Heroine, E. Indies; 413, Colombo, Ceylon.
,, Hon. Alan Hyde	III. 357, Hero; 359–61, Calder's actn. IV. 3–13, Strachan's actn.; 89, Warren's Sq. crsg.; 439, R.A. Blake, Scheldt exped.
,, Lord (A.) ...	III. 307–10. IV. 47, Com. Channel Flt.
Gardner, Hon. Francis Fayerman (P.C.)	IV. 13, Princess Charlotte, Jamaica.
Gardner, Thomas (L.)	V. 214, Semiramis, cutting out exped.

INDEX TO NAVAL OFFICERS 91

Gardoqui, Don Josef (C.) *Sp.*	III. 386, Sp. Santa Ana ; 393-8-405, Trafalgar.
Garland, James (L.) ...	IV. 414, Revenge, w. Basque Rds.
Garland, John (Mr.) ...	V. 194, Cornwallis, cutting out exped.
Garland, John (L.) ...	VI. 112, Detroit, k. Canadian Lakes.
Garland, Joseph Gulston (L.Com.)	III. 235, Escort, actn. with invas. flotilla.
Garlies, John (P.C.) ...	I. 344, Lively, Leghorn Rds.
Garlies, Lord (P.C.) ...	I. 241-6, Quebec, w. capture of Martinique ; 306-13, Lively, San Fiorenzo Bay. II. 34, Channel Flt. ; 90, Sq. crsg.
Garratt, George (Pr.)...	V. 327, Podargus, w. in actn.
Garreau, Pierre Elie (C.) *F.*	IV. 88, Alexandre, Sq. crsg. W. Indies.
Garrett, Edward Wm. (L.)	III. 410, Mars, w. Trafalgar. V. 1, Onyx recapts. Manly ; 2, pro. Cr.
Garrett, Henry (L.-Com.)	II. 133-5, Trial (cutter) des. Confiante (ashore). IV. 288, C. Royal Sovereign, Palermo.
Garrett, Henry (Cox.)	IV. 270, Renommée, w. cutting out exped.
Garrett, William (L.)...	III. 17, Defence, cutting out exped.
Garrety, James Henry (L.Com.)	III. 317, Plumper captd. by F. brigs. IV. 457, App.
Garroway, — (C.) *U.S.*	V. 369, U.S. Dash (priv.) capts. Whiting.
Garson, Geo. (act.Mr.)	V. 31, Topaze, cutting out exped.
Garth, Thomas (P.C.)	IV. 440, Impérieuse, Scheldt exped. VI. 27, Cerberus, crsg. Corfu.
Garthwaite, Edward Hancock (M.L.)	IV. 129, Egyptienne, cutting out exped.
Gascoigne, William (Mr.Mt.)	V. 416, Java, k. in actn.
Gascoyne, John (C.) ...	II. 100, Pelican, St. Domingo.
Gaspard, Mayor M. Pierre (C.) *F.*	II. 384-5, Vestale captd. by Clyde.
Gaspard, — (C.) *F.* ...	V. 352-4, Améthyste (priv.) captd. by Southampton, w. in actn.
Gassin, — (C.) *F.*	I. 141, Jacobin, Brest Flt.
Gaston, Don Miguel (C.) *Sp.*	III. 386, Sp. San Justo ; 389, 407-37-39, Trafalgar.
Gateshill, Henry (Mr.-Mt.)	VI. 113, Lady Prevost (sloop), w. Canadian Lakes.
Gaudolphe,—(L.Com.) *F.*	IV. 307, F. gbt. captd. off the Tagus.
Gaultier, André Louis (C.) *F.*	IV. 444, Austerlitz, Toulon Flt.
Gautier, Jacques (L.-Com.) *F.*	IV. 342, Griffon captd. by Bacchante.
Gaymore, Philip (Mid.)	IV. 367, Euryalus, cutting out exped.
Geall, Ebenezer (L.)...	III. 409, Belleisle, k. Trafalgar.
Geary, John (Mid.) ...	IV. 177, Monarch, w. in actn.
Geddes, John (L.)......	VI. 100-1, Ramillies, k. in actn.
Geddes, Peter (B.)......	V. 109, Phipps, cutting out exped.
Gell, John (R.A.)	I. 71, St. George ; 72-9, Medn. Flt. ; 100, Sq. crsg. Medn.
Gell, John (Mid.)	II. 323, k. at Acre.
Gelston, William (C.) *E.I.C.*	V. 54-61, E.I.C. Europe engages F. frigates.
Geltins, Thomas (Mr.)	III. 15, Lark (lugger), cutting out exped.
Génetière, Thos. Jos. Lamoureux (C.) *F.*	V. 47, Papillon captd. by Rosamond.
George, John (Mid.)...	V. 240, Volage, k. in actn.
Gerrard,Mark A.(M.L.)	II. 160, Fisgard, w. in actn. III. 15-17, cutting out expeds.
Gerraro, Don M.(C.)*Sp.*	II. 254-5, Sp. Santa Dorotea captd. by Lion.
Gettings,—(Mid.)......	VI. 274, Tyne, cutting out exped.
Geyt, George Le (C.)	IV. 27, Stork, crsg. Porto Rico ; 171, Cuba ; 380-1, actn. off St. Pierre.

Ghega, Anthonio (L.-Com.) *Ven.*	IV. 268, Safo (sloop) captd. by Porcupine.
Gibbings, Richard (Mr.Mt.)	IV. 378, Amethyst, k. in actn.
Gibbons, Wm. (Mid.)	III. 104, Venerable, k. Algesiras.
Gibbons, William H. (Mr.Mt.)	V. 340, Victorious, w. in actn.
Gibbs, George (Mr.)...	II. 375, Telegraph, in actn.
Gibbs, John (L.)	I. 95, Lowestoffe, in actn.
Gibbs, J. Blower (L.Com.)	IV. 457, Redbridge, fndrd. near Jamaica, drnd., crew saved.
Gibbs, — (Mr.)	III. 38, Admiral Pasley, w. in actn.
Gibson, Andrew (B.)...	III. 409, Belleisle, w. Trafalgar.
Gibson, James (Mr.Mt.)	V. 232, Cerberus, cutting out exped.
Gibson, John (L.Com.)	II. 34, Fox, St. Vincent ; 60, Cadiz ; 63-5, k. Santa Cruz ; 462, App.
Gibson, Robert (L.) ...	IV. 240-2, Galatea, cutting out exped. V. 256, Active, cutting out exped.
Gibson, William (L.)...	II. 433, Vestal, siege of Genoa.
Gibson, — (Mid.)	II. 262, Leander, k. in actn.
Giffard, John (P.C.) ...	IV. 123, Athénien, Sq. at Palermo.
Gilbert, Edmund Williams (L.)	VI. 288, Glasgow, w. Algiers.
Gilbert, George (As.S.)	IV. 239, Impérieuse, cutting out exped. ; 385-414, w. Basque Rds.
Gilbert, Robert (M.L.)	V. 41, Melpomène, cutting out exped.
Gilbert, Thos. (L.Com.)	III. 18, Boxer, Sq. off Dunkerque.
Gill, Charles (P.C.) ...	IV. 439, St. Domingo, Scheldt exped. VI. 83, Chesapeake Bay.
Gill, Charles (C.)	V. 1, Onyx recapts Manly, pro. P.C.
Gill, Richard (L.)	IV. 101, Superb, Dardanelles ; 104, pro. Cr.
Gill, Robert (Mid.) ...	III. 55, Elephant, w. Copenhagen.
Gill, Thomas (Mr.Mt.)	III. 188, Racoon, w. in actn.
Gillet, Maurice (C.) *F.*	II. 178, Franklin ; 191-2, the Nile.
Gilliland, Brice (L) ...	III. 406, Royal Sovereign, k. Trafalgar.
Gilmore, Andrew (B.)	II. 196, Majestic, k. the Nile.
Gilmour, John (L.) ...	V. 201, Caroline, capture of Banda Neira.
Gilson, Thos. (C.Ck.)	IV. 378, Amethyst, w. in actn.
Girardias, Joseph Maurice (C.) *F.*	IV. 175-6, Infatigable, actn. with Br. Sq.
Gittens, Richard (L.)	IV. 320, Tartarus, cutting out exped.
Gittins, Richard (L.)	IV. 168, Galatea, cutting out exped.
Glen, Nisbet (L.Com.)	III. 316, Clinker, Channel ; 324, actn. with invas. flotilla.
Glen, — (Mid.).........	I. 172, Leviathan, k. 1st June.
Glennie, Geo. R.(Mid.)	VI. 288, Granicus, w. Algiers.
Glenny, Gordon (Mid.)	III. 185, Naiad, cutting out exped.
Goddard, Robert Hendrick (C.Ck.)	IV. 263-4, Hydra, w. cutting out. exped.
Goddard, Thomas (L.)	I. 87, w. at Toulon.
Godfrey, George (L.)	V. 130, Kent, cutting out exped.
Godfrey, William (C.)	II. 350, Holland exped.
Godfrey, William (L.)	III. 443, Prince, Trafalgar ; 464, pro. Cr. IV. 205, C. Ætna (bomb.), Copenhagen ; 400, Basque Rds.
Godfrey, — (C.)	III. 29-30, Rover (priv.) capts. Sp. Santa Ritta.
Goff, John (A.B.)	VI. 270, Eliza, k. in actn.
Goldfinch, George (L.)	VI. 312-18-51, Burmese War.
Goldfinch, William (L.)	III. 55, Edgar, w. Copenhagen.
Goldfinch, W. J. (Mid.)	VI. 374, k. Navarino.
Goldie, John (L.Com.)	IV. 172, Sharpshooter, off St. Malo.
Golding, John (Mid.)	V. 126, Weazle, cutting out exped.
Gooch, George Thomas (Mid.)	VI. 41, Amelia, w. in actn.
Gooch, Samuel (C.) ...	II. 390-2, Rattlesnake engages Preneuse.

INDEX TO NAVAL OFFICERS

Good, John (L.)......... II. 253, Regulus, cutting out exped.
Goodall, Chas. (R.A.) I. 72, Princess Royal, Medn. Flt. ; 76-88, Gvr. at Toulon.
Goodall, Samuel Cranston (V.A.) I. 214, Princess Royal, Corsica ; 284, actn. off Genoa ; 290-7, Hyères.
Goode, Siphus (Mid.) V. 242, Active, w. actn. off Lissa.
Goodench, Jas. (Mid.) II. 49, Captain, k. St. Vincent.
Gooding, James George (L.Com.) IV. 462, Berbice (schooner), fndrd. off Demerara, crew saved.
Gooding, James Glassford (L.Com.) IV. 171, Flying Fish (schooner), actn. with F. privs.
Goodman, John (Mid.) II. 323, k. at Acre.
Goodridge, Richard (Mid.) V. 247, Unité, w. in actn.
Goodridge, — (C.) E.I.C. VI. 315-19, Burmese War.
Gordon, Alexander (C.) IV. 336, Moselle, crsg., recapts. Pike. V. 367, Rattler, crsg. VI. 387, Laurestinus, wrkd. off the Bahama Isles.
Gordon, Charles (C.) U.S. IV. 249-54, U.S. Chesapeake, actn. with Leopard. VI. 197, U.S. Constellation, Norfolk, U.S.
Gordon, Charles (P.C.) V. 66, Caroline, Persian Gulf ; 183-5-6, Ceylon captd. by F. Vénus, w. in actn.; 190, 203, act.C. Africaine, capture of the Isle of France.
Gordon, Henry (C.) ... III. 259-60, Wolverine captd. by F. Blonde (priv.) ; 261 pro. P.C.
Gordon, Henry Cranmer (L.Com.) VI. 247, St. Lawrence captd. by U.S. Chasseur.
Gordon, James Alexander (C.) IV. 326, Mercury, off Cadiz. V. 120, Active, crsg. ; 232-8, actn. off Lissa ; 261, Lissa ; 262-4, w. in actn. with F. frigates. VI. 175, Seahorse ; 181, Chesapeake Bay ; 183-4, Alexandria.
Gordon, Robert James (L.) IV. 327, Mercury, cutting out exped. V. 37-8, w. cutting out exped.
Gordon, Hon. William (P.C.) VI. 16, Magicienne, capture of St. Sebastian, Medn.
Gore, John (L.) .... I. 87, Toulon ; 212, Bastia, Corsica. II. 91, C. Triton ; 96, Warren's Sq.; 248, Sq. crsg.; 402, crsg. III. 65, Medusa, watching invas. flotilla ; 287, capture of Sp. frigates.
Gore, John (P.C.) ...... I. 295, Censeur, San Fiorenzo Bay ; 303-4, captd. by F. Sq. off St. Vincent.
Gore, John (P.C.) ...... I. 215, Windsor Castle, San Fiorenzo Bay ; 284-9-90, actn. off Genoa ; 297, off Hyères ; 303, San Fiorenzo Bay.
Gore, Sir John (P.C.) IV. 157, 175, Revenge, Sq. off Rochefort. V. 293, Tonnant engages F. Clorinde ; 312, Medn. Sq. VI. 35, Revenge, Adriatic.
Gore, William (Mid.) III. 66, k. in actn. invas. flotilla.
Gosselyn, Thomas Le Marchant (C.) I. 140, Kingfisher, Channel Flt. ; 262-3, Sq. off Ushant. IV. 116, Audacious, Sq. Barbadoes.
Gossett, Abraham (L.-Com.) I. 354-5, Aristocrat (lugger), in actn. at Herqui.
Gostling, Frank (L.) ... V. 349, Bacchante, cutting out exped. VI. 21-3-33, cutting out exped.
Gott, Thomas (C.)...... II. 456, Cormorant accidentally blows up at St. Domingo.
Gould, Davidge (P.C.) I. 284-90, Bedford, actn. off Genoa ; 297, Hyères. II. 171, Audacious ; 187-96, the Nile ; 306, Palermo ; 432, Genoa ; 438, Sq. blockading Malta.
Gourdon, Antoine Louis (C.) F. II. 286, Wattigny, Brest Flt. III. 68, Indivisible, Brest Flt. ; 368, R.A. ; 372, Ferrol. IV. 391-400, Foudroyant, Brest Flt.
Gourly, John (L.Com.) II. 457, Vanneau (brig), wrkd. at Porto Ferrajo; 60, C. Thunder (bomb.), at Cadiz.
Gourrège, Pierre Paul (C.) I. 356, Coquille, Sq. crsg. III. 69, Créole, Brest ; 342, Aigle, Cadiz Bay ; 386, 413-14, Trafalgar

Gower, Edward Leveson (P.C.)	II. 456, Active, wrkd. St. Lawrence River. III. 78, Pomone, capture of Carrère; 202, Shannon, wrkd. Cape La Hogue; 490, App. VI. 29, Elizabeth; 30, Adriatic.
Gower, Sir Erasmus (P.C.)	I. 262, Triumph, Sq. off Ushant.
Goy, Mathieu (C.) F.	III. 248, Grand Décidé (priv.) engages Eclair (schooner).
Grace, Percy (L.)	V. 214, Semiramis, cutting out exped.
Graham, Andrew (B.)	V. 186, Ceylon, w. in actn.
Graham, Charles (C.)	VI. 328, Diana (sloop), Burmese War.
Graham, Edward Lloyd (P.C.)	VI. 117, Caledonia, Medn. Fleet.
Graham, John Hore (M.C.)	VI. 29–30, Elizabeth, cutting out exped.
Graham, Thomas (C.)	VI. 91, Laurestinus, Chesapeake Bay.
Graham, — (L)	IV. 188, Cape of Good Hope exped.
Graham, — (As.S.)	VI. 274, Tyne, in actn
Grainger, Robert G. (M.L.)	VI. 41, Amelia, k. in actn.
Grandallana, — (V.A.) Sp.	III. 372, Sq. at Ferrol.
Granger, Wm. (act.C.)	II. 392–4, Jupiter engages Preneuse.
Grant, Charles (P.C.)	V. 107, Diana, off Havre. VI. 2, 117, Armada, Medn. Flt.; 302, Cmde. C.B.; 306 Liffey, Burmese War; 311, d.
Grant, Gregory (L.)	II. 61, Prince George, w. in actn.
Grant, James Ludovic (C.) E.I.C.	IV. 50, E.I.C. Brunswick captd. by F. Sq.
Grant, John (L.)	VI. 32, Milford, cutting out exped.
Grant, Patrick (M.L.)	IV. 383, Kent, cutting out exped.
Grant, Saml. (Mr.Mt.)	V. 378, Guerrière, w. in actn.
Grant, William (Mid.)	III. 434, Britannia, w. Trafalgar.
Grassin, — (C.) F.	IV. 337, Général Ernouf (priv.) capts. Barbara. V. 423–4, Diligent (priv.) capts. Laura.
Grave, William (Mr.)	III. 104, Cæsar, k. Algesiras.
Graves, Lawrence (Mid.)	II. 195, Goliath, w. the Nile.
Graves, Richard Wilcox (L.)	VI. 140, Eurotas, in actn.
Graves, Thomas (V.A.) „ Lord	I. 62, 139, Royal Sovereign, Channel Flt.; 154–62–7–73, 1st June; 174, w.; 199–200, created Baron.
Graves, Thomas (R.A.) „ Sir Thos.,K.B.	III. 44–6, Defiance; 51–8, Copenhagen; 64, K.B.; 215, Sq. off Brest. IV. 79, Com. Sq. off Rochefort.
Graves, Thomas (P.C.)	I. 408, Venus, N. American Sq. III. 201, Blenheim, Martinique. IV. 200, Brunswick, Copenhagen; 298, Baltic Flt.; 303, Nyborg.
Gravina, Don Frederico (R.A.) Sp.	I. 76, Toulon; 79–80–4, w. in actn. Toulon. III. 163, Brest; 305, 342, A. Sp. Argonauta, F. Sp. Flt. Toulon; 350–9, Calder's actn.; 370–8, 385–6, Sp. Principe de Asturias; 387–94, 407–9, 433–9, Trafalgar; 440, k. in actn.; 451–5.
Gray, Charles (Mr.Mt.)	IV. 448, Ville-de-Paris, cutting out exped.
Gray, George (L.)	III. 55, Defiance, k. Copenhagen.
Gray, H. B. (Mid.)	VI. 374, w. Navarino.
Gray, Joseph (Mid.)	VI. 374, w. Navarino.
Greaves, George (Mid.)	V. 297, Sir Francis Drake, cutting out exped.
Green, Andrew (C.)	VI. 6, Heligoland exped.
Green, James (L.)	III. 443, Defence, Trafalgar; 464, pro. Cr.
Green, John (Mr.Mt.)	IV. 168, Galatea; 240–1, w. cutting out exped.
Green, John (M.L.)	V. 48, Junon, k. in actn.
Green, Robert (M.L.)	III. 406, Royal Sovereign, k. Trafalgar.
Greenaway, Richard (L.)	VI. 29–31, Eagle, cutting out exped.
Greene, Pitt Barnaby (C.)	IV. 400, Foxhound, Basque Rds. VI. 44–6, Bonne Citoyenne, St. Salvador.

Greensword, Edward Nathaniel (L.Com.)	III. 235, Tigress, actn. off Ostende. IV. 369, captd. by Da. gbts. Great Belt ; 474, App.
Greenway, Chas. (Mid.)	VI. 136, Eurotas, k. in actn.
Greenway, Geo. (Mid.)	V. 398, Macedonian, w. in actn.
Greer, — (L.)	VI. 315, Burmese War.
Gregory, Charles Mars (March) (L.)	III. 13, Leviathan, cutting out exped. IV. 331, C. Carnation, captd. by Palinure ; 332, k. in actn.; 473, App.
Gregory, George (P.C.)	I. 128, Europa, Jamaica ; 251, St. Domingo. II. 75, Veteran, Camperdown.
Gregory, John (L.Com.)	IV. 139, Contest, Isle of Aix ; 400, Basque Rds. V. 442, fndrd. near America, drnd.
Greig, David (Mid.) ...	I. 186, Glory, k. 1st June.
Greig, — (C.) *Rus.* ...	II. 344, Rus. Ratvison, Holland exped. IV. 233–4, R.A. Rus. Rafael Flt. in the Dardanelles ; 235, Corfu.
Grénédan, Touissant Duplassis (C.) *F.*	I. 60, Côte D'Or, Brest Flt.
Greville, James (As.S.) *E.I.C.*	IV. 152, E.I.C. Warren Hastings, w. in actn.
Grey, Edward (L.) ...	II. 394–5, Adamant, cutting out exped.
Grey, Frederick (Mid.)	VI. 374, w. Navarino.
Grey, George (P.C.) ...	I. 240–3, Boyne, capture of Martinique exped.; 317, burnt at Spithead ; 443, App.
Grey, Hon. H. (C.) ...	II. 474, Weazle, wrkd. in Barnstaple Bay, drnd.
Grier, Thomas (Mid.)	III. 439, Revenge, k. Trafalgar.
Griffin, Charles William Griffith (L.)	VI. 206, w. Canadian Lakes.
Griffin, Philip (L.Com.)	IV. 467, Ignition (F.S.), wrkd. near Dieppe.
Griffinhoofe, Thomas Saville (Mid.)	IV. 37, Cambrian, w. cutting out exped.
Griffith, Edward (P.C.)	I. 270, London, Channel Flt. II. 30, Spithead mutiny; 231, Niger, Sq. convoy crsg. III. 346, Dragon, convoy escort ; 357–62, Calder's actn. IV. 55, Sq. crsg.; 445, Sultan, Medn. Sq. VI. 200, R.A. Dragon, Penobscot exped.
Griffith, John C. (Mid.)	V. 424, Laura, w. in actn.
Griffiths, Anslem John (L.)	II. 58, Culloden, St. Vincent, pro. Cr. III. 142, C. Atalante, crsg. Quiberon Bay. V. 30–1, Topaze, crsg. Adriatic ; 80, Isle St. Maura, Adriatic.
Griffiths, Thomas (Mr.)	III. 128, Phœbe, w. in actn.
Griffiths, Thos. (Car.)	IV. 333, Carnation, k. in actn.
Griffiths, Thomas H. (M.L.)	V. 340, Victorious, k. in actn.
Grimes, Edward (L.)	V. 163, Iphigenia, Isle of France.
Grimes, Joshua (As.-Secretary.)	VI. 287, Queen Charlotte, w. Algiers.
Grimshaw, Joseph (L.)	VI. 19, capture of Ponza.
Grindall, Richd. (P.C.)	I. 271–3, Irresistible, actn. off Isle Groix. II. 301, Ramillies, of Basque Rds. blockade. III. 384, Prince ; 440–1, Trafalgar.
Groot, — (C.) *Du.* ...	IV. 179, Du. Zeerop captd. by Caroline.
Gros, John Le (L.Com.)	III. 494, Hindostan (S.S.), burnt Medn.
Grose, Arthur (Mid.)	V. 248, Belle Poule, Sagone Bay.
Grote, — (L.)	VI. 342, Boadicea, Burmese War.
Grothschilling —, (L.) *Da.*	V. 229, Da. Sampsoe, actn. with Manly.
Groule, Thomas (L.)...	IV. 181, Culloden, cutting out exped.
Groves, James (L.) ...	V. 335–6, Venerable, N. Spain.
Groves, Jas. (L.Com.)	IV. 462, Belem captd. at Buenos Ayres.
Grubb, Chas. G. (Mid.)	VI. 287, Minden, w. Algiers.
Grubb, — (C.) *Swd.*...	IV. 299, Swd. Uladislaffe, Br. Swd. Flt., Oro Rds.
Guasteranus, — (C.) *Du.*	V. 193, Du. Mandarin captd. at Amboyna.
Guerin, Daniel (C.) ...	I. 412, Sirène, St. Domingo. II. 456, wrkd. in Honduras Bay, drnd.

Guignier, Jean François (L.Com.) *F*. — II. 98, Gaieté captd. by Arethusa.
Guillemet, François Charles (C.) *F*. — I. 273, Alexandre, Isle Groix actn.
Guillet, Pierre (L.) *F*. — IV. 23-4, Ville de Milan, w. in actn.
Guillotin, Jean Louis (C.) *F*. — II. 137-8, Franchise, Ireland exped.
Guion, Daniel Oliver (C.) — III. 83, Eurus, Egypt exped. V. 231, St. George, wrkd. Jutland, drnd ; 447, App.
Guion, Gardener Henry (L.) — V. 95-6, Armide, cutting out exped.; 97, pro. Cr. V. 84, C. Philomel, actn. with F. frigates.
Guiren, George (Mid.) — III. 410, Mars, w. Trafalgar.
Guise, George Martin (L.) — IV. 252, Leopard, in actn.
Guiyesse, Pierre (C.) *F*. — III. 131, Chiffonne captd. by Sibylle.
Gunn, Alex. (Mr.Mt.) — V. 104, Briseis, k. in actn.
Gunn, Alex. (Mid.) ... — V. 325, Sealark, w. in actn.
Gunning, Geo. W. (L.) — VI. 287, Superb, w. Algiers.
Gunter, George (Mid.) — V. 7, Horatio, k. in actn.
Gunter, Henry (C.) ... — II. 474, Nautilus, wrkd. off Flamborough Head.

Hackett, John (L.) ... — VI. 160, Epervier, w. in actn.
Haddon, Edward (Mid.) — II. 262, Leander, k. in actn.
Haggarty, William (Pr.) — V. 366, Alert, in actn.
Haggitt, Wm. (P.C.) — I. 304, Lutine, convoy escort.
Haggitt, William (C.) — II. 130, Orestes, St. Marcouf ; 474, fndrd., drnd.
Haig, William (M.L.) — V. 349-50, Bacchante, cutting out exped. VI. 21-3, cutting out exped. ; 119, w. in actn.
Haines, John (Mr.Mt.) — IV. 230, Standard, w. Dardanelles.
Halgan, Emmanuel (C.) *F*. — III. 250, Berceau, actn. with Dance's E.I.C. Sq. IV. 395, Hortense blockaded in Basque Rds.
Halkett, Peter (C.) ... — II. 75, Circe, Camperdown ; 474, Apollo, wrkd. on coast of Holland. IV. 200, Ganges, Copenhagen ; 238, Cmde. Sq. off the Tagus.
Hall, James (Mr.Mt.) — III. 18, Dart, w. cutting out exped.
Hall, James (L.) ...... — V. 35, Cyane, w. in actn.
Hall, John (Mid.) ...... — V. 248, Belle Poule, cutting out exped.
Hall, John Netherton O'Brien (L.) — IV. 440, capture of batteries, Flushing.
Hall, Robert (M.L.) ... — III. 279, Galatea, cutting out exped.
Hall, Robert (P.C.) ... — IV. 126, 425, Malabar, crsg. off Cuba.
Hall, Robert (C.) ...... — IV. 386, Lucifer (bomb.), Rosas Bay. V. 127, Rambler, Gibraltar Bay. VI. 20, Com. flotilla, Messina.
Hall, Roger (L.) ...... — VI. 289, Impregnable, Algiers ; 291, pro. Cr.
Hall, William (act.L.) — VI. 328, Burmese War.
Hall, William H. (L.) — VI. 343-53-4, Burmese War.
Hall, — (Mr.Mt.) ...... — III. 256, Emerald, w. cutting out exped.
Hall, — (L.) .... — IV. 259, Port d'Espagne engages Sp. priv.
Halliday, F. Alex. (C.) — VI. 381, Ferret, wrkd. near Leith.
Halliday, John (P.C.) — V. 85, Repulse, Sq. off Toulon.
Halliday Michael (L.) — II. 105, Phœbe, in actn., pro. Cr. ; 155, C. Mermaid, actn. with Loire.
Hallowell, Benjamin (P.C.) — I. 88, Leviathan, Toulon ; 212, Corsica ; 288, Lowestoffe, actn. off Genoa ; 294, Spezia Bay ; 297, Courageux, Hyères ; 351-2, wrkd. in the Straits of Gibraltar. II. 62, Lively, Santa Cruz Bay ; 171, Swiftsure, Flt. off Cadiz ; 190-6, the Nile ; 215-17, Alexandria ; 218, Aboukir Bay ; 306, Palermo ; 310, Naples Bay ; 315-20, St. Elmo ; 456, App. III. 12-13, Sq. off Cadiz ; 76-81, captd. by F. Medn. Sq. ; 203, Courageux, W. Indies ; 335, Tigre, Medn. Flt. ; 458, Sq. at Gibraltar ; 481, App. IV. 232, Alexandria exped. ; 445-7, Sq. in Rosas Bay. V. 315, R.A. Medn. Flt.

INDEX TO NAVAL OFFICERS

Hallowes, John (Mid.)	VI. 6, Heligoland exped.
Halsted, Lawrence William (P.C.)	I. 189, Hector, Channel Sq. ; 363-4, Phœnix capts. Du. Argo. III. 78, Medn. IV. 3-9, Namur, Strachan's actn. ; 89, Warren's Sq. crsq.
Halsted, William (M.L.)	IV. 448, Topaze, cutting out exped. V. 31, 127, cutting out expeds.
Halton, Thomas (L.)...	II. 88, Veteran, Camperdown, pro. Cr.
Haly, Richard Standish (Mid.)	III. 27, Minotaur, cutting out exped. IV. 328-9, L. Nymphe, cutting out exped.
Hamblin, Thos. (Mid.)	III. 68, w. cutting out exped.
Hambly, Richard (Mr.-Mt.)	V. 128, Blossom, w. cutting out. exped.
Hambly, Richard (L.)	V. 343, Leviathan, cutting out exped.
Hamelin, Jacques F. Em. (C.) *F.*	III. 316, Foudre ; 324-5, invas. flotilla. IV. 380, Cmde. Venus, crsg. E. Indies. V. 53, 62-3, Bay of Bengal ; 64, capts. E.I.C. Windham ; 65, Port Louis ; 131-65, Grand Port ; 166-7, capture of Iphigenia ; 184-6, capts. Ceylon ; 187, captd. by Boadicea.
Hamilton, Archibald (C.) *E.I.C.*	III. 250, E.I.C. Bombay Castle, actn. with Linois' Sq. E. Indies.
Hamilton, Arthur Philip (L.)	V. 101, Caledonia, cutting out exped.
Hamilton, Aug. Barrington (Mid.)	III. 33, Phaëton, w. cutting out exped.
Hamilton, Sir Charles (P.C.)	II. 164, Melpomène, Sq. crsg. ; 255, Isle Bas. III. 118, Gorée.
Hamilton, Charles Powell (P.C.)	I. 203-4, Canada, actn. with F. Sq. ; 271, Prince, Channel Flt.
Hamilton, Edward (C.) ,, Sir Edward (C.)	II. 405-6, Surprise, Puerto Cabello ; 407-10, cuts out late Br. Hermione ; 411, w. in actn. ; 412, kntd. III. 130, Trent, crsg. off Isles Bréhat.
Hamilton, Gawen Wm., C.B. (P.C.)	VI. 364-5-73, Cambrian, Navarino.
Hamilton, John (C.) *E.I.C.*	III. 22, E.I.C. Bombay Castle, actn. with F. frigates.
Hamilton, William (L.)	IV. 447, Tigre, cutting out exped. V. 337, C. Termagant, Sq. off Grenada.
Hamilton, Wm. (Mid.)	IV. 127, Franchise, cutting out exped.
Hamilton, — (L.)	II. 407, Surprise, cutting out of the Hermione.
Hamley, William (L.)	VI. 26, Havannah, cutting out exped.
Hammond, Charles (L.)	IV. 448, Topaze, cutting out exped. V. 31-2, cutting out exped.
Hammond, George (C.)	II. 103, Epervier (priv.) cut out by the bts. of Fairy.
Hammond, Thos. (Mr.-Mt.)	V. 416, Java, k. in actn.
Hammond, — (C.)	II. 381, Phœnix (lugger), priv. crsg. Spain.
Hamon, Joseph Pierre Marie (L.Com.) *F.*	IV. 76, Naïade captd. by Jason.
Hamond, Graham Eden (P.C.)	III. 44-6, Blanche, Copenhagen ; 287-8, Lively capts. Sp. Fama ; 375, Medn. IV. 439, Victorious, Scheldt exped.
Hanchett, John Martin (C.)	IV. 436-7, Raven, w. in actn. Scheldt exped. VI. 92, Diadem ; 93, w. in actn. Chesapeake Bay.
Hancock, Edw. (M.L.)	VI. 29, Saracen, Adriatic.
Hancock, John (L.) ...	VI. 119, cutting out exped., Adriatic.
Hancock, John (C.) ...	III. 171, Cruiser, crsg. ; 222-6-35, 321, actn. with invas. flotilla. IV. 290, Lavinia, watching Ganteaume's Flt.
Hand, George Sumner (Mid.)	VI. 343, Burmese War.
Hand, Thomas (C.) ...	II. 132, Hecla (bomb.), Ostende. III. 83, Tartarus (bomb.), Alexandria.
Handcock, Alex. Bell (Mid.)	III. 438, Swiftsure, w. Trafalgar.

H

Handfield, Philip Cosby (act. C.)	IV. 76, Egyptienne capts. Libre; 129, crsg. Spain; 294, C. Delight, k. in actn.; 474, wrkd. Calabria.
Hanickoff, — (V.A.) Rus.	IV. 298-301, Rus. Blagodath, Oro Rds., actn. with Br. Sq.
Hanlow, John (M.L.)...	IV. 383, Kent, cutting out exped.
Hanmer, David (L.-Com.)	VI. 6, Heligoland exped.
Hannay, Andrew (C.)	II. 244, E.I.C. Woodcot captd. by Preneuse.
Hansell, John (L.)......	IV. 138, Pallas, cutting out exped.
Hanson, James (C.) ...	III. 477, Brazen, wrkd. near Brighton, drnd.
Hanwall, P. G. (Mid.)	VI. 288, Leander, k. Algiers.
Hardiman, Henry(Mid.)	VI. 163, Reindeer, w. in actn.
Harding, James (A.B.)	II. 215, Alcmène rescues despatches.
Hardinge, Geo. Nicholas (Mid.)	II. 326, Acre. III. 172, Terror (bomb.), in actn. off Granville; 264, C. Scorpion; 265, cuts out Du. Atalante; 266, pro. P.C. Scorpion. IV. 188, Salsette; 307-11, San Fiorenzo capts. Piémontaise, k. in actn.
Hardy, Charles (Mid.)	II. 268, Leander, in actn.
Hardy, Hy. (C.) E.I.C.	VI. 303, Burmese War; 347, App.
Hardy, John Oakes (C.)	I. 385, Thisbe, Murray's Sq. crsg.
Hardy, Temple (C.) ...	I. 333-4, Echo, Cape of Good Hope exped.
Hardy, Thomas Masterman (L.)	I. 407, Minerve, in actn. II. 62, w. in cutting out Mutine; 63, pro. Cr.; 170, C. Mutine, Flt. off Toulon; 173, Naples; 174, Alexandria; 206, Vanguard; 306, Palermo; 311, Naples. III. 47, St. George, Copenhagen; 175, Amphion, Toulon; 177, Victory (2nd C.); 335, Flt. crsg.; 384-91-7-8-403-20-22, 447-8, Trafalgar; 464-66,
,, Sir Thomas M., Bart.	made Baronet. IV. 116, Triumph, Sq. at Barbadoes; 247, Sq. in Chesapeake Bay; 376, Isle Groix; 391, blockading Lorient. VI. 100, Ramillies off New London, U.S.; 193-4, Jamaica.
Hardyman, Lucius (L.)	II. 368, Sibylle, in actn.; 373, pro. Cr.; 375, pro. P.C. Forte. III. 481, wrkd. in the Red Sea. IV. 30, Unicorn, crsg. W. Indies; 279-80, Sq. at Monte Video; 400-13, Basque Rds. V. 95, Armide, Basque Rds.
Hare, Charles (C.)......	I. 86-7, Vulcan, Toulon; 433, destd.
Hare, John Edward (L.-Com.)	IV. 400, Fervent (brig), Basque Rds. actn.
Hare, Thomas (L.)......	V. 220, Exertion, cutting out exped.
Hargood, William (C.)	I. 105-6, Hyæna captd. by Concorde; 433, App. III. 241, Belleisle, off Toulon; 335, Flt. crsg.; 384-96, 406-9, Trafalgar. IV. 116-17, Sq. at Barbadoes capts. with consort F. Impétueux.
Harison, George (L.)...	I. 366, Santa Margarita, in actn. pro. Cr.
Harlowe, Thos. (Mid.)	III. 55, Monarch, w. Copenhagen.
Harman, William (L.)	VI. 7, Albacore, k. in actn.
Harman, — (C.) E.I.C.	V. 62, E.I.C. Orient (brig) captd. by Vénus.
Harness, Richard Stephen (Mid.)	IV. 448, Volontaire, cutting out exped.
Harper, John (L.)......	V. 35, Excellent, cutting out exped. VI. 29, C. Saracen; 33, 119, Adriatic.
Harrera, Don J. (C.) Sp.	III. 112, Sp. Argonauta, actn. in the Gut of Gibraltar.
Harrick, Edward (Mid.)	IV. 440, w. Scheldt exped.
Harriden, — (Mr.)......	I. 363, Spencer (sloop), in actn.
Harrington, Daniel (L.)	IV. 230, Standard, w. in actn. Dardanelles.
Harrington, Thomas Talbot (P.C.)	IV. 52, Ganges, actn. with F. Sq.
Harrington, Wm. (L.)	II. 438, act. C. Alexander; 439-40, blockade of Malta.
Harris, George (P.C.)	V. 296, Sir Francis Drake; 303-9, capture of Java exped. VI. 133, gun trials of Eurotas.
Harris, James (L.)......	IV. 101, Spencer, w. in actn.
Harrison, Jas. H.(M.C.)	VI. 175, Chesapeake Bay.

INDEX TO NAVAL OFFICERS

Harrison, Launcelot (Mid.)	VI. 374, w. Navarino.
Harrison, Thomas (L.)	I. 241, capture of Martinique.
Harry, James (Mr.Mt.)	III. 55, Amazon, w. Copenhagen.
Hart, George (C.)	II. 475, Grampus (T.S.), wrkd. near Woolwich.
Hart, George (P.C.) ...	II. 344, Monmouth, Holland exped. III. 175, Flt. off Toulon. IV. 213, Majestic, Heligoland exped.
Hartley, Edw. (Mr.Mt.)	III. 414, Bellerophon, w. Trafalgar.
Harvey, Booty (C.) ...	V. 109-10, Rosario capts. Mamelouck; 317, engages flotilla off Dieppe; 318, pro. P.C.
Harvey, Edward (L.)...	III. 262, loss of Apollo.
Harvey, Eliab (P.C.)...	I. 233, Santa Margarita, Sq. crsg.; 241, capture of Martinique. III. 384, Téméraire; 391-2, 409-19-20-6, 464-5, Trafalgar.
Harvey, George (Mid.)	VI. 16, Surveillante, in actn.
Harvey, Henry (P.C.)	I. 62, 139, Ramillies, Channel Flt.; 182-200, 1st June; 270, R.A. Prince of Wales, Channel Flt.; 280, Medn. II. 99, Martinique; 109-12, W. Indies; 116, Porto Rico; 461,
,, Sir Henry ...	App. III. 69, kntd., V.A. Channel Flt.
Harvey, James (L.Com.)	VI. 30, Haughty (brig), in actn., Adriatic.
Harvey, John (P.C.) ...	I. 62, 139, Brunswick, Channel Flt.; 178-80, 1st June, w. in actn.; 182, d.; 200, mentioned in despatches.
Harvey, John (P.C.) ...	II. 109, Prince of Wales, Sq. W. Indies. III. 357-62, Agamemnon, Calder's actn. IV. 109, Canada, Martinique; 445-6, Leviathan engages F. Sq. V. 207, Royal Sovereign, Medn. Flt.
Harvey, John (Mr.Mt.)	V. 343, Leviathan, cutting out exped.
Harvey, John (L.)	VI. 36, Swiftsure, k. in actn.
Harvey, John (L.)	VI. 166, Avon, w. in actn.
Harvey, John (Mid.)...	VI. 287, Albion, k. Algiers.
Harvey, John (L.Com.)	I. 440, Actif, fndrd. off Bermuda, crew saved.
Harvey, Robert (L.) ...	IV. 304, Superb, k. in actn.
Harvey, Thomas (P.C.)	IV. 214, Standard, Sq. crsg. Medn.; 289, Corfu; 292, 347, Medn.
Harward, John (C.) ...	II. 307, San León (brig), Sq. in Naples Bay.
Harward, Richard (L.-Com.)	III. 351, Netley, convoy escort. V. 207, C. Caledonia, Medn. Flt.
Harward, Richard (L.)	IV. 101, Northumberland, Duckworth's actn.; 104, pro. Cr.
Harwell, — (Mid.)......	IV. 225-35, Endymion, Dardanelles.
Harwood, Earle (M.L.)	III. 292-5, Theseus, w. Curaçoa.
Harwood, John (Mid.)	VI. 35, cutting out exped., Adriatic.
Hastings, Thomas (L.)	VI. 36, Undaunted, cutting out exped.
Haswell, John Stepney (M.L.)	V. 304, w. capture of Java.
Haswell, — (L.)	IV. 139, Pallas, cutting out exped.
Hatley, John (L.)	II. 69, St. George, Medn. Flt., pro. Cr. V. 59, C. Boadicea, Isle Bourbon; 141, superseded.
Hatton, Villiers T. (L.)	IV. 318, Seagull, w. in actn.
Haultain, Charles (L.)	VI. 6, Heligoland exped.
Haum, — (L.) *Du.* ...	V. 194, capture of Amboyna.
Haward, Richard (L.-Com.)	IV. 474, Delphinen, wrkd. on coast of Holland.
Hawes, James (L.Com.)	IV. 466, Moucheron, wrkd. Medn.
Hawker, Edward (P.C.)	V. 46, Melampus capts. Béarnais; 92, Sq. off Basse Terre. VI. 73, Bellerophon, crsg. Newfoundland.
Hawker, Thomas (L.)	I. 290, Windsor Castle, w. in actn.
Hawkes, Richard (L.)	III. 57, Dart, Copenhagen.
Hawkey, Joseph (L.)...	V. 40-1, Implacable, k. cutting out exped.
Hawkey, Richard (M.L.)	IV. 326, Alceste, cutting out exped. V. 119, actn. at Agaye.
Hawkey, William (1st Mt.) *E.I.C.*	V. 134, E.I.C. Astell, in actn.
Hawkins, Abel (L.) ...	VI. 237, Endymion, k. cutting out exped.

Hawkins, Abraham Mills (L.)	V. 328-9, Horatio, w. cutting out exped., pro. Cr.
Hawkins, Edward (C.)	IV. 178-9, Despatch engages Présidente.
Hawkins, John (L.) ...	III. 195, Atalante, cutting out exped.
Hawkins, John (Mid.)	VI. 287, Impregnable, k. Algiers.
Hawkins, Richard (Mid.)	I. 87, Toulon. II. 196-7, Theseus, w. the Nile ; 210, pro. Cr. V. 364, C. Minerva, convoy escort.
Hawkins, — (Mid.) ...	II. 249, Flora, cutting out exped.
Hawtayne, Chas. Sibthorpe John (P.C.)	V. 105, 220, Quebec, crsg. off the Texel.
Hay, Alexander (Mid.)	V. 217, Hotspur, k. in actn.
Hay, James (L.)	IV. 382, Amaranthe, cutting out exped.
Hay, Matthew (L.) ...	III. 432, Africa, w. Trafalgar.
Hay, Robt. (C.) *E.I.C.*	V. 132-6, E.I.C. Astell, w. in actn. with F. frigates.
Hay, Robert (L.)	VI. 289, Albion, Algiers ; 291, pro. Cr.
Hay, R. S. (L.)	VI. 374, w. Navarino.
Haye, George (L.)......	V. 232, Cerberus, cutting out exped.; 241, actn. off Lissa, w.; 256, Active ; 263-4, w. in actn.; 266, pro. Cr.
Hayes, Charles (Mid.)	V. 239, Amphion, k. in actn.
Hayes, Geo. (L.Com.)	II. 457, Experiment (brig) captd. by Sp. Sq. Medn.
Hayes, John (M.L.) ...	IV. 263, Hydra, cutting out exped.
Hayes, John (Cmde.)	V. 303, E.I.C. Malabar, capture of Java.
Hayes, John (P.C.) ...	V. 51, 87, Freija, Guadaloupe ; 332-3, Magnificent, off Basque Rds. ; 428, Majestic. VI. 144-7, capts. Terpsichore ; 237-8, 300, Sq. off New York.
Hayes, — (C.) *E.I.C.*	III. 151, capture of Ternate, E. Indies.
Hayman, Charles (L.)	III. 279-80, Galatea, k. cutting out exped.
Haymond, — (C.) *F.*	III. 125, Espérance engages Bordelais.
Hayward, Thomas (C.)	II. 462, Swift, fndrd. in the China Sea, drnd.
Head, Michael (L.) ...	IV. 367, Euryalus, cutting out exped. VI. 69, C. Curlew, crsg.
Hearne, William (A.B.)	V. 401, Macedonian, in actn.
Heathcote, George (C.)	III. 490, Suffisante wrkd. on Spike Island, Cork.
Heathcote, George Henry (Mid.)	VI. 288, Glasgow, w. Algiers.
Heathcote, Henry (P.C.)	III. 279-81, Galatea, Guadaloupe. V. 303, Lion, capture of Java. VI. 2, Scipion, Sq. off Toulon.
Heiden, Count de (R.A.) *Rus.*	VI. 359-65-73, Rus. Azof, Navarino.
Heighman, George (L.)	I. 155, Royal George, k. 29th May.
Heilberg, — (L.) *Du.*	II. 86, Du. Delft, captd. at Camperdown, fndrs.
Hellard, William (L.)	III. 443, Defiance, Trafalgar ; 464, pro. Cr.
Helpman, Thos. (Mr.-Mt.)	IV. 158, k. cutting out exped.
Heming, Samuel Scudamore (L.Com.)	IV. 256, Richmond capts. Sp. Galliard (priv.).
Henderson, James (L.)	V. 256, Active, cutting out exped.
Henderson, John (L.-Com.)	VI. 6, Heligoland exped.
Henderson, Robert (L.)	III. 195-6, Osprey, w. cutting out exped.; 298, Centaur, w. in actn. V. 203, act.C. Néréide, capture of the Isle of France. VI. 203, C. Tigris, crsg. Channel.
Henderson, William (L.)	V. 245, Active, in actn. off Lissa, pro. Cr.
Hendric, John (Mr.Mt.)	III. 119, Melpomène, w. cutting out exped.
Heneyman, W. (L.-Com.) *Du.*	V. 1, Du. late Br. Manly captd. by Onyx.
Henley, Jonathan (Mid.) *U.S.*	III. 303, w. in actn. at Tripoli.
Henley, Robert (C.) *U.S.*	VI. 213, U.S. Eagle (brig), Lake Champlain.
Hennah, William (L.)	III. 37, Magicienne, cutting out exped. ; 409, act.C. Mars ; 427, Trafalgar ; 464, pro. P.C.

INDEX TO NAVAL OFFICERS 101

Henniker, Major Jacob (C.)	III. 234, Albacore engages F. flotilla off Grosnez.
Henning, Alex. (Mid.)	V. 289, Galatea, w. in actn.
Henri, Antoine (C.) F.	IV. 88, Foudroyant, Sq. crsg.; 391, off Ushant; 444, Danube, Toulon.
Henry, Jean Baptiste (C.) F.	I. 60, Aquilon, Belleisle Rds. II. 5, Tourville, Ireland exped.; 286, Brest Flt. IV. 88, Diomède, Sq. St. Domingo; 102, destd. by Br. Sq.
Henry, John (P.C.) ...	I. 240, Irresistible, capture of Martinique.
Hepenstall, Wm. (L.)	II. 249, Flora, cutting out exped.
Herbert, Charles (Mid.)	I. 312, Blanche, w. in actn.
Herbert, Hon. Charles (P.C.)	II. 140, Amelia, crsg.; 376-7, actn. with F. frigates.
Herbert, Massey Hutchinson (Mr. Mt.)	IV. 264, Confiance, cutting out exped.
Herbert, Thomas (L.)	VI. 186, Euryalus, Alexandria.
Herbert, — (Mid.) ...	III. 468, Neptune, Trafalgar.
Herringham, William (Mid.)	III. 416, Colossus, w. Trafalgar.
Hervey, George W. (Mid.)	VI. 288, Glasgow, w. Algiers.
Hewett, John (M.L.)	VI. 206, actn. on the Canadian Lakes.
Hewett, William (B.)	IV. 39, Blanche, w. in actn.
Hewson, George (C.)	V. 445, Flêche, wrkd. off the Elbe.
Heywood, Edmund (L.)	III. 129, Phœbe, in actn.; 227, C. Harpy; 330, engages invas. flotilla; 315, Dunkerque. IV. 203-4, Comus capts. Da. Frederickscoarn; 473, Astræa, wrkd. W. Indies.
Heywood, Peter (P.C.)	IV. 281, Polyphemus, Buenos Ayres; 392, act.C. Donegal, Sq. off Chasseron.
Hibberd, I. (Mid.) ...	III. 104, Pompée, w. in actn.
Hibbert, Edward (Mid.)	VI. 32, Eagle, Adriatic; 287, Queen Charlotte, w. Algiers.
Hickey, Frederick (C.)	VI. 381, Atalante, wrkd. Halifax.
Hickman, John Collman (L.)	V. 248, Alceste, Parenza.
Hicks, Wm. (L.Com.)	VI. 222, Finch (gbt.), Lake Champlain.
Hicks, — (L.)	VI. 222, Confiance, Lake Champlain.
Higginson, James (L.-Com.)	IV. 94, Epervier, W. Indies.
Higginson, Montagu G. (L.Com.)	IV. 466, Pigmy (brig), wrkd. near Rochefort.
Higman, Henry (L.) ...	IV. 170, Arethusa, w. in actn. V. 451, C. Fly, wrkd. Anholt Island.
Hildyard, Richard (Mr.)	V. 37, Mercury, cutting out exped.
Hill, Henry (L.)	I. 87, Toulon.
Hill, John (L.Com.) ...	VI. 7, Landrail (cutter), crsg., chases Gloire.
Hill, John George (L.)	V. 343, Leviathan, Languelia.
Hill, Thomas (Mr. Mt.)	IV. 328, Nymphe, cutting out exped.
Hill, William (A.B.) ...	IV. 248-9, Halifax, deserter.
Hill, William (L.)	IV. 380, Amethyst, in actn. V. 16-17, in actn. pro. Cr.
Hill, — (M.Maj.)	I. 335, America, in actn.
Hillier, — (Mr.Mt.) ...	III. 104, Pompée, w. in actn.
Hillier, — (Gunner) ...	IV. 139, Pallas, Isle of Aix.
Hills, Alexander (L.)...	III. 448, Victory, Trafalgar.
Hills, John (P.C.)	I. 252, Hermione, St. Domingo.
Hills, John B. (L.) ...	III. 181, Hercule, crsg.; 292, Curaçoa.
Hills, William (P.C.)...	II. 412, Orpheus capts. Du. Zeelast and Zeevraght.
Hillyar, James (C.) ...	III. 27-9, Niger (en flûte), Barcelona; 83-9, Egypt exped. V. 203, Phœbe, capture of Isle of France; 283-6, actn off Madagascar; 303-10, capture of Java. VI. 150-5, capts. U.S. Essex Junior.
Hilton, George (C.) ...	VI. 197, Nimrod, Buzzard's Bay.

Hinton, John (L.)	I. 300, Victory, w. in actn. III. 235, L.Com. Blazer, off Ostende.
Hinxt, — (C.) *Du.* ...	II. 76-9, Du. Beschermer, Camperdown.
Hoare, Edward Wallis (P.C.)	V. 297-303, Minden, capture of Java.
Hoare, George (Mid.)	III. 55, Ardent, k. Copenhagen.
Hoare, — (Mr.Mt.) ...	VI. 207, Montreal (gbt.), k. Canadian Lakes.
Hobbes, — (L.).........	III. 89, Egypt exped., k. in actn.
Hobson, — (L.).........	VI. 269-72, Tyne, W. Indies.
Hockly, Wm. (M.L.)	VI. 26, Havannah, cutting out exped.
Hodder, Edward (L.)	III. 57, Polyphemus, Copenhagen ; 64, pro. Cr.
Hodder, Henry (act.-Mr.)	VI. 311, Larne, Burmese War.
Hodge, Andrew (C.) ...	IV. 330-1, Supérieure engages Pilade.
Hodge, John (Mid.) ...	III. 441, Defiance, w. Trafalgar.
Hodge, J. T. (1st.cl. Vol.)	III. 409, Belleisle, w. Trafalgar.
Hodge, Wm. (L.Com.)	IV. 109, Dolphin (S.S.), convoy escort.
Hodgskins, Thos. (L.)	IV. 328, Nymphe, cutting out exped. V. 99, Nemesis, cutting out exped.
Hoffman, Frederick (C.)	V. 318-19, Apelles (sloop), invas. flotilla.
Hoffmeister, John M. (Pr.)	VI. 113, Detroit (gbt.), w. Canadian Lakes.
Hogg, Daniel (Pr.) ...	II. 268, Leander, in actn.
Holbrook, Geo. (Mid.)	IV. 229, Royal George, w. Dardanelles.
Holbrook, Thomas (L.)	VI. 29, Eagle, cutting out exped.
Hole, Lewis (L.)	III. 443, Revenge, Trafalgar ; 464, pro. Cr.
Holgate, Robert (Mid.)	III. 424, Téméraire, Trafalgar.
Holland, J. (Mid.)......	I. 177, Queen Charlotte, w. 1st June.
Holland, John Wentworth (L.)	III. 128, Phœbe, w. in actn.; 129, pro. Cr.
Holland, — (C.) *Du.*	II. 76-9, Du. Wassenaer, Camperdown ; 82, k. in actn.
Hollingsworth, John (L.Com.)	II. 105, Growler captd. by F. privs., k. in actn.; 462, App.
Hollis (or Holles) Askew Paffard (P.C.)	III. 112-16, Thames, actn. in the Gut of Gibraltar. IV. 431, Standard, Scheldt exped. V. 208, Achille, Medn. Flt.
Holloway, John (P.C.)	I. 72, Britannia, Medn. Flt.; 213, off Bastia ; 215, Gourjean Bay ; 284, Flt. in Leghorn Rds.; 297, Hyères. III. 109, R.A. Ferris' court-martial at Portsmouth.
Holloway, Richard (L.)	I. 87, Toulon.
Holm, — (C.) *Da.* ...	V. 229, Da. Loland with consorts capts. Manly.
Holman, William (L.)	II. 253, Regulus, cutting out exped. V. 207, act.C. Hibernia, Medn. Flt.
Holmes, Charles (M.L.)	V. 23, Bacchante, cutting out exped.
Holmes, James (B.) ...	V. 398, Macedonian, k. in actn.
Holmes, John Henry (L.)	III. 27, Courageux, w. cutting out exped.
Holmes, Wm. (Mid.)	V. 126, Weazle, cutting out exped. VI. 29, L. Saracen, crsg. Adriatic.
Holmes, Wm. (Mr.Mt.)	V. 213, Diana, cutting out exped.
Holstein, — (L.) *Da.*	V. 223-5, k. in actn. Anholt.
Holt, David (M.L.) ...	IV. 221, Pompée, Dardanelles.
Holt, William (Mid.)	IV. 155, Minerva, cutting out exped.
Holtoway, — (M.C.)	VI. 206, k. in actn. Canadian Lakes.
Home, Roddam (P.C.)	I. 412, Africa, Léogane, St. Domingo.
Hony, George M. (C.)	IV. 269, Herald, crsg. Adriatic.
Honyman, Robert (L.)	I. 290, St. George, w. in actn. off Genoa. III. 174, C. Leda, crsg. in Channel ; 227, 315, watching invas. flotilla. IV. 186, exped. to the Cape of Good Hope ; 279, exped. to Monte Video ; 473, wrkd. Milford Haven.
Hood, Alex. (P.C.) ...	II. 120-22, Mars capts. Hercule, k. in actn

INDEX TO NAVAL OFFICERS 103

Hood, Sir Alexander, K.B. (V.A.)	I. 62, 139, Royal George, Channel Flt. ; 149–55, 29th May ; 162–86, 1st June ; 199, created Viscount Bridport ; 200, A. ; 206, Spithead ; 271–2, Medn. ; 273–7, actn. off Isle Groix ; 280, Spithead ; 441, App. II. 11, 24, Flt. crsg. ; 25–31, Spithead mutiny ; 91, Flt. off Ushant ; 120, Channel Flt. ; 285–7, off Ushant ; 427, resigns command of the Channel Flt.
Hood, Lord (V.A.) ...	I. 68–73, Victory, Medn. Flt. ; 74–96, at Toulon ; 206–14, Com. Medn. Flt. ; 215, resigns.
Hood, Samuel (P.C.)...	I. 216–17, Junon, Toulon ; 305, Aigle, off Smyrna. II. 63–6, Zealous, Santa Cruz ; 171–2, crsg. ; 183–96, the Nile ; 206, Alexandria ; 215–16, 306, Palermo ; 450, Courageux, Ferrol. III. 98, Venerable ; 100–5, Algesiras ; 116–18, in actn. Gut of Gibraltar ; 203, Centaur, Cmde. Sq. W. Indies ; 244–9, Fort Royal ; 296, Surinam. IV. 89, Sq. crsg. ; 115, off Rochefort ; 157, 175–6, actn. with F. frigate Sq. ; 177, w. in actn. ; 200–10, Copenhagen ; 275, R.A. capture
,, Sir Samuel, K.B.	of Madeira ; 298, made K.B., Baltic Flt. ; 299–302, 321, actn. with Rus. Flt. ; 459, App.
Hood, Silas Thomson (L.)	V. 350, Bacchante, cutting out exped. VI. 21–3, w. cutting out exped.
Hoope, John (Mid.) ...	V. 7, Horatio, w. in actn.
Hooper, Benjamin (L.)	V. 326, Calypso, in actn.
Hooper, John Sackett (Mid.)	V. 327, Dictator, w. in actn.
Hope, David (L.)	V. 88–9, Freija, cutting out exped. ; 396, Macedonian ; 398, 401–5, w. in actn. VI. 156, Com. Shelburne (schooner), capture of U.S. Frolic.
Hope, George (P.C.)...	I. 294, Romulus, Spezia Bay. II. 206, Alcmène, Aboukir Bay ; 215, off Alexandria ; 307, Majestic, Sq. crsg. III. 384, Defence ; 438–9, Trafalgar. IV. 298, Victory, Baltic Flt.
Hope, Henry (P.C.) ...	IV. 447, Topaze, Rosas Bay. VI. 193, Endymion, New London, U.S. ; 200, Penobscot exped. ; 237, off New York ; 239–46, actn. with U.S. President.
Hope, William (P.C.)	I. 139, Bellerophon, Channel Flt. ; 144–52, 29th May ; 162–200, 1st June. II. 345, Kent, Holland exped. III. 81, Egypt exped.
Hope, William (Mt.) E.I.C.	IV. 152, E.I.C. Warren Hastings, w. in actn.
Hopkins, Harry (L.)...	II. 62, Minerve, cutting out exped.
Hopkins, John (M.C.)	II. 196, Bellerophon, w. the Nile.
Hopkins, Matthew (Ck.)	VI. 288, Infernal (bomb.), w. Algiers.
Hore, Jas. Rivers (M.L.)	IV. 384–6, Impérieuse, crsg. Spain.
Horn, Philip (Mr.Mt.)	III. 55, Amazon, w. Copenhagen.
Horncastle, James (C.) E.I.C.	I. 218, E.I.C. Princess Royal captd. by F. privs.
Horne, — (C.Ck.)......	III. 24, Seine, w. in actn.
Horniman, Robt. L. (Pr.)	IV. 338, Redwing, w. in actn.
Hornsey, John (L.) ...	II. 61, Seahorse, w. in actn.
Horton, John (Mid.)...	V. 297, Sir Francis Drake, capture of Java.
Horton, Joshua Sydney (L.)	I. 324, Lowestoffe, in actn, pro. Cr. II. 102–3, C. Fairy, crsg. in the Channel. III. 3–7, actn. with Pallas ; 8, pro. P.C.
Hosack, Alex. (As.S.)	IV. 447, Tigre, cutting out exped.
Hoskins, Thomas (Mr.)	III. 130, Trent, cutting out exped.
Hoste, Thomas Edward (1st cl.Vol.)	V. 37, Amphion, cutting out exped. ; 120, Mid., cutting out exped. ; 239, w. in actn. VI. 21–3, Bacchante, cutting out exped.
Hoste, William (C.) ...	II. 307, Mutine, Medn. Sq. IV. 125, Amphion, Calabria ; 344, actn. Rosas Bay. V. 9, crsg. Adriatic ; 28, 36, crsg.; 120, Trieste ; 123–5, Sq. crsg. ; 233–9, actn. off Lissa, w.;
,, Sir William, Bart.	244–5, 349, Bacchante, off Istria. 446, App. VI. 21–33, 119–21, Adriatic. VI. 294, Albion, force of.

Hotham, Henry (L.)...	I. 212, Corsica. III. 142, C. Immortalité, capture of Invention (priv.). IV. 392, Defiance, actn. with F. frigates.
Hotham, Hon. Henry (P.C.)	IV. 4-8, Révolutionnaire, Strachan's actn. V. 312, Northumberland, Medn. Sq.; 320-3, des. Arienne and Andromaque. VI. 246, R.A. Com. N. American Sq.
Hotham, William (V.A.)	I. 71-2, Britannia, Medn. Flt.; 213, Bastia; 215, Gourjean Bay; 282, Corsica; 284-93, actn. off Genoa; 297, A.; 298-303, actn. off Hyères; 306, returns home; 321-8, Com. Medn. Flt.; 441, App.
Hotham, William (C.)	I. 297, Cyclops, Medn. Flt.; 305, Smyrna. II. 75-6, Adamant, Camperdown; 129, St. Marcouf; 394, des. Preneuse.
Hotham, William (L.)	VI. 29-31, Eagle, cutting out exped., Adriatic.
Hough, John James (L.)	V. 8, Horatio, in actn.
Houghton, William (L.)	V. 40, Implacable, cutting out exped.
Howard, John (Gunner)	IV. 170, Bacchante, cutting out exped.
Howard, Thos. (Mr. Mt.)	VI. 287, Superb, k. Algiers.
Howden, Matthew (M.L.)	V. 60, Raisonable, k. Isle of Bourbon.
Howe, Richard, Earl of (A.)	I. 61-2-5, Queen Charlotte, Channel Flt. crsg.; 67, Spithead; 138-40, off Ushant; 142-5, 28th May; 151-4, 29th May; 159-83, 1st June; 187, Spithead; 199-202, 270-7, Com. Channel Flt.; 437, App. II. 25, 30-1, Spithead mutiny.
Howell, Joseph Benjamin (L.)	VI. 289, Minden, Algiers; 291, pro. Cr.
Hownam, Joseph Robt. (L.)	VI. 19, Undaunted, capture of Ponza; 35, cutting out exped.
Hubert, Jean Joseph (C.) F.	III. 334, Indomptable, Toulon; 386-9, 455-6, Trafalgar.
Hubert, Paul Mathieu (C.) F.	IV. 159, Guerrière; 160-2, captd. by Blanche.
Hubert, Richard (A.B.)	IV. 249, Halifax, deserter.
Hudson, John (Mid.)...	VI. 31, Eagle, w. in actn.
Hudson, William (Mr.)	III. 408, Belleisle, Trafalgar.
Hudson, — (C.) E.I.C.	I. 219, E.I.C. Houghton captd. by F. privs.
Huell, Ver. (R.A.) Du.	III. 223-5, flotilla, actn. off Ostende; 315, A.; 318-26, invas. flotilla.
Huggell, William (L.)	I. 325, Réunion, in actn.
Hugget, William (C.)...	II. 462, Resolution, fndrd., drnd.
Hughes, John (Mid.)...	I. 186, Royal George, k. 1st June.
Hughes, William (B.)...	V. 329, Horatio, w. cutting out exped.
Hughes, William James (L.Com.)	IV. 166-7, Phosphorus (F.S.) beats off F. priv., w. in actn., pro. Cr.
Hughes, William Rand. (Mr. Mt.)	IV. 184, Success, cutting out exped.
Hughes, — (Pr.)	III. 6, Fairy, w. in actn.
Hugon, — (C.) F.......	VI. 365-70-3, Armide, Navarino.
Huguet, Simon Auguste (L.) F.	IV. 332, Palinure, in actn.
Huguet, — (C.) F. ...	I. 141, Scipion, Brest Flt.
Huijs, — (C.) Du.......	II. 343, Du. De Ruyter blockaded in the Texel.
Huish, George (L.) ...	III. 33, Phaëton, cutting out exped.
Hull, Isaac (C.) U.S....	V. 362, 370-9, 383, 408, U.S. Constitution capts. Guerrière. VI. 54, 77, Cmde. at Boston.
Hull, — (Mid.)	III. 93, Ajax, k. in actn.
Humble, James (B.) ...	V. 417, Java, w. in actn.
Hume, Joseph (Mid.)...	IV. 448, Topaze, cutting out exped.
Humphreys, Salusbury Pryce (L.)	II. 383-4, Latona, cutting out exped. IV. 250, C. Leopard; 251-4, actn. with U.S. Chesapeake.
Hunt, Anthony (C.) ...	I. 212, Corsica; 330, Concorde, crsg.; 357, Pellew's Sq. crsg.; 439, App.
Hunt, Harry (M.L.) ...	VI. 17-19, 36, Undaunted, cutting out expeds., Adriatic.

INDEX TO NAVAL OFFICERS

Hunt, Richard (Mid.)	VI. 6, w. Heligoland exped.
Hunt, Wm. Buckly (C.)	V. 327, Britomart (sloop), crsg. Heligoland.
Hunte, Francis Le (L.)	VI. 20, Pietra Nera, Calabria.
Hunter, Charles Newton (L.Com.)	V. 423, Laura captd. by Diligent (priv.); 451, App.
Hunter, Hugh (Mid.)...	V. 45, Pelorus, cutting out exped.
Hunter, Jas. (Mr.Mt.)	VI. 234, w. cutting out exped.
Hunter, John (P.C.)...	I. 62, Queen Charlotte, Channel Flt. III. 493, Venerable, wrkd. in Torbay.
Hunter, William (Mr.)	I. 288, Captain, w. in actn.
Hurdis, — (Mid.)......	I. 182, Brunswick, w. 1st June.
Hurst, George (L.) ...	VI. 36, Guadeloupe (brig), cutting out exped.
Husband, John (M.L.)	IV. 312, Emerald, cutting out exped.
Huskisson, Thomas (C.)	V. 45, Pelorus, crsg. W. Indies; 450, Barbadoes, wrkd. on Sable Island.
Hussey, Paul (M.L.)	III. 85, w. Egypt exped.
Hussey, Thomas (M.C.)	VI. 19, capture of Ponza.
Hutchinson, Duncan (Mid.)	V. 255, Unité, cutting out exped.
Hutchinson, Massey (Mid.)	IV. 32, Loire, cutting out exped.
Hutchinson, Wm. (Mid.)	VI. 27-9, Apollo, Adriatic.
Hutchinson, William (L.Com.)	VI. 73, Highflyer (schooner) captd. by U.S. President; 382, App.
Hutchinson, Wm. (L.)	VI. 96, Mohawk, cutting out exped.
Hutt, John (P.C.)	I. 127, Queen, Sq. at Martinique; 139, Channel Flt.; 150-1, 29th May; 155, w. in actn.
Hutton, Hugh (M.L.)	III. 17, Defence, cutting out exped.
Huys, — (C.) *Du*.......	II. 76-9, Du. Ambuscade captd. at Camperdown.
Iago, John Sampson (L.)	VI. 287, Queen Charlotte, w. Algiers.
Ibrahim Pasha (A.) *Turk.*	VI. 361-3, 372-8, Navarino.
Illingworth, John (Mr.-Mt.)	V. 100, Surveillante, cutting out exped.
Imbert, — (C.)	VI. 20, flotilla Messina.
Imbert, — (C.) *F.*......	I. 75, Apollon, Toulon.
Incledon, Richard (P.C.)	I. 246, Ceres, capture of the Saintes Guadeloupe.
Indjee-Bey (C.) *Turk.*	III. 12, Turk. ship destd. by Peterel.
Infernet, Louis Ant. Cyprien (Cmde.) *F.*	III. 386, Intrépide; 430, Trafalgar. IV. 11, 444, Donawerth, Toulon Flt.
Ingestre, Viscount (Cr.)	VI. 365, Philomel; 373-8, Navarino.
Inglefield, John Nicholson (P.C.)	I. 213, Victory, Medn. Flt.
Inglefield, Samuel Hood (L.)	II. 323, Acre. IV. 342, C. Bacchante, capts. Griffon.
Inglis, Charles (C.) ...	III. 83, Peterel, Egypt exped. IV. 292, Canopus, Sq. Syracuse; 445, Catalonia. V. 32, Sq. off Procida.
Inglis, George (L.) ...	VI. 113, Detroit, in actn. Canadian Lakes.
Inglis, John (P.C.) ...	II. 75-80-1, Belliqueux, Camperdown.
Inglis, Peter (Mr.)......	II. 12, Cumberland (merchant) captd. by Droits de l'Homme.
Ingram, William (L.)	VI. 154, Phœbe, k. in actn.
Inkpen, Benjamin (A.B.)	VI. 270, Eliza, w. in actn.
Inman, Henry (C.) ...	I. 77, Aurore (prize), Toulon. II. 121, Ramillies, crsg. III. 17, Andromeda, off Dunkerque; 19-20, cuts out Désirée; 46, Désirée, Copenhagen; 357, Triumph; 362, Calder's actn. IV. 89, Sq. crsg.
Innes, Thomas (L.) ...	III. 104, Pompée, w. Algesiras. IV. 457, Com. Woodlark, wrkd. near St. Valery.
Irby, Hon. Charles Leonard (Mid.)	IV. 280, w. in actn. Monte Video.

Irby, Hon. Frederick Paul (P.C.)	IV. 393-4, Amelia, actn. with F. frigates; 399, Basque Rds. V. 27, capts. Mouche; 211, crsg. VI. 37-9, engages Aréthuse; 40-3, w. in actn.
Ireland, Thomas (L.)	I. 186, Royal George, w. 1st June.
Irvine, George (C.) ...	II. 469, Rover, wrkd. Gulf of St. Lawrence.
Irvine, — (L.) Canadian	VI. 112, in actn. Canadian Lakes.
Irwin, David (Mid.) ...	V. 74, Confiance, Cayenne.
Irwin, John (P.C.)......	II. 34, Prince George, Channel Flt.; 39-48, St. Vincent; 293, Queen Charlotte, Medn. Flt. IV. 425, Gambier's court-martial.
Irwin, Robert (M.L.)	III. 185, Naiad, cutting out exped.
Irwin, Thomas (L.) ...	II. 196, Minotaur, w. the Nile.
Irwin, William (Mid.)	I. 301, Victory, w. in actn. Hyères.
Isacke, Matt. (C.) E.I.C.	IV. 308, E.I.C. Metcalfe, in actn.
Isatt, John (Mid.)	VI. 374, w. Navarino.
Ives, Edmund (Mr.) ...	II. 326-9, Tiger, in actn. Acre.
Ivey, William (Mid.)...	I. 174, Royal Sovereign, k. 1st June.
Jackson, Bartholomew (Mr.)	II. 61, Ville de Paris, in actn.
Jackson, George Vernon (L.)	V. 53, Junon, in actn.
Jackson, James (M.L.)	V. 174-8, Africaine, w. in actn.
Jackson, John (L.Com.)	VI. 394, Whiting (cutter), wrkd. near Padstow.
Jackson, Robert (P.C.)	VI. 133, gun trials of Eurotas.
Jackson, Robert Milborne (L.)	VI. 131, Hebrus, in actn., pro. Cr.
Jackson, Samuel (L.)	II. 432, act.Cr. Chameleon, blockading Savona. III. 116, Superb, in actn. Gut of Gibraltar, pro. Cr.; 173, C. Autumn; 227, crsg. in the Channel. IV. 288, Renown, Strachan's Sq. crsg.; 298, Superb, Baltic Flt.; 304, Nyborg.
Jackson, Thos. (Mid.)	IV. 100, Superb, w. in actn.
Jackson, — (A.B.) ...	III. 9, Danaë captd. at Brest through mutiny.
Jacob, Louis Léon (C.) F.	II. 139, Bellone, Ireland exped.; 147, captd. by Ethalion. III. 10, 317, invas. flotilia. IV. 393-4, Calypso destd. by Br. Sq.
Jacobs, Chapman (L.)	I. 200, Majestic, 1st June, pro. Cr.
Jacobs, Jules (C.) F. ...	V. 104, Sans Souci (priv.) captd. by Briseis.
Jacobson, — (C.) Du.	II. 76, Cerberus, Camperdown.
Jager, — (C.) Du.......	IV. 179-80, Du. Maria Riggersbergen captd. by Caroline.
Jagerfelt, — (C.) Swd.	IV. 299, Swd. Adolph. Frederic, Br. Swd. Flt., Oro Rds.
Jagerschold, — (C.) Swd.	IV. 299, Swd. Aran, Br. Swd. Flt., Oro Rds.
Jago, Samuel (Mid.) ...	III. 409, Belleisle, w. Trafalgar.
Jallineaux, — (C.) F....	I. 219, Résolu (priv.), actn. with E.I.C. ships.
James, Hugh (act. Mr.Mt.)	VI. 77, Boxer, in actn.
James, Peter Paumier (L.)	IV. 155, Minerva, cutting out exped.
James, Tobias (B.)......	I. 108, Nymphe, k. in actn.
Jance, Pierre François (C.) F.	IV. 330, Palinure engages Gorée, w. in actn; 331-2, capts. Carnation, k. in actn.
Jane, Henry (L.)	III. 16, Renown, cutting out exped. VI. 247-53, C. Arab (sloop), crsg. Boston Bay.
Janverin, Richd. (Mid.)	II. 324, w. Acre. III. 98, L. Calpé, Medn.
Jardine, George (L.) ...	II. 197, Goliath, the Nile; 210, pro. Cr.
Jardine, John (Mid.)...	VI. 287, Albion, k. Algiers.
Jarratt, Thomas (Car.)	II. 265, Leander, in actn.
Jarvis, Alex. (M.L.)...	VI. 19, capture of Ponza.
Jay, Charles (Mid.) ...	IV. 230, active, w. Dardanelles.

INDEX TO NAVAL OFFICERS

Jeakes, — (C.), *E.I.C.*	V. 66, E.I.C. Mornington, Persian Gulf.
Jeans, John (L.).........	II. 196, Audacious, w. the Nile.
Jeffery, Robert (A.B.)	IV. 273-4, Recruit, left on a desert island.
Jeffrey, Samuel (Vol.)	V. 120, Amphion, cutting out exped.
Jeffrey, Samuel (Pr.)	V. 240, Cerberus, k. in actn.
Jeffries, — (L.)	V. 193, Dover, w. capture of Amboyna.
Jenkins, George (L.)...	V. 52, Blonde, k. in actn.
Jenkins, Henry (P.C.)	II. 273-5, Ambuscade captd. by Baïonnaise; 278-80, w. in actn.; 469, App.
Jenkins, John (Mid.)...	III. 410, Mars, w. Trafalgar.
Jenkins, John (Mr.) ...	V. 166, Sirius, Grand Port, Isle of France.
Jenkins, Michael (L.-Com.)	V. 448, Guachapin, wrkd. at Antigua.
Jenkins, Wm. (L.Com.)	V. 103, Snapper (schooner), crsg. off Ushant.
Jennings, Ulick (L.) ...	II. 80, Powerful, w. Camperdown; 88, pro. Cr.
Jephcott, Wm. (M.L.)	I. 275, Sans Pariel, w. in actn.
Jermy, Charles Deyman (L.Com.)	V. 45, Bacchus (schooner), Sq. crsg. Guadaloupe.
Jervis, James (Mid.) *U.S.*	III. 2, U.S. Constellation, k. in actn.
Jervis, Sir John, K.B. (V.A.)	I. 68-239, Boyne, Com. at Barbadoes; 243-5, capture of Martinique; 248, Guadeloupe; 306, A.; 307, Com. Medn. Flt.; 317, Boyne, burnt; 342-6, Medn.; 349, Rosas Bay; 353, Tagus; 371, off Toulon; 437, App. II. 33-4, Victory; 35-52, St. Vincent; 55, Lagos Bay; 58, Lisbon, created Earl St. Vincent II. 59, Ville de Paris, off Cadiz; 166, 219-36, 291-3, Com. Medn. Flt.; 427, Com. Channel Flt.; 461, App. III. 21, 65, 72, Channel Flt.; 137, 148, 212, First Lord of the Admiralty. IV. 117, Com. off Brest; 236, Lisbon.
Jervis, Wm. Hy. (P.C.)	III. 493, Magnificent, wrkd. near Brest.
Jessen, — (C.) *Da.* ...	IV. 202, Da. Prindts Christian Frederic, Copenhagen; 319, captd. by Stately and Nassau.
Jewell, John (M.L.) ...	II. 196, Minotaur, w. the Nile. III. 27, cutting out exped.
Jewell, Wm. N. (Mid.)	III. 414, Bellerophon, w. Trafalgar.
Jewers, Richard Francis (Mr.Mt.)	IV. 405, Theseus, w. in actn. Basque Rds.
Johns, James (M.L.)...	VI. 58-66, Shannon, in actn. with Chesapeake.
Johnson, David (L.) ...	II. 81, Russel, w. Camperdown.
Johnson, Edmund (L.)	III. 55, Edgar, k. Copenhagen.
Johnson, Edward (L.-Com.)	IV. 467, Magpie (cutter) captd. at Perros.
Johnson, Edward J. (1st cl. Vol.)	IV. 319, Nassau, w. in actn.
Johnson, Geo. (Mr.Mt.)	V. 220, Alert (cutter), cutting out exped.
Johnson, James (P.C.)	V. 303, Scipion, capture of Java exped.
Johnson, John (Gunner)	V. 120, Cerberus, cutting out exped.
Johnson, Joshua (L.)...	III. 55-7, Edgar, w. Copengagen.
Johnson, Urry (L.) ...	IV. 385-6, Impérieuse, cutting out exped., Spain. V. 450, C. Avenger, wrkd. Newfoundland.
Johnson, William (Mr.) *U.S.*	VI. 232-3, U.S. Seahorse (schooner), Chandeleur Isles.
Johnson, — (Mid.) ...	III. 224, Aimable, k. in actn.
Johnston, Charles James (P.C.)	IV. 357, Cornwallis, Isle of France.
Johnston, Frederick John (L.)	VI. 287, Queen Charlotte, k. Algiers.
Johnstone, James (L.-Com.)	III. 148, Lark, crsg. off Cuba. V. 137, C. Leopard, Isle of France.
Johnstone, — (C.)	II. 366, actn. of Sibylle and Forte (passenger).
Joille, Le (C.) *F.*	II. 178, Généreux; 193-4, the Nile; 214, Corfu; 260-1, capts. Leander.

Joliff, Eman. H. Le (C) F. — II. 357, Prudente captd by Dædalus.
Joliffe, George (L.) ... — II. 196, Bellerophon, k. the Nile.
Joly, Jean Joseph Maurice (L.) F. — III. 247, Curieux, w. in actn.
Jones, Charles (Mid.) — III. 55, Isis, w. Copenhagen.
Jones, Chas. (Mr.Mt.). — V. 416, Java, k. in actn.
Jones, Hon. Charles (P.C.) — I. 370, Doris, capture of Légère. II. 10, crsg. Channel.
Jones, David (Mr.Mt.) — V. 33, Cyane, k. in actn.
Jones, Edmund (Mid.) — III. 265, Scorpion, w. cutting out exped.
Jones, George Matthew (L.) — V. 36, Amphion, cutting out exped.
Jones, Jacob (C.) U.S. — V. 390-1, U.S. Wasp capts. Frolic; 393, 434, captd. by Poictiers. VI. 98, U.S. Macedonian, Sq. crsg.; 195-6, Lake Ontario.
Jones, James (Mr.Mt.) — III. 124, Bordelais, w. in actn.
Jones, Jenkin (Mr.Mt.) — V. 174, Africaine, cutting out exped.; 178, w. in actn. VI. 394. L.Com. Julia, wrkd. off Tristan d'Acunha.
Jones, John (L.) ...... — IV. 259, Pomone, cutting out exped.
Jones, Joshua (Mr.) ... — IV. 382, Amaranthe, w. in actn.
Jones, Lewis Tobias (Mid.) — VI. 288, Granicus, w. Algiers.
Jones, Richard (L.) ... — II. 197, Defence, the Nile; 210, pro. Cr.
Jones, Robert (C.) ...... — III. 65-7, invas. flotilla.
Jones, Thomas L. ...... — V. 327, Briseis, cutting out exped.
Jones, Thos. Ap Catesby (L.Com.) U.S. — VI. 232, Chandeleur Isles.
Jones, Thomas William (L.Com.) — VI. 9-10, Alphea, k. in actn. with Renard; 382, App.
Jones, William (S.) ... — I. 87, Toulon.
Jones, Wm. (Mr.Mt.) — IV. 230, Windsor Castle, w. Dardanelles.
Jones, — (Mid.) ... .. — II. 81, Triumph, w. Camperdown.
Jones, — (Mid.)......... — II. 326-9, Tigre, Acre.
Jopete, Don R. (C.) Sp. — III. 112, Sp. San Augustin, actn. Straits of Gibraltar.
Jordain, John (S.) ...... — II. 114, Magicienne, cutting out exped.
Jordon, Don Josef (C.) Sp. — II. 110, Sp. San Damaso captd. by Br. Sq.
Jorgenson, Jorgen (C.) Da. — IV. 307, Da. Admiral Yawl captd. by Sappho.
Jortis, Martin (C.) F. — VI. 9, Invincible (priv.) captd. by Mutine.
Joy, William (B.) ...... — III. 55, Ganges, w. Copenhagen.
Joyce, John (C.)......... — IV. 400-5, Redpole, Basque Rds. V. 450, Manilla, wrkd. off the Texel.
Jugan, Nicolas (C.) F. — IV. 164-75, Thémis, crsg. W. Indies; 444, Magnanime, Toulon Flt.
Julian, Don Joseph (L.Com.) Sp. — IV. 136, Sp. Vigilante cut out by the bts. of Renommée.
Jump, Robert (L.Com.) — III. 72, Sprightly; 483, captd. by F. Sq.

Keats, Richard Goodwin (P.C.) — I. 62, London, Channel Flt.; 235, Galatea, crsg.; 279 Quiberon exped.; 355-6, actn. with F. frigates; 381-3, des. Andromaque. II. 139, Boadicea, crsg.; 302, actn. Isle of Aix. III. 10, crsg.; 98-110, Superb, Sq. off Cadiz; 175-8, Toulon; 236, Algiers; 335-46, Medn. Flt. IV. 90-1, Sq. off Teneriffe; 165, Cmde., crsg. W. Indies; 200, Ganges; 201-7-11, Great Belt; 239 Chasseron; 298, Superb, R.A. Baltic Flt.; 303-5, Nyborg; 396, made K.B.
„ Sir Richard Goodwin, K.B. — IV. 433-8, Scheldt exped. VI. 73, V.A. Bellerophon, crsg. Newfoundland.

INDEX TO NAVAL OFFICERS 109

Keay, — (Mid.).........	VI. 288, Glasgow, w. Algiers.
Keele, Charles (L.) ...	VI. 313–14–21–8–9, Burmese War ; 353–4, App.
Keele, Edward (Mid.)	V. 417, Java, k. in actn.
Keenor, George (L.) ...	II. 80, Bedford, w. Camperdown.
Keilly, Richard (C.) ...	IV. 465, Busy, fndrd. off Halifax, drnd.
Keith, Sir George Morat, Bart. (L.Com.)	IV. 187, Protector (brig), Cape of Good Hope. V. 220, Redbreast, Sq. off the Texel. VI. 6, capture of Gluckstadt.
Keith, Lord, K.B. (A.)	*See* Hon. George Keith Elphinstone.
Kellet, Augustus Hy. (L.)	VI. 312–17–22–3–8–9–38, Burmese War ; 352, App.
Kelly, Benedictus Marwood (C.)	V. 303, Dasher, capture of Java.
Kelly, Edward (L.) ...	V. 42, Lynx, cutting out exped.
Kelly, William (L.) ...	III. 79, Minerve, actn. off Vado.
Kelly, William Hancock (P.C.)	I. 241, Solebay, capture of Martinique ; 313, 332, Veteran, crsg. II. 289, Gibraltar, Flt. off Cadiz. III. 73, Medn.
Kempthorn, Charles Henry (Mid.)	V. 37, Amphion, cutting out exped.
Kempthorne, William (L.Com.)	V. 43, Diana capts. Du. Zephyr ; 45, pro. Cr. ; 445, wrkd. E. Indies. VI. 278, Belzebub (bomb.), Algiers.
Kenah, Richard (C.) ...	V. 195, 202, Barracouta, capture of Banda Neira. VI. 181, Ætna (bomb.), Potomac exped. ; 190–2, k. in actn. Baltimore.
Kendall, Geo. (M.L.)	V. 40, Bellerophon, cutting out exped.
Kenkin, Klaas (C.) *Du.*	IV. 163, Du. Vittoria captured by Harrier and consort.
Kennan, Thomas (C.)	VI. 313, Burmese War.
Kennedy, Thomas (L.)	III. 443, Téméraire, Trafalgar ; 464, pro. Cr.
Kennedy, Thomas Fortescue (L.)	II. 241, Sibylle, Com. prize Corrigidore Isle.
Kennicott, Chas. (Mid.)	VI. 41, Amelia, k. in actn.
Kennicott, Gilbert (Mid.)	III. 406, Royal Soverign, w. Trafalgar.
Kent, Bartholomew (L.)	V. 380–6, Guerrière, w. in actn.
Kent, R. (M.C.)	IV. 225–9, Canopus, k. Dardanelles.
Kentish, Samuel (L.)...	VI. 15, Royalist, w. in actn.
Ker, George Lewis (L.Com.)	III. 317, Teazer captd. by F. gbts. IV. 457, App.
Kerangoué, — (L.) *F.*	V. 17, Niemen, in actn.
Keranguen, Bertrand (C.) *F.*	I. 60, Achille, Brest Flt.; 141, Eole ; 163, 1st June.
Kerdaniel, G. E. L. Le Marant (L.Com.) *F.*	IV. 242, Favourite captd. by Jason. V. 23–5, Furieuse captd. by Bonne Citoyenne, w. in actn.
Kergre, Joseph Normand. (L.Com.) *F.*	V. 47, 50, Loire (en flûte) destd. at Anse la Barque by the Br.
Kerguelen, Yves. J. (R.A.) *F.*	I. 60, Auguste, Brest Flt.; 135, imprisoned ; 194, 258–64–76, 386, Isle of France. III. 96, A. Brest Flt.
Kerimel, François Louis (L.Com.) *F.*	III. 180, Bacchante captd. by Endymion.
Kerjulien, Julien M. Cosmao (Cmde.) *F.*	II. 286, Jemmappes, Brest Flt. III. 334, Annibal, Toulon Flt.; 361, Pluton, Calder's actn.; 386–9, 409–11, Trafalgar, 455, Cadiz Bay. IV. 444, R.A. Commerce de Paris, Toulon
„ Baron J. M. Cosmao	Flt. VI. 1, created Baron, Wagram ; 2–3, actn. off Toulon ; 117, Toulon.
Kerr, Alex. Robert (L).	I. 112, Boston, w. in actn. II. 386, Clyde, in actn. pro. Cr. IV. 391, C. Valiant, blockading Sq. in Orient Rds. ; 396, Revenge, Basque Rds. actn. V. 98, Unicorn capts. Laurel. VI. 99, Acasta, New London ; 247, Boston Bay ; 252, W. Indies.
Kerr, James (Mr.)......	V. 359, Belvidera, in actn.
Kerr, Lord Mark Robt. (C.)	II. 219–20, Cormorant, capture of Minorca.

Kersteman, Lambert (L.)	IV. 282, Psyche, cutting out exped.
Kerwal, — (C.) *Du*....	I. 221, Du. Amazone, off Java.
Khrom, Jos. H. Isidore (Cmde.) *F.*	IV. 88, Patriote, Sq. crsg.; 287, Isle of Aix.
Kidd, Joseph (L.Com.)	IV. 474, Hirondelle, wrkd. near Tunis.
Killkert, — (A.) *Du.*	III. 267, Sq. in the Texel.
Killogrivoff, — (L.) *Rus.*	III. 16, St. Croix, Penmarcks, Vol. cutting out exped.
Kindall, Bernard (M.L.)	IV. 378, Amethyst, k. in actn.
King, Andrew (L.) ...	III. 54-7, Désirée, Copenhagen; 418, 443, Victory, Trafalgar; 464, pro. Cr. IV. 439, act.C. Venerable, Scheldt exped.
King, Hon. Edward (C.)	III. 319, Ariadne, Sq. off Gravelines. IV. 167-8, Alexandria, Rio de la Plata, cutting out exped.
King, Edward Durnford (L.)	I. 370, Dryad, in actn. pro. Cr.
King, George Morison (L.)	VI. 287, Queen Charlotte, Algiers.
King, Henry (L.)	VI. 186, Seahorse, Alexandria.
King, Norfolk (Mid.)	IV. 221, Dardanelles. VI. 167, L.Com. Ballahou (cutter), captd. by U.S. Perry (cutter); 388, App.
King, Sir Richard (V.A.)	I. 125, Stately, Com. N. American Sq.
King, Richard (P.C.)	II. 10, Druid, crsg.; 270, Sirius capts. Du. Waakzaamheid. III. 123, capts. with consorts Dédaigneuse; 375, Achille,
,, Sir Richard, Bart.	off Cadiz; 384-9, 416-17, 464, Trafalgar. IV. 175, Sq. off Rochefort. VI. 2, R.A. Medn., San Josef; 117, Medn. Flt.
King, Robert (Mr.Mt.)	V. 7, Horatio, w. in actn.
King, William (L.) ...	III. 254, act.Cr. Drake, crsg. Martinique; 256, Guadaloupe; 298, Centaur, w. capture of Surinam. IV. 186, C. Espoir, Cape of Good Hope exped.; 466, Prospero (bomb.), fndrd. North Sea, drnd.
King, William (P.C.)	IV. 189, Diadem, capture of Buenos Ayres.
King, W. Elletson (L.Cr.)	V. 451, Sentinel, wrkd. Isle of Rugen.
Kingdom, John (Mid.)	V. 100, Surveillante, cutting out exped.
Kingston, John (M.L.)	III. 426, Téméraire, k. Trafalgar.
Kingston, Robert (Mid.)	V. 244, Active, actn. off Lissa.
Kinneer, — (Mid.) ...	I. 185, Queen, w. 1st June.
Kippen, George (C.) ...	VI. 201, Peruvian, Penobscot exped.
Kirby, Edward (Mr.)	II. 196, Bellerophon, w. the Nile.
Kirby, Wm. (L.Com.)	V. 448, Chichester (S.S.), with invas. flotilla, wrkd. Madras Rds.
Kirby, William (Mr.)	III. 66, w. in actn.
Kirchner, John G. (L.)	II. 196, Minotaur, k. the Nile.
Kirk, Edward B. (Mid.)	VI. 264, Penguin, in actn.
Kirkpatrick, John (C.) *E.I.C.*	III. 250, E.I.C. Henry Addington, actn. with Linois' Sq. E. Indies.
Kittoe, Edward (C.) ...	IV. 433, Sabrina (sloop), Scheldt exped.
Kittoe, W. Hugh (C.)	I. 439, Espion captd. by F. frigates.
Knapman, Edwd. (Mid.)	III. 437, Spartiate, w. Trafalgar.
Knapman, William Stephens (M.L.)	V. 240, Volage, w. in actn. off Lissa.
Kneeshaw, Joshua (L.)	VI. 6, in actn. Cuxhaven.
Knight, Hood (L.) ...	IV. 204, Comus, in actn.; 244, cutting out exped.
Knight, John (P.C.) ...	I. 72, Victory, at Toulon; 213, Corsica; 297, Hyères. II. 75, Montagu; 81, Camperdown; 289, Flt. off Cadiz. III. 346, R.A. Queen, Flt. at Madeira.
Knight, Thomas Edward (Mr.Mt.)	IV. 316, Childers, cutting out exped.

INDEX TO NAVAL OFFICERS

Knight, Wm. (Mid.)	I. 87, Toulon. II. 323, 325, L., w. in actn. Acre.
Knowles, Sir Charles H. Bart. (P.C.)	II. 34, Goliath, Channel Flt.
Kolff, — (C.) *Du*.......	II. 76, Du. Mars, Camperdown; 343, Du. Utrecht, Flt. blockaded in the Texel.
Krabbe, — (C.) *Du*. ...	III. 41, Du Freya engages Nemesis.
Kraft, — (C.) *Du*.......	II. 76-9, Du. Alkmaar captd. at Camperdown.
Krebs, — (Mr. Mt.) ...	III. 87, k. in actn. Egypt.
Krusenstjerna, — (C.) *Swd*.	IV. 299, Swd. Gustav. IV. Adolph., Br. Swd. Flt. Oro Rds.
Kynaston, Charles R. (Mid.)	IV. 101, Donegal, k. in actn.
Kynson, Joshua (Mr.-Mt.)	IV. 447, Tigre, cutting out exped.
Laar, Paul R. Cantz (C.) *F*.	VI. 12, Weser, actn. with Br. brigs.
Labatul, — (C.) *F*. ...	I. 60, Convention, Brest Flt.
Labretonnière, Guillaume Botherel (L. Cr.) *F*.	V. 2, Hébé captd. by Loire.
Lacaille, Chas. Nicolas (C.) *F*.	IV. 391, Tourville, Brest Flt.; 417-29, Basque Rds.
Lacey, — (B.)	V. 16, Amethyst, w. in actn.
Laconture, Martin Antoine (C.) *F*.	II. 139, Sémillante, Rochefort Sq.
Lacroix, Louis G. Prevost de (C.) *F*.	IV. 88, Eole, Sq. crsg. W. Indies.
Lafon, Jean Baptiste (C.) *F*.	IV. 395, Calcutta (en flûte), Sq. blockaded in Basque Rds. 411-12, actn. in Basque Rds. ; 429, executed.
Lafont, Galien (C.) *F*.	V. 105-6, Jeune Louise captd. by Quebec, k. in actn.
Laforey, Francis (C.) ,, Sir Francis, Bart.	I. 228-9, Carysfort capts. Castor; 379, Beaulieu, crsg. II. 128, Hydra St. Marcouf; 133, off Havre ; 134-5, des. Confiante. III. 347, Spartiate, Antigua ; 384, 410-36-7, 464, Trafalgar. IV. 288, Sq. at Palermo. V. 32, Medn.
Laforey, Sir John (V.A.)	I. 126-7, Trusty, Com. at Barbadoes ; 409-10, A. Martinique exped., resigns command.
Lagarde, René J. M. Denis (C.) *F*.	VI. 131-6, Clorinde captd. by Eurotas.
Lagerstrale, —(C.) *Swd*.	IV. 299, Swd. Gustav. IV. Adolph., Br. Swd. Flt. Oro Rds.
Lahalle, Pierre Nicolas (C.) *F*.	V. 3, Topaze captd. by Cleopatra and consorts ; 77, Cayenne. VI. 44, Hortense, Brest.
Laignel, Gaspard (C.)*F*.	IV. 88, Jupiter, Sq. crsg. W. Indies ; 444, Borée, Toulon Flt.
Laing, David (Mr.) ...	V. 250, Alacrity, w. in actn.
Lake, John (L. Com.)	III. 316, Locust, Channel, invas. flotilla.
Lake, Hon. Warwick (L.)	III. 197, Blanche, cutting out exped. IV. 273-4, C. Recruit, crsg. W. Indies; 275, dismissed (1810). V. 22, Intrepid, crsg. (1809).
Lake, Willoughby Thos. (P.C.)	IV. 112, Gibraltar, Sq. crsg. V. 336, Magnificent, w. capture of Santander. VI. 133, gun trials of Eurotas.
Lallemand, Felix L. (C.) *F*.	II. 414, Guerrier (priv.) captd. by Courier.
Lalonde, — (C.) *F*. ...	III. 96, Formidable ; 100-5, k. in actn. Algesiras.
Lamandé, — (Mr.) *F*.	II. 20, loss of Droits de l'Homme.
Lamarque, Chas. (C.) *F*.	III. 276, Dame Ambert (priv.) capts. Lilly.
Lamb, John (Mid.)......	IV. 127, Franchise, cutting out exped. ; 314, L. Aigle, w. in actn.
Lamb, Thomas (Mid.)	II. 329, drnd. at Acre.
Lamb, William (L.) ..	II. 88, Isis, Camperdown, pro. Cr.
Lambert, Alexandre (C.) *F*.	IV. 159, Syrène, Sq. crsg.

Lambert, Arthur (Mid.)	II. 323, k. at Acre.
Lambert, Henry (C.)...	III. 267–9, Wilhelmina engages Psyché ; 271, pro. P.C. IV. 18–19, San Fiorenzo capts. Psyché. V. 137, Iphigenia ; 145, Port Louis ; 158-62-7-70, Grand Port ; 409, Java ; 412-15, captd. by U.S. Constitution, w. in actn. ; 421-2, d. ; 445, 450, App.
Lambert, Robert (P.C.)	I. 336, Suffolk, Ceylon ; 414, capture of Amboyna. III. 47, Saturn, Copenhagen. VI. 117, Duncan, Medn. Flt.; 133, gun trials of Eurotas.
Lambour, Bernard Isodore (C.) F.	III. 222, Ostende, invas. flotilla ; 319, Dunkerque.
Lamel, — (C.) F.	I. 141, Indomptable ; 152, 29th May ; 197, 1st June.
Lamond, Daniel (Mr.)	III. 55, Isis, k. Copenhagen.
Lamphier, Vernon (L.)	V. 80, w. capture of St. Maura.
Lancaster, Henry (Mid.)	IV. 448, Apollo, cutting out exped.
Lancaster, Robt. Daniel (L. Com.)	VI. 167, Landrail (cutter) captd. by U.S. Syren (priv.) ; 388, App.
Lancaster, — (C.) Du.	II. 76–9, Du. Monnikendam captd. at Camperdown.
Landais, — (R.A.) F.	I. 60, Bretagne, Brest Flt. ; 135, in actn. Belle Isle.
Landolphe, Jean François (Cmde.) F.	III. 22, Concorde, capture of E.I.C. ships.
Landry, François Timothée (L.Cr.) F.	II. 295, Salamine captd. by Br. Flt.
Lane, George D. (Mid.)	IV. 346, Porcupine, cutting out exped.
Lane, Richard (P.C.)...	I. 411, Astrea, W. Indies.
Lane, William (L.) ...	II. 88, Agincourt, Camperdown, pro. Cr.
Lanfesty, — (Mid.) ...	II. 196, Zealous, w. the Nile.
Lang, Jack (A.B.)......	V. 391, U.S. Wasp, in actn., deserter.
Langara, Don Juan de (A.) Sp.	I. 80–5, 93, Toulon ; 345–6, Medn.; 349, Toulon ; 441, App. II. 36, Toulon.
Langdon, John (L.) ...	IV. 230, Endymion, w. Dardanelles.
Langford, Frederick (L.)	III. 66, w. in actn. IV. 91, C. Lark, crsg.
Langford, George (C.)	IV. 307, Sappho capts. Da. Admiral Yawl.
Langland, Roger (Mr.)	V. 257, Pilot, cutting out exped. ; 341-2, cutting out exped., pro. L.
Langlois, Claude Marie (C.) F.	I. 60, 141, Tourville, Brest Flt.
Langlois, Jean Jacques Jude (C.) F.	IV. 175, Armide captd. by Br. Sq.
Langton, Thomas Wm. (Mid.)	V. 349, Bacchante. VI. 23, cutting out expeds.
Langton, William (Mid.)	V. 299, Minden, w. capture of Java exped.
Lanier, Pierre J. B. M. (C.) F.	V. 122-4, Uranie, Sq. crsg. off Lissa.
Lapenotiere, John Richards (L.Com.)	III. 384, Pickle (schooner), Flt. off Cadiz. V. 104, C. Orestes, capts. Loup Garou (priv.)
Lapointe, — (C.) F. ...	III. 280-1, Général Ernouf, Guadaloupe. IV. 26-7, destd. by Renard.
Larans, James (S.)......	V. 329, Horatio, k. in actn.
Larcom, Joseph (L.)...	I. 200, Thunderer, 1st June, pro. Cr.
Larcom, Thomas (P.C.)	I. 271-5, Russel, actn. off Isle Groix. II. 285, Prince, Channel Flt. ; 297, Triumph, Minorca.
Larkan, John (L.)......	I. 200, Defence, 1st June, pro. Cr.
Larkan, Robert (L.)...	I. 199, Leviathan, 1st June, pro. Cr.
Larkins, Thomas (C.) E.I.C.	III. 250-4, E.I.C. Warren Hastings, actn. with Linois' Sq., E. Indies. IV. 149-54, captd. by Piémontaise, w. in actn.
Larmour, John (L.) ...	III. 83, Diadem, Egypt exped.
Laroche, Christopher (P.C.)	IV. 259-63, Uranie, crsg. off Cherbourg.
Laronier, Clement (C.) F.	II. 5, Pégase, Brest Flt.

INDEX TO NAVAL OFFICERS 113

Laroque, Jean B. M. (C.) *F.* — II. 91, Résistance captd. by San Fiorenzo and Nymphe.
Larrégny, — (C.) *F.* ... I. 141, Mucius, Brest Flt.
Latour, — (C.) *F.* ...... I. 389–94, Seine, k. in actn. with two Br. 74's.
Laugharne, Thos. Lamb Polden (L.) — V. 58, Otter, cutting out exped.; 138, Néréide, cutting out exped.; 365–6, C. Alert, captd. by U.S. Essex; 450, App.
Launder, William (L.) — II. 196, Bellerophon, k. the Nile.
Laurence, Norbez (C.) *F.* — V. 110, Mamelouk (priv.) captd. by Rosario.
Laurie, James (M.L.)... — VI. 206, in actn. Canadian Lakes.
Laurie, Sir Robt., Bart. (P.C.) — IV. 20–6, Cleopatra captd. by Ville de Milan; 456, App.
Lavie, Thomas (P.C.) — IV. 160–1, Blanche capts. Guerrière; 162, kntd.; 179, Sq. crsg.; 465, wrkd. off Ushant.
,, Sir Thomas ...
Law, John (M.L.)...... — VI. 58–66, Shannon, in actn. with Chesapeake.
Lawford, John (P.C.)... — I. 439, Convert, wrkd. W. Indies. II. 345, Romney, Holland exped. III. 46, Polyphemus, Copenhagen. IV. 313, Impétueux, Medn.
Lawless, Paul (L.)...... — IV. 301, Centaur, w. in actn. Baltic.
Lawless, Peter (C.) ... — VI. 387, Vautour, fndrd., drnd.
Lawrence, Daniel (L.) — IV. 334, Heureux, cutting out exped.
Lawrence, James (L.-Com.) — IV. 336, Rook (schooner) captd. by F. privs., k. in actn.; 475, App.
Lawrence, James (L.) *U.S.* — III. 301–2, U.S. Constitution at Tripoli. V. 356, C. Hornet, Sq. crsg.; 408, off St. Salvador. VI. 44–5, St. Salvador; 46–7, capts. Peacock; 52–60, U.S. Chesapeake captd. by Shannon; 61, w. in actn.; 66–9, d. at Halifax.
Lawrence, Jeremiah (Mid.) — IV. 100, Northumberland, w. in actn.
Lawrence, John (M.Art.L.) — VI. 178, A.D.C. battle of Bladensburg.
Lawrence, John (A.B.) — IV. 253, U.S. Chesapeake, k. in actn. (deserter).
Lawrence, Thomas Lewis (M.Art.L.) — V. 336, capture of Santander.
Lawrie, Robert (L.) ... — I. 155, Queen, 29th May. III. 130, C. Cleopatra, crsg.
Lawrie, William (M.L.) — IV. 221, Dardanelles.
Lawson William (Mr.) — II. 196, Alexander, w. the Nile.
Lawson, Wm. (Mr.Mt.) — IV. 37, Cambrian, w. in actn.
Lawson, Wm. (Mid.) — VI. 16, capture of St. Sebastian.
Layman, William (C.) — III. 494, Weazle, wrkd. in Gibraltar Bay. IV. 456, Raven, wrkd. in Cadiz Bay. V. 428, Sq. crsg.
Leach, James (L.Com.) — IV. 475, Millbrook, wrkd. on the Burlings.
Leake, Henry Martin (Mid.) — VI. 66, Shannon, in actn. with Chesapeake.
Leake, Henry Martin (L.Com). — III. 267, Swift captd. by Espérance (priv.)
Lebastard, Jean M. P. (L.Com.) *F.* — II. 139, Biche (schooner), Brest. III. 182, C. Créole, captd. by Br. Sq.
Lebeau, Pierre Mandé (C.) *F.* — I. 141, Républicain, Brest Flt.
Lebozec, Charles (C.) *F.* — II. 286, Convention, Brest Flt. IV. 391, Jean Bart, Brest.
Lebrun, Jean Marie (C.) *F.* — II. 5, Pluton, Ireland exped.
Lecamus, Felix M. L. A. J. J. (L.Com.) *F.* — VI. 18, Fortune destd. by Euryalus.
Leckey, John (Mr.Mt.) — II. 262, Leander, w. in actn.
Lecolier, Jean Bap. L. (L.Com.) *F.* — II. 134–6, Vésuve, actn. with Hydra and consorts.
Leddon, Wm. (M.L.) — III. 417, Achille, w. Trafalgar.
Leduc, Amand (Cmde.) *F.* — IV. 159–62, Revanche, Medn.

I

Lee, John (C.)	II. 390-2, Camel (en flûte), Algoa Bay.
Lee, Michael (Mr.) ...	II. 262, Leander, w. in actn.
Lee, Richard (P.C.) ...	III. 485, Assistance, wrkd. Dunkerque. IV. 3-9, Courageux, Strachan's actn. ; 157, Monarch, Sq. off Rochefort ; 175-6, capture of F. frigates ; 236, Sq. off the Tagus. V. 230, Sq. crsg.
Lee, W. V. (Mid.)......	VI. 374, w. Navarino.
Leech, Andrew (Mr.)...	VI. 143-4, Primrose, w. in actn.
Leech, Robert (Mid.)	V. 178, Africaine, w. in actn.
Leef, Thomas (C.)	III. 18-19, Comet (F.S.) destd. in Dunkerque Rds. ; 477, App.
Leeke, Henry John (Mid.)	IV. 448, Ville de Paris, cutting out exped. Rosas Bay.
Lefroy, Christopher H. B. (Mid.)	IV. 19, San Fiorenzo, k. in actn.
Legge, Hon. Arthur Kaye (P.C.)	I. 139, Niger, Channel Flt. ; 329-30, Latona, crsg. III. 357, Repulse ; 358-62, Calder's actn. IV. 89, Sq. crsg ; 217-19-21-8, Dardanelles ; 292, Sq. Syracuse ; 439 Scheldt exped.
Leggett, John (S.)	I. 318, Hebe, w. in actn.
Legrand, Jean François (C.) F.	II. 139, Immortalité, Ireland exped ; 152-3, crsg. ; 160-1, captd. by Fisgard, k. in actn.
Legras, François (C.) F.	IV. 444, Robuste, Toulon Flt. VI. 3, Wagram, Toulon Flt.
Leigh, Thos. (Mr. Mt.)	V. 126, Pilot, cutting out exped.
Leissegues, Corentin Urbain (V.A.) F.	IV. 88-90, Imperial, Sq. crsg. ; 94-5, actn. with Duckworth's Sq. ; 97, destd. ; 102-3-8, 133, tactics of.
Lejoille, — (C.) F.......	I. 283-4, Alceste, w. in actn. with Berwick. II. 260-4, Cmde., Généreux capts. Leander ; 304, Brindisi, k. in actn.
Lelarge, — (R.A.) F.	I. 60, Côte d'Or, Brest Flt. ; 135, executed.
Lemaître, Joseph (L.) F.	VI. 136, Clorinde, in actn.
Lemaresquier, Jean François (C.) F.	IV. 371-3, Diligent engages Recruit. V. 91-2, Néréide, Isle of France ; 282-9, actn. off Madagascar ; 291, k. in actn.
Lemprière, George (Mid.)	II. 268, Leander, in actn. III. 490, L.Com. Redbridge, captd. by F. Sq.
Lennock, George Gustavus (C.)	V. 220, Raven, Sq. crsg. off the Texel ; 324, actn. with invas. flotilla.
Lennox, Charles (C.) E.I.C.	II. 89, E.I.C. Woodford and consorts beat off F. Sq.
Lenox, Joseph (L.) ...	I. 363, Spencer (sloop), in actn.
Leopard, Thos. (Mid.)	II. 81, Ardent, w. Camperdown.
Leriche, William (Pr.)	IV. 170, Bacchante, cutting out exped.
Lesby, William (Mr.)	V. 156, Néréide ; 161, 169, w. in actn. Grand Port.
Lester, William (L.) ...	VI. 35, Furieuse, cutting out exped.
L'Estrille, Dumisuilde (C.L.) Du.	II. 76, Du. Heldin, Camperdown.
Letchmere, Wm. (P.C.)	III. 357, Thunderer ; 358-62, Calder's actn. ; 384, Trafalgar.
Letellier, Jean Marie (C.) F.	III. 334 Formidable, Toulon Flt. ; 386, 433-4, Trafalgar. VI. 3, Agamemnon, Toulon Flt.
Letellier, — (L.) F. ...	VI. 366-9-74, Navarino.
Lett, — (Mr.Mt.)	VI. 312, Burmese War ; 328, 343, Mid., Burmese War.
L'Evêque, Chas. (C.) F.	III. 326, invas. flotilla.
Lévêque, Jean Pierre (C.) F.	I. 60, Impétueux, Brest Flt.
Lew, Henry (Mid.) ...	V. 256, Active, cutting out exped.
Lew, James (Mid.) ...	V. 244, Active, in actn. off Lissa.
Lewis, Alexander (Mr.)	VI. 36, Guadeloupe, cutting out exped.
Lewis, Fredk. (C.Ck.)	V. 239, Amphion, w. in actn.
Lewis, Geo. (M.Maj.)	V. 171, Chesapeake Bay.
Lewis, Henry (M.L.)	V. 289, Astrea, w. in actn.
Lewis, John (Mid.) ...	VI. 373, k. Navarino.

INDEX TO NAVAL OFFICERS 115

Lewis, Joseph (L.) ...	IV. 167-8, Alexandria, w. cutting out exped.
Lewis, Thomas (P.C.)...	II. 306, Minotaur, cutting out exped.
Lewis, William (Mid.)	V. 349, Minstrel, cutting out exped.
L'Héritier, Louis(C.)*F.*	I. 141, America, Brest Flt. II. 5, Cmde. Constitution, Ireland exped.; 121-3, Hercule captd. by Mars; 285, Invincible, Brest.
L'Hermite, Jean M. Adrien (C.) *F.*	I. 163, Tamise, 1st June; 287, Vertu, Santa Cruz. II. 244, Preneuse capts. E.I.C. ships; 390-1, actn. with Camel (en flûte) and consort,; 392-3, actn. with Jupiter; 394, destd. by Tremendous and Adamant. IV. 178, Cmde. Regulus, Sq. crsg. W. Indies. V. 207, R.A.; 315, Toulon Flt.
L'Huillier, — (C.) *F.*	I. 228-9, Castor captd. by Carysfort.
Libby, Edward (L.) ...	II. 49, Blenheim, w. St. Vincent.
Liddon, Matthew (Mid.)	V. 126, Thames, cutting out exped. VI. 84, L. Maidstone, cutting out exped.
Lilburne, James (L.)...	III. 443, Swiftsure, Trafalgar; 464, pro. Cr. V. 211-16, C. Goshawk, off Havre.
Lillenshield, — (C.L.) *Da.*	III. 58, Da. Hielpern, Copenhagen.
Lillicrap, James (L.)...	III. 116, Venerable, in actn. Gut of Gibraltar, pro. Cr. VI. 140, C. Eurotas, capture of Clorinde.
Lily, Peter (M.C.)......	III. 439, Revenge, w. Trafalgar.
Liming, John (B.)	IV. 319, Stately, w. in actn.
Lind, James (P.C.) ...	III. 271-82, Centurion, Vizagapatam Rds.; 284, engages Marengo and consorts.
Lindguist, Wm. (Pilot)	VI. 303-8-18-22, Burmese War.
Lindsay, Charles (C.)	II. 34-7-8, Bonne Citoyenne, St. Vincent.
Lindsay, James (L.) ...	IV. 383, Kent, cutting out exped.
Lindsey, David (C.Ck.)	III. 105, Hannibal, k. Algesiras.
Linois, Charles A. L. Durand (C.) *F.*	I. 135, Atalante; 227-8, captd. by Swiftsure; 273, Formidable captd. in actn. off Isle Groix; 275, w.; 356-8, Unité captd. by Révolutionnaire and consorts. II. 5, Cmde. Nestor, Ireland exped.; 286, R.A. Brest Flt. III. 96-109, Algesiras; 164, St. Domingo exped.; 208, Marengo, Pondicherry; 210, Isle of France; 251-4, actn. with E.I.C. ships, E. Indies; 283-6, actn. with Centurion. IV. 20, 50, Isle of France; 51, crsg.; 52, engages Blenheim; 130, captd.
,, Comte Charles A. L. Durand	by London and consorts; 131, w. in actn. VI. 229, Comte, V.A., Gvr. of Guadaloupe.
Linthorne, Thomas (L.)	II. 88, Montagu, Camperdown, pro. Cr.
Linthorne, — (Mid.)...	I. 175, Marlborough, w. 1st June.
Linzee, Robert (P.C.)	I. 72, Alcide, Medn. Flt.; 94, Cmde.; 95-6, exped. to Corsica; 207, Corsica; 214, R.A. Medn. Flt.; 215, Windsor Castle; 284, Flt. in Leghorn Rds.; 297, V.A. actn. off Hyères.
Linzee, Samuel Hood (C.)	I. 305, Nemesis captd. by Sensible and Sardine; 443, App. III. 123, Oiseau, crsg.; 357-62, Warrior, Calder's actn. IV. 200, Maida, Copenhagen.
Lions, Ambrose (Mr.)	III. 149, Pasley, k. in actn.
Lions, John (Mid.) ...	III. 124, Bordelais, w. in actn.
Little, James (L.)	IV. 264, Hydra, cutting out exped.
Little, John (L.Com.)	V. 447, Firm (brig), wrkd. France. VI. 394, Telegraph (brig), wrkd. on Mount Batten, drnd.
,, ,, C. B. ...	
Little, Richard (B.) ...	III. 412, Tonnant, w. Trafalgar.
Little, Robert John (M.L.Art.)	V. 102, cutting out exped.
Little, — (C.) *U.S.* ...	III. 32, U.S. Boston capts. F. Berceau.
Littlehales, Bendall Robert (L.)	II. 19, Amazon, in actn. pro. Cr. III. 203, C. Centaur, W. Indies.
Littlejohn, Adam (P.C.)	I. 282, Berwick captd. by F. Flt.; 283, k. in actn.; 443, App.

Littlejohn, David (Mid.)	VI. 66, Shannon, in actn. with Chesapeake.
Liven, Thomas (Mid.)	V. 212, Scylla, w. in actn.
Livermore, Samuel (act. Chaplain) *U.S.*	VI. 61, U.S. Chesapeake, w. in actn. with Shannon.
Livingstone, George A. (M.L.)	II. 49, Culloden, k. St. Vincent.
Livingstone, Sir Thos., Bart. (P.C.)	III. 74, Athénien, Medn. ; 323, Renommée, actn. off Calais. IV. 136, 270, Carthagena.
Lloyd, Edward (L.) ...	V. 60, Raisonable, w. in actn. VI. 298, C. Esk, crsg.
Lloyd, Henry (L.)......	I. 382, Galatea des. Andromaque. II. 232, Aurora, cutting out exped.
Lloyd, James L. (L.)...	III. 437, Dreadnought, w. Trafalgar.
Lloyd, John (Mr.Mt.)	III. 258, Hippomenes, w. in actn.
Lloyd, Meyricke (Mid.)	IV. 143, Sirius, w. in actn.
Lloyd, Richard (L.) ...	V. 248, Alceste, in actn. Parenza.
Lloyd, Robert (C.) ...	II. 415, Racoon capts. Intrépide. VI. 149, 223, Plantagenet, crsg. Western Isles.
Lloyd, Robert (L.) ...	III. 435-6, Conqueror, k. Trafalgar.
Lloyd, Samuel (M.L.)	VI. 29-31, Elizabeth, w. in actn. Adriatic.
Lloyd, Walter Griffith (M.L.)	V. 119, Alceste, cutting out exped. VI. 196, Hogue, cutting out exped.
Lloyd, William (Mid.)	VI. 374, w. Navarino.
Lobb, William Grenville (P.C.)	II. 412-13, Crescent, actn. with Sp. Sq.
Lochner, John Christopher (C.) *E.I.C.*	III. 250, E.I.C. Ocean, actn. with Linois' Sq., E. Indies.
Lock, Andrew (B.) ...	V. 7, Horatio, w. in actn.
Lock, Francis Erskine (C.)	VI. 128, Sparrow, crsg. off St. Malo.
Lock, George (M.L.)...	V. 297, Sir Francis Drake, capture of Java.
Lockyer, Nicholas (L.)	III. 278, Tartar, cutting out exped. IV. 304, C. Hound (bomb.), Nyborg. VI. 231, Sophie, Chandeleur Isles ; 232-3, actn. with U.S. gunboats ; 234, pro. P.
Lodwick, Wm. (Car.)	IV. 387, Impérieuse, in actn. at Rosas.
Logan, John (C.) *E.I.C.*	III. 283, E.I.C. Princess Charlotte, Vizagapatam Rds.
Long, Beaulieu le (C.) *F.*	II. 365-9, Forte captd. by Sibylle.
Long, Charles (L.) ...	I. 318, Niger, w. in actn. II. 220, C. Peterel ; 221, captd. by Sp. Sq. ; 469, App.
Long, George (L.)......	I. 362-3, Niger, w. cutting out exped. III. 80-1, C. Vincejo, k. Egypt.
Long, Henry (M.L.)...	III. 55, Isis, k. Copenhagen.
Longer, Pierre Jacques (C.) *F.*	I. 141, Terrible, Brest Flt.
Lopez, Don Jesse (L.-Com.) *Sp.*	IV. 155, Sp. gbt. captd. by Minerva.
Lord, A. Bliss W. (L.-Com.)	V. 442, Claudia (cutter), wrkd. Norway.
Loring, John (C.)	I. 433, Conflagration (F.S.), destd. at Toulon. III. 186, Cmde. Bellerophon ; 204-6, Sq. off St. Domingo ; 489, App.
Loring, John Wentworth (Mid.)	I. 87, w. at Toulon. IV. 159, C. Niobe, capts. Néarque. V. 107, crsg. off Havre ; 108, actn. with F. frigates ; 212, crsg., Amazone destd.
Losack, George (P.C.)	I. 416, Jupiter, Sq. Cape of Good Hope. II. 358, Com. at the Cape.
Losack, Woodley (L.)	III. 137-8, Ville de Paris, cutting out of the Chevrette ; 141, pro. Cr. V. 283, C. Galatea ; 284-94, actn. off Madagascar ; 407, escapes U.S. frigates.
Louis, John (L.).........	III. 185, Naiad, cutting out exped.

INDEX TO NAVAL OFFICERS 117

Louis, Thomas (P.C.)	I. 62, Cumberland, Channel Flt.; 189-90, Minotaur, Sq. off Ushant. II. 171, Flt. off Cadiz; 432-5, blockade of Genoa. III. 27, Barcelona Rds.; 81, Egypt exped.; 228, R.A. Leopard, off Boulogne; 339, Canopus, Gulf of Palma; 379-80, Medn.; 458, off Cadiz. IV. 2, Medn.;
,, Sir Thomas, Bart.	90-101, Duckworth's actn.; 104, created Baronet; 117, Sq. off Belleisle; 178, capts. Présidente; 214, Malta; 217-25, Dardanelles; 233, Alexandria, Egypt exped., d. on board Canopus; 459, App.
Louthean, Alex. (Mr.)	VI. 186, Seahorse, Alexandria.
Louvel, Auguste François (C.) *F.*	IV. 444, Suffren, Toulon Flt. V. 10, Toulon.
Loveday, Edwd. (Mid.)	IV. 367, Cruiser, cutting out exped.
Lowdon, — (Mid.) ...	VI. 288, Leander, k. Algiers.
Lowry, James (Mid.)...	III. 27, Minotaur, cutting out exped.
Lucadore, — (C.) *F.*...	I. 141, Patriote, Rochefort Sq.
Lucas, Engelburtus (R.A.) *Du.*	I. 415-17, Du. Dordrecht captd. by Br. Sq. Cape of Good Hope.
Lucas, James (Mid.) ...	I. 182, Brunswick, k. 1st June.
Lucas, Jean Jacques Et. (C.) *F.*	III. 386, Rédoutable; 402-3, 418, 421, w. Trafalgar; 461, 501, App. IV. 11, 391, Regulus, Brest Flt.
Lucas, Mark Robinson (L.Com.)	IV. 321-2, Swan des. Da. cutter.
Lucas, Richard (P.C.)	I. 189, Arrogant, Channel Sq.; 333, Cape of Good Hope; 390-3, actn. with F. Sq.
Luckraft, Alfred (Mid.)	III. 410, Mars, w. Trafalgar.
Luckraft, John (L.-Com.)	IV. 457, Pigeon (schooner), wrkd. off the Texel.
Ludlow, Augustus Charles (L.) *U.S.*	VI. 61, U.S. Chesapeake captd. by Shannon; 67, w. in actn.; 69, d.
Ludlow, Charles (C.) *U.S.*	V. 273, U.S. President; 275-80, actn. with Little Belt.
Luke, George (L.)......	I. 108-9, Nymphe, w. in actn.
Luke, William (P.C.)	II. 289, Namur, Flt. off Cadiz; 428, Thames, Quiberon. IV. 175, Mars, Sq. off Rochefort; 201, Copenhagen; 298, Baltic Flt.
Lumley, John Richard (L.)	III. 275, Seahorse, cutting out exped. VI. 90, 169, C. Narcissus, Chesapeake Bay; 237, Pomone, New York; 240-1, actn. with U.S. President.
Lumsdaine, George (P.C.)	I. 101, Iris engages Citoyenne Française.
Lund, Thomas (Mid.)	II. 49, Captain, w. St. Vincent.
Luscombe, Sam. (Mid.)	II. 248, Jason, w. in actn.
Luthill, Hungerford (Mid.)	IV. 448, Topaze, cutting out exped.
Lutkin, — (R.A.) *Da.*	V. 230, Com. Da. Sq.
Lutkin,—(L.Com.)*Da.*	V. 229, Da. Alsen with consorts capts. Manly. VI. 5, Da. Jonge Troutman captd. by Br. bts.
Lutman, Chas. (Mid.)	IV. 320, Tartarus, cutting out exped.
Lutwidge, Skeffington (P.C.)	I. 72, Terrible, Medn. Flt. III. 42, V.A. Com. Downs station.
Lydiard, Charles (L.)	I. 371-2, Southampton capts. Utile, pro. Cr. IV. 114, C. Anson, engages Foudroyant; 169-70, engages Sp. Pomona and gbts.; 275-8, capture of Curaçoa; 465, wrkd. in Mounts Bay.
Lye, Wm. Jones (P.C.)	IV. 355, Terpsichore, Ceylon. V. 203, Doris, capture of Isle of France; 284-303, capture of Java exped.
Lyford, H. James (C.)	V. 442, Proselyte (bomb.), wrkd. in the Baltic.
Lynne, Henry (L.) ...	IV. 365, in actn. V. 172, Emma (T.S.), Isle of France 204, act.C. Eclipse, capture of the Isle of France.
Lyons, Ebenezer (B.-Mt.)	IV. 256, Richmond, cutting out exped.

Lyons, Edmund (Mid.)	IV. 221, Dardanelles. V. 199, capture of Banda Neira; 297, Minden; 298-9, capture of Java; 300, pro. Cr.
Lyons, — (L.)	VI. 374, w. Navarino.
Mabroux, — (C.) *F.* ...	II. 400, Iphigénie (priv.) destd. in actn. with Trincomalé.
M'Adam, David (M.L.)	V. 126, 256, Thames, cutting out expeds.
Macartney, Lord (Gvr.)	II. 117, Cape of Good Hope.
M'Auley, Angus (Passenger)	V. 26, Bonne Citoyenne, in actn.
M'Beath, Alex. (L.) ...	II. 114, Regulus, cutting out exped.
Macbride, John (R.A.)	I. 40, 62-5, Cumberland, Channel Flt.; 99, Com. Holland exped.; 372, Com. at Sheerness. II. 119, Minotaur, armament of.
M'Call, Edwd. R. (L.) *U.S.*	VI. 76, U.S. Enterprise, in actn.
M'Carthy, John (B.) ...	IV. 22, Cleopatra, w. in actn.
M'Carty, — (L.Com.)	I. 443, Mosquito (floating battery), wrkd. Jersey, drnd.
M'Caul, Abraham (Mid.)	IV. 326, Alceste, cutting out exped.
M'Cawley, Daniel (B.)	IV. 174, Constance, w. in actn.
M'Clintock, Hy. (Mid.)	VI. 285, Queen Charlotte, Algiers.
M'Cloud, — (Mid.) ...	III. 148, Lark, w. cutting out exped.
M'Creery, David (L.)	VI. 76, Boxer, in actn.
M'Cuin, Wm. (Mr.Mt.)	III. 130, Andromache, k. in actn.
M'Cullock, Andrew (Mid.)	III. 437, Dreadnought, w. Trafalgar. IV. 168, L. Galatea, cutting out exped.
M'Curdy, John (L.) ...	V. 248, Belle Poule, in actn. Parenza.
M'Daniel, Jeremiah (Mr.Mt.)	VI. 178, w. battle of Bladensburg.
M'Dermeit, James (L.)	III. 18, Dart, w. in actn.; 20, pro. Cr.
M'Dermott, John (A.B.)	VI. 270, Eliza, k. in actn.
Macdonald, Archibald (M.L.)	III. 24, Seine, w. in actn.
Macdonald, Colin (C.)	V. 217, Redpole, actn. with invas. flotilla. VI. 12-13, Scylla and consorts capts. Weser.
M'Donald, James (L.)	VI. 263, Penguin, in actn.
M'Donald, John (Mr.-Mt.)	V. 105, 220, Quebec, cutting out expeds.
Macdonel, Don Enrique (Cmde.) *Sp.*	III. 386-9, 456, Sp. Rayo, Trafalgar.
Macdonough, Thomas (Cmde.) *U.S.*	VI. 213-14-19-23, U.S. Saratoga, Lake Champlain.
M'Doual, Robert (P.C.)	I. 410, Ganges, capture of St. Lucie, W. Indies.
M'Dougal, John (L.) ...	V. 255-61-2, Unité, cutting out exped.
M'Dougall, John (P.C.)	II. 291, Edgar, Medn.
M'Dougall, John (L.)	VI. 254-8-9, Leander, crsg.; 287, Superb, w. Algiers.
M'Dougall, John (Mr. Mt.)	IV. 448, Ville de Paris, cutting out exped.
M'George, John (C.) ...	V. 36, Pultusk, Sq. at Basse Terre.
M'Ghie, Jas. (L.Com.)	V. 212-22, Chubb (cutter), Lake Champlain.
M'Gie, David (L.Com.)	III. 83, Cruelle (cutter), Egypt exped.
Macgregor, —(Mr.Mt.)	V. 267, Anjier, Straits of Sunda.
M'Guffock, John (Mid.)	I. 318, Syren, k. in actn.
M'Gwier, — (B.)	III. 181, Loire, w. in actn.
M'Inerheny, John (C.)	II. 462, Marie Antoinette (cutter) captd. by the F., crew mutiny.
M'Intyre, John (Mr.)	IV. 306, Découverte, cutting out exped.
Mackaroff, — (V.A.) *Rus.*	II. 223, Rus. Sq. North Sea.
Mackau, Ange René A. De (L.Com.) *F.*	V. 249-51, Abeille capts. Alacrity; 252, pro. C.
M'Kay, Charles (L.) ...	V. 392, Frolic, k. in actn.

M'Kean, Jas. (Mr.Mt.)	VI. 21-3, Bacchante, cutting out expeds.
M'Keene, Isaac (L.-Com.) *U.S.*	VI. 232, U.S. gbt. Chandeleur Isles.
Mackellar, John (P.C.)	II. 131-3, Minerva (en flûte), reverse at Bruges.
M'Kellar, Peter (L.) ...	I. 199, Royal Sovereign, 1st June, pro. Cr.
M'Kenzie, Adam (C)...	II. 382-3, Pylades with consorts capts. Du. Crash. IV. 94, P. Magicienne, crsg. ; 200, Prince of Wales, Copenhagen.
M'Kenzie, David(Mid.)	VI. 234, w. in actn. with U.S. gbts.
Mackenzie, Geo. Chas. (C.)	IV. 126-7, Wolf capts. F. privs. ; 367, Cruiser, Baltic ; 461, App. VI. 124, Creole ; 125-8, actn. with F. frigates.
M'Kenzie, James (L.-Com.)	IV. 269-70, Anne (cutter), actn. with Sp. gbts.
Mackenzie, James (C.)	V. 441, Foxhound, fndrd., drnd.
Mackenzie, Kenneth (L.)	III. 120-1, cutting out exped. ; 272-4, C. Hippomenes, w. in actn. with Buonaparte (priv.) ; 296, Guachapin, capture of Surinam. IV. 109, Carysfort, convoy escort.
Mackenzie,Thos. (P.C.)	I. 139, Gibraltar ; 163-76-7, 1st June.
M'Kenzie, Thomas H. (Mr.Mt.)	IV. 244, Bacchante, w. in actn.
M'Kerlie, John (L.) ...	III. 443, Spartiate, Trafalgar ; 464, pro. Cr. V. 104,C.Calliope, capts. F. priv.
Mackey, Charles (Mid.)	V. 120, Cerberus, Agaye exped.
Mackey, Michael (L.-Com.)	II. 223-4, George captd. by Sp. privs. ; 470, App.
M'Killier, John (Mid.)	II. 81, Ardent, w. Camperdown.
M'Kinlay Geo. (Mid.)	III. 55, Isis, k. Camperdown.
M'Kinley George (L.-Com.)	I. 354-5, Liberty, actn. at Herqui. V. 444, C. Lively, wrkd. near Malta. VI. 133, gun trials of Eurotas.
M'Kinnon, Hugh (Mr.-Mt.)	II. 48, Irresistible, w. St. Vincent.
M'Lachlan, Archibald (M.C.)	V. 102, Caledonia, cutting out exped.
M'Lean,Rawdon(Mid.)	III. 416, Colossus, w. Trafalgar.
M'Lean, Thos. Henry (Mid.)	IV. 326, Alceste, cutting out exped.
M'Leod, Daniel (C.)...	III. 172, Sulphur (bomb.), off Granville, Channel. IV. 201, Superb, Copenhagen.
M'Mullen, John (S.)...	II. 407-11, Surprise cuts out Hermione.
Macnamara, Jas. (P.C.)	I. 325-6, Southampton, actn. with Vestale ; 371-2, capts. Utile. II. 34, St. Vincent ; 404-5, Cerberus, actn. with F. frigates. IV. 303-4, Edgar, Nyborg. V. 211-12, Berwick des. Amazone.
Macnamara, — (A.B.)	III. 412, Tonnant, Trafalgar.
M'Pherson, Geo. (C.)	V. 448, Thistle, wrkd. New York.
M'Pherson, Geo. (L.)	VI. 289, Glasgow, Algiers, pro. Cr.
M'Pherson,James (Mr.)	V. 99, Belvidera des. Da. gbts.
M'Queen, Jas. (act.Mr.)	V. 277, Little Belt, w. in actn.
Macquet, Joseph Jean (C.) *F.*	V. 2, Iris captd. by Aimable.
M'Rensey, — (L.)......	II. 231, Victorieuse, cutting out exped.
M'Taggart, John (L.)	II. 88, Director, Camperdown, pro. Cr.
M'Veagh, Patrick (M.-L.)	VI. 207, Canadian Lakes.
Madden, Lewis Pryse (M.L.)	V. 214, Diana, in actn.
Maddox, — (Pr.)	IV. 18, Curieux, k. in actn.
Magee, — (Mr.).........	I. 102, Iris, k. in actn.
Magendie, Jean Jacques (C.) *F.*	I. 122, Uranie, capture of Thames. III. 128, Africaine captd. by Phœbe, w. ; 334, Bucentaure, Toulon Flt. ; 386, 398, 401, Trafalgar.
Magnae, — (C.) *F.* ...	I. 265-6, Zélé, actn. with Mars.

Magon, Charles (Cmde.) F.	I. 386-8, Preneuse, Isle of France. II. 237, Vertu, crsg. III. 224, Com. Ostende flotilla; 350, R.A. Algésiras, Guadaloupe; 377, 386-9, 410-12, k. Trafalgar; 501, App.
Magui, Joseph (Mr. Mt.)	IV. 230, Repulse, w. Dardanelles.
Mahé, Jean Michel (L.-Com.) F.	III. 298-9, Oncle Thomas capts. Gorée. IV. 164-5, C. Hermione, Sq. W. Indies; 395, Patriote, Basque Rds. VI. 3, Borée, Medn.; 4, w. in actn. with Br. Sq.
Main, Dawson (L.) ...	II. 275, Ambuscade, k. in actn.
Main, Robert (Mid.) ...	III. 119, Melpomène, k. in actn.
Maingon, Jacques Remy (C.) F.	IV. 391, Aquilon, Brest Flt.; 411-14, k. in actn. Basque Rds.
Mainwaring, Benjamin (Mid.)	VI. 35, Revenge, cutting out exped.
Mainwaring, Jemmett (C.)	I. 377-8, Aimable engages Pensée. II. 225, Babet, crsg. Martinique. III. 482, fndrd. W. Indies, drnd.
Mainwaring, T. Fraser Charles (P.C.)	VI. 2, 117, Royal George, Medn. Flt.
Maistral, Désiré Marie (C.) F.	II. 139, Hoche, Ireland exped.; 141-5, captd. by Br. Sq.
Maistral, Esprit Tranquille (Cmde.) F.	II. 5, Fougueux, Ireland exped.; 286, Mont Blanc, Brest Flt. III. 334, Neptune, Medn.; 386, 401, 455, Trafalgar. IV. 12, Strachan's actn.
Maitland, Hon. Anthony (Mid.)	III. 66, w. in actn. invas. flotilla. VI. 198-200, C. Pique, crsg.; 278-88, Glasgow, Algiers; 291, made C.B.
Maitland, Frederick Lewis (L.Com.)	II. 298-9, Penelope captd. by Sp. Carmen; 469, App. III. 84, Egypt; 180, C. Loire; 282, capts. Blonde (priv.). IV. 32, crsg. Spain; 33-6, Muros; 76, crsg.; 311, Emerald, Vivero, Spain; 393, crsg.; 400-25, Basque Rds. V. 13, crsg.; 428, Goliath. VI. 227, Bellerophon, surrender of Buonaparte.
Maitland, John (P.C.)	III. 187-8, Boadicea engages Duguay Trouin. IV. 3, crsg.; 90, convoy escort. VI. 2, 117, Barfleur, Medn. Flt.
Majeur, — (L.)	II. 243, Sibylle, in actn.
Majoribanks, Geo. (L.)	V. 301, Procris, cutting out exped.
Malbon, Micajah (C.) ...	II. 428, Cynthia, Quiberon exped. III. 320-1, Hebe engages invas. flotilla.
Malcolm, Charles (P.C.)	IV. 313, Narcissus, Medn. Sq. V. 334-6, Rhin, Sq. N. Spain.
,, Sir Charles ...	VI. 279, Com. Rhin. 1812.
Malcolm, Pulteney (P.C.)	II. 237-9, Fox, at Manilla; 240-2, at Samboangon. III. 236, Royal Sovereign, Medn.; 335, Donegal, Medn. Flt.; 383, Gibraltar; 456-7, Cadiz Bay. IV. 90-6-7-8, 101, Duckworth's actn.; 392-6, Basque Rds. V. 106-8, 216, Royal Oak, off Cherbourg. VI. 133, Cmde. Queen Charlotte, Com. Brest blockade; 174, R.A. Royal Oak, Chesapeake Bay; 192-3, Jamaica; 385, App.
Malin, Joseph Pierre André (C.) F.	II. 5, Eole, Ireland exped.
Malina, Don J. (C.) Sp.	III. 112-13, Sp. San Fernando, Saumarez's actn.
Maling, Thomas James (L.)	II. 62, Minerve, cutting out exped. VI. 2, C. Mulgrave, Medn. Flt.
Mallard, Edward (M.L.)	VI. 19, capture of Ponza.
Mallet, — (C.) F.	VI. 146, Atalante, Medn.
Mallock, Samuel (M.L.)	IV. 32-3, Loire, cutting out exped.
Malone, Edmund (L.)	V. 186, Ceylon, in actn.
Malone, William (L.) ...	V. 327-8, Osprey, cutting out exped.
Man, Antony Willem De (C.) Du.	VI. 279, Du. Melampus, Algiers.
Manby, Thomas (C.) ...	III. 124, Bordelais capts. Curieux.
Manderston, Patrick (L.Com.)	III. 222-6, Minx (gbt.), off Calais.
Manger, Nicholas (L.)	II. 390-2, Sibylle, in actn.

INDEX TO NAVAL OFFICERS 121

Mangin, Micheli (L.-Com.) *Ital.*	IV. 347, Volpé (gbt.) captd. by Standard.
Manley, Jas. B. (act. Mr.)	VI. 321, Arachne, Burmese War.
Manley, John (P.C.) ...	I. 98, Syren, Holland; 370, Apollo, capture of Légère. II. 301, Mars, blockade of Aix.
Mann, Robert (P.C.)...	I. 72, Bedford, Medn. Flt.; 96–9, Genoa; 214, Flt. at Corsica; 297–300, R.A. Victory, actn. off Hyères; 303–6, Medn.; 345–6, Gibraltar.
Manners, Charles (L.)	IV. 158, Revenge, k. cutting out exped.
Manners, William (C.)	V. 357, Reindeer, convoy escort. VI. 161–3, captd. by U.S. Wasp, k. in actn.; 226, 387, App.
Mansel, Robert (C.) ...	III. 125–7, Penguin engages F. ships.
Mansel, Thomas (Mid.)	II. 48, Orion, w. St. Vincent.
Mansell, Robt. (Mr. Mt.)	III. 275, Narcissus, w. cutting out exped.
Mansfield, Charles J. Moore (P.C.)	II. 90, Andromache capts. Algrn. ship. III. 180, Minotaur capts. Franchise; 384, 436–7, Trafalgar. IV. 201, Copenhagen.
Mant, Robt. M. (M.L.)	IV. 123, Juno, cutting out exped.
Maples, John (L.)	II. 114, Magicienne, cutting out exped.
Maples, John Fordyce (C.)	VI. 78–81, Pelican capts. U.S. Argus; 82, pro. P.
Mapleton, David (L.)	IV. 139, Pallas, cutting out exped.; 239, Impérieuse, cutting out exped.; 385, off Spain. VI. 34, in actn. at D'Anzo.
Maren, Jacob Van (C.) *Du.*	VI. 12–13, Du. Trave engages Achates; 14, captd. by Andromache, w. in actn.
Marinier, — (Mid.) *F.*	IV. 418, Tourville, in actn. Basque Rds.
Markham, Geo. (Mid.)	VI. 287, Queen Charlotte, w. Algiers.
Markham, Thos. (P.C.)	II. 219–20, Centaur, capture of Minorca; 292, Port Mahon; 471, App.
Markland, John Duff (C.)	V. 35, Bustard, off Trieste; 208, Rodney, Medn. Flt. VI. 30–2, Milford, blockade of Trieste.
Marks, John (B.)	III. 192–3, Sheerness (cutter), actn. off Brest.
Marley, Robert (Mid.)	IV. 30, Gracieuse, w. in actn.
Marrie, James (M.L.)	III. 55, Monarch, w. Copenhagen.
Marryat, Fredk. (Mid.)	IV. 387, Impérieuse, Rosas Bay. VI. 302, 303–11, C. Larne; 334–5, Burmese War; 344, made C.B.; 347, App.
Marsden, Mark (Pr.)...	IV. 414, Impérieuse, w. Basque Rds.
Marsh, Digby (Mid.)...	V. 100, Surveillante, cutting out exped. VI. 16, St. Sebastian.
Marsh, John (L.)	I. 100, Gibraltar, 1st June, pro. Cr.
Marsh, Stephen (Mr.)	II. 414, Courier, k. in actn.
Marshall, Jas. (L. Com.)	III. 315, Watchful, off Ambleteuse, Channel.
Marshall, John (L.) ...	IV. 156, Port Mahon, cutting out exped. V. 417, Com. Java, w. in actn. VI. 6, C. Shamrock, Sq. at Heligoland.
Marshall, John (Mid.)	V. 128–9, Blossom, cutting out exped.
Marshall, John Houlton (C.)	VI. 387, Halcyon, wrkd. Jamaica.
Marshall, John Willoughby (C.)	V. 42, Lynx, crsg. off Denmark.
Marshall, Sampson (L.)	VI. 190, w. in actn. at Baltimore.
Marshall, Sam. (Mid.)	IV. 168, Gracieuse, w. in actn.
Marshall, Thos. (M.L.)	IV. 230, Repulse, w. Dardanelles.
Marshall, — (Mr.)......	II. 227, 396, Speedy, in actn.
Marsingal, Sam. (Mid.)	IV. 19, San Fiorenzo, w. in actn.
Mart, — (Car.)	V. 40, Bellerophon, cutting out exped.
Martin, Alexander (L.)	V. 250, Alacrity, in actn.
Martin, Andrew (Mr.)	IV. 318, Seagull, k. in actn.
Martin, Antoine (C.) *F.*	II. 229, Revanche (priv.) captd. by Recovery.
Martin, Claude Jean (C.) *F.*	II. 178–85, Sérieuse, the Nile.
Martin, Daniel (A.B.)	IV. 252, Melampus, Chesapeake Bay.

Martin, George (P.C.)	II. 34, Irresistible, Channel Flt.; 38–48, St. Vincent; 93, capts. Sp. Ninfa and St. Elena; 289, Northumberland, Flt. off Cadiz; 307, Palermo; 438–44–5, capture of Malta. III. 81, Egypt exped. Barfleur; 358, Calder's actn. IV. 290, R.A. Canopus; 292, Syracuse; 293, Palermo; 445–6, St. Sebastian. V. 32–3, 79, Medn. Flt.
Martin, George Bohun (Cr.)	VI. 365–73, Mosquito, Navarino.
Martin, John (Mid.) ...	I. 96, Ardent, k. in actn.
Martin, Pierre (L.Com.) *F.*	II. 400, Buonaparte captd. by Echo.
Martin, Thomas Byam (P.C.)	I. 365–6, Santa Margarita capts. Tamise; 400, capture of Buonaparte. II. 112, Tamer, Sq. at St. Kitts; 160–1, Fisgard capts. Immortalité. III. 15, 142, crsg. Spain. IV. 298, Implacable, Baltic; 301, capture of Rus. Sewolod. V. 40–1, crsg. Finland; 327, R.A. Baltic Flt.
Martin, — (R.A.) *F.*	I. 214, Medn.; 283–6–92, actn. off Genoa; 295, V.A.; 296–9, 302, actn. off Hyères.
Martinencq, Jules François *F.*	II. 205, Aboukir. III. 96, Muiron, Medn.
Masefield, Joseph Ore (L.)	III. 57, Amazon, Copenhagen; 194, C. Atalante, crsg. IV. 175, Sq. off Rochefort; 287, Raleigh, off Rochefort.
Mason, Francis (C.) ...	III. 222–5, Rattler engages invas. flotilla. IV. 320, Daphne, crsg. Denmark. VI. 16, Présidente, Sq. off St. Sebastian.
Mason, Samuel (C.) ...	II. 462, Pandora, fndrd. North Sea, drnd.
Massaredo, Don Joseph (A.) *Sp.*	II. 60–1, 70, 219, Cadiz; 298, Medn. III. 109–10, Cadiz.
Massey, George (Mid.)	II. 80, Monarch, w. Camperdown. III. 115, Venerable, w. Saumarez's actn.
Massieur, François Nicolas (L.Com.) *F.*	V. 174, Isle of France.
Masters, James (L.) ...	IV. 249, Halifax, Chesapeake Bay.
Masters, Thos. Jas. Poole (L.)	V. 328–9, Horatio, w. cutting out exped.
Mather, William (L.)...	III. 136–7, Mercury, cutting out exped.; 224, Cruiser, w. in actn. VI. 381, Tweed, wrkd. Newfoundland.
Mathias, — (B.)	II. 262, Leander, w. in actn.
Matson, Henry (Mid.)	I. 87, Toulon. III. 120, C. Cyane, W. Indies.
Matson, Richard (C.)	III. 120, Daphne, W. Indies.
Matterface, Wm. (L.)	VI. 224, Rota, k. in actn.
Matthews, Henry Bathurst (L.)	VI. 307, Slaney, w. Burmese War.
Matthews, John (P.C.)	I. 88, Courageux, Toulon; 94, Corsica exped.
Matthews, Wm. T. I. (M.C.)	VI. 18, Berwick, cutting out exped.
Matthias, Thomas Joseph (Ck.)	V. 417, Java, k. in actn.
Maude, John (P.C.) ...	I. 99–100, Leopard and Bedford.
Maude, Hon. J. Ashley (L.)	IV. 448–9, Ville de Paris, w. cutting out exped. VI. 92, C. Nemesis, Chesapeake; 365–73, Glasgow, Navarino.
Maude, William (P.C.)	V. 3, 4, Jason, capture of Topaze.
Maujouen, Jos. François Léon (C.) *F.*	IV. 371–2, Espiègle captd. by Sibylle.
Maule, John (M.L.) ...	VI. 19, capture of Ponza.
Maunsell, Robert (C.)	V. 300–4, Procris, capture of Java.
Maurice, F. Moore (C.)	V. 451, Magnet, fndrd. Halifax, drnd.
Maurice, James Wilkes (L.)	III. 245, Centaur, Com. 'Diamond Rock'; 349, capture of 'Diamond Rock' by the F. V. 222, C., Gvr. of Anholt; 223–6, defence of Anholt.
Maurice, — (C.) *F.* ...	VI. 365–73, Trident, Navarino.
Maw, Henry Lister (L.)	VI. 307, A.D.C.; 348–51, Burmese War.

INDEX TO NAVAL OFFICERS 123

Maxey, Lewis (L.Com.)	V. 368-9, Whiting (schooner), Sandy Hook; 451, captd. by Diligent (priv.).
Maxtone, Thomas (C.)	I. 385, Bermuda, Sq. crsg. II. 457, fndrd. Gulf of Florida, drnd.
Maxwell, Henry (Mid.)	V. 248, Belle Poule, in actn. Parenza.
Maxwell, John (Gunner)	II. 407, Surprise; 409-11, w. in cutting out Sp. Hermione.
Maxwell, Keith (L.) ...	III. 138-40, Beaulieu bts. cut out Chevrette; 141, pro. Cr. III. 278, C. Tartar, capts. Hirondelle; 320-1, Arab engages invas. flotilla. IV. 438, Nymphen, Scheldt exped.
Maxwell, Murray (P.C.)	III. 244, Centaur, crsg.; 296-7, capture of Surinam. IV. 326, Alceste, off Cadiz; 444, Medn. V. 85, Toulon; 119, Agaye; 247, Parenza; 261-5, actn. with F. frigates, made
,, ,, C.B.	C.B. VI. 381, Dædalus, wrkd. Ceylon; 394, Alceste, wrkd. China Sea.
Maxwell, Robt. (Mid.)	VI. 35, Revenge, cutting out exped.
Maxwell, William (B.)	VI. 287, Queen Charlotte, w. Algiers.
Mayne, Anthony De (Mr.)	VI. 40-1, Amelia, w. in actn.
Mayne, Dawson (Mid.)	VI. 288, Leander, w. Algiers.
Mayston, —(L.) *E.I.C.*	VI. 269, E.I.C. Nautilus, k. in actn.
Meade, John (L.)	IV. 251-2, Leopard, in actn.
Meadway, John Allen (L.)	III. 6, Loire, w. in actn. IV. 440, Scheldt exped.
Meares, John (M.L.)...	V. 239, Active, w. in actn.
Mears, James (L.)	V. 121, Active, cutting out exped.
Mears, Peter (M.L.)...	V. 232, 256, Active, cutting out expeds.
Mears, Roger (L.)......	I. 200, Orion, 1st June, pro. Cr.
Meech, Giles (M.L.)...	IV. 312, Emerald, cutting out exped.
Meerton, Henry (M.L.)	IV. 137, Renommée, cutting out exped.
Meillerie, Antoine F. Z. La Marre (C.) *F.*	V. 122, Favorite, Sq. crsg. Adriatic; 240, k. in actn. off Lissa.
Meillerie, Louis C. A. La Marre la (C.) *F.*	III. 352-3, Hortense, Sq. W. Indies. IV. 14-16, capts. Arrow; 120, Sq. crsg.; 164, Cmde.; 165, W. Indies; 166, Bordeaux; 444, Annibal, Toulon Flt.
Mein, James (C.)	V. 441, Primrose, wrkd. Falmouth, drnd.
Mekeek, Thomas (Mr.- Mt.)	IV. 403, in actn. Basque Rds.
Melhuish, John (L.) ...	I. 87, Toulon.
Melville, Lord (1st Lord Admiralty)	III. 25, 337-41, (1800). IV. 74 (1805).
Menager, — (L.) *F.* ...	V. 188, Vénus, in actn.; 443, App.
Menard, Chas. Leonard (L.Com.) *F.*	IV. 76, Cyane captd. by Princess Charlotte.
Mendel, Philip (L.) *Rus.*	III. 429, Conqueror, w. Trafalgar.
Mendoza, Don Geronimo (C.) *Sp.*	II. 110, Sp. San Vincente destd. to prevent capture, W. Indies.
Mendoza, Don Juan de (C.) *Sp.*	II. 401-2, Sp. Thetis captd. by Ethalion.
Mends, Robert (L.) ...	I. 275, Colossus, w. in actn. off Isle Groix. V. 12, C. Arethusa, crsg. N. Spain.
Mends, Thomas (As.S.)	VI. 287, Albion, k. Algiers.
Mends, William Bowen (C.)	VI. 195, Loup Cervier and U.S. Hornet.
Mends, — (M.L.)	IV. 127, Franchise, cutting out exped.
Menses, — (R.A.) *Du.*	II. 76-9, 82, Du. Jupiter, w. Camperdown.
Menzies, Chas. (M.L.)	IV. 154-5, Minerva, cutting out exped.
Mercer, Edward Smith (M.L.)	V. 31, Topaze, cutting out exped.
Mercer, John (M.L.)...	I. 249, w. n actn. Guadaloupe.

Mercier, Chas. (Mid.)...	V. 178, Africaine, w. in actn.
Meriton, Henry (C.) E.I.C.	III. 22-3, E.I.C. Exeter capts. with consorts Médée; 250-1, actn. with Linois' Sq. East Indies. V. 132-4, E.I.C. Ceylon captd by F. Sq.; 135, w. in actn.
Metcalfe, George (Mr.)	I. 186, Glory, k. 1st June.
Metherell, Anthony (Mr.)	IV. 332-4, 366, Carnation, k. in actn.
Metluist, John (C.) ...	III. 172, Perseus (bomb.), off Dieppe.
Meuse, Pieter (C.) *Du.*	II. 412, Du. Zeevraght captd. by Orpheus.
Meynne, François Jac. (C.) *F.*	II. 286, Jean Bart, Brest Flt. III. 68, Egypt exped.; 223, Ville d'Aix (prame), invas. flotilla.
Middleton, Sir Charles (Comptroller)	I. 53 (1783), afterwards Lord Barham.
Middleton, Henry B. (Mr. Mt.)	V. 103, Dreadnought, k. cutting out exped.
Middleton, James (Pr.)	II. 103, Fairy, w. cutting out exped.
Middleton James (Mr.-Mt.)	III. 143, Victor, w. in actn.
Middleton, Robert Gambier (L.)	I. 87, Toulon; 321-4, C., Lowestoffe with Dido capts. Minerve. II. 249, Flora, bts. cut out Mondovi; 251, Santa Cruz.
Middleton, Wm. (Car.)	IV. 448, Scout, cutting out exped.
Miell, Charles (Mid.)	II. 196, Orion, w. the Nile.
Milbanke, Henry (Mr.-Mt.)	III. 416, Colossus, w. Trafalgar.
Milbourne, Charles Robert (Mid.)	IV. 447, Cumberland, cutting out exped. VI. 119, L. Saracen, capture of Cattaro.
Mildmay, George William St. John (L.)	VI. 259, Leander and U.S. frigates.
Mildridge, Herbert (Mid.)	IV. 32, Loire, cutting out exped.
Mildridge, Matthew (Mid.)	IV. 32, Loire, cutting out exped.; 312, Mr. Mt. Emerald, w. cutting out exped.
Miles, Jeaffreson (Mr.-Mt.)	IV. 245, Comus, cutting out exped.
Miles, Lawford (Mid.)	IV. 378, Amethyst, w. in actn.
Miles, Thomas (L.) ...	I. 288, Bedford, w. in actn.
Milius, Pierre Bernard (C.) *F.*	III. 350, Didon, Martinique. IV. 56, 63, crsg.; 65-9, captd. by Phœnix, 70-3, suppresses mutiny.
Milius, — (C.) *F.*	VI. 365-73, Scipion, Navarino.
Millard, William (Mid.)	IV. 100, Northumberland, w. in actn.
Miller, Daniel (L.-Com.)	V. 445, Racer, wrkd. on the coast of France.
Miller, George (C.) ...	II. 440, Minorca, Malta. III. 83, Egypt exped. V. 45, Thetis; 46-50, crsg.; 92, off the Saintes.
Miller, John (Mid.) ...	V. 120, Cerberus, cutting out exped.
Miller, Joseph (Mr.) ...	V. 34, Cyane, in actn.
Miller, Ralph Willett (L.)	I. 87, Toulon; 215, Corsica. II. 34, C. Captain; 42-5, St. Vincent; 61-3, Theseus, Teneriffe; 66, Santa Cruz; 171, Flt. off Cadiz; 320, Alexandria; 322, 330, k. in actn. at Acre.
Millet, Richard (Mid.)	V. 220-2, Quebec, w. cutting out exped.
Mills, George (L.)......	IV. 388, Wanderer, in actn. Isle St. Martin.
Mills, John (Mid.)......	VI. 234, k. in actn.
Mills, Thomas (Mid.)	IV. 72, Amaranthe, w. in actn.
Milne, David (L.)	I. 310-11, Blanche, in actn.; 313, pro. Cr. II. 247-8, C. Pique, in actn. with Seine; 249, with Jason capts. Seine; 469, App. III. 23-5, Seine capts. F. Vengeance; 490, wrkd. off the Texel. VI. 278, R.A. **Impregnable**;
,, Sir David, K.C.B.	285, Algiers; 291, made K.C.B.
Milne, George (L.) ...	III. 24, Seine, k. in actn.
Milne, James (C.)......	I. 244, Avenger, k. capture of Martinique.

INDEX TO NAVAL OFFICERS 125

Milne, James (Mr.Mt.) II. 81, Belliqueux, k. Camperdown.
Milne, Thomas (Mid.) V. 42, w. cutting out exped.
Milner, William (L.-Com.) V. 442, Carrier (cutter), wrkd. on the coast of France.
Minchin, Paul (P.C.) I. 318, Hébé, crsg. off France.
Minchin, William (L.) III. 55, Monarch, w. Copenhagen.
Mindham, Wm. (A.B.) VI. 56-9, Shannon, in actn. with Chesapeake.
Mingay, — (L.) .... IV. 188, actn. Cape of Good Hope.
Minto, Wm. (M.Maj.) III. 85, w. in actn. Egypt.
Missiessy, Burgues (R.A.) F. III. 242-50, Rochefort. IV. 47, Rochefort; 78-81, Dominique; 84-5, Guadaloupe; 432-5-8, Sq. in the Scheldt. V. 207, V.A. Com. Flt. in the Scheldt.
Mitchel, Hugh (Mid.) III. 55, Elephant, w. Copenhagen.
Mitchell, Andrew(V.A.) II. 344-5, Isis; 347-50, Com. Holland exped; 351, made
" Sir Andrew, K.B. ; 388, 472, App.
K.B.
Mitchell, Charles (Cmde.) E.I.C. I. 218-21, E.I.C. William Pitt, actn, with F. privs.
Mitchell, Charles (act.-L.) IV. 22, Cleopatra, w. in actn. VI. 303-7, C. Slaney, Burmese War.
Mitchell, Edwd.Jas.(C.) III. 227, Inspector, watching invas. flotilla Channel.
Mitchell, Frederick Thomas (L.) VI. 284-9, Queen Charlotte, Algiers; 291, pro. Cr.
Mitchell, John (L.-Com.) IV. 23, Haughty, Guadaloupe.
Mitchell, Lewis Dunbar (Mid.) VI. 288, Granicus, w. Algiers.
Mitchell, Matthew (Mr.Mt.) VI. 163, Reindeer, w. in actn.
Mitchell, Peter (Pilot) VI. 369-74-6, k. Navarino.
Mitchell, Thos. (M.C.) VI. 34, Impérieuse, cutting out exped.
Mitchell, William (Mr.) I. 155, Queen, k. 29th May.
Mitchell,William(P.C.) II. 75-80, Isis, Camperdown. 456, Salisbury, wrkd. St. Domingo.
Mitchell, — (C.) Por. II. 211, Por. San Sebastian, Medn.
Mitford, Henry (P.C.) III. 493, York, fndrd. North Sea, drnd.
Mitford, Robert (C.) ... V. 32-5, Espoir engages F. gbts; 113-14, Medn.
Mix, Mervine P. (Mid.) U.S. VI. 193, U.S. Constellation, Chesapeake Bay.
Moffat, Richard (Mid.) IV. 367, Euryalus, cutting out exped.
Moffat, Thos. (L.Com.) VI. 122-4, Jason (prize), actn. with F. frigates.
Moffat, William (C.) E.I.C. III. 250-3, E.I.C. Ganges, actn. with Linois' Sq., E. Indies.
Moire, Don Juan de (C.) Sp. IV. 137, Sp. Giganta cut out by the bts. of Renommée.
Molesworth, Bouchier (L.) V. 343, America, cutting out exped.
Molesworth,Francis(L.) V. 126, Thames, cutting out exped.
Moller, A. (C.) Rus. II. 344, Rus. Mistisloff, Holland exped.
Molloy, Anthony James Pye (P.C.) I. 62, Ganges, Channel Flt.; 100, Medn.; 139, Cæsar, Channel Flt.; 149-55, 29th May; 159-62-3-71, 1st June; 201, 277, court-martialled; 435, App.
Molyneux, Richard (M.-Sergeant) VI. 57, Shannon, in actn. with Chesapeake.
Monconsu, — (C.) F. I. 259, Rédoutable, Brest Flt. II. 5, Ireland exped.; 286, Brest Flt. III. 68, Cmde. Indomptable; 69-72, Medn.; 73, Toulon; 96-102, Algesiras; 105, k. in actn.
Mondragon, Don Francisco (C.) Sp. III. 342, Sp. Terrible, F. Sp. Flt. Toulon.
Money, Rowland (C.) VI. 175, Chesapeake Bay; 177, Bladensburg; 188, Baltimore.
Monios, Don (C.) Sp.... III. 342, España, F. Sp. Flt. Toulon.
Monk, John (Mid.) ... VI. 18, Euryalus, cutting out. exped.

Monke, George Paris (P.C.)	V. 92, Castor, Guadaloupe ; 445, Pallas, wrkd. in the Firth of Forth.
Monkton, John (L.) ...	I. 175-99, Marlborough, 1st June ; 200, pro. Cr. ; 271, C. Colossus ; 272-5, actn. off Isle Groix ; 315, crsg. II. 285, Mars, off Ushant.
Montagu, George (P.C.)	I. 127, Hector, Martinique ; 138, R.A. ; 142-3, crsg. ; 160, 187-8, Plymouth ; 189-91-98, Sq. off Ushant.
Montagu, James (Mid.)	IV. 447, Tigre, cutting out exped. V. 266, L. Alceste, in actn.
Montagu, John Wm. (L.)	VI. 28, Cerberus, cutting out exped.
Montagu, Robt. (P.C.)	I. 62, Sampson, Channel Flt.
Montagu, William Augustus (P.C.)	IV. 359-62, Terpsichore engages Sémillante. V. 191, Cornwallis ; 194, Amboyna ; 204, capture of the Isle of France.
Montalan, Ant. M. François (C.) *F.*	I. 222-3, Résolue, actn. with Br. Sq. ; 224, Morlaix. IV. 444, Génois, Toulon Flt.
Montalan, Guillaume S. A. (C.) *F.*	I. 314, Tourterelle captd. by Lively.
Montes, Don Francesco (Cmde.) *Sp.*	II. 413, Sp. Asia, in actn. III. 342, Sp. San Rafaël, F. Sp. Flt. Toulon.
Montfort, Gilles François (L.Com.) *F.*	III. 180, Venteux captd., w. in actn. V. 10-11, C., Pauline with Pénélope capts. Br. Proserpine ; 262-3, actn. with Br. frigates ; 264, Ancona.
Montgomery, Archibald (L.)	III. 124, Bordelais, in actn.
Montgomery, Augustus (P.C.)	I. 284, Courageux ; 288-9, actn. off Genoa ; 303-4, Bedford, convoy escort.
Monthazin, L. C. G. B. de (L.Com.) *F.*	V. 46, Béarnais captd. by Melampus.
Montresor, Henry (C.)	VI. 232-3, Manly, actn. with U.S. gbts ; 234, pro. P.C.
Moodie, Robert (L.) ...	V. 343, America, cutting out exped.
Moor, Henry (Mr.) ...	III. 20, Ann (cutter), cutting out exped.
Moore, Charles (L.) ...	VI. 32, Eagle, Adriatic.
Moore, George (Mid.)	V. 256, Active, cutting out exped.
Moore, Graham (P.C.)	I. 318, Syren, Jersey. II. 142, Melampus, crsg. ; 151-3, capts. Résolue ; 226, capts. Volage. III. 287-8, Indefatigable capts. Sp. treasure ships ; 493, App. IV. 236, Marlborough, Sq. at Lisbon ; 238, Rio Janeiro. V. 422, R.A. Portsmouth.
Moore, Howard (Mr.)	V. 248, Belle Poule, in actn. Parenza.
Moore, Humphrey (M.-L.)	V. 220-2, Quebec, w. cutting out exped.
Moore, John (Mid.) ...	I. 185, Montagu, w. 1st June.
Moore, John (Mid.) ...	IV. 320, Daphne, cutting out exped.
Moore, John (Mid.) ...	VI. 184, Seahorse, in actn. Alexandria.
Moore, Ogle (L.)	III. 275, Maidstone, cutting out exped. IV. 154, Minerva, cutting out exped.
Moore, Thomas (M.L.)	V. 28, Spartan, cutting out exped. ; 36, 120-1, Amphion, cutting out expeds. ; 239, C., w. in actn. off Lissa. VI. 374, w. Navarino.
Moore, Thos. W. (Mid.)	VI. 234, k. in actn. with U.S. gbts.
Moore, — (Mid.)	I. 289, Illustrious, w. in actn. off Genoa.
Moore, — (Mid.)	IV. 230, Thunderer, w. Dardanelles
Moorsom, Constantine R. (C.)	IV. 278-84, Fury (bomb.), Algiers.
Moorsom, Robert (P.C.)	III. 384, Revenge ; 438-9, w. Trafalgar.
Moralez, Count de los Rios (V.A.) *Sp.*	II. 52, St. Vincent ; 59, dismissed.
Morce, William (L.) ...	III. 57, Ganges, Copenhagen ; 64, pro. Cr.
Moreau, Charles (L.) *F.*	IV. 153-4, Piémontaise, in actn.
Morel, — (C.) *F.*	I. 141, Téméraire, Rochefort.
Morell, John Arthur (L.)	IV. 124, Eagle, Isle of Capri.
Moreno, Don Juan J. de (V.A.) *Sp.*	III. 97, Cadiz ; 110-12-16-17, Saumarez's actn.
Moresby, Fairfax (L.)	IV. 383, Kent, cutting out exped. VI. 32, C. Wizard, Adriatic.

INDEX TO NAVAL OFFICERS

Morey, George (Mid.)	VI. 96, cutting out exped.
Morgan, Benjamin (L.)	II. 81, Lancaster, w. Camperdown.
Morgan, George (Mid.)	III. 55, Monarch, w. Copenhagen.
Morgan, Henry (Mid.)	III. 410, Mars, w. Trafalgar.
Morgan, James (L.)	I. 87, Toulon.
Morgan, Jeremiah (Mr.-Mt.)	I. 362, Niger, cutting out exped.
Morgan, Wm. (M.L.)	V. 220, Naiad, w. in actn.
Morgan, Wm. M. (M.L.)	VI. 288, Granicus, k. Algiers.
Morgan, Wm. Thos. (L.)	VI. 246, Endymion, in actn., pro. Cr.
Morgan, — (Mr. Mt.)	II. 115, Magicienne, w. cutting out exped.
Moriarty, Redmond (Mid.)	V. 256, Active, cutting out exped. ; 266, act. L., in actn.
Moriarty, Wm. (Mid.)	IV. 329, Nymphe, w. cutting out exped.
Morice, Nicolas (L.-Com.) *F.*	IV. 363, Jéna, Isle of France ; 366, captd. by Modeste. V. 132, C. Victor, crsg.; 133-5, actn. with E.I.C. ships; 152, Isle de la Passe ; 184-7, with Vénus capts. Ceylon ; 443, App.
Moriencourt, Jos. Salvador (L.)	I. 78, Princess Royal, Toulon.
Moring, Jas. (C.) *E.I.C.*	IV. 189, E.I.C. Comet, Cape of Good Hope.
Morris, Amherst (L.)	I. 109, Nymphe, in actn., pro. Cr.
Morris, Charles (Mid.) *U.S.*	III. 301-2, U.S. Intrepid, at Tripoli. V. 370, pro. L. U.S. Constitution, crsg. ; 378-80, w. in actn. with Guerrière. VI. 201-3, C. U.S. Adams, destd. Penobscot exped.
Morris, Edward (Mid.)	II. 325, k. at Acre.
Morris, Edw. (L. Com.)	IV. 466, Griper, wrkd. off Ostende, drnd.
Morris, Fred. (Chapln)	II. 330, Theseus, w. at Acre.
Morris, George (L.) ...	II. 88, Ardent, Camperdown, pro. Cr. III. 257, C. Penguin, des. Renommée (priv.). V. 441, Magnet, wrkd. in the Baltic.
Morris, James Nicoll (P.C.)	II. 469, Lively, wrkd. near Cadiz ; 432, Phaëton, Genoa. III. 33-4, off Malaga, Spain; 375, Colossus, Sq. crsg. ; 384, 415-16, w. Trafalgar. IV. 288, Medn.
,, Sir James Nicoll (V.A.)	I. 114, V.A. when James was writing, evidently same as above.
Morris, John Row (L.-Com.)	IV. 400-12, Insolent, Basque Rds.
Morrison, Alexander (L)	V. 248, Belle Poule, in actn. Parenza.
Morrison, Arthur (M.L.)	V. 80, w. in actn. Toulon.
Morrison, Isaac Hawkins (C.)	VI. 13-14, Achates engages Trave ; 135, capture of Clorinde.
Morrison, John (P.C.)	III. 83-9, Thisbe, Egypt exped. IV. 93, Northumberland, W. Indies.
Morrison, John (C.) ...	IV. 461, Heureux, fndrd. Halifax, drnd.
Morrison, John (Mid.)	IV. 280, Diadem, w. in actn. Buenos Ayres.
Morrison, Robt. (M.L.)	IV. 8, Cæsar, k. in Calder's actn.
Morrison, — (Mid.) ...	VI. 258, Leander and U.S. frigates.
Mortimer, John (L.) ...	II. 58, Excellent, St. Vincent, pro. Cr.
Mortlock, Charles (C.) *E.I.C.*	V. 63-5, E.I.C. Charlton captd. by Manche and consorts.
Mortlock, Lewis (C.)...	II. 132, Wolverine, watching invas. flotilla ; 352-3, k. in actn. with F. privs.
Morton, — (Mr. Mt.)...	II. 249, Flora, cutting out exped.
Morton, — (B.)	IV. 302, Centaur, w. in actn.
Moss, John Ralph (C.)	II. 280, Merlin, at Honduras.
Mosse, Jas. Robt. (P.C.)	III. 46-51-4-5, Monarch, k. Copenhagen.
Motard, Léonard Bertrand (C.) *F.*	III. 250-3, Sémillante, Linois' actn. with E.I.C. ships, E. Indies ; 283-5, capts. E.I.C. Princess Charlotte. IV. 52-3, actn. with Phaëton and consort ; 355-6, Isle of France ; 357-8, engages Dédaigneuse ; 359-61, actn. with Terpsichore ; 362, reaches France.
Mott, Andrew (L.) ...	III. 57, Ardent, Copenhagen ; 64, pro. Cr.

Mottley, Samuel (L.)...	VI. 202, Bulwark, Penobscot exped.
Moubray, Richard Hussey (P.C.)	III. 237, Active, Medn. ; 333, Toulon. IV. 215, Malta ; 221-9, Dardanelles ; 289, Medn. V. 80, Montagu, Isle St. Maura ; 125, Com. in the Adriatic ; 208, Repulse, Channel Flt. VI. 17, cutting out exped. Medn.
Moulac, Vincent (L.) *F.*	VI. 136, Clorinde, in actn.
Mould, James (L.)......	III. 426, Téméraire, w. Trafalgar. VI. 278-84, C. Mutine, Algiers.
Mould, Rich. Cotton (L.)	IV. 273, Recruit, Isle Sombrero.
Moulston, Jean (Cmde.) *F.*	I. 365-9, Tribune captd. by Unicorn.
Mounsey, William (C.)	V. 23-6, Bonne Citoyenne capts. Furieuse ; 27, pro. P.C. VI. 19, Furieuse, capture of Ponza.
Mounsher, Eyles (L.)...	III. 443, Leviathan, Trafalgar ; 464, pro. Cr.
Mounteney, John B. (Mid.)	V. 41, Melpomène, k. in actn.
Mousnier, Jean Bap. A. (L. Com.) *F.*	V. 86-7, Oreste captd. by Scorpion.
Mowat, Henry (P.C.)	I. 385, Assistance, Murray's Sq. crsg.
Mowbray, George (L.)	III. 443, Polyphemus, Trafalgar ; 464, pro. Cr.
Mowbray, William (Mr.)	IV. 101, Atlas, w. in Duckworth's actn.
Moyase, James (Mr.)...	IV. 206, Charles (T.S.), k. Copenhagen.
Moysey, Henry George (L.)	IV. 309, San Fiorenzo, w. in actn. V. 441, C. Curieux, wrkd. W. Indies.
Muddle, Richard Henry (L.)	III. 292, Theseus, Curaçoa.
Mudge, Zachary (P.C.)	III. 196-7, Blanche, St. Domingo ; 199-201, Mancenille Bay ; 291, Curaçoa. IV. 38, W. Indies ; 39-46, captd. by Topaze ; 287, Phœnix ; 375, off Rochefort ; 456, App. V. 49, actn. of Junon.
Mudie, David (L.)......	III. 57, Defiance, Copenhagen ; 64, pro. Cr.
Mugg, Francis John (Mid.)	III. 417, Achille, k. Trafalgar.
Muggridge, James (Mr.-Mt.)	V. 220-2, Princess Augusta (cutter), w. cutting out exped.
Muir, Thomas (L.)......	IV. 272, Curieux, in actn.
Mulberry, — (S.)	II. 264, Leander, in actn.
Mulcaster, William Howe (L.)	IV. 154-5, Minerva, cutting out exped. V. 74-6, Confiance, capture of Cayenne ; 450, C. Emulous, wrkd. Sable Island. VI. 109, Canadian Lakes.
Mulgrave, Lord (1st Lord Admiralty)	IV. 74 (1805), 396-8, 425-8 (1809).
Mullah, Henry (L.) ...	III. 278, Tartar, cutting out exped.
Mullins, Thos. (Mr. Mt.)	IV. 158, cutting out exped.
Mullins, William (B.)	V. 126, Thames, cutting out exped.
Mullon, Jean (C.) *F.*...	I. 105-7, Cléopâtre captd. by Nymphe ; 108, k. in actn.
Mulso, William (C.) ...	II. 462, Hermes, fndrd., drnd.
Munbee, Valentine (Mid.)	VI. 35, Revenge, cutting out exped.
Mundy, George (P.C.)	III. 171, Hydra, crsg. off Havre. IV. 119-20, capts. Furet ; 263-4, off Catalonia.
Munro, Thomas (Mid.)	V. 349, Menelaus, k. cutting out exped.
Munroe, Daniel (A.B.)	II. 108, loss of Tribune.
Murat, Jean Bapt. B. (C.) *F.*	V. 3, Galatée, Toulon.
Murray, George (V.A.)	I. 385, Resolution, Sq. crsg.
Murray, George (P.C.)	I. 222-4, Nymphe, actn. with F. Sq. II. 34, Colossus, Channel Flt.; 38, 40-3-8, St. Vincent ; 212, blockade of Malta ; 285, Achille, Sq. off Brest ; 469, Colossus, wrkd. Sicily. III. 46, Edgar ; 50-5, Copenhagen ; 63, Carlscrona ; 177, Victory, Medn. Sq. ; 335, R.A. Medn. Flt. IV. 281, Polyphemus, Com. Buenos Ayres exped. (repulsed).

INDEX TO NAVAL OFFICERS

Murray, Hon. George (P.C.)	I. 127, Duke, Martinique exped.
Murray, Henry (L.Com.)	IV. 475, Bacchus, captd. Leeward Isles.
Murray, James (L.) ...	IV. 27-8, Stork, w. cutting out exped. V. 220, Com. Exertion, Holland exped. ; 451, wrkd. in the Elbe. VI. 279, C. Satellite, Algiers.
Murray, Jas. (C.) *E.I.C.*	IV. 308, E.I.C. Devonshire, Colombo.
Murray, Hon. Jas. (P.C.)	III. 482, Jason, wrkd. St. Malo.
Murray, John (L.)	IV. 447, Cumberland, cutting out exped.
Murray, John (Mid.) ...	V. 126, Thames, cutting out exped. VI. 388, L.Com. Herring (cutter), fndrd. near Halifax, drnd.
Murray, Hon. John (P.C.)	IV. 129, Franchise bts. cut out Sp. Raposa.
Murray, Robert (Mid.)	VI. 312-18-26, Sophie, Burmese War.
Murray, Timothy (B.)	IV. 137, Renommée, cutting out exped.
Murray, William Bowman (Pr.)	II. 275, Ambuscade, in actn.
Murray, — (L.Com.) ...	III. 3, Seaflower, crsg. off St. Malo.
Murray, — (L.)	IV. 172, Supérieure, cutting out exped.
Muskein, — (C.) *F.* ...	II. 127-9, 131-6, invas. flotilla.
Musquetier, — (C.) *Du.*	II. 76-9, Du. Leyden, Camperdown.
Nagle, Edmund (L.) ...	IV. 167-8, Alexandria, w. cutting out exped.
Nagle, Sir Edmund (P.C.)	I. 233-5, Artois, Warren's Sq., capture of Révolutionnaire ; 355-6, 381, Warren's Sq. crsg. II. 95, Sq. off Ushant; 462, wrkd. on the coast of France.
Nailor, — (Mid.)	II. 262, Leander, w. in actn.
Nairne, John (P.C.) ...	IV. 146, Cambrian, Sq. off New York.
Nankivee, Thos. James (Mr. Mt.)	V. 398, Macedonian, k. in actn.
Napier, Charles (L.-Com.)	III. 316, Starling, off Boulogne, watching invas. flotilla. IV. 372-3, C. Recruit, w. in actn. with Diligente. V. 19-20-2, engages D'Haupoult ; 71, capture of Martinique ; 255, Thames ; 258-9, Medn. ; 342, capture of Sapri. VI. 18-19, Euryalus, capture of Ponza ; 174, Chesapeake Bay ; 181-5, w. Alexandria exped. ; 191, Baltimore.
Napier, Charles Frederick (L.)	II. 400-1, Echo, cutting out exped.
Napier, Hon. William J. (Mid.)	IV. 239, Impérieuse, cutting out exped.
Napper, Thos. (Mid.)	IV. 31, Seahorse, cutting out exped.
Nares, Wm. Hy. (L.)	VI. 28-9, Apollo, cutting out exped.
Nash, James (L.)	II. 58, Namur, St. Vincent, pro. Cr. III. 120, C. Hornet, Guadaloupe ; 296, Pandour, capture of Surinam. V. 428, Saturn, rasé. VI. 238, crsg. Halifax.
Nauckhoff, — (R.A.) *Swd.*	IV. 299, Swd. Gustav. IV. Adolph, Br. Swd. Flt, Oro Rds.
Nazer, Kelly (L.)	VI. 83, cutting out exped.
Neale, Sir Harry, Bart. (P.C.)	II. 91, San Fiorenzo and consort capts. Résistance and Constance off Brest ; 248, off Rochelle ; 302, actn. off Isle of Aix ; 376, Medn. IV. 89, London, Sq. crsg. ; 129-31, capts. Marengo ; 395, Caledonia ; 403-11-20, Basque Rds. actn. ; 421, returns to England ; 428. V. 101, Basque, Rds. ; 320, R.A. Com. off Brest.
Neame, William (Mid.)	IV. 101, Spencer, w. Duckworth's actn. V. 247, L. Scout, w. in actn.
Nearne, John (L.)	V. 343, America, cutting out exped.
Neirop, — (C.) *Du.* ...	II. 270, Du. Waakzaamheid captd. by Sirius.
Nelson, Abraham (Mid.)	I. 175, Marlborough, k. 1st June.

K

Nelson, Horatio (P.C.)	I. 72, Agamemnon, Medn. Flt.; 117-18, engages F. Sq. off Sardinia; 211-13, w. in actn. at Corsica; 284-6-90, actn. off Genoa; 296-8, actn. off Hyères; 303-5, Cmde. Sq. crsg. off Italy; 343, actn. off Oneglia; 344-5, Captain, Porto Ferrajo; 348, Bastia; 350-3, Com. at Porto Ferrajo; 406-7, Minerve capts. Sp. Sabina. II. 34-5, Captain;
,, Sir Horatio, K.B.	38-47, St. Vincent; 48-9, Irresistible; 58, kntd., made K.B.; 60, R.A.; 61, bombardment of Cadiz; 63, Theseus; 64-6-7-9, w. at Santa Cruz; 166-7, Vanguard, St. Pietro, Medn.; 169-72, Com. Medn. Flt.; 175-7-82-3-6-8, the
,, Lord	Nile; 197, w.; 202-6, 209, created Baron; 210-11, honours; 212-13, capture of Goza; 214-19, 259-65, 291-4-7, 305-6, Palermo; 307, crsg. off Sicily; 309, Foudroyant 310-14-17, Naples; 437-8, blockade of Malta; 440, England; 448, 466, App. III. 43, V.A. St. George; 44, Elephant; 45-55, Copenhagen; 58-62, Carlscrona; 63, returns to England; 64-5, Com. Channel defence; 175, Victory, Com. Medn. Flt.; 176-8, off Toulon; 179, Agincourt Sound; 236, 238-41, blockading Toulon; 243, 267-308, 333-5-42, 347-8, 352-5, in pursuit of M. Villeneuve; 357, 371-9, Medn. Flt.; 380, off Cadiz; 381-402, Trafalgar; 403, w. in actn.; 404-12-21-2-6-8, 443-8, d.; 449-51-55-7, Trafalgar; 462-3, honours; 465-7, 469-71, Nelson's tactics, 497-8, 502, App. IV. 38, Blanche carries despatches to Nelson; 59-62, Lord Wm. Fitzroy's despatches. VI. 260, Nelson's disregard of signal.
Nepean, Edmund (M.L.)	VI. 30, Elizabeth, in actn. Adriatic.
Nes, Jan Van (C.) *Du.*	IV. 277, Du. Surinam captd. by Anson.
Nesbett, Alexander (L.)	IV. 137, Renommée, cutting out exped.
Nesham, Christopher J. William (L.)	II. 88, Adamant, Camperdown, pro. Cr. V. 69, C. Intrepid, capture of Martinique.
Netley, — (C.) *F.*	IV. 306, Dorade (priv.) captd. by Découverte.
Netrel, Jacques Gab. La (C.) *F.*	V. 45, Nisus, cut out by Thetis.
Neve, Augustus Wm. H. Le (Pr.)	IV. 316, Childers, cutting out exped.
Neville, Martin (L.) ...	III. 139-40, Uranie, w. cutting out exped.
Neville, Ralph, Viscount (C.)	V. 204, Actæon, capture of the Isle of France.
Nevin, Charles I. (C.)	III. 38, Admiral Pasley captd. by Sp. gbts.
New, Thomas (C.)......	III. 482, Bonetta, wrkd. Isle of Cuba.
Newcombe, Francis (L.Com.)	III. 477, Albanaise captd. by mutiny off Malaga. IV. 400, C. Beagle; 405, 413, Basque Rds. actn.
Newcome, Henry (P.C.)	I. 226, Orpheus capts. Duguay-Trouin; 336-8, capture of Amboyna.
Newman, James Newman (P.C.)	I. 412, Ceres, St. Domingo. II. 154, Mermaid; 155-8, actn. with Loire; 247, Sq. crsg. III. 4-7, Loire with consorts capts. Pallas. IV. 396, Hero, Sq. blockading Basque Rds. V. 232, wrkd. off the Texel, drnd.; 447, App.
Newman, Robert Amyett (Mid.)	VI. 84, San Domingo, cutting out exped.
Newton, Vincent (C.)	VI. 175, Manly, Chesapeake Bay.
Nicholas, Harry (Mid.)	IV. 448, Topaze, cutting out exped.
Nicholas, Robert (C.)	V. 441, Lark, fndrd., drnd.
Nicholl, Robt. (Gunner)	IV. 316, Childers, cutting out exped.
Nichols, Henry (P.C.)	I. 62, 139, Royal Sovereign, Channel Flt.; 167, 73-4, 200, 1st June.
Nichols, John (Mr.Mt.)	IV. 230, Canopus, w. Dardanelles.
Nicholson, James (L.-Com.)	III. 36, Soworrow (lugger), Sq. crsg., 369, brings to England despatches of Calder's actn.
Nicholson, Richard St. Loo (L.)	IV. 440, Scheldt exped.

INDEX TO NAVAL OFFICERS 131

Nicholson, Robert (L.)	V. 214, Semiramis, cutting out exped.
Nicholson, — (Mid.)...	II. 241, Fox, drnd. at Samboangon.
Nicolas, John Toup (C.)	V. 125-7, Pilot, actn. with F. gbts. ; 257-8, Gulf of Taranto ; 341, off Palinuro. VI. 227-9, actn. with Légère.
Nicolas, Keigwin (L.)	VI. 228, Pilot, in actn.
Nicolas, Robert (C.) ..	IV. 183-4, Drake, crsg. ; 243, Lark, w. cutting out Sp. gbts.
Nicolls, Edward (M.L.)	III. 197-9, Blanche, w. cutting out exped. ; 292-4, Curaçoa. IV. 221, Standard, Dardanelles ; 347, C. cutting out exped.; 431, Scheldt exped. VI. 231, Maj. Chandeleur Isles.
Nielly, Joseph Marie (R.A.) F.	I. 140, Sans Pareil ; 142-7, Rochefort, Sq. crsg. ; 161-2, Républicaine ; 163-8, 1st June ; 191, 203, Sq. crsg. ; 204-5, capts. Alexander ; 228-9, 259, Brest Flt.
Nind, George (Mid.) ...	III. 409, Belleisle, k. Trafalgar.
Nisbet, Josiah (P.C.)...	II. 219, Dolphin, capture of Minorca.
Nisbett, Samuel (Mid.)	IV. 78, Serpent, cutting out exped. V. 99, L. Belvidera, cutting out exped. ; 451, L.Com. Chubb, fndrd. near Halifax, drnd.
Niza, Marquess de (R.A.) Por.	II. 211-12-18, Por. Principe-Real, Br. Por. Sq. blockade of Malta.
Noble, Christopher (M.C.)	V. 337, w. in actn. Santander (taken prisoner).
Noble, Francis (L.) ...	V. 304, capture of Java.
Noble, James (L.)	I. 343, w. cutting out exped. ; 406, Minerve, w. in actn.
Noble, Mark G. (B.)	V. 214, Diana, in actn.
Nodin, —(Mid.)(late)F.	I. 123, on board Antelope (packet), in actn.
Noel, Frederick (Mid.)	IV. 447, Tigre, cutting out exped.
Nops, John George (L.-Com.)	V. 442, Defender, wrkd. off Folkestone.
Norates, Don Manuel (C.) Sp.	III. 13, captd. by Leviathan ; 476, App.
Norcock, J. H. (Mid.)	VI. 309-28, Burmese War ; 349, App.
Nordenankar, — (C.) Swd.	IV. 299, Swd. Manligheten, Br. Swd. Flt. Oro Rds.
Norman, Chas. R. (L.)	VI. 224, Rota, k. cutting out exped.
Norman, George R. (L.)	V. 144, Sirius, cutting out exped. ; 146-8, k. capture of Isle de la Passe.
Norman, Samuel (L.-Com.)	III. 18-19, Biter, w. in actn. (also named William Norman).
Norman, Thos. (M.C.)	III. 410, Mars, w. Trafalgar.
Norris, George (Mr.)...	I. 119, Thames, w. in actn.
Norris, Wm. (M.Maj.)	II. 49, Captain, k. St. Vincent.
North, George (A.B.)	IV. 249, Halifax, deserter.
Northesk, Earl of (P.C.) ,, ,, K.B.	II. 72, Monmouth, Sheerness. III. 384, R.A. Britannia ; 389, 433-4, 443, Trafalgar ; 463, made K.B.
Norton, George (L.) ...	IV. 170-1, Bacchante, cutting out exped.; 466, Com. Inveterate, wrkd. near St. Vallery en Caux.
Norton, John (L.)	IV. 139, Frisk (cutter), Isle of Aix ; 244, Mediator, St. Domingo.
Norton, Nathaniel (Mr.-Mt.)	IV. 326, Virginie, in actn., pro. L.
Norway, John A. (Mid.)	I, 108, Nymphe, w. in actn.
Nott, Francis John (Mid.)	I. 275, Sans Pareil, actn. off Isle Groix.
Nourse, Charles (Mid.)	V. 263, Alceste, k. in actn.
Nourse, Joseph (L.) ...	III. 27, Courageux, w. in actn.; 351, C. Barbadoes, convoy escort. VI. 124, Severn, convoy escort; 170-5-6, engages flotilla, Chesapeake Bay.
Noyes, John (Mid.) ...	VI. 264, Penguin, w. in actn.
Nugent, Charles Edmund (P.C.)	I. 62, Veteran, Channel Flt.; 240-3, capture of Martinique.
Nugent, John (L.Com.)	IV. 172, Strenuous, crsg. off St. Malo.
Nurse, Hugh (Mt.) ...	VI. 269-70, Eliza, w. in actn.

K 2

Oades, Lewis (Car.) ...	III. 426, Téméraire, k. Trafalgar.
Oates, Mark (M.L.) ...	IV. 221, Pompée, in actn. Dardanelles.
Oates, Martin (B.)......	IV. 101, Spencer, k. in actn.
Obet, Yves Louis (C.) F.	I. 60, Suffren, Brest Flt.
O'Brien, Donat Henchy (L.)	V. 120, Amphion, cutting out exped.; 238–41, actn. off Lissa; 349–50, Bacchante, cutting out exped. VI. 21, cutting out exped. pro. Cr.
O'Brien, Edwd. (P.C.)	II. 75-8-81, Monarch, Camperdown.
O'Brien, James (P.C.)	III. 255, Emerald, crsg.; 297, capture of Surinam.
O'Brien, — (C.)	VI. 348, Moira, Burmese War, App.
O'Bryen, Edward (L.)	I. 233, Romney, in actn. III. 83, C. Cameleon, Egypt exped.; 175–6, Kent, Medn. Sq.
O'Bryen, James (C.) ...	II. 255, Childers, crsg. off Isle Bas.
O'Connor, Richard James L. (C.)	VI. 204, Prince Regent, Canadian Lakes.
O'Donnel, Robt. (Mid.)	IV. 374, Maria, k. in actn.
Ogilvie, David (Mid.)...	III. 422, Victory, Trafalgar.
Ogilvie, Henry (Mid.)	IV. 101, Donegal, w. Duckworth's actn.
Ogilvy, William (L.)...	I. 200, Glory, 1st June, pro. Cr.; 412, C. Lark, St. Domingo. II. 112–13, Thunderer des. Hermione, St. Domingo. III. 36, Magicienne, capture of Réolaise.
Ogle, Charles (Mid.)...	VI. 190, w. in actn. at Baltimore.
Ogleby, Rd. (Mr.-Mt.)	III. 84, w. Egypt exped.
O'Kane, W. F. (Mid.)	VI. 374, w. Algiers.
Oldfield, Thos. (M.C.)	II. 61, Theseus, w. in actn.; 64, Santa Cruz; 324, Maj., k. in actn. at Acre.
Oldham, Thomas Widlock (Mt.) E.I.C.	V. 134, E.I.C. Ceylon, w. in actn.
Oldmixon, John William (Mid.)	V. 308, Phaëton, capture of Java.
Oliver, B. S. (Mid.) ...	V. 349, Minstrel, cutting out exped.
Oliver, Robert (L.) ...	V. 113, Success, cutting out exped.
Oliver, Robert Dudley (L.)	I. 236, Artois, in actn. pro. Cr. III. 10, C. Mermaid, crsg. in Marseille Bay; 227, Melpomène, off Havre. IV. 165–6, Mars capts. Rhin. V. 101, Valiant, Basque Rds. VI. 99, 100, off New London.
Oliver, Thomas (L.) ...	III. 66, w. in actn. with invas. flotilla. IV. 28, Bacchante, cutting out exped.; 29, pro. Cr.
Oliver, William (Mr.)	V. 186, Ceylon, w. in actn.
Oliver, Wm. Sandford (L.)	II. 381, Alcmène, cutting out exped.
Ollivier, Louis François (C.) F.	VI. 36, Rubis chases Daring; 37, goes ashore Isles de Los.
Ommanney, John Acworth (P.C.)	VI. 365-8-73, Albion, Navarino.
O'Neale, John (L.) ...	V. 220, Alert (cutter), cutting out exped.
O'Neil, Don Felix (Cmde.) Sp.	II. 254, Sp. Pomona, actn. with Lion.
Onslow, Sir Richard (V.A.)	I. 307, Port A. at Plymouth. II. 454, App.
Onslow, Richard (V.A.)	II. 75-8-80, Camperdown; 88, created Baronet.
Orchard, J. (L.Com.)	IV. 457, Barracouta, wrkd. Isle of Cuba.
Orde, Sir John (V.A.)	III. 333-42-5, Glory, Sq. off Cadiz.
O'Reilly, Dowell (act.-L.)	IV. 184, Success, w. cutting out exped. V. 335, L. Surveillante, San Nicolas, Spain. VI. 16, St. Sebastian; 120, Com. Lyra, Spain.
O'Reilly, John (Mid.)	VI. 234, w. in actn. with U.S. gbts.
Ormond, Francis (L.)	VI. 201, Endymion, Penobscot exped.
Ormsby, Charles C. (L.Com.)	III. 235, Conflict, wrkd. Isle of Wight; 494, App.
Orso, Don Francisco de (C.) Ital.	II. 256–7, Liguria captd. by Espoir, w. in actn.

Orvilliers, De — (A.) F. I. 196, 240, Keppel's actn. (1778).
Osborn, Edward Oliver (P.C.) I. 416, Trident, Sq. in Simon's Bay. IV. 235, Kent, crsg. off Isle Lemnos, Dardanelles.
Osborn, John (P.C.) ... II. 394, Tremendous des. Preneuse, Port Louis. III. 208, Pondicherry. IV. 143-4, actn. with Canonnière.
Osborne, Geo. (Mid.) V. 263, Active, k. in actn.
Osborne, George (M.-Corporal) VI. 57, Shannon, in actn. with Chesapeake.
Osborne, Samuel (P.C.) I. 226, Centurion, Sq. Isle of France; 236-7, actn. with Cybèle; 336-8, Ceylon; 414, Amboyna.
Osborne, Thomas (L.) IV. 9, Namur, w. Strachan's actn.
Oswald, James (C.) ... II. 307-8, Perseus (bomb.), Palermo; 320, Alexandria. IV. 160, Phœbe, Shetland Isles.
Otter, Charles (L.) ... I. 116, Crescent, in actn. IV. 293, C. Proserpine, Medn. V. 10-12, captd. by Pénélope and Pauline; 441, App.
Ottley, Edward (L.) ... II. 273, Perdrix, in actn,
Ottley, John (L.Com.) IV. 171, Pike, off Cuba; 336, captd. by F. Marat (priv.); 467, App.
Otway, Robert Waller (L.) I. 177, Impregnable, 1st June; 320-1, C. Thorn, capts. Courier National; 378-80, Mermaid, actn. with Vengeance; 412, W. Indies. II. 113, Jean Rabel exped.; 376, Trent, Porto Rico. III. 47, London, Copenhagen; 313, Montagu, Channel Flt. IV. 116, Sq. at Barbadoes; 292, Syracuse; 294, Scylla. V. 81-2, Ajax, Medn.; 129, Palamos; 245-6, capts. Dromadaire.
Otway, William Albany (R.A.) IV. 434, Monarch, Scheldt exped.
Ouchakow, — (V.A.) Rus. II. 214, Isle Cerigo.
Oughton, James (C.)... II. 132, Tartarus (bomb.), off Ostende; 345, Isis, Holland exped.
Overend, Henry (Mr.-Mt.) IV. 170, Bacchante, cutting out exped.
Overton, Edward (Mr.) III. 413-14, Bellerophon, k. Trafalgar.
Overton, Robert (C.-Ck.) II. 196, Majestic, w. the Nile.
Owen, Edw. Wm. CampbellRich.(P.C.) III. 171-2, Immortalité, actn. off Dieppe; 227-9, 320-1-3, off Boulogne, watching invas. flotilla. IV. 265, Clyde, crsg. off France; 436-9, Scheldt exped.
Owen, John (M.L.) ... II. 394, Adamant, cutting out exped. III. 408-9, C. Belleisle, w. Trafalgar. V. 343-4, Leviathan, cutting out exped.
Owen, William Fitz-William (L.) IV. 181, Seaflower, cutting out exped. V. 303, C. Barracouta, capture of Java.

Paddon, Silas Hiscutt (Mid.) III. 20-1, Viper, w. cutting out exped. IV. 313, L.Com. Cuckoo, Medn. V. 445, wrkd.
Page, Benjamin (L.) ... V. 386, borne on the register of U.S. Navy.
Page, Benjamin Wm. (C.) I. 338, Hobart, capture of Molletive, Ceylon; 415, Banda Neira.
Paget, Hon. Chas. (C.) II. 75, Martin, Channel Flt. III. 180, Endymion capts. Bacchante. IV. 129, Egyptienne, crsg. Spain; 391, Revenge, off Brest. V. 106, off Cherbourg. VI. 196, Superb, Buzzard's Bay, U.S.
Paget, Hon.Wm.(P.C.) I. 231, Romney capts. Sibylle.
Paimpéni, — (C.) F. ... III. 272-3, Buonaparte (priv.), actn. with Hippomenes
Pain, Reuben (Mid.)... III. 55, Isis, w. Copenhagen. VI. 185, L., w. Alexandria.
Pakenham, Edward (P.C.) I. 226, Resistance, E. Indies; 336, capture of Malacca; 414, Amboyna. II. 240, crsg.; 245, Resistance blows up, k.; 469, App.
Pakenham, John (P.C.) I. 297, Gibraltar; 299, actn. off Hyères; 351, Gibraltar.

Pakenham, John (L.-Com.)	VI. 394, Bermuda, wrkd. in the Gulf of Mexico.
Pakenham, Hon. Thos. (P.C.)	I. 65, 139, Invincible, Channel Flt.; 149-54, 29th May; 159, 30th May; 162-6-76-7, 200, 1st June; 206, Spithead.
Pakenham, Hon. Wm. (P.C.)	V. 441, Greyhound, wrkd. Luconia; 447, Saldanha, wrkd. Ireland.
Paley, Cornwallis (Mid.)	V. 120, Amphion, cutting out exped.
Palicuccia,—(C.)*Ital.*	V. 122, Carolina, Sq. crsg., Adriatic.
Pallière, Jean A. Christy (C.) *F.*	III. 68, 73, Desaix, Egypt exped.; 96, Toulon; 112, Saumarez's actn.
Palmer, Alexander (Mid.)	III. 425, Victory, k. Trafalgar.
Palmer, Edmund (C.)	IV. 232, Wizard, Egypt exped.; 465, wrkd. Medn. VI. 128, Hebrus; 129-30, capts. Etoile; 175-6, Chesapeake Bay;
,, ,, (C.B.)	177-8, Bladensburg; 278, C.B., Algiers.
Palmer, Edward (C.)	IV. 136, Nautilus, off Carthagena; 215, Azire Bay.
Palmer, Edward Gascoigne (L.)	V. 112, Rinaldo, in actn.
Palmer, Geo. (C.)*E.I.C.*	II. 89, E.I.C. Boddam repels with consorts F. Sq.
Palmer, George H. (L.)	VI. 26, Kingfisher, cutting out exped.
Palmer, John (C.)	IV. 280, Pheasant, Buenos Ayres.
Palmer, Joseph (Mid.)	III. 295, k. in actn. Curaçoa.
Palmer, Mark (B.)......	IV. 230, Active, w. Dardanelles.
Palmer, Nesbit (L.) ...	I. 283, Berwick captd. by F. Flt. V. 248-9, C. Alacrity, captd. by Abeille; 250, w.; 251, d.; 325, 447, App.
Palmer, Thomas (L.)...	I. 368, Unicorn, in actn., pro. Cr.
Palmer, William (L.)...	III. 119, Melpomène, k. cutting out exped.
Palmer, William (Mid.)	V. 327, Briseis, w. cutting out exped.
Papin, André (C.) *F.*	II. 137, Concorde, Rochefort Sq.
Papineau, Jean Alex. (L.Com.) *F.*	V. 213, Teazer recaptd. by Diana.
Pardoe, Charles (Mid.)	III. 115, Venerable, w. in actn.
Pardoe, — (Mr.Mt.)	I. 175, Marlborough, w. 1st June.
Parejas, Don Antonio (Cmde.) *Sp.*	III. 386, Sp. Argonauta, Trafalgar.
Parish, John (L.)	IV. 170, Arethusa, in actn. Havana; 279, at Curaçoa, pro. Cr.
Park, Thomas (M.L.)	VI. 224, Rota, w. cutting out exped.
Parker, Charles (Mid.)	IV. 317, Childers, w. in actn.
Parker, Christopher (P.C.)	I. 271, Valiant, Channel Flt.
Parker, Edward Thornborough (P.C.)	III. 65-6, k. in actn. with invas. flotilla.
Parker, Frederick (C.)	V. 67-9, Derwent, drnd. off Sénégal.
Parker, Fred.Aug. Hargood (L.)	V. 38, Tartar, cutting out exped.
Parker, George (L.) ...	I. 116, Crescent, in actn., pro. Cr. IV. 319, C., Stately with Nassau des. Da. Prindts-Christian-Frederic. VI. 117, Aboukir, Medn. Flt.
Parker, Henry H. (C.)	II. 462, Vipère, fndrd off the Shannon, drnd.
Parker, Sir Hyde (R.A.)	I. 72, Victory, Medn. Flt.; 84, Toulon; 214-15, St. George, Corsica; 262, Raisonable, Channel Flt.; 284, V.A. St. George, actn. off Genoa; 297, Hyères; 305-6, Com. at Leghorn. II. 112-13, Queen; 405, A.; 406-11-15, Com. at Jamaica. III. 43, London; 45-7-50-1, Com. Copenhagen exped.; 61-2, Carlscrona; 63-4, returns to England; 481, App.
Parker, Hyde (L.)	III. 275, Narcissus, cutting out exped. VI. 51-2, C. Tenedos, crsg. Boston Bay; 200, Marblehead; 201, Penobscot exped.; 238-41, crsg. off Sandy Hook.
Parker, J. Stevens (Mid.)	IV. 326, Alceste, cutting out exped.
Parker, Kenyon Stevens (M.L.)	VI 32, Milford, in actn. Adriatic.

INDEX TO NAVAL OFFICERS 135

Parker, Sir Peter (A.)	I. 317, Port A. at Spithead.
Parker, Peter (P.C.) ...	V. 38-40, Melpomène, crsg. ; 203, Menelaus, capture of the
,, Sir Peter, Bart.	Isle of France ; 315, Baronet ; 350, w. in actn. Toulon batteries. VI. 146-7, Medn. ; 175, Chesapeake ; 186-7, k. in actn.
Parker, Richard (P.C.)	I. 416, Swiftsure, St. Domingo exped.
Parker, Richard (A.B.)	II. 71-2, mutiny at the Nore ; 73, executed.
Parker, Richard Wm. (L.)	II. 395-6, Speedy, cutting out exped. III. 133-4, w. in actn., pro. Cr.
Parker, Samuel (Mr.) ...	V. 178, Africaine, k. in actn.
Parker, Thomas (L.) ...	IV. 158, Indefatigable, w. cutting out exped. VI. 381, C. Sarpedon, fndrd., drnd.
Parker, William (P.C.)	I. 62, 139, Audacious, Channel Flt. ; 144-7, engages Révolutionnaire ; 148, Plymouth ; 200, 29th May. II. 24, R.A. Prince George, Gibraltar ; 34-7-9, 42-6, 50, St. Vincent ;
,, Sir William, Bart.	58, created Baronet ; 289, V.A. Flt. off Cadiz.
Parker, William (P.C.)	III. 236, Amazon, Sardinia. IV. 129, Neale's Sq. crsg.
Parker, William (Mid.)	V. 37, Mercury, cutting out exped.
Parker, Sir William George (L.)	IV. 137-8, Renommée, cutting out expeds. V. 318, C. Rinaldo, Sq. off Boulogue, in actn.
Parker, — (L.) U.S. ...	V. 418, U.S. Constitution, in actn.
Parkinson, John (B.) ...	VI. 41, Amelia, w. in actn.
Parkinson, W. S. (L.)	II. 311-12, Foudroyant, Naples.
Parkyns, George (Mid.)	IV. 221, Pompée, Dardanelles.
Parr, John (P.C.)	I. 409, Malabar, capture of Demerara. II. 456, fndrd. W. Indies, crew saved.
Parr, — (Gunner)	II. 218, Swiftsure, Alexandria.
Parry, Henry (Mr.Mt.)	IV. 346, Porcupine, cutting out exped.
Parry, Richard (M.L.)	II. 249, Flora, w. cutting out exped. III. 85, w. Egypt.
Parry, William (Mid.)	VI. 74, Dominica, k. in actn.
Parson, John (L.)	VI. 289, Granicus, Algiers ; 291, pro. Cr.
Parsons, Robert White (L.)	V. 214, Diana, in actn.
Parster, I. (S.Mt.)	III. 35, Milbrook, w. in actn.
Paschaligo, — (C.) Ven.	V. 122, Corona, Sq. crsg. Adriatic ; 233-9, 244, captd. in actn. off Lissa ; 316, Regenitore launched at Venice.
Pasco, John (L.)	III. 425, Victory, w. Trafalgar. VI. 102, C. Tartarus, Quebec.
Pasco, — (B.)	I. 123, Antelope (packet), in actn.
Pascoe, William R. (L.-Com.)	VI. 36-41, Daring, k. in actn. ; 381, App.
Pasley, James (L.)	III. 139, Beaulieu, cutting out exped.; 148-9, Lark, cutting out exped.
Pasley, Thomas (P.C.)	I. 65, Bellerophon, Channel Sq. ; 67, Spithead ; 139, R.A. Channel Flt.; 144-6, 28th May ; 149-53, 29th May; 162-72,
,, Sir Thos., Bart.	w. 1st June ; 199-200, created Baronet.
Pater, Charles Dudley (L.)	I. 87, Toulon. IV. 3, C. Bellona ; 12-13, Strachan's actn. V. 41, Princess Caroline, Baltic Sq. ; 231, Cressy, off Jutland.
Pater, Henry Dudley (P.C.)	I. 295, Ça-Ira, San Fiorenzo Bay. II. 456, destd. by fire.
Paterson, William (C.)	IV. 382, Star, W. Indies. V. 92, St. Domingo ; 204, capture of the Isle of France. VI. 278, Minden ; 283-7, Algiers ;
,, William, C.B.	291, made C.B.
Patey, Benjamin (L.) ...	III. 443, Mars, Trafalgar ; 464, pro. P.C.
Patey, Joseph (Mid.) ...	II. 255, Lion, w. in actn. III. 494, L.Com. Cerbère, wrkd. off Berry Head.
Patfull, William (L.) ...	III. 222, Stag (cutter), off Ostende. IV. 78, Serpent, cutting out exped.
Patriarch, Charles (L.)	IV. 100, Superb, w. in actn.
Patterlo, — (B.)	I. 176, Impregnable, w. 1st June.
Patterson, Daniel T. (C.)	V. 386, borne on the register of U.S. Navy.

Patterson, William Love (L.)	IV. 320, Tartarus, cutting out exped.
Patton, Andrew (C.) E.I.C.	II. 89, E.I.C. Ocean escapes a F. Sq.
Patton, James (Mid.)...	I. 362-3, Niger, w. cutting out exped.
Paul, Robert (C.)	III. 172, Explosion (bomb.), actn. off Dieppe.
Paulet, Lord Henry (P.C.)	I. 240, Vengeance, capture of Martinique; 315-16, Astræa capts. Gloire; 329, Thalia, crsg. II. 289, Defence, Flt. off Cadiz. III. 15, Warren's Sq. crsg.; 47-53, Copenhagen. IV. 89, Terrible; 116, Barbadoes.
Paulin, Paul François (C.) F.	V. 9-10, F. Var captd. by Belle Poule.
Payler, Francis R. (Mid.)	II. 159, Anson, w. in actn.
Payne, James (Schoolmaster)	II. 195, Goliath, w. the Nile.
Payne, John Willet (P.C.)	I. 65, 139, Russel, Channel Flt.; 144-7, 28th May; 149-50, 29th May; 162, 172-3, 200, 1st June.
Payne, Samuel J. (M.L.)	III. 426, Téméraire, w. Trafalgar. IV. 378, Amethyst, w. in actn.
Peace, Richard (Mr. Mt.)	V. 113, Success, cutting out exped.
Peachey, Francis (L.)...	III. 120-1, Cyane, cutting out exped.
Peachy, Henry John (L.)	V. 194-5, Cornwallis, cutting out exped.; 303, C. Hecate, capture of Java.
Peacock, James (B.) ...	II. 49, Blenheim, w. in actn.
Peacock, Philip (Mid.)	IV. 100, Northumberland, w. in actn.
Peake, J. G. (M.L.)...	III. 425, Victory, w. in actn.
Peake, Thos. Ladd (L.)	V. 339, Victorious, in actn.; 341, pro. Cr.
Peake, William (C.) ...	VI. 46-50, Peacock captd. by U.S. Hornet, k. in actn.; 381, App.
Pearce, Geo. (L.Com.) U.S.	VI. 204, U.S. Growler, Canadian Lakes.
Pearce, John (L.Com.)	VI. 388, Decoy captd., date unknown.
Pearce, Joseph (C.) ...	VI. 201, Rifleman, Penobscot exped.
Pearce, Robert (L.) ...	VI. 186, Menelaus, Chesapeake Bay.
Pearce, Wm. Isaac (L.)	III. 18-20, Dart, cutting out exped.
Pearce, — (Mid.)	I. 186, Royal George, w. 1st June.
Pearce, — (L.)	IV. 188, capture of the Cape of Good Hope.
Peard, Shuldham (P.C.)	II. 33, St. George, Lisbon; 68-9, off Cadiz; 289, Success, Medn.; 380, crsg.; 438-9, Sicily; 444, Malta. III. 72, captd. by F. Sq. Medn.; 98-105, Audacious, Algesiras; 482, App.
Pearl, James (L.)	IV. 405, Mediator (bomb.), w. Basque Rds.
Pearse, Henry Whitmarsh (C.)	IV. 185-6, Halcyon capts. Sp. Neptuno.
Pearse, Richd. (Mr. Mt.)	I. 108, Nymphe, k. in actn.
Pearson, Charles (L.)...	VI. 155, Phœbe, in actn., pro. Cr.
Pearson, George (Mid.)	III. 414, Bellerophon, w. Trafalgar.
Pearson, Hugh (Mr. Mt.)	II. 61, w. in actn. Cadiz.
Pearson, Hugh (L.) ...	V. 12-13, Arethusa, coast of Spain.
Pearson, James (act. L.)	VI. 201, Dragon, Penobscot exped.
Pearson, Richard Hy. (P.C.)	III. 179, Doris captures Affronteur (lugger).
Pearson, Wm. Henry (Mr. Mt.)	III. 409, Belleisle, w. Trafalgar.
Pechell, Samuel John (P.C.)	V. 3, Cleopatra, capture of Topaze; 71, capture of Martinique; 273, Guerrière, crsg.; 384. VI. 92, San Domingo, Chesapeake.
Pedlar, George (L.) ...	VI. 201, Dragon, Penobscot exped.
Peebles, George (M.L.)	III. 85, w. Egypt exped.
Peebles, Thomas (L.)	IV. 39-43, Blanche, w. in actn.
Peel, Jonathan Haworth (Mid.)	VI. 236, w. in actn. St. Mary's, U.S.
Peffers, Peter (B.)......	II. 49, Excellent, k. St. Vincent.

INDEX TO NAVAL OFFICERS 137

Pegge, George (Mr. Mt.) III. 417, Achille, w. Trafalgar.
Pelabonde, François Aug. (L.Com.) *F.* III. 11, Ligurienne captd. by Peterel, k. in actn.
Pell, Watkins Owen (Mid.) III. 6, Loire, w. in actn. IV. 326, L. Mercury, cutting out exped. V. 37-8, w. cutting out exped. VI. 14, C. Thunder (bomb.), capts. Neptune (lugger).
Pellew, Edward (P.C.) I. 106-8, Nymphe capts. Cléopâtre; 109, kntd.; 222-33-5,
,, Sir Edward, Knt. Arethusa, Sq. crsg.; 259, Sq. off Brest; 357-8, Indefatigable, off Ushant; 361, capture of Virginie; 437, App. II. 7-8, off Brest; 12-16, engages Droits de l'Homme; 23, Falmouth; 31, off Brest; 102, capts. Hyène; 258, capts. Vaillante; 285, Impétueux; 297-300, Brest; 427, Quiberon exped.; 450, Ferrol. III. 20-1, Port Louis; 188, Cmde., crsg.; 191, Tonnant, crsg. IV. 51, R.A. Com. at Ceylon; 93, 180, E. Indies; 282-3, capture of Gres-
,, Sir Edward, Bart. sie, Java, created Baronet; 460-3, App. V. 207-9, Caledonia, V.A. Com. Flt. off Toulon; 260-97, 315, 375, 427, Medn. VI. 1, 2, 4-19, off Toulon; 117-18,
Exmouth, Lord, G.C.B. Medn.; 226, created Lord Exmouth; 278, A., G.C.B., Queen Charlotte; 279-90, Algiers; 291, created Viscount.
Pellew, Fleetwood B. Reynolds (P.C.) IV. 181-2, Psyche, Java; 283, capts. Du. ships at Java, kntd., made C.B. V. 296, Phaëton; 303-9, capture of Java.
,, Sir Fleetwood B. Reynolds, C.B. VI. 34, Resistance, Adriatic.
Pellew, Israel (C) ...... I. 109, on board Nymphe at capture of Cléopâtre, pro. P.C.; 395, Amphion blows up at Plymouth. II. 456, App. III. 130, Andromache, crsg. Cuba; 335, Conqueror, Medn.; 384, 427-9, Trafalgar. IV. 157, Sq. off Rochefort; 236, Lisbon exped. V. 207, R.A. Caledonia, Flt. off Toulon. VI. 2, 117, Medn.
Pellew, Pownoll B. (C.) IV. 456, Fly, wrkd. Gulf of Florida.
Pelley, P. R. M. Et Dumanoir le (Cmde.) *F.* II. 5-10, Révolution, Ireland exped.; 127, invas. flotilla; 174-5, Alexandria; 215, 336, Corsica. III. 97, R.A. Cadiz; 109-10, 241, Formidable, Toulon; 334, Toulon; 386-7, 433-6, 447, 467, Trafalgar. IV. 1-3, 6-12, w. Strachan's actn.
Pellowe, Richard (L.) I. 107-9, Nymphe, in actn.
Pelly, Charles (L.) ... III. 66, w. in actn. invas flotilla; 265, C. Beaver off the Texel. V. 303, Bucephalus; 306-7, capture of Java.
Pender, Francis (P.C.) I. 385, Resolution, Murray's Sq. III. 458, Queen, Cadiz.
Pendergrass, James (C.) *E.I.C.* III. 250, E.I.C. Hope, actn. with Linois' Sq. E. Indies.
Pengelly, Edw. (M.L.) IV. 263, Hydra, cutting out exped.
Pengelly, John (L.Com.) II. 92, Viper capts. Sp. Maria; 419 20, capts. Furet.
Penrose, Charles Vinicombe (Cmde.) V. 111, Com. at Gibraltar. VI. 120, R.A. Sq. off Spain; 290-1, Algiers, kntd.
Penruddock, Geo. (L.) V. 126, Pilot, cutting out exped.
Percival, Edw. (Mr. Mt.) VI. 26, Havannah, k. cutting out exped.
Percival, Hon. George James (Mid.) IV. 447, Tigre, cutting out exped. VI. 201, L. Tenedos, Penobscot exped.; 278, C. Infernal (bomb.), Algiers.
Percy, Hon. Henry William (C.) VI. 231, Hermes destd. at Mobile, U.S.; 387, App.
Percy, Josceline (P.C.) V. 216, Hotspur, actn. with F. brigs.
Peregrine, Hugh (M.L.) V. 289, Galatea, k. in actn.
Perez, Don Pablo (C.) *Sp.* II. 359, Sp. Santa Teresa captd. by Argo.
Péridier, Jean Alexandre (C.) *F.* V. 233-8, 244, Flore, actn. off Lissa.
Perkins, Henry Augustus (L.) VI. 288, Granicus, w. Algiers.
Perkins, John (C.) ...... II. 113, Drake, St. Domingo. III. 150, Arab, W. Indies; 186, Tartar, St. Domingo.
Perkyns, Edw. (Mid.) IV. 138, Pallas, cutting out exped.

Perrée, — (Cmde.) *F.*	I. 117, Sq. crsg. Medn.; 282, Toulon; 321–2 Minerve captd. by Dido and consort; 323–4, w. in actn. II. 176–8, 215, Com. gbts. on the Nile; 295, R.A., Junon captd. by Br. Sq.; 324–5, 330–1, 377–9, Sq. crsg.; 438, Généreux captd. by Br. Sq.; 439, k. in actn.
Perrin, Jas. (M.Private)	VI. 187, k. in actn.
Perrot, Samuel (M.L.)	III. 292–5, Hercule, w. Curaçoa.
Perroud, Jacques (C.) *F.*	IV. 156, Bellone captd. by Powerful; 355–6, Isle of France. V. 97, Confiance captd. by Valiant.
Perry, Oliver Hazard (C.) *U.S.*	VI. 109–14, Canadian Lakes; 183–8, Potomac; 208–10–23, Canadian Lakes.
Perry, Philip Luscombe (M.L.)	II. 114, Magicienne, cutting out exped.
Peschell, Thos. John (L.)	IV. 127, Franchise, cutting out exped.
Peter, Robert (M.L.)	IV. 462, Dominica captd., date unknown.
Peters, Andrew (A.B.)	V. 136, E.I.C. Astell, k. in actn.
Petit, Jean Nicolas (C.) *F.*	IV. 48, Jemmappes, Sq. crsg.; 444, Ajax, Toulon Flt. V. 10, Medn.
Petit-Thouars Arist. Aub. du (Cmde.) *F.*	II. 178, F. Tonnant; 186–9, 191–4–99, k. the Nile.
Petit-Thouars Georges du (C.) *F.*	VI. 124, F. Sultane; 125–7, actn. with Br. frigates.
Petley, — (Mid.)	II. 249, Flora, cutting out exped.
Petrona Bey (A.) *Turk*	VI. 363, Navarino.
Pettel, Mark (Mr.Mt.)	VI. 234, w. in actn.
Petterson, — (C.) *Swd.*	IV. 299, Swd. Gustav. III. Br. Swd. Flt. Oro Rds.
Pettet, Robert (C.) ...	III. 354, Termagant, bearer of news of F. Flt. to Nelson's Flt. at Ceuta.
Pettet, Robert (L.) ...	V. 42, Cerberus, cutting out exped.
Pettman, Thomas (L.)	V. 103, Dreadnought, cutting out exped.
Pevrieux, Etienne (C.) *F.*	I. 222–5, Pomone captd. by Br. Sq.; 365–9–70, Proserpine captd. by Dryad. II. 134–7, Confiante destd. by Hydra and consorts. III. 66, 230, invas. flotilla.
Peyton, John (P.C.)...	II. 171, Defence, Medn. Flt.
Peyton, John Strutt (C.)	V. 346–9, Minstrel, Medn.
Peyton, — (A)	II. 103, Com. Channel Sq.
Phibbs, Matthew (Mid.)	V. 297, Sir Francis Drake, cutting out exped.
Phillibert, Pierre Henri (C.) *F.*	VI. 124–7, Etoile, in actn.; 129–30, captd. by Hebrus.
Phillimore, George (L.)	III. 271, Wilhelmina, in actn.
Phillimore, John (P.C.)	VI. 14, Eurotas, crsg., capture of Trave; 132–3, actn. with Clorinde; 134, w.; 135–41, 385, App.
Phillips, Edward (Mid.)	IV. 71, Phœnix, in actn.
Phillips, Jas. Robt. (L.)	III. 282, Centurion, in actn.
Phillips, Wm. (Mr.Mt.)	III. 140, w. cutting out exped.
Phillott, Charles George Rodney (L.)	V. 9. Amphion, Adriatic; 28, 36–7, cutting out exped., pro. Cr. VI. 142–4, C. Primrose; 236, w. in actn. St. Mary's, U.S.
Philpot, Robert (C.) ...	II. 400–1, Echo, crsg. Porto Rico.
Pichot, Sébastian L. M. (C.) *F.*	III. 1, F. Vengeance engages U.S. Constellation; 23–5, captd. by Seine.
Pickering, Wm. (Mr.)	IV. 100, Superb, w. in actn.
Pickerwell, Thos. (Mr.-Mt.)	IV. 300, Implacable, w. in actn.
Pickett, Stephen (Car.)	V. 220, Raven, cutting out exped.
Pickett, Wm. W. (Ck.)	VI. 288, Leander, w. Algiers.
Pickey, Valentine (Mid.)	VI. 317–18, Arachne; 328, 342, L. Alligator, Burmese War.
Pickford, Charles (L.)	III. 299, Inconstant, Gorée. V. 441, C. Glommen, wrkd. Barbadoes.
Pickmore, Francis (P.C.)	IV. 89, Ramillies, Sq. crsg. V. 208, R.A. Téméraire, Medn. Flt.
Pierce, Jesse (Mr.) *U.S.*	IV. 147, U.S. Richard (sloop), actn. with Leander.

Pierce, John (A.B.) *U.S.*	IV. 147, U.S. Richard (sloop), k. in actn. with Leander.
Pierce, William (L.) ...	III. 273, Hippomenes, in actn. with Buonaparte.
Piercy, R. (C.)	I. 439, Hound captd. W. Indies.
Pierrepont, Charles Herbert (C.)	II. 224–5, Kingfisher capts F. Betsy (priv.).
Pierrepont, William (P.C.)	II. 269, Naiad with consort capts. Décade; 401–2, capture of Sp. treasure ships.
Pigot, George (C.)	IV. 327, Blossom, off Lisbon; 328, cutting out exped.; 329, pro. P. IV. 465, Java, fndrd East Indies, drnd.
Pigot, Hugh (P.C.) ...	II. 111, Hermione, Porto Rico; 113–16, k. mutiny of crew; 462, App.
Pigot, Hugh (P.C.) ...	IV. 331–2, Circe, crsg.; 387, Guadaloupe. V. 5, Latona, crsg.; 20–3, capts. Félicité. VI. 147, Orpheus, Rhode Island; 156–7, capts. U.S. Frolic.
Pigot, Robert (L.)	IV. 36–7, Cambrian, w. cutting out exped, pro. Cr.
Pigot, — (L.)	IV. 188, capture of the Cape of Good Hope.
Pigott, James (P.C.) ...	I. 65–139, Tremendous, Channel Flt.
Piguement, Saml. (Pr.)	II. 273, Perdrix, in actn.
Pilastre, Jean François (C.) *F.*	I. 141, Audacieux, Rochefort.
Pilch, Robert (L.)	V. 40, Bellerophon, cutting out exped. Finland.
Pilcher, John M. (M.L.)	IV. 170, Bacchante, cutting out exped.
Pilford, John (L.)	III. 384, Ajax, Trafalgar; 464, pro. P.C.
Pilford, John (L.)	II. 428, Impétueux, cutting out exped.
Pilkington, — (Mid.)...	VI. 234, k. in actn. with U.S. gbts.
Pillet, Louis Gabriel (L.-Com.) *F.*	I. 356, Cigogne, Sq. crsg.
Pillon, Don Antonio (C.) *Sp.*	II. 401–3, Sp. Santa Brigida captd. by Naiad.
Pin, M. de la Tour (M.L.)	II. 407–9, Surprise, cutting out exped.
Pine, Horace (L.)	I. 355, Diamond, in actn. Herqui.
Pinsum, Jacques (C.) *F.*	IV. 376–7, Thétis captd. by Amethyst; 379, w. in actn.
Pinto, Thomas (C.) ...	V. 45, Achates, crsg. Guadaloupe; 445, wrkd. W. Indies.
Pinto, — (C.) *Por.* ...	V. 66, Por. Minerva captd. by F. Bellone and consorts.
Pipon, Philip (L.)	II. 19–22, wrkd. in Droits de l'Homme. III. 142–3, Fisgard, cutting out exped., pro. Cr.; 172, C. Kite. VI. 131, Tagus, capture of Cérès.
Pipon, Philip (L.)	IV. 326, Alceste, cutting out exped.
Pipon, Philip (M.L.)...	V. 258–60, Impérieuse, w. cutting out exped.
Pistock, Thomas (C.)	II. 271–2, Herald (priv.) engages F. privs.
Pitts, William (Mid.)...	III. 426, Téméraire, k. Trafalgar.
Place, La (C.) *F.*	III. 278, Hirondelle (priv.) captd. by Tartar.
Placiard, — (C.) *F.* ...	III. 257–8, Egyptienne (priv.) captd. by Hippomenes.
Plaine, John (Mid.) ...	I. 108, Nymphe, w. in actn.
Plampin, Robert (P.C.)	III. 482, Lowestoffe, wrkd. W. Indies. IV. 90, Powerful, Sq. crsg.; 156, capts. Bellone (priv.); 180, Java. VI. 117, Ocean, Medn. Flt.
Plant, Wm. (Mr. Mt.)	IV. 448, Apollo, cutting out exped.
Pletz, — (C.) *Du.*	II. 270, Du. Furie captd. by Sirius.
Plowman, George (L.-Com.)	IV. 261, Defender, in actn. off Cherbourg.
Plumridge, James Hanway (L.)	V. 38, Melpomène, cutting out exped.
Plymsell, Amos (L.) ...	VI. 274, Tyne, in actn. Isle of Cuba.
Pocock, Edw. O. (Mid.)	VI. 21, Bacchante, cutting out exped.
Pococke, George H. A. (Mid.)	VI. 288, Hebrus, k. Algiers.
Poe, George (M.L.) ...	VI. 187, w. in actn. Baltimore.
Pogson, Hy. F. Young (C.)	VI. 388, Racer, wrkd. Gulf of Florida.
Polders, Johannes Martinus (C.) *Du.*	VI. 279, Du. Dageraad, Algiers.

Pole, Charles Morice (P.C.)	I. 72, Colossus, Medn. Flt.; 189, Sq. off Ushant; 378, R.A. Carnatic, Guadaloupe. II. 28, Spithead mutiny; 285, Royal George, Sq. off Brest; 302, Basque Rds. III. 63–4, V.A. Com. Baltic Flt.
,, Sir Charles Morice	
Polkinghorne, Jas. (L.)	VI. 84, San Domingo, w. cutting out exped.
Pollet, — (C.) *F.*	III. 196, Sept Frères (priv.) destd. by Merlin.
Pommier, Zavier (C.)*F.*	II. 62, Mutine cut out by the bts. of Minerve.
Ponée, François (L.)*F.*	V. 291–2, Néréide, in actn.
Pooke, James (Gunner)	III. 149, Pasley, k. in actn.
Pool, — (C.) *Du.*	IV. 322–4, Du. Guelderland captd. by Virginie; 325, dismissed.
Pope, John (L.)	VI. 40–1, Amelia, k. in actn.
Popham, Sir Home (P.-C.)	II. 350, Holland exped. III. 235, Antelope, off Calais. IV. 187, Cmde. Diadem; 189–91, Cape of Good Hope exped.; 192, court-martialled; 200, Prince of Wales; 208–79, Copenhagen; 433, Venerable; 434–7, Scheldt exped.; 459, App. V. 334, Com. Sq. N. Spain.
Popham, Home Riggs (P.C.)	II. 131, Expedition (en flûte), off Ostende.
,, Sir Home Riggs	III. 91, Romney, Egypt exped.
Popham, Stephen (L.)	V. 105, Quebec, cutting out exped. VI. 204, C. Montreal; 206–7, w. in actn. Canadian Lakes.
Popham, William (C.)	VI. 278, Hecla (bomb.), Algiers.
Porcel, Don Fraquin (C.) *Sp.*	III. 13, Sp. Carmen captd. by Leviathan; 476, App.
Porte, La (L.Com.) *F.*	II. 258, Vaillante captd. by Indefatigable.
Porter, David (C.) *U.S.*	V. 84, 362–8, U.S. Essex capts. Alert; 408, St. Salvador. VI. 149–50, Valparaiso; 151–6, 161, captd. by Phœbe and consort; 183–88, 245, Potomac exped.
Portlock, Nathaniel(C.)	II. 388–9, Arrow capts Du. Draak.
Poulain, Jean B. J. Remi (C.) *F.*	III. 386, Héros; 434, k. Trafalgar.
Poulden, Richard (C.)	II. 220, Calcutta (T.S.), Minorca exped.
Pound, Richard (Pr.)...	IV. 243, Lark, w. cutting out exped.
Pourquier, Honoré (C.) *F.*	II. 295, F. Junon captd. by Br. Sq.
Powell, Geo. (Mr.Mt.)	V. 349, Bacchante, cutting out exped. VI. 21, cutting out exped.
Powell, Herbert B. (C.)	VI. 286, Vol. on board Impregnable, Algiers.
Powell, James (Mid.)...	V. 327, Calypso, w. in actn.
Powell, Walter (M.L.)	IV. 30, Unicorn, cutting out exped.
Power, Richard (L.) ...	II. 88, Triumph, Camperdown, pro. Cr.
Poyntz, Stephen (P.C.)	II. 414–15, Solebay capts. F. gbts. III. 137, Beaulieu, off Brest. IV. 116, Melampus, Strachan's Sq. crsg.
Praed, B. M. (L.Com.)	II. 469, Crash captd. on the coast of Holland.
Prater, Richard (L.) ...	II. 58, Colossus, St. Vincent, pro. Cr.
Pratt, George (L.)	V. 199, capture of Banda Neira. VI. 233–4, Seahorse, k. in actn. Chandeleur Isles.
Pratt, Robert (Mid.) ...	VI. 288, Granicus, k. Algiers.
Preble, — (Cmde.) *U.S.*	III. 299–301, Com. Sq. at Tripoli.
Prendergrast, John (L.)	VI. 166, Avon, k. in actn.
Prenet, — (L.) *F.*	IV. 145, F. Canonnière, w. in actn.
Prescott, Henry (C.) ...	V. 125–6, Weazle, cutting out exped.; 127, pro. P.C.
Pressland, Thomas (C.)	II. 220, Ulysses (T.S.), capture of Minorca.
Preston, Abraham (Pr.)	IV. 252, Leopard, in actn. with U.S. Chesapeake.
Preston, D'Arcy (P.C.)	I. 343, Blanche, Medn.; 406–8, actn. with Sp. Cérès.
Preston, Robert F. (C.)	V. 4, Asp, crsg. off the Virgin Isles.
Préville, Martres (L.-Com.) *F.*	III. 185, F. Providence cut out by the bts. of Naiad.
Price, Charles Papps(L.)	II. 128–30, Badger, in actn. off St. Marcouf; 131, pro. Cr.
Price, David (L.)	V. 216, Hawk, cutting out exped. VI. 190, C. Volcano (bomb.), Baltimore.

INDEX TO NAVAL OFFICERS 141

Price, Francis S. (Mr.-Mt.)	III. 426, Téméraire, w. Trafalgar.
Price, George (L.)	IV. 268, 345, Porcupine, cutting out expeds.; 346, w. pro. Cr. V. 266-7, C. Sabine, crsg. Cadiz.
Price, John (L.)	II. 153, Melampus, in actn. III. 227, Archer, off Boulogne. IV. 321, act.Cr. Falcon, crsg. Denmark.
Price, Richard (Car.)...	II. 116, Hermione, mutiny of crew.
Price, Thomas (M.L.)	VI. 29-30, Elizabeth, Adriatic.
Price, Thomas (L.Com.)	IV. 467, Fire Fly, fndrd. Sp. Main, drnd.
Price, William (L.) ...	III. 15, Unicorn, cutting out exped.; 316, Com. Archer, watching invas. flotilla, Channel.
Prickett, John (L.)	I. 313, Blanche, in actn.
Priest, Joseph (L.)	I. 87, Toulon.
Prieur, Peter Stephen (L.)	IV. 30, Papillon, in actn. Jamaica.
Pring, Daniel (C.)	VI. 212-13, 221-2, Linnet, captd. Lake Champlain.
Pringle, James (C.) ...	V. 129, Sparrowhawk, in actn. off Palamos.
Pringle, Thomas (P.C.)	I. 139, Valiant, Channel Flt.; 183, 200, 1st June; 342, R.A. Sq. crsg.; 416-17, Tremendous, Sq. in Simon's Bay. II. 117, Com. at the Cape of Good Hope.
Pringle, William (L.)...	I. 376, Glatton, in actn. with F. frigates.
Prior, Edward (M.L.)	IV. 131, London, k. in actn.
Prior, Francis (Mr.) ...	IV. 61, Æolus, in actn.
Proby, Granville (Mid.)	III. 442, Foudroyant, w. in actn.
Proby, Lord (C.)	III. 4-5, Danaë, crsg.; 9-10, captd. by mutiny of crew; 477, App.
Proctor, Jas. (L.Com.)	V. 442, Sealark, wrkd. North Sea.
Proctor, Peter (Mid.)...	III. 55, Edgar, w. Copenhagen. IV. 274, L.Com. Thistle, Halifax. V. 90-1, capts. Du. Havik, pro. Cr.
Proctor, William Beauchamp (P.C.)	IV. 357-8, Dédaigneuse engages Sémillante; 359, court-martialled.
Proteau, Guillaume M. (C.) *F.*	IV. 391, Indienne, Brest Sq.; 406, 422, destd. Basque Rds.; 429, court-martialled.
Prothers, William (Mid.)	III. 6, Railleur, k. in actn.
Provost, — (L.Com.)*F.*	II. 22, Arrogante, crsg. off the Penmarcks.
Prowse, Thomas (C.)...	IV. 461, Martin, fndrd. Barbadoes, drnd.
Prowse, William (L.)...	I. 176, Barfleur, w. 1st June. II. 34, C. Raven, St. Vincent. III. 357, Sirius; 359, Calder's actn.; 384, Trafalgar. IV. 142-3, capts. Bergère.
Prynn, Parkins (L.) ...	III. 417, Achille, w. Trafalgar.
Prytherck, Sam. (M.L.)	V. 16, Amethyst, w. in actn.
Puget, Peter (P.C.) ...	IV. 200-5, Goliath, Copenhagen; 298, Baltic Flt.
Pullibank, A. (L.Com.)	I. 433, Pigmy, wrkd. on the Motherbank.
Pulling, George Christopher (C.)	III. 134-5, Kangaroo, actn. off Spain.
Pulling, John King (C.)	II. 99-100, Penguin capts. Oiseau.
Pullman, John (L.) ...	V. 372, Guerrière, Com. a prize.
Purnel, John (C.Ck.)...	V. 325, Sealark, k. in actn.
Purvis, John Child (P.C.)	I. 72, Princess Royal, Medn. Flt.; 78, Toulon; 214, Flt. at Corsica; 284-5, actn. off Genoa; 297, off Hyères. II. 289, London, Flt. off Cadiz; 450, Sq. at Ferrol. IV. 238, R.A.; 288-95, off Cadiz.
Puver, John (L.Com.)	III. 384, Entreprenante (cutter), Trafalgar.
Puysigur, — (C.) *Por.*	II. 211, Por. Principe-Real, Sq. in the Medn.
Pye, Thomas Robert (M.L.)	V. 60, Boadicea, w. Isle Bourbon; 149-51-54, Isle de la Passe.
Pym, Samuel (L.)	II. 225-6, Babet, w. cutting out exped. IV. 93, C. Atlas, Martinique. V. 59, Sirius; 61, 141-4, Isle Bourbon; 145-8, Isle of France; 149-53, Port Louis; 157-69, Grand Port; 170, court-martialled; 445, App.
Pyne, Harry (L.)	VI. 196, Borer, cutting out exped., pro. Cr.
Quelch, Thomas (Mid.)	VI. 35, Revenge, cutting out exped.

Querangel, Pierre M. J. (Cmde.) *F.*	II. 5, Mucius, Ireland exped.; 286, Duquesne, Brest Flt. III. 186, captd. by Bellerophon and consort.
Quevedo, Don Josef (C.) *Sp.*	III. 386, Sp. San Leandro, Trafalgar.
Quilliam, John (L.) ...	III. 398, Victory; 443, Trafalgar; 464, pro. P.C.
Quin, Michael (L.)......	VI. 27, Weasel, Adriatic.
Quinn, Henry (Mid.)...	VI. 287, Impregnable, w. Algiers.
Quinton, Cornelius (C.)	III. 482, Légère, wrkd. S. America. V. 357, Polyphemus, convoy escort.
Raccord, Pierre Paul (C.) *F.*	II. 178, Peuple Souverain; 188-9, w. the Nile. III. 10-11, Lejoille, Marseille Bay.
Rackum, — (B.)	II. 107, loss of Tribune.
Radcliffe, Coples (L.)...	VI. 211, Netley, k. Canadian Lakes.
Radelet, Georges (C.) *F.*	III. 124-5, Curieux captd. by Bordelais, k. in actn.
Raffi, René Guillaume (L.Com.) *F.*	II. 255, Adventurier cut out by the bts. of Melpomène.
Raggett, Richard (C.)	II. 132, Dart, off Ostende. IV. 201, Africaine, Copenhagen. V. 173, 181, Plymouth.
Rainier, Jas. Sprat (C.)	I. 414, Swift, capture of Amboyna.
Rainier, John Sprat (P.C.)	II. 337, Centurion, Suez. III. 208, Pondicherry; 282-5, actn. with Marengo and consorts.
Rainier, Peter (P.C.)...	I. 62, Suffolk, Channel Flt.; 138, convoy escort; 336, R.A. Com. at Madras; 414-15, capture of Amboyna. II. 89-90. III. 208, V.A.; 209-10, Madras; 268-83, Wilhelmina, E. Indies. V. 198, A., capture of Banda Neira.
Rainier, Peter (P.C.)...	IV. 179-80, Caroline capts. Du. Maria-Riggersbergen; 282, Gressie, Java. VI. 131-2, Niger with consort capts. F. Cérès.
Raitt, William (C.) ...	IV. 447, Scout, Rosas Bay. V. 29-30, Marseille Bay.
Ralph, James (B.)	V. 86, Cherokee, w. in actn.
Ram, Thomas (Mid.)	III. 55, Isis, k. Copenhagen.
Ram, William (L.) ...	III. 421-5, Victory, k. Trafalgar.
Ramage, Edward (C.)	I. 413, Rattlesnake, Colombo exped.
Ramage, James (L.) ...	V. 386, borne on the register of U.S. Navy.
Ramsay, Robert (C.) ...	VI. 175, Chesapeake Bay; 188, Baltimore.
Randall, Thos. (Mr. Mt.)	IV. 448, Volontaire, cutting out exped.
Randall, Wm. (Mr. Mt.)	V. 301, Procris, w. cutting out exped.
Ranelagh, Lord (P.C.)	II. 142, Doris, crsg. Channel.
Raoul, Joseph François (C.) *F.*	IV. 374-5, Département des Landes capts. Maria. V. 305-6, Cmde. Nymphe, actn. off Java.
Raper, Henry (P.C.)...	II. 416-18, Aimable engages Sirène.
Rasmusen, — (L.Com.) *Da.*	V. 99. Da. Thor (gbt.) cut out by the bts. of Belvidera.
Ratford, Jenkin (A.B.)	IV. 249, Halifax, deserter; 252-5, executed.
Rathbone, William (L.)	I. 288, Captain, w. in actn. IV. 3, C. Santa Margarita; 4-9, Strachan's actn.
Ratsey, Edward (C.) ...	IV. 52-3, Harrier, actn. with Sémillante.
Rattray, James (C.) ...	VI. 96, Contest, Chesapeake Bay.
Raven, Michael (Mr.Mt.)	IV. 328, Nymphe, cutting out exped.
Ravenshaw, George (L.)	IV. 101-4, Spencer, Duckworth's actn., pro. Cr.
Rawle, Richard (L.) ...	VI. 224, Rota, w. cutting out exped.
Rawlence, Roger R. (L.)	I. 177, Queen Charlotte, k. 1st June.
Rawlins, William (L.)	IV. 448, Topaze, cutting out exped.
Rawlinson, RogerA.(L.)	I. 155, Queen Charlotte, k. 29th May.
Ray, Joseph (Mid.) ...	V. 340, Victorious, w. in actn.
Ray, Julien Le (Cmde.) *F.*	II. 5, Trajan, Ireland exped.; 286, Constitution, Brest Flt. III. 109, Cadiz; 112-14, St. Antoine, w. in actn. Gut of Gibraltar; 229-30, 326, invas. flotilla Boulogne.
Raybaun, — (C.) *F.* ...	III. 125, Mutine, W. Indies.
Raymond, Geo. (Mid.).	VI. 66, Shannon, in actn. with U.S. Chesapeake.

Rayner, Edmund (L.)	III. 6, Loire, in actn.
Raynor, John (C.)	III. 477, Railleur, fndrd. Channel, drnd.
Raynsford, Robt.(P.C.)	IV. 461, Athénien, wrkd. near Tunis, drnd.
Rea, Charles (M.L.)...	II. 81, Isis, w. Camperdown.
Rea, Henry (M.C.) ...	IV. 383, Kent, cutting out exped. V. 343, America, cutting out exped.
Read, James (Mr.)	II. 81, Triumph, w. Camperdown.
Read, John (M.L.) ...	V. 74–5–6, Confiance, k. capture of Cayenne.
Ready, Henry (Mr.Mt.)	III. 412, Tonnant, w. Trafalgar. V. 380, L. Guerrière, k. in actn.
Reala (Bey) *Turk.* ...	VI. 363, Navarino.
Redding, Thos. (Mid.)	V. 248, Alceste, Parenza.
Reding, Edward (L.)...	IV. 124, Pompée, Isle of Capri.
Redmill, Robert (P.C.)	III. Polyphemus; 407, 442, Trafalgar. IV. 157, Sq. off Rochefort.
Reece, Thos. G. (Mid.)	III. 416, Colossus, w. Trafalgar.
Reed, Archibald (Mid.)	VI. 312–19–23–28, Burmese War.
Reed, Thos. (L.Com.)	III, 494, Mallard captd. near Calais.
Rees, Thomas Gwynne (L.)	V. 250, Alacrity, k. in actn.
Rees, William Lee (Mid.)	V. 37, cutting out exped. VI. 22–3, Mr. Mt. Bacchante, cutting out exped. ; 119, act.L., crsg. in the Adriatic.
Reeve, Samuel (P.C.)	I. 72, Captain, Medn. Flt. ; 96, Genoa ; 97, capts. Impérieuse ; 214, Flt. at Corsica ; 284–9, actn. off Genoa ; 297–301, actn. off Hyères.
Reeve, William (L.) ...	VI. 40–41, Kangaroo, w. in actn.
Reeves, Lewis Buckle (M.L.)	III. 425, Victory, w. Trafalgar.
Reeves, Thomas (M.L.)	VI. 19, capture of Ponza.
Reid, Andrew (Mr.Mt.)	VI. 185, Fairy, w. in actn.
Reid, Curtis (act.L.) ...	V. 94, Avon, w. in actn.
Reid, James (Mr.)	II. 114, Regulus, cutting out exped.
Reid, Samuel (L.)	II. 111, Hermione, cutting out exped.
Reid, — (Mr.)	III. 28, Minotaur, w. cutting out exped.
Renaud, Gabriel (C.) *F.*	III. 120, Sans Pareille captd. by Mercury.
Renaud, Jean Marie (C.) *F.*	I. 218–21, F. Prudente capts. E.I.C. ships ; 236–7, Isle of France. II. 416–19, Sirène engages Aimable. IV. 21–3, Ville de Milan capts. Cleopatra, k. in actn.
Renaudin, — (C.) *F.* ...	I. 141 Vengeur ; 183, captd. 1st June ; 205, Brest ; 258–9–62, Toulon ; 295, R.A. Formidable.
Renfrey, Wm. (M.L.)	VI. 288, Granicus, k. Algiers.
Rennie, George (L.) ...	IV. 440, k. Scheldt exped.
Rennie, George (L.) ...	V. 38–40, Melpomène, cutting out exped. ; 240, act.C. Hecate, capture of the Isle of France.
Rennie, James (C.) ...	II. 347, Victor, Holland exped.
Rennie, James (Mr.Mt.)	V. 232–3, Cerberus, cutting out exped.
Rennie, John (P.C.) ...	III. 481, Invincible, wrkd. near Yarmouth.
Renou, Adrian (L.) ...	I. 200, Barfleur, 1st June, pro. Cr. II. 420, C. Prince of Wales, capture of Surinam.
Renou, Timothy (Mid.)	III. 416, Colossus, w. Trafalgar. V. 214, Mr.Mt. Semiramis, cutting out exped.
Renou,— (C.) *F.*	III. 119, Sénégal cut out by the bts. of Melpomène.
Renton, William (L.)	II. 88, Venerable, Camperdown, pro. Cr.
Renwick, James (M.L.)	IV. 345–7, Porcupine, k. cutting out exped.
Retalick, James (L.)...	II. 80, Monarch, w. Camperdown.
Retalick, Richard (P.C.)	III. 46, Defiance, Copenhagen.
Reynolds, Barrington (C.)	V. 302–4, Hesper, capture of Java.
Reynolds, George (C.)	II. 470, Etrusco, fndrd. W. Indies. V. 98, Tribune engages Da. gbts.
Reynolds, John (L.-Com.)	V. 451, Nimble, fndrd. in the Cattegat, crew saved.

Reynolds, Robert Carthew (P.C.)	I. 357-8, Amazon with consort capts. Unité. II. 7, Sq. crsg. Ireland; 12-14-16, engages Droits de l'Homme; 18-19, wrkd.; 224, Pomone capts. Cheri; 462, App. V. 231, R.A. St. George, wrkd. Jutland, drnd.; 447, App.
Reynolds, Robert Carthew (L.)	III. 245, Centaur; 246, w. in cutting out Curieux; 247, pro. Cr.; 248, d.
Reynolds, Wm. (Mid.)	II. 260, Leander, in actn.
Reyntjes, — (V.A.) *Du.*	II. 76-9, Du. Jupiter captd. at Camperdown.
Rhubende, — (C.) *Du.*	I. 415-16, Du. Revolutie captd. at the Cape of Good Hope.
Ribouleau, Peter (P.C.)	III. 83, Astræa, Egypt exped.
Rice, George (L.)	I. 200, Valiant, 1st June, pro. Cr.
Rich, J. W. (L.Com.)	I. 440, Spitfire, fndrd. St. Domingo, drnd.
Richards, George Spencer (L.)	IV. 174, Constance, w. in actn.
Richards, H. Lord (L.Com.)	VI. 382, Fearless, wrkd. Spain.
Richards, Jacob (Mid.)	IV. 367, Euryalus, cutting out exped.
Richards, Peter (L.) ...	VI. 285-89, Queen Charlotte, Algiers; 291, pro. Cr.; 374, Navarino.
Richards, William (L.)	VI. 35, Revenge, cutting out exped.
Richardson, CæsarWm. (Mid.)	II. 268, Leander, in actn. V. 52, L. Blonde, w. in actn.
Richardson,Charles(C.)	III. 296-7, Alligator, capture of Surinam. IV. 89, Cæsar, Sq. crsg.; 116, Barbadoes; 288, Sq. at Palermo; 392-6, 425, Basque Rds.; 435, 440, Scheldt exped. V. 213-14, Semiramis des. Pluvier.
Richardson,Geo. (Mid.)	VI. 6, actn. with Da. gbts.
Richardson, Henry (L.-Com.)	III. 227, Bloodhound, watching invas. flotilla. IV. 123, C. Juno, off Gaeta, Italy.
Richardson, John Geo. (M.L.)	IV. 370, Africa, w. in actn.
Richardson,Philip(Mid.)	II. 196, Zealous, w. the Nile.
Richardson,Sam.(Mid.)	VI. 23, Bacchante, cutting out exped.
Richardson, Wm. (L.)	II. 197, Leander, the Nile; 210, pro. Cr.
Richardson, Wm. (L.)	V. 343, America, cutting out exped.
Richardson, — (Mr.)...	VI. 206, w. in actn. Canadian Lakes.
Richer, Jean Bap. Edm. (L.Com.) *F.*	II. 273, Baïonnaise; 275-9, capts. Ambuscade.
Richery, — (C.) *F.* ...	I. 60, Bretagne, Flt. Quiberon Bay; 295, Toulon; 303-5, Victoire, Cadiz; 345, N. America; 408-9, Newfoundland. II. 3-7, R.A. Pégase, Ireland exped. III. 385.
Riches, John (C.Ck.)...	VI. 6, w. in actn. Cuxhaven.
Riches, Thos. (Mr.Mt.)	VI. 6, w. in actn. Cuxhaven.
Richmond, Henry (L.)	VI. 259, Leander, crsg.
Richmond,Thos.F.(L.)	I. 87, Toulon.
Ricketts, James Wm. Otto (Mid.)	IV. 367, Euryalus, cutting out exped.
Ricketts, William (C.)	III. 136-7, Corso, in actn. Gulf of Venice.
Ricketts, Wm. Henry (P.C.)	II. 114-15, Magicienne, St. Domingo.
Riddell, Robert (C.) ...	VI. 278, Britomart, Algiers.
Ridge,John Jas. (Mid.)	III. 55, Edgar, w. Copenhagen.
Ridge, Thomas R. (C.)	V. 441, Harrier, fndrd. E. Indies, drnd.
Ridgeway,David (Mid.)	IV. 100, Northumberland, k. Duckworth's actn.
Ridley, — (M.L.)	II. 355, loss of Proserpine.
Rigny, H. de (R.A.) *F.*	VI. 359-61-71-6-9, Navarino.
Rioms, D'Albert de (C.)	II. 268, Pluton, in actn. with Leander.
Rion, Edward (C.)	I. 243, Rose, capture of Martinique.
Rion, Henry (P.C.) ...	III. 46, Amazon; 49-52, 55, k. Copenhagen.
Rippe, James de (C.)...	V. 283, Racehorse; 287-92, actn. off Madagascar.
Riverij, — (C.) *Du.* ...	II. 343, Du. Ambuscade, Sq. blockaded in the Texel.
Rivers, William (Mid.)	III. 425, Victory, w. Trafalgar.

INDEX TO NAVAL OFFICERS

Rivière, Vicomte de la (C.) *F. Royalist*	I. 128, Ferme, Trinidad.
Rivington, Robert (C.) *E.I.C.*	III. 31, E.I.C. Kent captd. by Confiance, k. in actn.
Rix, Geo. Albert (Mid.)	VI. 41, Amelia, w. in actn.
Roberts, Benjamin (C.)	I. 342, Espiègle, crsg. off the Texel.
Roberts, Hugh (Mid.)	II. 442, Lion, k. in actn.
Roberts, John Walter (C.)	VI. 271–4, Thracian, exped. to Cuba, W. Indies.
Roberts, Joseph (C.Ck.)	IV. 317, Childers, w. in actn.
Roberts, Mitchell (L.)	VI. 29–30, Elizabeth, cutting out exped.
Roberts, Samuel (L.)...	V. 96, Armide, cutting out exped. VI. 181, C. Meteor (bomb.), Alexandria; 190, Baltimore; 232–4, Chandeleur
,, ,, C.B.	Isles; 393, C.B. Tay, wrkd. Gulf of Mexico.
Roberts, William (C.)	III. 186, Snake, crsg. Cape François. V. 20–1, Castor, capture of D'Haupoult; 50, Guadaloupe.
Roberts, William Gilbert (L.)	VI. 234, w. in actn.
Robertson, George (L.)	IV. 27, Stork, cutting out exped.
Robertson, James (L.)	V. 45, Hazard, cutting out exped. VI. 222, Lake Champlain.
Robertson, John (L.)...	VI. 217–19–22, Confiance, in actn. Lake Champlain.
Robertson, Lewis (P.C.)	I. 249, Veteran, k. in actn. Guadaloupe.
Robertson, Patk. (M.L.)	VI. 287, Queen Charlotte, w. Algiers.
Robertson, William (C.)	IV. 466, Speedwell, fndrd. off Dieppe.
Robertson, — (M. L.)	VI. 85, Chesapeake Bay.
Robilliard, Thomas (1st cl.Vol.)	V. 327, Dictator, w. in actn.
Robilliard, Wm. (Mid.)	II. 159, Anson, w. in actn. V. 325–6, C. Podargus, actn. with Da. gbts.; 327, pro. P.C.
Robinson, Batty (Mr.)	V. 417, Java, w. in actn.
Robinson, Charles (C.)	I. 439, Scout captd. by two F. frigates.
Robinson, Edw. (Mid.)	III. 84, k. in actn. Egypt.
Robinson, Edward (Mr.Mt.)	VI. 41, Amelia, w. in actn.
Robinson, George (L.)	I. 119, Thames, w. in actn.
Robinson, George (Mr.)	II. 395, Unity (T.S.), Sq. off the Tagus.
Robinson, James (B.)...	III. 437, Minotaur, w. Trafalgar.
Robinson, John (Mr. Mt.)	IV. 143, Sirius, w. in actn.
Robinson, Katly (Mr.)	V. 36, Bustard, w. in actn.
Robinson, Mark (P.C.)	III. 335, Swiftsure, Medn. Flt.
Robinson, Parker (C.)	III. 477, Trompeuse, fndrd. Channel, drnd.
Robinson, Raby (M.L.)	II. 67, 261, Leander, k. in actn. Teneriffe.
Robinson, Thomas (B.)	III. 414, Bellerophon, w. Trafalgar.
Robinson, Wm. (Mid.)	V. 103, Dreadnought, k. cutting out exped.
Robinson, Wm. Todd (Mid.)	V. 256, Active, cutting out exped.
Robinson, — (Mid.) ...	VI. 274, Tyne, cutting out exped.
Robotham, Thos. (Mid.)	V. 52, Blonde, w. in actn.
Robotier, Anthony Richard (L.)	II. 248, Jason, k. in actn.
Robson, John (Gunner)	IV. 156, Port Mahon, cutting out exped.
Robson, William (Mr.)	III. 255–6, Drake, k. cutting out exped.
Robson, Wm. (Mr.Mt.)	V. 118, Spartan, k. in actn.
Robyns, John (M.C.)...	VI. 171–5–6, Chesapeake; 188–90, w in actn. Baltimore.
Roch, — (M.L.)	V. 309, capture of Java.
Roche, Thomas Owen (Mid.)	III. 275, k. cutting out exped.
Rodd, John Tremayne (P.C.)	III. 311, Indefatigable, off Ushant. IV. 139, Isle of Aix; 158, off the Gironde; 400–18, Basque Rds.
Rodgers, Geo. William (L.) *U.S.*	V. 391, U.S. Wasp, in actn.

L

Rodgers, John (Cmde.) U.S.	V. 84, 273-6, 279-81, U.S. President engages Little Belt; 356-8, w. in actn. with Belvidera; 360-2, 370, 393-4, crsg.; 407, chases Galatea; 422, Boston. VI. 69-72, crsg.; 73, Rhode Island; 86, 147-9, crsg.; 183-4, 188, Potomac; 245, 296, U.S. North Carolina, Medn.
Rodney, Hon. Edw. (L.)	III. 36-7, Magicienne, cutting out exped.
Roebuck, Hy. (Mr. Mt.)	V. 398, Macedonian, w. in actn.
Rogers, Daniel (Mid.)	II. 80, Powerful, w. Camperdown.
Rogers, Josias (P.C.)...	I. 246, Quebec, Guadaloupe; 333, capture of Grenada.
Rogers, Matthew (Gunner)	VI. 64, found serving on board U.S. Chesapeake.
Rogers, Thomas (L.)...	I. 241, capture of Martinique. III. 119, C. Mercury, crsg. Gulf of Lyons; 135-7, crsg. Adriatic. IV. 288, Kent, Palermo; 383, crsg. Italy. V. 129, off S. Spain; 208, Medn. Flt.
Rogers, Wm. (act. C.)	IV. 266-7, Windsor Castle (packet) capts. Jeaune Richard (priv.).
Rolfe, William (Mid.)	VI. 35, Revenge, cutting out exped.
Rolland, Pierre Nicolas (C.) F.	II. 286, Révolution, Brest Flt. III. 334, Atlas, Medn. Flt. IV. 391, Océan, Brest Flt.
Rolles, Robert (P.C.)...	VI. 2, 117, Union, Medn. Flt.
Rollier, Lewis (Mid.)...	V. 120, Cerberus, Agaye.
Romney, Francis Darby (L.)	V. 327, Leveret, cutting out exped. VI. 6, in actn. Cuxhaven.
Roncière, Nicolas C. de la (C.) F.	II. 139, Embuscade, Ireland exped. IV. 391, Tonnerre, Brest; 429, Basque Rds.
Rondeau, Jacques Mélanie (Cmde.) F.	I. 231, Sibylle captd by Romney; 305-6, Sensible, Smyrna.
Roodneff, — (C.) Rus.	IV. 300, Rus. Sewolod captd. by Implacable.
Rooke, William (Mid.)	IV. 131, London, k. in actn.
Roper, George B. (L.)	V. 213, Diana, cutting out exped.
Roper, Richard (L.)...	VI. 6, in actn. Cuxhaven.
Roper, — (C.) E.I.C.	I. 218, E.I.C. Nautilus, Singapore.
Roquebert, Dominique (L.Com.) F.	III. 316, Audacieuse, in actn. Channel.
Roquebert, François (Cmde.) F.	V. 47-9, Renommée, capture of Junon; 53, Brest; 282-4, 288, 291-3, captd. in actn. off Madagascar; 289, k.
Rorie, John James (L.)	II. 400, Echo, cutting out exped.
Rosamel, C. C. M. Ducamp (C.) F.	V. 262-3, Pomone captd. by Alceste and consort; 264-5, w. in actn.
Rose, Hector (Mid.)...	V. 101, Surveillante, cutting out exped.
Rose, James (L.)	II. 81, Isis, w. Camperdown. VI. 6, C. Hearty, Cuxhaven.
Rose, Jonas (C.).........	II. 475, Espion (T.S.), wrkd. on Goodwin Sands. III. 46-9, Jamaica, Copenhagen. IV. 110, Agamemnon, Sq. crsg.; 201, Copenhagen; 238, off the Tagus. V. 441, wrkd. Rio de la Plata.
Rose, Joseph (C.Ck.)...	III. 55, Amazon, w. Copenhagen.
Rosenhagen, Philip L. J. (C.)	IV. 341, Volage capts. Requin.
Rosily, — (V.A.) F. ...	III. 243, 378, Toulon. IV. 1, Com. at Cadiz; 11, Paris; 120, Cadiz; 295, Héros captd. at Cadiz by the Sp.
Roskruge, Francis (L.)	III. 434, Britannia, k. Trafalgar.
Ross, C.B. Hodgson (C.)	III. 477, Diligence, wrkd. Havana.
Ross, Charles Henry (Mid.)	V. 37, Amphion, cutting out exped.; 120, Mr. Mt. cutting out exped.
Ross, Francis (L.)......	I. 176, Tremendous, k. 1st June.
Ross, John (C.)	V. 327, Briseis, crsg. Baltic.
Ross, William (L.Com.)	II. 229-30, Recovery capts. Revanche (priv.).
Ross, William B. Hodgson (P.C.)	III. 291-3, Pique, Curaçoa. IV. 134-5, capts. Phaëton and Voltigeur. VI. 84, Marlborough, Chesapeake Bay; 168, Albion, Chesapeake Bay; 227, Northumberland, St. Helena.

INDEX TO NAVAL OFFICERS 147

Rossen, Van (C.) *Du.*...	II. 76-9, Du. Vryheid, Camperdown ; 82, w. in actn., d.
Rotheram, Edward (L.)	I. 200, Culloden, 1st June, pro. Cr. III. 375, C. Dreadnought, off Cadiz ; 384, Royal Sovereign ; 395-7, Trafalgar.
Rothery John Carpenter (L.)	II. 427, Repulse, dismissed.
Roulette, Francis (L.)	VI. 113, Lady Prevost, w. in actn. Canadian Lakes.
Rous, Hon. Hy. I. (Mid.)	VI. 21, Bacchante, cutting out exped.
Rouse, John Wood (Mid.)	IV. 229, Royal George, w. Dardanelles.
Rousel, — (C.) *F.*......	II. 230, Brutus (priv.) captd. by Victorieuse.
Rousseau, Bernard Louis (C.) *F.*	V. 107-8, actn. off Havre ; 211-12, destd by Berwick and consorts.
Rousseau, Jean B. Augustin (L.Com.) *F.*	I. 363, Ecureuil, destd. in actn. IV. 380, C. Junon, crsg. V. 4-5-7, captd. by Horatio and consorts ; 8, k. in actn.
Roussin, Albert René (L.) *F.*	V. 163, Bellone, in actn. Grand Port
Roussin, Albin René (C.) *F.*	VI. 6-9, Gloire capts. Albacore.
Roux, De (C.) *F.*	VI. 9-10, Renard (priv.) des. in actn. Alphæa.
Rowe, A. J. T. (Mid.)	VI. 374, Dartmouth, k. Navarino.
Rowe, Henry Nathaniel (L.)	II. 61, Diadem, w. in actn. Cadiz. IV. 206, Valiant, w. Copenhagen.
Rowe, James (Mid.) ...	VI. 23, Bacchante, d. cutting out exped.
Rowe, John (C.)	II. 400, Trincomalee blows up in actn., k.; 474, App.
Rowe, Thomas (L.) ...	V. 108, Diana, cutting out exped.
Rowe, Thomas (Pr.)...	VI. 228, Pilot, w. in actn.
Rowed, Henry (L.Com.)	III. 192-4, Sheerness capts. F. gbt.
Rowley, Bartholomew S. (P.C.)	I. 122, Penelope, capture of Inconstante ; 129, St. Domingo ; 297, Cumberland, actn. off Hyères.
Rowley, Charles (P.C.)	IV. 123-4, Eagle, capture of Capri ; 288-94, Sq. at Palermo. V. 260, capts. Corceyre ; 351, Cape Maistro, Ancona.
,, Sir Charles ...	VI. 29-32, Adriatic. VI. 270, R.A., kntd., Com. in the W. Indies.
Rowley, Josias (P.C.)...	III. 357-62, Raisonable, Calder's actn. IV. 44, chases Topaze ; 186-7, Cape of Good Hope exped. ; 189, capture of Buenos Ayres ; 279, of Monte Video ; 365, Cape of Good Hope. V. 58-61, Isle of France ; 140-1, Boadicea ; 166-9, 171-3-5-80-3-7, capts. Vénus, Isle of France ; 203-4, capture of the Isle of France ; 343, America, in actn. Languelia. VI. 119, kntd., capture of Genoa.
,, Sir Josias	
Rowley, S. Campbell (P.C.)	V. 450, Laurel, wrkd. in the Teigneuse Passage.
Roxburgh, Robert (Mr.)	III. 104, Pompée, k. Algesiras.
Royer, Charles (L.) ...	V. 288-91, Astræa, actn. off Madagascar
Royle, Charles (Mid.)...	II. 196, Majestic, w. the Nile.
Rudall, William (Mid.)	IV. 101, Donegal, w. Duckworth's actn.
Rudduck, Alexander (L.)	I. 175, Marlborough, w. 1st June ; 199, pro. Cr. II. 92, C. Hazard, capts. F. Hardi and Musette (privs.) ; 93, pro. P.C.
Ruell, John Godfrey (M.L.)	V. 46, Thetis, cutting out exped.
Runciman, — (Mid.)...	III. 299, Inconstant, cutting out exped.
Rundle, Charles (Pr.)	IV. 30, Unicorn, cutting out exped.
Rushworth, Edwd. (C.)	IV. 171-2, Supérieure, in actn. Isle of Cuba. V. 216, Barbadoes, actn. off Cherbourg.
Russel, Jeremiah (Mr.-Mt.)	II. 268, Leander, in actn.
Russel, Robert (C.) ...	VI. 391, Cygnet, wrkd. Courantine River.
Russel, William (L.)...	II. 249, Flora, cutting out exped. IV. 320, C. Tartarus, crsg. off Denmark.
Russel, — (A.)	I. 21, Com. Channel Flt. (1691)

Russell, Charles (Mid.)	VI. 374, k. Navarino.
Russell, John (A.B.)...	V. 280, Little Belt, in actn. with U.S. President.
Russell, Robert (S.) ...	IV. 440, k. Scheldt exped.
Russell, Thomas Macnamara (P.C.)	II. 109–10, Vengeance, Sq. at Trinidad. IV. 213, V.A. Majestic, capture of Heligoland.
Russell, — (L.)	IV. 172, Supérieure, in actn. Isle of Cuba.
Rutherford, Alexander (Mr.Mt.)	III. 66, k. in actn. with invas. flotilla.
Rutherford, Geo. (L.)	II. 241, Com. Sp. gbt. (prize), fndrd., drnd.
Rutherford, Wm. Geo. (P.C.)	III. 384, 438, Swiftsure, Trafalgar.
Rutherford, William Gordon (L.)	I. 241, capture of Martinique.
Ruysen, — (C.) *Du*....	II. 76–9, Du. Gebykheid captd. at Camperdown.
Ryan, Eugene (Pr.) ...	V. 345, Swallow, w. in actn.
Ryder, Charles (L.) ...	I. 343, cutting out exped. Vado.
Rye, Peter (L.)	I. 116, Crescent, in actn.
Rysoort, Van (C.) *Du*.	II. 76–9, Du. Hercules captd. at Camperdown.
Ryves, Geo. Fredk. (C.)	I. 411, Bulldog (bomb.), capture of St. Vincent. III. 175, Gibraltar, Medn. Flt. ; 177–8, discovery of Agincourt Sound, Magdalena Isles. VI. 302–3, Sophie ; 316-18-19-
,, ,, ,, C.B.	21-4-7-9, 335, Burmese War ; 344, made C.B.

Sabbin, James (Mid.)	III. 437, Dreadnought, w. Trafalgar.
Sacker, Isaac (Mr.) ...	VI. 74, Dominica, k. in actn.
Sadler, Peter (B.)	II. 196, Orion, w. the Nile.
Saillard, — (C.) *F*. ...	II. 416, Intrepide (priv.) captd. by Racoon.
Sainburn, William (L.)	IV. 306, Meleager, cutting out exped.
St.Clair,Hon. Mat. (C.)	III. 477, Martin, fndrd. North Sea, drnd.
St. Cricq, Jacques (L.-Com.) *F*.	IV. 133–4, Voltigeur captd. by Pique. V. 47–8, C. Clorinde, capture of Junon ; 282, Isle de la Passe ; 291, actn. off Madagascar ; 293, Brest ; 295, dismissed.
St. Faust, — (L.Com.) *Du*.	III. 194, Du. Union, actn. with Princess Augusta (cutter).
St. Felix,— (Cmde.)*F*.	I. 132, Cybèle, Mahé Rds.
St. George,Wm.M.(L.)	III. 435, Conqueror, k. Trafalgar.
St. Hacuen, Yves M. G.P.LeC.(Cmde.)*F*.	II. 285, Terrible, Brest Flt.
St. Julien, — (R.A) *F*	I. 72–6, Com. at Toulon.
St. Vaast, Page (L.) *F*.	V. 214, Pluvier cut out by the bts. of Semiramis.
St. Vincent, Earl (A.)	*See* Sir John Jervis, K.B.
Saizien, Louis P. F. R. B. (C.) *F*.	V. 317, Boulogne flotilla, actn. with Rosario.
Salgado, — (C.) *Por*....	V. 73, Por. Voader (brig), capture of Cayenne.
Salkeld, Thomas (act.-L.)	VI. 17, Undaunted, in actn. Carri, Medn.
Salmon, John (Mr.) ...	III. 249, Eclair, actn. with Grand Décidé (priv.).
Salmon, John (L.Com.)	IV. 461, Clinker, fndrd. off Havre, drnd.
Salmond, Wm. (Mid.)	V. 417, Java, k. in actn.
Salomon,VictorAmédée (L.Com.)	IV. 172–3, Salamandre destd. by Br. brigs ; 174, k. in actn.
Salter, — (L.) *E.I.C.*	V. 66, E.I.C. Ariel, capture of Sénégal.
Salzeco, — (R.A.) *Sp*.	III. 341, Sp. Sq. at Carthagena.
Salzedo, Don Josef (C.) *Sp*.	III. 386, Sp. Montanes ; 416–17, Trafalgar.
Samson, Joseph (L.-Com.) *F*.	III. 276, Charente destd. by Aigle.
Samwell, John (Mid.)	VI. 57, Shannon ; 60–6, k. in actn.
Sandell, — (Gunner)...	V. 38, Mercury, cutting out exped.
Sanders, George (C.)...	III. 316–17, Falcon, actn. with invas. flotilla. IV. 197, off Dantzic.

INDEX TO NAVAL OFFICERS 149

Sanders, James (C.) ...	II. 306, Espoir, Palermo; 364–5, capts. Sp. Africa. VI. 83, Junon, Lynhaven; 90, Hampton Rds.; 96–7, Delaware Bay.
Sanders, Thomas (L.)	VI. 289, Leander, Algiers; 291, pro. Cr.
Sanders, William (L.)	IV. 101, Donegal, Duckworth's actn.; 104, pro. Cr.
Sanderson, Wm. (Mr. Mt.)	V. 194, Cornwallis, cutting out exped.
Sandes, John T. (Mid.)	VI. 187, Menelaus, k. in actn. Baltimore.
Sandiland, Alex. (L.)	VI. 18, Euryalus, cutting out exped.
Sandom, William (L.)	V. 26, Bonne Citoyenne, in actn.
Sandwith, George Augustus Edw. (M.L.)	IV. 244, Glatton, cutting out exped.
Sandys, George (Mid.)	IV. 447, Tigre, cutting out exped.
Sandys, John (M.L.)...	II. 81, Lancaster, w. Camperdown.
Sandys, Rchd. Edw. (L.)	III. 56, Dart, k. Copenhagen.
Sargent, William (C.)	VI. 130, on board Hebrus, in actn.; 278, Cordelia, Algiers.
Sarradine, George (C.)	III. 67, Hound, off Boulogne, invas. flotilla.
Sarsfield, Barry (Mr. Mt.)	IV. 240–1, Galatea, w. cutting out exped.
Sartorius, Geo. Rose (L.)	V. 113–14, Success, cutting out expeds.
Satie, Jsph. André (C.) F.	V. 262–5, Persanne captd. by Alceste and consort.
Sauce, Robert (P.C.)	III. 91, Sensible, Egypt exped.; 485, wrkd. Ceylon.
Saulce, Louis H. Freycinet (L.Com.) F.	IV. 133–4, Phaëton captd. by Pique; 135, w. in actn. V. 107–8, C. Eliza, destd. by Diana.
Saulnier, — (C.) F. ...	II. 178, Guillaume Tell; 193–4, the Nile; 440–2, captd. by Br. Sq. off Malta. III. 127–8, Cmde., Africaine captd. by Phœbe; 129, k. in actn.
Saumarez, James (P.C.)	I. 114–15, Crescent capts. Réunion; 116, kntd.; 230–1, actn.
,, Sir James	with F. Sq.; 271, Orion; 273–5, actn. off Isle Groix; 329–30, crsg. II. 34–7–8, 40–3, 46–8, St. Vincent; 93, off Cadiz; 164, Cæsar, Sq. crsg.; 171, Orion, Medn. Sq; 183–5–9, the Nile; 196, w. in actn.; 206–11–12, Malta; 285, Cæsar, Sq. off Brest. III. 97, R.A. Com. Sq. off Cadiz; 98, 102–6–12, Algesiras; 113–15, actn. in the Gut
,, ,, K.B.	of Gibraltar; 116–17, made K.B.; 172, Cerberus, invas.
,, ,, Bart.	flotilla; 479–80, App. IV. 297–8, V.A., Baronet, Victory, Com. Baltic Flt.; 302–3, blockade of Rogerswick; 368, 431, Com. Baltic Flt. V. 41, 79, Com. Baltic Flt.
Saunders, Alex. (M.C.)	I. 182, Brunswick, k. 1st June.
Saunders, Henry (A.B.)	IV. 249, Halifax, deserter.
Saunders, James (L.)...	V. 412, Java; 417, w. in actn.
Saunders, Samuel (Mid.)	VI. 118, Boyne, w. in actn.
Saunders, Thomas (L.)	V. 319, Bermuda, in actn. Boulogne.
Saurin, Edw. (Mr. Mt.)	IV. 312, Emerald, cutting out exped.
Sauveur, Bois (C.) F.	I. 60, Superbe, Brest Flt.
Savage, Henry (P.C.)	I. 372–5, Albion, crsg. off Helvoetsluys. II. 462, Albion (F.S.), wrkd. in the Swin.
Savage, Patrick (M.L.)	VI. 90, Narcissus, cutting out exped.
Savage, R. H. (Mid.)	II. 328, Theseus, in actn. at Acre.
Savary, Daniel (Cmde.) F.	II. 137–9, 164–5, Concorde, Ireland expeds. III. 326, R.A. invas. flotilla Boulogne.
Saville, John G. (C.)	III. 83, Experiment, Egypt exped.
Savory, Thomas (Pr.)	V. 74–5, Confiance, capture of Cayenne.
Sawyer, Charles (P.C.)	I. 249, Vanguard, Sq. at capture of Guadaloupe; 333, Blanche, capture of Grenada.
Sawyer, Herbert (P.C.)	II. 285, Russel, Sq. off Brest; 301, blockading Aix.
Sawyer, — (R.A.)......	V. 275, Com. at Bermuda; 360–8–9, 424, V.A. Com. at Halifax.
Sayer, George (L.)......	I. 229, Carysfort, in actn. II. 163, Ethalion, in actn., pro. Cr. IV. 168–9, C. Galatea, Guadaloupe; 239–42, capts. Lynx. V. 297, Leda; 300–3, capture of Java.
Scallon, Robert (L.) ...	III. 130, Trent, cutting out exped.
Scandril, Kichuc Ali (C.) Turk.	IV. 350–4, Turk. Badere Zaffer captd. by Seahorse.

Scanlan, James (B.) ...	IV. 168, Galatea, cutting out exped.
Schanks, — (C.)	II. 353, gun designer.
Schilds, Jean J. B. (L.Com.) *F.*	V. 212, Canonnier captd. by Scylla, k. in actn.
Schomberg, Alexander Wilmot (L.)	I. 241, capture of Martinique; 376, Glatton, in actn. V. 2, C. Loire, capts. Hébé.
Schomberg, Charles Marsh (L.)	II. 197, Minotaur, the Nile; 210, pro. Cr. III. 27–9, cutting out exped.; 175, C. Agincourt, Medn. Flt. IV. 236, Hibernia, Sq. off the Tagus. V. 283, Astræa, Port Louis, 284-7-8-92-4, actn. off Madagascar; 446, App.
Schomberg, Isaac (P.C.)	I. 139, Culloden; 162, 176, 182, 1st June.
Schutter, — (C.) *Du.*	II. 343, Du. Amphitrite, Sq. blockaded in the Texel.
Scott, Charles Kittoe (Mid.)	VI. 318–28, Burmese War; 351, App.
Scott, Eleazer (Mid.)...	V. 45, Pelorus, cutting out exped.
Scott, George (P.C.) ...	III. 83, Stately, Egypt exped. V. 5, Horatio; 6–9, with consorts capts. Junon, w. in actn.; 97, capts. Nécessité.
Scott, George (L.)......	V. 295, Phœbe, in actn., pro. Cr.
Scott, George (C.)......	IV. 465, Boreas, wrkd. near Guernsey.
Scott, Isaac William (L.Com.)	III. 194, Princess Augusta, k. in actn. with Du. gbts.
Scott, James (Mid.) ...	II. 81, Belligueux, w. Camperdown.
Scott, James (Mr.Mt.)	V. 72, Pompée, w. capture of Cayenne.
Scott, James (L.)	VI. 84, Marlborough, Chesapeake Bay; 178, Albion, Bladensburg.
Scott, John (Nelson's Secretary)	III. 397, Victory; 403–425, k. Trafalgar.
Scott, John Nicholas C. (Pr.)	V. 26, Bonne Citoyenne, in actn.
Scott, Matthew Henry (C.)	I. 246, Rose, capture of the Saintes; 410, Hebe, Martinique; 439, App. IV. 54, Niobe; 59, Channel Flt.
Scott, Octavius (M.L.)	V. 12, Arethusa, cutting out exped.
Scott, Robert (L.)......	II. 415, Solebay, in actn.
Scott, Robert (Mr.) ...	V. 380, Guerrière, w. in actn.
Scott, Thomas (A.B.)	II. 245–6, loss of Resistance.
Scotten, — (Car.)	V. 257, Pilot, cutting out exped.
Scriven, Tim. (L.Com.)	VI. 11, Telegraph, actn. with Flibustier; 394, C. C.B. Erne,
,, ,, (C.B.) ...	wrkd. Cape de Verdes.
Scriven, Thomas (Mr.)	III. 416, Colossus, k. Trafalgar.
Scriven, Thomas (Pr.)	III. 78, Serpent, cutting out exped.
Scroeder, Christopher (Mr.Mt.)	II. 326, Tigre at Acre.
Seagrove, James (L.)...	V. 127, Rambler, cutting out exped. VI. 146, Menelaus and F. Atalante, Concarneau Bay.
Seale, Chas. Hen. (L.)	VI. 6, in actn. Cuxhaven.
Searle, John Clarke (C.)	I. 396–7, Pelican, actn. with Médée; 410, at Martinique. II. 474, Ethalion, wrkd. Penmarcks.
Searle, Richd. (Gunner)	II .116, mutiny of Hermione.
Searle, Thos. (L.Com.)	II. 379–80, Courier capts. Ribotteur (priv.); 382, recapture of Crash; 413–14, capts. Guerrier (priv.), pro. Cr. IV. 270–1, C. Grasshopper, capts. Sp. San Josef; 326, off Cadiz; 329–30, off Portugal.
Seaward, Thos. (Mr.-Mt.)	IV. 336, Rook, k. in actn.
Seccombe, Thos. (P.C.)	IV. 244, Glatton, Isle of Tenedos; 294, k. at Palermo.
Secker, — (M.Sergeant)	III. 403, Victory, Trafalgar.
Sedley, John (L.Com.)	IV. 467, Elizabeth, fndrd. W. Indies, drnd.
Segbourne, Thomas (Schoolmaster)	II. 330, Theseus, burnt at Acre, k.
Segges, James (Gunner)	IV. 405, Mediator, k. Basque Rds.
Segond, Adrien Joseph (C.) *F.*	II. 139–147, Loire, Ireland exped.; 154–7, engages Mermaid; 158–9, captd. by Anson.

INDEX TO NAVAL OFFICERS 151

Segourney,—(L.Com.) U.S. VI. 96, U.S. Asp, k. Chesapeake Bay.
Selby, William (L.) ... II. 58, Victory, St. Vincent, pro. Cr.; 61, w. at Cadiz. III. 172, C. Cerberus, invas. flotilla. IV. 387-8, Guadaloupe; 431, Owen Glendower, Scheldt exped.
Selwyn, Chas. William (Mid.) IV. 100, Northumberland, w. Duckworth's actn. V. 442, L.Com., Haddock, captd. by Génie.
Senden, Van (C.) Du. II. 343, Batavia, blockaded in the Texel.
Senes, Louis André (L.Com.) F. III. 32, Berceau captd. by U.S. Boston.
Senez, André (C.) F. ... II. 137, Vénus, Ireland exped.
Senhouse, Henry Fleming (C.) VI. 97, Martin, in actn. Delaware Bay.
Senhouse, Wm. Wood (L.Com.) II. 99, Alexandrian capts. Coq (priv.); 101, capts. Epicharis (priv.).
Seniavin, — (V.A.) Rus. IV. 217, Sq. in the Dardanelles; 230-3-5, actn. with Turk. Sq.; 238-296, Sq. in the Tagus; 348, Isle of Tenedos.
Sennequier,—(L.Com.) F. II. 251-3, Lodi, actn. with Br. brig.
Septford, John (Mid.) IV. 320, Tartarus, cutting out exped.
Sercey, Pierre C. C. Guillaume (R.A.) F. I. 60-3, Eole, Sq. in the W. Indies; 69, Brest; 386-7 Santa Cruz; 389, Ceylon; 390-4, Sq. actn. with two Br. 74's; 395, W. Indies. II. 3, coast of Malabar; 89-90; 236-8, Isle of France; 356, 365, Batavia.
Serocold, Walter (L.) I. 80, in actn. Toulon; 211-13, C. Prosélyte (floating battery), destd. at Bastia, k. in actn.
Seton, — (L.Com.) ... I. 443, Flying Fish captd. by F. privs.
Settimo, — (C.) Neap. II. 432, Neap. Strombolo (brig), blockade of Savona.
Settle, Thomas (Mr.)... V. 266, Sabine, cutting out exped.
Seward, Charles (Mid.) II. 196, Majestic, w. the Nile.
Sewell, Henry (Mid.) V. 174, Africaine, w. cutting out exped.
Seymour, Geo. Francis (L.) IV. 100, Northumberland, w. Duckworth's actn.; 140, C. Kingfisher, Isle of Aix; 400, Pallas; 418, actn. Basque Rds.
Seymour, Hon. Hugh Conway (P.C.)
„ Lord Hugh I. 72, Leviathan, Medn. Flt.; 139-40, Lord Hugh, Channel Flt.; 146-9, 151-2, 29th May; 167-72-3, 200, 1st June; 271, R.A. Sans Pareil, actn. off Belleisle; 277, off Isle Groix. II. 26, Spithead mutiny; 284, V.A. off Brest.; 420-1, Prince of Wales, capture of Surinam.
Seymour, Michael (L.)
„ Sir Michael, Bart. I. 175, Marlborough, w. 1st June. IV. 376-9-80, C. Amethyst, capts. Thetis; 392, off Isle Groix; 433, Baronet; 438, Scheldt exped. V. 13-17, capts. Niemen. VI. 128-30, Hannibal capts. Sultane; 133, gun trials of Eurotas.
Seymour, Richard (L.) IV. 131, Amazon, k. in actn.
Seymour, Stephen (C.) II. 456, Arab, wrkd. near Brest.
Seymour, Thos. (Mid.) II. 196, Vanguard, k. the Nile.
Shadwell, William (Pr.) III. 224, Aimable, w. in actn.
Shapland, — (Mid.) ... VI. 274, Tyne, cutting out exped., pro. L.
Sharp, Alex. (M.C.) ... III. 54, Bellona, w. Copenhagen.
Sharpe, Alexander Renton (C.) V. 246, Scout, Corsica.
Shaw, Charles (L.) ... II. 392, Camel, in actn. V. 346, C.Philomel, crsg. Spain.
Shaw, Isaac (L.) ...... VI. 17-18, Volontaire, w. cutting out exped.
Shaw, John (C.)......... V. 386, borne on the register of the U.S. Navy.
Shaw, — (L.) .... IV. 244, Mediator, cutting out exped.
Sheckley, John (A.B.) IV. 253, U.S. Chesapeake, k. in actn.
Shekel, John (L) ...... IV. 8, Cæsar, w. Strachan's actn. V. 40, Bellerophon, cutting out exped. VI. 382, C. Bold, wrkd. Prince Edward's Island.
Sheppard, Richard S. (Mr.) U.S. VI. 232, U.S. Alligator, in actn. Malheureux Isles.

Sheppardson, Ralph (L.)	IV. 158, Indefatigable, w. cutting out expe
Sheridan, John (L.) ...	III. 202, Merlin, cutting out exped. V. 40, Bellerophon, cutting out exped. VI. 190, C. Terror (bomb.), Baltimore; 235, St. Mary's, U.S.
Sherman, Thos. (M.C.)	V. 102, Caledonia, cutting out exped. VI. 19, capture of Ponza.
Sherrard, Thos. (Pilot)	II. 81, Veteran, w. Camperdown.
Sherriff, John (C.)	IV. 271-2, Curieux, k. in actn. with Revanche.
Sherwin, Daniel (Mid.)	II. 80, Monarch, w. Camperdown.
Sherwood, Wm. (Mid.)	V. 120, Cerberus, cutting out exped.
Shield, Wm. (P.C.) ...	I. 214-15, Berwick, Corsica; 297, Audacious, actn. off Hyères. IV. 292, Malta, Syracuse.
Shiells, Ludlow (L.) ...	I. 96, Courageux, k. in actn.
Shiels, David (L.Com.)	IV. 320, Forward, crsg. off Denmark.
Shillibeer, John (M.L.)	V. 88-9, Freija, cutting out exped.
Shipley, Charles (Vol.)	IV. 328-9, on board Nymphe, cutting out exped.
Shipley, Conway (C.)	III. 258, 274, Hippomenes capts. Egyptienne (priv.); 296, capture of Surinam. IV. 201, Nymphe, crsg.; 244-5, Comus, crsg.; 327, Nymphe, off Lisbon; 328-9, k. cutting out exped.
Shippard, Alexander (L.Com.)	III. 174, Admiral Mitchell, actn. off Boulogne. IV. 473, C. Banterer, wrkd. in the St. Lawrence.
Shirly, Thos. (L.Com.)	III. 315, Gallant, watching invas. flotilla.
Shirreff, Wm. Hy. (C.)	IV. 387, Lily, W. Indies. VI. 91, Barrosa, actn. in Chesapeake Bay.
Shivers, Thomas Revell (P.C.)	II. 293, Defiance, Medn. Flt.
Shorbridge, Wm. (B.)	IV. 230, Standard, w. Dardanelles.
Short, John Ides (C.)...	II. 474, Contest, wrkd. Holland.
Shortland, John (P.C.)	V. 47-8, 52-3, Junon captd. by F. frigates, k. in action; 441, App.
Shortland, Thos. Geo. (L.)	II. 255, Melpomène, cutting out exped.; 256, pro. Cr. IV. 214, C. Canopus, Malta.
Shortland, — (Mid.)...	I. 175, Marlborough, w. 1st June.
Shovel, Sir Cloudesley (A.)	I. 14 (1571), on naval terms.
Shuldham, Molyneux (L.Com.)	IV. 461, Adder, captd. by going ashore near Abreval.
Shuldham, Wm. (Mid.)	III. 298, Centaur, k. in actn.
Sibly, Edward Reynolds (L.)	IV. 158, Centaur, w. cutting out exped.; 159, pro. Cr. V. 81, C. Shearwater, Sq. off Toulon; 345-6, Swallow, actn. with Renard and Goéland. VI. 33, crsg. Adriatic.
Sibrell, John (L.Com.)	IV. 368, Piercer, actn. with Da. gbts.
Sibthorpe, — (Mid.)...	II. 441, Penelope, w. in actn. Malta.
Sillans, De (C.)F.......	I. 239-40, Pégase captd. by Foudroyant.
Simens, Thomas (L.) ..	III. 441, Defiance, k. Trafalgar.
Siméon, Gabriel (C.)F.	II. 286, Gaulois, Brest Flt.
Simiot, Etienne Stanislaus (C.) F.	VI. 3, Pauline, Toulon Flt.
Simkin, Wm. (Mr.Mt.)	VI. 25, Weasel, w. in actn.
Simmonds, Richard William (L.Com.)	V. 229-30, Manly captd. by Da. gbts.; 329-30, Attack, actn. off Calais; 331, captd. by Da. gbts; 448, 451, App.
Simmonds, Robert (L.Com.)	II. 220, Coromandel (T.S.), capture of Minorca.
Simmons, John (Mid.)	III. 414, Bellerophon, k. Trafalgar.
Simms, Samuel (Mid.)	II. 326, Tigre, in actn. Acre.
Simon, Isaac (Mr.) ...	V. 255, Cephalus, w. cutting out exped.
Simonds, Wm. J. (L.)	II. 135, Hydra, cutting out exped.
Simonot, Edme Louis (C.) F.	VI. 3, Pénélope, Medn.
Simpkins, Wm. (Mid.)	V. 256, Active, cutting out exped.

INDEX TO NAVAL OFFICERS 153

Simpson, Henry Pierson (Mr. Mt.)	V. 257, Pilot, cutting out exped.
Simpson, John (L.) ...	V. 42, Cerberus, cutting out exped.
Simpson, John (M.L.)	VI. 41, Amelia, w. in actn.
Simpson, Slingsby (C.)	IV. 146, Driver, crsg. off New York.
Sinclair, Alexander(C.)	V. 447, Fancy, fndrd. in the Baltic, drnd.
Sinclair, Arthur (L.) U.S.	IV. 249, U.S. Chesapeake, Norfolk, U.S. V. 356, 394, C. U.S. Argus, Sq. crsg. VI. 208-9, Com. at Lake Erie.
Sinclair, David (Mr. Mt.)	IV. 221, in actn. Dardanelles.
Sinclair, James (M.L.)	III. 139-40, Beaulieu, k. cutting out exped.
Sinclair, Sir John Gordon (C.)	VI. 17, Redwing, cutting out exped. ; 19, capture of Ponza.
Sinclair, Patrick (P.C.)	I. 122, Iphigenia, St. Domingo ; 129, Port Louis ; 252, St. Domingo.
Sinclair, — (M.L.) ...	II. 275, Ambuscade, w. in actn.
Singleton, — (Mid.) ...	I. 227, Orpheus, k. in actn.
Sison, Samuel (L.)......	IV. 448, Volontaire, cutting out exped.
Sitford, William (Mid.)	III. 54, Bellona, w. Copenhagen.
Skeffington, L. (R.A.)	I. 214, Terrible, Flt. at Corsica.
Skelton, Jeremiah (L.)	III. 66, w. in actn. with invas. flotilla.
Skene, Alexander(P.C.)	IV. 337, Guerrière, crsg. Gulf of Florida.
Skinner, Fitzherbert Geo. (C.)	V. 27, Goldfinch, actn. with Mouche.
Skinner, George A. E. (L.Com.)	IV. 244, Hirondelle, off Isle of Tenedos.
Skinner, John (C.)......	II. 233, Princess Royal (packet), actn. with Aventurier (priv.).
Skinner, John W. (C.)	IV. 368, Tickler captd. by Da. gbts, k. in actn. ; 474, App.
Skottowe, George (L.)	III. 36-7, Magicienne, cutting out exped. ; 494, C. Sterling, wrkd. near Calais.
Skynner, Lancelot (P.C.)	I. 410, Beaulieu, W. Indies. II. 474, Lutine, wrkd. Holland, drnd.
Slade, Charles (Mid.)	II. 80, Monarch, w. Camperdown.
Slade, Henry (L.)......	VI. 202, Bulwark, Penobscot exped.
Slade, James (L.)	II. 383, Latona, cutting out exped.
Slaughter, William (L.)	V. 36, Amphion ; 120-1, cutting out expeds.
Sleigh, John (Mid.) ...	VI. 84, w. in actn. Chesapeake Bay.
Slenner, Hy. Geo.(Mr.)	V. 118, Spartan, in actn.
Sloan, David (L.)......	IV. 319, Stately, capture of Da. Prindts-Christian-Frederic. V. 450, C. Belette, wrkd. Isle of Lessoe, drnd.
Slocum, — (C.) U.S.	VI. 54, bearer of challenge to U.S. Chesapeake.
Slout, Samuel (L.)......	V. 220-2, Raven, k. cutting out exped.
Smedley, Henry (C.) E.I.C.	II. 244, E.I.C. Raymond captd. by Preneuse.
Smith, Alfred (Mr.Mt.)	IV. 167-8, Alexandria, k. cutting out exped.
Smith, Charles (C.) ...	I. 439, Alert capt. by Unité.
Smith, Charles Thomas (Mid.)	V. 349, Minstrel, cutting out exped.
Smith, Francis (Mid.)	III. 142, Atalante, cutting out exped. IV. 268, L. Porcupine ; 345-7, cutting out expeds.
Smith, Henry (Mid.)	IV. 280, w. in actn. Buenos Ayres.
Smith, Isaac (P.C.) ...	I. 131, Perseverance, Mangalore, E. Indies.
Smith, James (L.)	II. 273, Perdrix, in actn.
Smith, James (L.)......	IV. 75, Swift, cutting out exped.
Smith, Jas. Edwd. (L.)	III. 298, Centaur, k. capture of Surinam.
Smith, James J. (M.L.)	II. 80, Monarch, w. Camperdown.
Smith, John (L.)	II. 88, Bedford, Camperdown, pro. Cr.
Smith, John (P.C.) ...	II. 344, America, Holland exped.
Smith, John (Mr.Mt.)	III. 199-200, Blanche, cutting out exped.
Smith, John (L.)	III. 428, 443, Africa, Trafalgar ; 464, pro. Cr. VI. 16, C. Beagle, Sq. off St. Sebastian.
Smith, John (Mr.)......	V. 216, Hawk, cutting out exped.

Smith, John (C.) *U.S.*	V. 356, U.S. Congress, Sq. crsg.; 408, crsg. Bermuda. VI. 73, Portsmouth, U.S.
Smith, John B. (Mid.)	IV. 29–30, Gracieuse, in actn. Jamaica.
Smith, John Sam.(Mid.)	III. 437, Minotaur, w. Trafalgar.
Smith, J. S. (P.C.) ...	I. 125, Stately, St. John's, Newfoundland.
Smith, Marmaduke(L.)	V. 99, Belvidera, cutting out exped.
Smith, Matthew (P.C.)	I. 236–8, Diomede, actn. off Isle of France, court-martialled; 337, Malacca exped.; 443, wrkd. Ceylon.
Smith, Matthew (L.-Com.)	III. 34, Millbrook, actn. with Bellone (priv.); 35, pro. Cr.
Smith, Robert (Mid.)	III. 425, Victory, k. Trafalgar.
Smith, Robert (L.) ...	V. 164, Magicienne, in actn. VI. 134, Eurotas, in actn.; 138, pro. Cr.
Smith, Spencer (L.) ...	VI. 374, w. Navarino.
Smith, Sydney (L.) *U.S.*	IV. 252, U.S. Chesapeake, in actn. VI. 115, Canadian Lakes.
Smith, Thomas (Mid.)	IV. 221, Pompée, Dardanelles.
Smith, William (P.C.)	I. 282, Berwick, dismissed ship.
Smith, William (Mid.)	II. 196, Swiftsure, w. the Nile. IV. 312, L. Emerald, in actn. Spain.
Smith, Wm. (Mr.Mt.)	IV. 230, Active, Dardanelles.
Smith, Wm. (Act.L.)	IV. 167–8, Gracieuse, cutting out exped.
Smith, William (Mr.)	IV. 381, Circe, cutting out exped.
Smith, William (Mid.)	V. 217, Hotspur, k. in actn.
Smith, William (L.) ...	VI. 36, Swiftsure, cutting out exped.
Smith, William (Mid.)	VI. 58–9, Shannon, actn. with U.S. Chesapeake; 66, pro. L.
Smith, William (L.) ...	VI. 342, Boadicea, Burmese War.
Smith, William (L.) ...	VI. 373, k. Navarino.
Smith, Wm. (L.Com.)	IV. 457, Pigmy, wrkd. Jersey.
Smith, Sir Wm. Sidney (P.C.)	I. 85–7, Toulon; 233–5, Diamond, Sq. crsg.; 259–60, Brest Rds.; 358–9, off Havre; 360–1, taken prisoner; 455, App. II. 128, St. Marcouf; 231, 266, escapes; 291, off Alexandria; 321–32, at Acre; 333, Aboukir; 336, Cyprus; 340–2, Damietta; 378, Tigre; 445–7, capture of Malta. III. 11, 81-4-7-8, 92–5, Egypt exped.; 220–2, Cmde. Antelope; 223–6, Sq. off Ostende; 315, invas. flotilla. IV. 122, R.A. Pompée; 123–4, Com. Sq. at Sicily; 217–22–30, Dardanelles; 236–8, Lisbon. V. 73, Com. at the Brazils. VI. 117, V.A. Hibernia, Medn. Flt.
Smith, — (L.)	VI. 336–7, Alligator, Burmese War; 354, App.
Smithies, Thomas (L.-Com.)	III. 229, Bruiser, off Boulogne.
Smyth, — (L.)	VI. 368, Dartmouth, Navarino.
Smythe, Brown (Mid.)	VI. 374, k. Navarino.
Sneedorf, — (C.) *Da.*	IV. 202, Da. Princessen Louisa Augusta, Fredrickswaern, Norway.
Snell, Francis Jackson (C.)	III. 490, Avenger, fndrd. off the Weser, crew saved.
Snell, John (Mr.)	III. 115, Venerable, w. in actn.
Snell, John (Mr.Mt.)	III. 440, Thunderer, w. Trafalgar.
Snellgrove, Henry (Mid.)	III. 416, Colossus, w. Trafalgar.
Sneyd, Clement (C.) ...	V. 313, Myrtle, crsg. off Ushant.
Sneyd, Ralph (L.)	II. 81, Montagu, w. Camperdown.
Snow, William John (Mid.)	III. 417, Achille, w. Trafalgar. V. 380, Mr.Mt. Guerrière, w. in actn.
Snowe, William Havisand (M.C.)	V. 81, w. in actn. Toulon.
Sobriel, John (L.)	II. 81, Ardent, w. Camperdown.
Solano, — (R.A.) *Sp.*	I. 345, Sp. Flt. Cadiz Bay.
Soleil, Elénore Jean Nic. (C.) *F.*	II. 178, Diane, F. Flt. Aboukir Bay. IV. 48, Lion, Allemand's Sq. crsg.; 175–6, Cmde., Gloire captd. by Br. Sq.

INDEX TO NAVAL OFFICERS 155

Solsby, — (Mr.)	II. 257, Espoir, k. in actn.
Somervell, James (C.)	VI. 175, in actn. Chesapeake Bay.
Somerville, Philip (C.)	III. 65, invas. flotilla, Channel. IV. 438, Rota, Scheldt exped. VI. 223, crsg. Western Isles; 235, St. Mary's, U.S.
Sorondo, Don Gabriel (C.) *Sp.*	II. 110, Sp. Gallardo destd. at Trinidad.
Sotheby, Thos. (P.C.)	I. 353, Bombay Castle, wrkd. in the Tagus. II. 289, Marlborough, Flt. off Cadiz; 428, wrkd. Belleisle; 429, courtmartialled; 456 App. III. 476, App. V. 102-3, R.A. Dreadnought, crsg. off Ushant.
Sotheron, Frank (P.C.)	II. 382, Latona, crsg. Holland. III. 178, Excellent, off Toulon; 346, Naples Bay. IV. 122, Palermo.
Sottomayor, Don M. d'Acunha (V.A.) *Por.*	IV. 237, Por. Principe-Real, Lisbon.
Soulanges, Comte de (C.) *F.*	I. 239, Protecteur, convoy escort.
Sous, Rais Mahomet (C.) *Tripolitan*	III. 160-1, Tripolitan ship captd. by U.S. Enterprise.
Souters, — (C.) *Du.* ...	II. 76-9, Du. Batavier, Camperdown.
Southcomb, John (C.) *U.S.*	VI. 83, U.S. Lottery (priv.) captd. by Maidstone, k. in actn.
Southcott, Edwd. (Mr.)	II. 116, mutiny of the Hermione.
Southey, Thos. (Mid.)	II. 122, Mars, w. in actn. III. 54, L. Bellona, w. Copenhagen.
Spargo, Stephen (B.)...	IV. 101, Atlas, w. Duckworth's actn.
Sparrow, Benjamin (L.)	II. 7-8, Duke of York (lugger), off Brest.
Sparrow, Francis (L.)	V. 213, Diana, cutting out exped.
Sparrow, — (C.) *F.* ...	III. 15, Imprenable (priv.) capts. Lark.
Spea, John Linzee (M.L.)	III. 85, k. in actn. Egypt exped.
Spear, John (P.C.)......	IV. 108, Northumberland, Martinique.
Spear, Joseph (C.)	IV. 330, Goree, actn. with F. brigs. V. 208, Téméraire, Medn. Flt.
Spear, Richard (L.) ...	III. 454, Conqueror, Trafalgar. V. 229, C. Chanticleer, actn. with Da. gbts.
Spearing, George Augustus (Mr. Mt.)	III. 56, Alcmène, w. Copenhagen. IV. 388, L.Com. Subtle, k. in actn.
Spearman, Robert (1st cl. Vol.)	V. 37, Amphion, cutting out exped.; 239, 245, Mid., k. in actn. off Lissa.
Spedden, Robert (L.) *U.S.*	VI. 232, in actn. Chandeleur Isles.
Spence, Charles (L.)...	IV. 184, Success, cutting out exped.
Spence, — (Mid.)	III. 125, Bordelais, capture of Curieux, drnd.
Spencer, Benj. (M.L.)	III. 55, Edgar, k. Copenhagen.
Spencer, Earl (1st Lord Admiralty)	II. 27, 67-8 (1797); 210, 222 (1798).
Spencer, Hon. Frederick (P.C.)	VI. 362-5-73, Talbot, Navarino.
Spencer, Richard (Mid.)	I. 275, Sans Pareil, w. in actn. Isle Groix. IV. 467, L.Com. Crafty, captd. in the Straits of Gibraltar. V. 191-3, C. Samarang, capture of Amboyna.
Spencer, Sir Robert (P.C.)	VI. 274-5, Naiad capts. Algrn. Tripoli.
Spencer, Hon. Robert Cavendish (C.)	VI. 19, Kite, in actn. Cassis, Medn.
Spencer, Hon. Robert Churchill (Mid.)	IV. 447, Tigre, cutting out exped. VI. 231, C. Carron, Chandeleur Isles.
Spencer, R. (1st cl. Vol.)	III. 104, Spencer, k. in actn. Algesiras.
Spens, Nathaniel (C.) *E.J.C.*	III. 22, E.I.C. Neptune, in actn.

Spicer, Peter (B.)	II. 49, Excellent, k. St. Vincent.
Spilsbury, Francis Brockwell (L.)	V. 337, Hyacinth, crsg. Spain. VI. 105, C. Beresford; 204-7, Niagara, Canadian Lakes.
Spottiswood, Robert (C.) *E.I.C.*	III. 191, E.I.C. Lord Nelson captd. by Bellone (priv.), recaptd. by Pellew's Sq.
Spranger, John William (C.)	I. 333-4, Rattlesnake, Cape of Good Hope exped.; 417, Crescent, Madagascar. IV. 91, Sq. off Cadiz; 449, Warrior, capture of Cephalonia. V. 32, Sq. in the Medn.
Spratley, Samuel (Mid.)	III. 66, w. in actn. with invas. flotilla.
Spratt, James (Mr. Mt.)	III. 441, Defiance, w. Trafalgar.
Spurin, John (M.C.) ...	VI. 35, Revenge, cutting out exped.
Spurking, Jeremiah (Mid.)	VI. 136, Eurotas, k. in actn.
Spurling, John (Mr.)...	VI. 202, Bulwark, Canadian Lakes.
Stackpoole, Hassard (L.)	II. 405, Cerberus, in actn. III. 483, L.Com. Iphigenia (T.S.), burnt at Alexandria. V. 361, C. Statira, crsg. VI. 83, Chesapeake Bay; 193-4, off New London, U.S.
Staines, Thomas (C.)	V. 32-5, Cyane, w. in actn. with Espoir.
Staines, Wm. H. (Mid.)	III. 417, Achille, w. Trafalgar.
Staines, — (Mr. Mt.)...	I. 227, Orpheus, w. in actn.
Stamp, Thomas (L.) ...	III. 15, Defence, cutting out exped.
Standelet, Pierre Jean (C.) *F.*	II. 178, Artémise; 193, 204, captd. at the Nile; 323, in actn. at Acre.
Standley, Robert (C.)	VI. 387, Crane fndrd. West Indies, drnd.
Standly, Robert (Mid.)	IV. 22, Cleopatra, w. in actn.
Stanfell, Francis (C.)	V. 50, Scorpion, off Basse Terre; 86, capts. Oreste; 92, Guadaloupe. VI. 200, Bacchante, Penobscot exped.
Stanhope, Edwyn Francis (Mid.)	V. 101, Surveillante, cutting out exped.
Stanhope, Henry Edwin (P.C.) ,, Sir H.E., Bart.	I. 416, Ruby, Sq. Simon's Bay. IV. 200, V.A. Pompée, Copenhagen; 210, created Baronet; 425, Gambier's courtmartial.
Stanhope, John (P.C.)	I. 65, Vanguard, Channel Flt.
Stanley, Edwd. (Mid.)	VI. 287, Queen Charlotte, w. Algiers.
Stanning, Richd. (Mr.)	II. 242, Sibylle, k. in actn.
Stannus, John (M.C.)	IV. 124, Eagle, in actn. coast of Italy.
Stanton, Anthony Collings (Mid.)	III. 33, Phaëton, cutting out exped.
Stap, William (C.)......	II. 456, Scourge, fndrd. off Holland, crew saved.
Stapledon, Arth. (Mid.)	III. 104, Pompée, w. Algesiras.
Starck, M. A. Newton de (L.Com.)	III. 196, Milbrook, actn. off Calais.
Steel, George (C.)......	IV. 461, Seaforth, fndrd. Leeward Island Station, drnd.
Steel, — (Gunner)......	III. 276, Aigle, in actn. des. F. ships.
Steele, Elms (L.)	V. 13, Arethusa, crsg. N. Spain.
Steele, Henry (M.L.)	IV. 70, Phœnix, w. in actn. with Didon.
Stéeling, Jean (L.Com.) *Du.*	V. 91, Du. Havik captd. by Thistle.
Steffen, Von (L.) *Da.*...	IV. 209, Copenhagen.
Stephens, Athelstan (M.L.)	VI. 171, in actn. Bladensburg; 288, Glasgow, w. Algiers.
Stephens, C. J. (C.) ...	VI. 374, k. Navarino.
Stephens, Edward (C.)	VI. 387, Picton captd. by U.S. Constitution.
Stephens, John (Mr.)...	V. 392, Frolic, k. in actn.
Stephens, William (L.)	III. 443, Royal Sovereign, Trafalgar; 464, pro. Cr. V. 80, C. Imogene, w. capture of St. Maura.
Stephenson, John (Mid.)	II. 61, Audacious, w. in actn. Cadiz.
Sterling, John (Mid.)...	V. 37, Mercury, cutting out exped.
Sterrett, Andrew (L.-Com.) *U.S.*	III. 160, U.S. Enterprise capts. Tripolitan ship.
Steuart, Hew (C.)	IV. 205, Mutine, Copenhagen.

INDEX TO NAVAL OFFICERS 157

Steuart, Don Jacobo (C.) *Sp.*	I. 406, Sp. Sabina captd. by Minerve.
Stevens, William (B.)	VI. 57–60, Shannon, k. in actn. with U.S. Chesapeake.
Stevenson, Cornelius James (M.L.)	IV. 9, Hero, w. Strachan's actn.
Stevenson, James (C.)	I. 411, Charon (S.S.), capture of Grenada. III. 83, Europa; 89–92, Egypt exped.
Steward, — (Mid.) ...	III. 104, Pompée, k. Algesiras.
Stewart, Allen (L.) ...	IV. 326–7, Alceste, cutting out exped.
Stewart, Charles (L.-Com.) *U.S.*	III. 302, U.S. exped. to Tripoli. V. 382, C. construction of ships. VI. 83, U.S. Constellation, Norfolk, U.S.; 193, Chesapeake; 197–9, U.S. Constitution, crsg.; 247, Boston Rds.; 248–50, capts. Cyane and Levant; 251–2, Isle of Mayo; 254–6, crsg.; 257, Boston.
Stewart, Chas (L.Com.)	IV. 466, Jackal, wrkd. near Calais.
Stewart, George (L.)...	IV. 280, w. in actn. Buenos Ayres.
Stewart, Houston (Mid.)	IV. 239, Impérieuse, cutting out exped.; 385–7, in actn. Rosas Bay.
Stewart, Hugh (Mr.) ...	IV. 320, Daphne, cutting out exped. V. 321, Northumberland des. F. frigates.
Stewart, James (B.) ...	V. 247, Unité, w. in actn.
Stewart, James (Mid.)	VI. 21–5, Weasel, w. cutting out exped.; 374, L., w. Navarino.
Stewart, James Pattison (L.Com.)	IV. 259, Port d'Espagne, in actn. Gulf of Paria. V. 224, C. Sheldrake, capture of Anholt; 325–6, Dictator, actn. off Norway.
Stewart, John (L.)......	II. 429–30, loss of Queen Charlotte. III. 82, C. Mondovi, Egypt exped. IV. 348, Seahorse; 349–53, capts. Turk. Badere Zaffer.
Stewart, John (C.) *E.I.C.*	V. 63–4, E.I.C. Windham captd. by Vénus; 132–6, actn. with F. frigates.
Stewart, Robert (Mr.)	III. 55, Ganges, k. Copenhagen.
Stewart, Walter (L.)...	V. 386, borne on the register of U.S. Navy.
Stewart, William (C.)	V. 128, Blossom, crsg. Cape Sicie, Medn; 342, cutting ou exped. VI. 2, 117, San Josef, Medn. Flt.
Stewart, — (Mid.)......	II. 80, Venerable, w. Camperdown.
Stewart, — (Mid.)......	III. 185, Naiad, cutting out exped.
Stiddy, John (Mid.) ...	IV. 448, Tuscan, cutting out exped.
Stiles, John (L.).........	I. 87, in actn. at Toulon.
Stirling, Charles (P.C.)	I. 280, Jason, Isle d'Yeu. II. 96, Warren's Sq. crsg.; 121, Channel Flt.; 247–8, capture of Seine, w. in actn.; 285, Pompée, Sq. off Brest; 297, Medn.; 469, App. III. 98, 100–4, Algesiras; 310, R.A. off Rochefort; 356, Glory, Calder's Flt.; 358–61–2–8, Calder's actn.; 372, off Rochefort. IV. 47, Sq. off Aix; 279, Diadem, Com. Sq. capture of Monte Video; 281, Buenos Ayres exped.
Stirling, James (L.) ...	V. 41, Prometheus, k. cutting out exped.
Stocker, Chas. M. (L.)	I. 275, Sans Pareil, k. in actn. Isle Groix.
Stockham, John (L.)...	III. 384, act.C. Thunderer; 439–40, Trafalgar; 464, pro. P.C.
Stoddart, Pringle (C.)	IV. 205, Cruiser, Copenhagen.
Stokes, Henry (Mid.)...	IV. 100, Northumberland, w. Duckworth's actn.
Stokes, James (L.)......	II. 323–5, in actn. at Acre; 340, in actn. Damiette, Nile.
Stokes, John (L.Com.)	V. 100–1, Constant, actn. off Morbihan. VI. 11, off Bayonne; 16, St. Sebastian; 112–13, w. in actn. Canadian Lakes.
Stone, James (Mid.) ...	III. 414, Bellerophon, w. Trafalgar.
Stone, — (C.)	II. 211, Por. Rainha-de-Portugal, Sq. off Malta.
Stoney, Joseph (Mid.)	V. 120, Cerberus, cutting out exped.
Stopford, Edward (C.)	IV. 247–8, Chichester (S.S.), Gosport, Virginia. V. 54, Victor; 65–6, captd. by Bellone; 304, w. capture of Java; 441, App.

Stopford, Hon. Robert (P.C.)	I. 67, Phaëton, Channel Flt.; 139, Aquilon, Channel Flt.; 262, Phaëton, Sq. off Ushant; 387, capture of Bonne Citoyenne. II. 106, crsg. France; 228, Warren's Sq. crsg.; 248, crsg.; 269, capts. Flore. III. 335, Spencer, Medn.; 380, 458, Gibraltar. IV. 90-5-6-8, 101, w. Duckworth's actn.; 200, Copenhagen; 392, R.A. Cæsar; 393-5, actn. with F. frigates; 396, 405-15-16-28, Basque Rds. V. 283, 300, Com. at the Cape; 302-5-9, Scipion, Com. Sq. capture of Java; 439, App.
Storey, — (R.A.) *Du.*	II. 76-8, Du. States General, Camperdown; 343-8, Du. Washington, Sq. captd. in the Texel.
Stovin, George Charles (Mid.)	IV. 385-7, Impérieuse, in actn. Rosas Bay.
Stovin, George S. (C.)	III. 477, Chance, fndrd., drnd.
Straaten, Jakob A. Van der (C.) *Du.*	VI. 279, Du. Frederica, Algiers.
Strachan, John (A.B.)	IV. 252, Melampus, deserter.
Strachan, Richard John (P.C.)	I. 67, Phœnix, crsg. Channel; 131, Baronet; 132, E. Indies; 222-5, Warren's Sq. frigate actn.; 318, Melampus, actn. off Jersey; 329, crsg. II. 128, Diamond, off St. Marcouf; 136, off Havre; 293, Captain, Medn.; 428, off Belleisle; 450, Ferrol. III. 36, crsg.; 175, 237, Donegal, Medn.; 213, Cæsar, invas. flotilla. IV. 2-10, Strachan's actn.; 12,
,, Sir R. J., Bart.	
,, ,, ,, K.B.	pro. R.A., K.B.; 64, 74, Strachan's actn.; 89, Com. Sq. crsg. St. Helena; 115-16, at Barbadoes; 287, Rochefort; 288, Palermo; 292, Adriatic; 433-8, St. Domingo; 439, Scheldt exped.; 454, App. V. 79, Com. Sq. crsg. off Flushing; 207, relieved by Admiral Young; 311, V.A. Com. off Flushing.
Strachey, Christopher (L.Com.)	III. 171, Jalouse, actn. with F. brigs. IV. 198, C. Dauntless, captd. by the F. at the capture of Dantzic; 465, App.
Strangeways, Henry Ludlow (M.C.)	I. 375, Glatton, k. in actn.
Stratton, Hy.(Mr.)*U.S.*	I. 385, U.S. Martha Brand at Plymouth.
Street, Benj. (L.Com.)	V. 175, Staunch, crsg. Isle Bourbon; 204, act.-C. Emma, capture of the Isle of France.
Strode, Edward (Mr.)	IV. 301, Centaur, in actn. with Rus. Sewolod.
Strong, Charles Burrough (L.)	IV. 436, Clyde, Scheldt exped.
Strong, John (B.)	V. 161, Néréide, w. in actn.
Strong, Thomas (L.)...	IV. 265, Clyde, cutting out exped.
Stuart, Lord George (P.C.)	IV. 456, Sheerness, wrkd. Ceylon. V. 2, Aimable capts. Iris; 328-9, Horatio, off Norway; 429, Newcastle. VI. 247, Sq. in Boston Bay; 252-3-4-60, crsg., chases U.S. Constitution.
Stuart, Henry (P.C.)...	II. 338, Fox, Kosseïr Bay.
Stuart, James (L.)	III. 443, Minotaur, Trafalgar; 464, pro. Cr.
Stuart, John (P.C.) ...	III. 335, Royal Sovereign, Medn. Flt. IV. 116, Décade, Strachan's Sq. Barbadoes.
Stuart, Richard (L.) ...	IV. 447-9, Cumberland, w. cutting out exped.
Stuart, Lord William (C.)	III. 136, Champion recapts. Bulldog (bomb.). IV. 437-40, Lavinia, Scheldt exped.
Studd, Edw.(C.)*E.I.C.*	II. 89, E.I.C. Taunton Castle, actn. with F. ships.
Studdert, John Fitzgerald (C.)	VI. 338, Burmese War.
Stupart, Gustavus (L.)	II. 380, Success, w. cutting out exped.
Sturgeon, Philip (L.)...	VI. 374, w. Navarino.
Sturt, Henry (Mid.) ...	VI. 288, Leander, w. Algiers.
Sturt, H. R. (L.)	VI. 374, w. Navarino.
Styles, John (L.)	I. 212, w. in actn. Corsica.
Subjado, Don Josef (C.) *Sp.*	II. 365, Sp. Africa captd. by Espoir, w. in actn.

INDEX TO NAVAL OFFICERS

Suckling, Maurice W. (L.) — I. 343, Meleager, cutting out exped.
Sudbury, John (Mr.Mt.) — VI. 234, w. in actn. Chandeleur Isles.
Suett, Thomas Richard (Mr.Mt.) — VI. 29, Cerberus, k. cutting out exped.
Sullivan, Charles (Mid.) — IV. 282, Psyche, cutting out exped.
Sullivan, Thomas Ball (L.) — IV. 279, Anson, in actn. pro. Cr. VI. 104, C. Woolwich (T.S.), Quebec; 175, Chesapeake Bay; 188, Baltimore; 382, wrkd. Barbuda.
Summers, James (L.)... — II. 330, Theseus, burnt at Acre, w.
Surcouff, — (C.) F. ... — III. 31, Confiance capts. E.I.C. Kent.
Surridge, Thos. (P.C.) — II. 338, Leopard, Mocha. III. 90–1, Egypt exped.; 208, Trident, Pondicherry, E. Indies.
Sutherland, Andrew (P.C.) — I. 72, Diadem, Medn. Flt.
Sutherland, James (Mr.) — IV. 138–9, Pallas, cutting out exped.
Sutherland, — (L.) ... — IV. 188, Cape of Good Hope exped.
Sutton, Charles Thos. (Mid.) — VI. 15, Royalist, w. in actn.
Sutton, John (P.C.) ... — I. 214, Egmont, Medn. Flt.; 297, off Hyères; 343, Toulon; 348, Bastia. II. 34–8, 41–3, 48, St. Vincent; 285, Superb, Sq. off Brest; 297, Gibraltar. III. 114, Superb, armament of. IV. 45, court-martial of Captain Mudge; 425, R.A., Gambier's court-martial.
Sutton, Robt. Manners (P.C.) — I. 72, Ardent, Medn. Flt.; 94, Sq. off Corsica; 207, blows up off Corsica, k.; 439, App.
Sutton, Samuel (P.C.) — II. 297, Prince, Medn. Flt. III. 46, Alcmène, Copenhagen; 176–7, Victory capts. Embuscade; 287, capture of Sp. treasure ships.
Swaffield, Wm. (P.C.) — I. 395, Overyssel, k. by Amphion blowing up at Plymouth. II. 456, App.
Swaine, Spelman (C.) — III. 494, Raven, wrkd. Medn. VI. 391, Statira, wrkd. Isle of Cuba.
Swaine, Thos. (L.Com.) — IV. 132, Attack, off Isle Groix; 287, off Rochefort.
Sweedland, Henry Johnston (L.) — VI. 18, Berwick, cutting out exped.
Sweeting, Wm. (Mid.) — VI. 287, Superb, w. Algiers.
Swimmer, Henry (Mid.) — III. 55, Monarch, w. Copenhagen.
Swiney, William (L.)... — II. 262–8, Leander, w. in actn.
Syder, George (M.L.) — V. 328–9, Horatio, k. cutting out exped.
Syer, Day Richard (Mid.) — IV. 447–9, Tigre, w. cutting out exped. VI. 17, L. Redwing, cutting out exped.
Sykes, John (Cox.)...... — II. 46, Captain, St. Vincent; 61, w. in actn. at Cadiz.
Sykes, John (L.)......... — V. 358, Belvidera, in actn.; 362, pro. Cr.
Sykes, Thomas (L.) ... — IV. 323, Tartar, cutting out exped. V. 38, cutting out exped. VI. 387, C. Fantome, wrkd. near Halifax.
Symes, Aaron Stark (Mid.) — VI. 285–8, Hebrus, w. Algiers.
Symes, Benjamin (L.) — II. 394, Tremendous, cutting out exped.
Symes, Joseph (L.)...... — V. 26, Bonne Citoyenne, in actn. pro. Cr.
Symonds, James (L.)... — VI. 202, Bulwark, Penobscot exped.
Symons, Henry (Mid.) — VI. 234, k. in actn. Chandeleur Isles.
Symons, Jeremiah J. (C.) — II. 457, Helena, fndrd. on the coast of Holland, drnd.

Tailour, John (L.) ...... — IV. 447–9, Tigre, w. cutting out exped., pro. Cr.
Tainsh, Robert (S.) ... — II. 330, Theseus, burnt at Acre, w.
Tait, Dalhousie (L.) ... — IV. 158, Monarch, w. cutting out exped.; 448–9, Volontaire, k. cutting out exped.
Tait, James (L.)......... — IV. 30, Unicorn, cutting out exped.
Tait, Walter (M.L.) ... — III. 130, Trent, cutting out exped.
Talbot, James Hugh (L.Com.) — IV. 400, Encounter, in actn. Basque Rds. V. 451, wrkd. San Lucar, Spain.

Talbot, John (L.)	I. 316, Astræa, in actn. pro. Cr. II. 129, C. Eurydice, St. Marcouf. IV. 24, Leander capts. Ville de Milan and recapts. Cleopatra; 214, Thunderer, Malta; 288-94, Sq. at Palermo. V. 338-40, Victorious capts. Rivoli, w. in actn.; 341, kntd.
,, Sir John	
Tancock, — (Gunner)	II. 249, Flora, cutting out exped.
Tanes, Charles (L.) ...	IV. 361, Terpsichore, w. in actn.
Tapley, Edwd. (Mr. Mt.)	IV. 400-3, Nimrod (cutter), in actn. Basque Rds.
Tapping, Charles (C.)	V. 441, Fama, wrkd. in the Baltic.
Tarbell, — (C.) U.S.	VI. 90-1, Chesapeake Bay.
Tardy, — (C.) F.	I. 141, Gasparin, Brest Flt.
Tarrant, John (L.)......	IV. 448, Scout, cutting out exped.
Tartue, — (C.) F.	I. 119, Uranie, k. in actn. with Thames.
Tatham, Sandford (C.)	I. 244, Dromedary (T.S.), w. in actn. Martinique.
Tattnall, James Barnwell (L.)	VI. 233-4, Tonnant, cutting out exped.
Taupier, Pierre Isaac (L.Com.) F.	III. 188, Lodi captd. by Racoon.
Tause, Charles (Mid.)	III. 432, Orion, w. Trafalgar.
Tayler, Joseph Needham (L.)	V. 108, Donegal, cutting out exped. VI. 15, C. Sparrow, off Castro de Urdeales.
Taylor, Benjamin William (L.Com.)	III. 477, Dromedary, wrkd. Trinidad.
Taylor, Bridges Watkinson (L.)	II. 262-8, Leander, w. in actn. IV. 44, C. Camilla, capture of Faune; 160, Thames, Shetland Isles; 447, Apollo, Rosas Bay. V. 338, capts. Mérinos (S.S.). VI. 27-8, Adriatic; 119, capture of Isle Paxo, Adriatic.
Taylor, Geo. (Mr. Mt.)	II. 31, Veteran, w. Camperdown.
Taylor, Henry (L.Com.)	V. 448, Olympia captd. off Dieppe.
Taylor, Henry Packhurst (Mr. Mt.)	V. 31, Topaze, cutting out exped.
Taylor, John (A.B.) ...	II. 215, Alcmène, rescues despatches.
Taylor, John (Mid.) ...	V. 35, Cyane, w. in actn.
Taylor, John (C.)	VI. 46, Espiègle off Demerara River; 49, court-martialled.
Taylor, JohnGeo. (Mid.)	II. 196, Vanguard, k. the Nile.
Taylor, Joseph (L.) ...	III. 130. Andromache, k. cutting out exped.
Taylor, Leonard (B.)...	IV. 378, Amethyst, w. in actn.
Taylor, Thomas (P.C.)	I. 303-4, Fortitude, convoy escort, actn. with Richery's Sq.
Taylor, Thos. (Mid.)...	III. 135, Speedy, k. cutting out exped.
Taylor, William (Car.)	V. 74, Confiance, cutting out exped.
Temple, Francis (L.)...	III. 180, Loire, cutting out exped.; 181, pro. Cr.
Temple, John (C.)......	I. 343, Peterel, Nelson's Sq. off Vado. IV. 473, Crescent, wrkd. Jutland.
Templeton, Richd. (A.B.)	III. 246, Centaur, cutting out of the Curieux.
Terragut, Don Juan (Mr.) Sp.	IV. 31, Sp. Ordnance, brig cut out by the bts. of Seahorse.
Terrason, Jean Elie (Cmde.) F.	I. 60, Juste, Brest Flt.
Terry, George (Mid.)...	VI. 118, Boyne, k. in actn.
Tetley, Joseph Swabey (L.)	V. 68, Derwent, capture of Sénégal; 209-10, act. C. Perlen, in actn. off Toulon; 253, C. Guadeloupe, actn. with F. brigs; 254, pro. P.C.
Thaarup, Christian (L.-Com.) Du.	V. 131, Du. Echo captd. by Sylvia.
Theed, John (Mr. Mt.)	V. 178, Africaine, w. in actn.
Thesiger, Sir Fredk. (Cr.)	III. 53-4, A.D.C. to Lord Nelson, Copenhagen.
Thévenard, Henri Alexandre (C.) F.	I. 235, Révolutionnaire captd. by Br. Sq., w. in actn.; 413, Cmde. Sq. at Cape François. II. 5, Wattigny, Ireland exped.; 178, Aquilon; 188, k. the Nile.
Thévenard, Vincent (L.-Com.) F.	IV. 148, Diligent captd. by Renard.

INDEX TO NAVAL OFFICERS 161

Thèvenard, — (C.) F. I. 141, Mont Blanc, Brest Flt. IV. 11, V.A. Dumanoir's court-martial; 194, A. ordnance invention.
Thicknesse, John (C.) IV. 173, Sheldrake with consorts des. Salamandre.
Thierry, — (Pilot) F.... II. 97-8, revolt of convict ship Lady Shore.
Thistlewayte, Frederick (Mid.) III. 416, Colossus, w. Trafalgar.
Thomas, A. Wantner (L.Com.) III. 490, Grappler, wrkd. on the Isles de Chosey.
Thomas, Edw. F. (L.) III. 443, Bellerophon, Trafalgar; 464, pro. P.C.
Thomas, George (L.)... III. 84, w. Egypt exped. V. 349, Minstrel, cutting out exped.
Thomas, Guillaume (C.) F. I. 60, F. Northumberland, Brest Flt.; 413, Sq. at Cape François.
Thomas, Henry (Mid.) VI. 34, Swallow, cutting out exped.
Thomas, Joseph (Mr.) III. 194, Princess Augusta (cutter), actn. off the Texel. V. 99-100, Queen Charlotte (cutter), actn. with F. brig.
Thomas, Morgan (Pr.) IV. 331-3, Carnation, k. in actn.
Thomas, Richard (P.C.) IV. 292, Ocean, Collingwood's Sq. at Syracuse. V. 342, Undaunted, cutting out exped. Agaye.
Thomas, Saml. (L.Com.) V. 445, Alban captd. by Da. gbts.
Thompson, Andw. (L.) II. 48, Irresistible, w. St. Vincent.
Thompson, Charles (Cmde.) I. 240-3-5, Vengeance, Jervis' Sq. capture of Martinique; 249, Guadaloupe.
Thompson, Charles (L.) III. 79, Phœnix, in actn.
Thompson, Grenville (Mid.) III. 406, Royal Sovereign, w. Trafalgar. V. 30, Mr. Mt. Scout, cutting out exped.
Thompson, Henry Clement (L.) III. 196, Merlin, cutting out exped.; 202, des. Shannon (ashore).
Thompson, James Rob. (M.L.) VI. 36, Swiftsure, w. cutting out exped.
Thompson, John (A.B.) II. 46, Captain, St. Vincent.
Thompson, John (L.)... II. 17, Indefatigable, w. in actn.; 19, pro. Cr.
Thompson, John (M.L.) III. 17, Renown, w. cutting out exped.
Thompson, John (Mr.) III. 12, Peterel, in actn.; 189-90, Racoon, w. cutting out exped. IV. 134-5, Pique, k. in actn.
Thompson, John (L.)... III. 275, Narcissus, cutting out exped.
Thompson, John (Gunner) V. 72, Amaranthe, w. in actn.
Thompson, John (C.)... V. 368, Colibri, Sandy Hook, New York. VI. 381, wrkd. at Jamaica.
Thompson, Josiah (L.) V. 331, Medusa, cutting out exped.
Thompson, Norborne (P.C.) IV. 236, Foudroyant, Sidney Smith's Sq. off the Tagus; 438, Perlen, Scheldt exped.
Thompson, Rob. (Mr.Mt.) III. 55 Glatton, w. Copenhagen.
Thompson, Thos. (L.) I. 362, Niger, cutting out exped.
Thompson, Thomas Boulden (P.C.) II. 63-4, 66-7, Leander, Nelson's Sq. at Santa Cruz, w. actn.; 70, at Algiers; 171, Nelson's Flt.; 182-3, 191, 201, the Nile; 205, 259, bears despatches to Earl St. Vincent, Com. Medn. Flt.; 261-4, 266, captd. by Généreux; 267, court-martialled; 268, kntd.; 293, Medn. Flt.; 469, App.
„ Sir Thomas Boulden III. 46, 51, 54, Nelson's Flt., w. Copenhagen.
Thompson, Thomas Brown (L.) III. 135, Kangaroo, w. cutting out exped.
Thompson, William A. (Mid.) IV. 138, Pallas, cutting out exped.
Thompson, — (R.A.) I. 341, London, Com. Sq. off Brest.
Thornborough, Edward (P.C.) I. 66, Latona, crsg.; 139, Channel Flt.; 171, 1st June; 271, Robust, Channel Flt. II. 142-4-5, 162-3, Warren's Sq., capture of Hoche; 297, Formidable, Medn. Flt. III. 264-6, R.A. off the Texel; 381, V.A. Sq. Cadiz. IV. 138, Sq. off the Isle of Aix; 288, Sq. in Palermo Bay; 290-2, Collingwood's Flt. Syracuse; 293, blockading Toulon. VI. 81, Com. at Cork, Ireland.

M

Thorpe, George (L.) ...	II. 67, Terpsichore, w. in actn. Santa Cruz.
Thrakstone, Henry (L.Com.)	V. 448, Snapper captd. off Brest.
Thréouart, Pierre Julien (C.) *F.*	I. 133, Cybèle, Pondicherry ; 388, Port Louis. II. 89–90, repulsed by E.I.C. ships.
Thurn, Count (Cmde.) *Neap.*	II. 312, Caraccioli's court-martial.
Tierro, Don Juan Christovel (C.) *Sp.*	IV. 78, Sp. San Christovel Pano cut out by the bts. of Serpent.
Tillard, James (C.)......	V. 441, Alaart captd. by Da. gbts.
Tiller, John (L.Com.)	III. 482, Blazer captd. in the Baltic.
Timmins, George (Mid.)	V. 161–9, Néréide, k. in actn. Grand Port.
Timmins, John Fam. (C.)*E.I.C.*	III. 250, E.I.C. Royal George, actn. with Linois' Sq. E. Indies.
Tincombe, George (L.)	VI. 309, Liffey, Burmese War.
Tindale, Joseph (L. Com.)	IV. 475, Crane, wrkd. West Hoe.
Tindall, William (L.)...	III. 55 Glatton, w. Copenhagen.
Tinkler, Robert (L.) ...	III. 57, Isis, Copenhagen ; 64, pro. Cr.
Tinley, J. P. (Mid.) ...	II. 80, Monarch, w. Copenhagen.
Tiphaigne or Tiphaine (C.) *F.*	I. 60, 141, Neptune, Brest Flt.
Tippet, George (L.) ...	III. 271, Wilhelmina, in actn.
Tippet, James (C.)	IV. 456, Hawke, fndrd. in the Channel, drnd.
Titterton, Thomas (Pr.)	IV. 9, Cæsar, w. Strachan's actn.
Tobin, George (P.C.)...	IV. 75–6, Princess Charlotte capts. Cyane. VI. 14, Andromache capts. Trave ; 133, gun trials of Eurotas.
Toby, James (B.)	VI. 25, Weasel, k. in actn.
Todd, Andrew (L.) ...	I. 334, Monarch, capture of the Cape of Good Hope ; 413, C. Echo, Colombo exped. II. 429, Queen Charlotte, Keith's Sq. ; 430–8, lost by fire. III. 476, App.
Toker, Thos. Richd. (L.)	III. 443, Colossus, Trafalgar ; 464, pro. Cr.
Tom, Robt. Brown (L.)	III. 57, Glatton, Copenhagen ; 64, pro. Cr.
Tomkinson, James (L.)	IV. 372, Comet, in actn. V. 172, C. Otter, Isle de la Passe ; 175, Isle Bourbon ; 204, act. C. Ceylon, capture of the Isle of France.
Tomlinson, Jas. Ward (Mid.)	VI. 312–26–28, Burmese War.
Tomlinson, Nicholas (C.)	I. 364–5, Suffisante capts. Revanche.
Tomlinson, Philip (Mr.-Mt.)	IV. 206, k. in actn. Copenhagen.
Tonyn, Patrick (L.) ...	I. 325, Stag, in actn.
Toohig, John (Mr.-at-Arms)	III. 426, Téméraire, Trafalgar.
Tooley, Robert (Mid.)	II. 61, Prince George, w. in actn. Cadiz.
Torin, Robt. (C.)*E.I.C.*	III. 22, E.I.C. Coutts, in actn. ; 250, actn. with Linois' Sq. E. Indies.
Torkington, Robert (M.C.)	III. 85, w. Egypt exped.
Torrens, Robert (M.C.)	V. 222–3–5, capture of Anholt.
Torres, Don Antonio de (L.Com.) *Sp.*	IV. 271, Sp. San Josef captd. by Grasshopper.
Torres, Don Josef de (C.) *Sp.*	II. 59, St. Vincent, degraded.
Torris, Don Francisco de (C.) *Sp.*	III. 133, Sp. Gamo captd. by Speedy.
Toruquist, — (C.) *Swd.*	IV. 299, Swd. Dristigheten, Br. Swd. Flt. Oro Rds.
Tothill, John (M.L.)...	VI. 28, Apollo, cutting out exped.
Totty, John (P.C.) ...	I. 410, Alfred, Christian's Sq. capture of Grenada.
Totty, Thomas (P.C.)	II. 112, Alfred, Porto Rico. III. 481, R.A. Invincible, wrkd. near Yarmouth.

INDEX TO NAVAL OFFICERS 163

Touch-Tréville René Madeleine La (R.A.) F. — III. 64, Com. invas. flotilla, Boulogne; 163, Com. St. Domingo exped.; 176, V.A. Toulon; 237, Bucentaure; 239-40, Com. at Toulon; 241, d.

Touffet, Claude (L.) F. — II. 304, Généreux, Ancona. III. 186-7, C., Duguay-Trouin engages Boadicea; 386, 434, Trafalgar. IV. 3-5-8, captd. in Strachan's actn.; 9, k. in actn.

Touffet, Nicolas (C.) F. — VI. 227-8, Légère, actn. with Pilot.

Tourelles, De (Pilot) F. — I. 243, capture of Martinique.

Tourneur, Laurent (L.-Com.) F. — III. 219, invas. flotilla; 220, pro. C. VI. 3, Magnanime, Toulon Flt.

Tourpie, — (C.) F. ... — III. 30, Quidproquo (priv.) captd. by Gipsy.

Tower, John (P.C.) ... — IV. 157, Iris, off Rochefort. V. 344, Curaçoa, capture of Languelia.

Townshend, Lord Jas. (L.) — IV. 101, Atlas, Duckworth's actn.; 104, pro. Cr.; 248-9, C. Halifax, Norfolk, U.S. V. 369, Æolus, Halifax.

Towry, George Henry (C.) — I. 214, Dido, Corsica; 321, off Toulon; 322-4, capture of Minerve; 343, Diadem, Nelson's Sq. blockading Genoa. II. 34-8, 42-4-8, St. Vincent; 302, Uranie, in actn. Isle of Aix.

Tozer, Aaron (Mid.) ... — IV. 70, Phœnix, w. in actn. VI. 17, L. Undaunted; 19, w. capture of Ponza.

Tozer, Caleb Evans (Mid.) — VI. 96, Contest, cutting out exped.

Tracey, John (Mr.Mt.) — II. 81, Ardent, w. Camperdown. IV. 305, L.Com. Linnet, capts. Courier. VI. 8-9, captd. by Gloire, pro Cr.; 381, App.

Tracs, Chas. (Mr.Mt.) — IV. 78, Serpent, cutting out exped.

Tracy, Francis M'Mahon (L.) — III. 171, Hydra, cutting out exped.

Tracy, John (Mid.) ... — III. 247, Centaur, w. cutting out exped.

Tranquelléon, — (C.)F. — I. 60, Révolution, Brest Flt.

Travers, Eaton (Mid.) — III. 294, Hercule, in actn. Curaçoa. IV. 440, L. Scheldt exped. V. 258-60, Impérieuse, cutting out expeds. VI. 34-5, in actn. Adriatic.

Travers, John (Mid.)... — VI. 166, Avon, w. in actn.

Travis, Samuel (C.) U.S. — VI. 90, U.S. Surveyor cut out by the bts. of Narcissus.

Treacher, Samuel Sharpe (L.Com.) — VI. 388, Holly, wrkd. off St. Sebastian.

Trefahar, John (L.-Com.) — II. 457, Berbice, wrkd. Dominica.

Tremenhere, Walter (M.L.) — I. 241, capture of Martinique.

Tremlett, Wm. Henry Brown (P.C.) — V. 441, Alcmène, wrkd. off Nantes.

Treslong, Bloys Van (Cmde.) Du. — III. 298, capture of Surinam.

Treslong, Van (C.) Du. — II. 76-9, Du. Brutus, Camperdown; 87-8, actn. with Endymion.

Triplet, William (B.)... — IV. 331, Carnation, in actn.

Tripp, George (P.C.)... — II. 268, Captain, Captain Boulden Thompson's court-martial.

Tripp, George (C.) ... — II. 475, Nassau (T.S.), wrkd. Holland.

Trippe, — (L.) U.S.... — III. 303, w. in actn. at Tripoli.

Trist, Robert (Mr.Mt.) — IV. 307, Confiance, cutting out expcd., pro. L.

Tritton, Ewell (C.) ... — V. 30, Kingfisher, Adriatic; 263, crsg. VI. 26, Adriatic.

Trogoff, Comte de (R.A.) F. — I. 73, Com. Flt. at Toulon; 76, superseded.

Trogoff, — (C.) F. ... — III. 268-9-71, Psyché (priv.) engages Wilhelmina.

Trolle, — (C.) Swd. ... — IV. 303, Swd. Camilla, Br. Swd. Flt. at Nyborg.

Trollope, George (L.) — II. 81, Triumph, w. Camperdown. IV. 294, C. Electra, Medn.; 474, wrkd. Sicily. V. 317-18, Griffon, actn. with invas. flotilla, Dieppe.

Trollope, Henry (P.C.)	I. 40–4–5, Rainbow capts. Hébé; 342, Glatton, crsg.; 372–5, actn. with F. frigates; 376, kntd. II. 75–8, 81, Russel, Camperdown; 88, created knight.
,, Sir Henry ...	
Troubridge, Thomas (P.C.)	I. 142, Castor captd. by F. Sq.; 161, 186, prisoner on board F. Sans Pareil, 1st June; 206, Culloden, Spithead mutiny; 229, recapture of Castor; 297–8, 300, actn. off Hyères; 306, Troubridge's Sq. off Cape Matapan, N. Archipelago; 350–1, Straits of Gibraltar; 439, App. II. 34–5–7–9, 43, 45–8, 58, St. Vincent; 63–7, Nelson's Sq. Santa Cruz; 171–3–6, Medn. Flt.; 183–90, the Nile; 210, Naples; 219, Medn.; 305–6, blockade Naples; 307, Palermo; 315–16, at St. Elmo; 320–1, 325, blockade of Alexandria; 440–4, blockade of Malta. IV. 51, R.A., Baronet, Blenheim, Com. at Madras; 465, V.A. Blenheim, fndrs. E. Indies, drnd.
,, Sir Thomas, Bart.	
Troude, Amable Gilles (C.) *F.*	III. 112, Formidable; 115–17, actn. in the Gut of Gibraltar; 118, pro. C. de vaisseau; 479, App. IV. 48, Suffren, Sq. crsg.; 391–3, Medn. V. 18, D'Haupoult; 21–2, captd. by Pompée and consorts.
Troughton, Thomas (Mr.)	I. 275, Irresistible, w. Isle Groix. II. 81, Russel, w. Camperdown.
Trounce, Stephen (Mr.)	III. 434, Britannia, w. Trafalgar.
Trowbridge, Edward Thomas (P.C.)	IV. 162–4, Greyhound, capture of Du. Pallas. VI. 232, Armide, Chandeleur Isles.
Truguet, Laurent Jean François (R.A.) *F.*	I. 49, exped. to Italy. II. 2–3, 32, V.A., Minister of Marine. III. 170, Vengeur, Brest; 215, Com. at Brest.
Trullet, Jean F. Timothée (sen.) (C.) *F.*	II. 178, Guerrier; 186–7, 199, the Nile.
Trullet, Jean F. Timothée (jun.) (C.) *F.*	II. 178, Timoléon; 193–5, destd. at the Nile.
Truscott, Wm. (P.C.)	I. 189, Ganges, Montagu's Sq. off Ushant.
Trusson, Charles A. (M.L.)	IV. 244, Glatton, cutting out exped.
Truxton, Thos. (Cmde.) *U.S.*	II. 363–4, U.S. Constellation capts. F. Insurgente. III. 1–2, actn. with F. Vengeance; 3, Sheriff of Philadelphia. V. 268, U.S. Constellation.
Tryon, Robert (L.) ...	V. 109, Phipps, w. in actn.
Tucker, Edward (P.C.)	V. 191, Dover; 194, capture of Amboyna; 447, wrkd. Madras Rds.
Tucker, Nicholas (L.)	II. 359, Dædalus, in actn.
Tucker, Robert (C.) ...	III. 290–1, Surinam captd. by the Du. at Curaçoa; 490, App.
Tucker, Thomas Tudor (Mid.)	IV. 30, Northumberland, cutting out exped.; 380, C. Epervier, off St. Pierre. V. 23, Cherub, Guadaloupe. VI. 150–2–3, capture of U.S. Essex; 154, w. in actn.
Tucker, Tudor (C)......	II. 462, Hunter, wrkd. Virginia.
Tucker, — (L)	I. 352, Gibraltar, Straits of Gibraltar.
Tucket, Hon. George (Mid.)	III. 55, Amazon, k. Copenhagen.
Tuckey, Jas. Kingston (L.)	II. 370, Fox, on board Sibylle in actn. with Forte.
Tullidge, Joseph Crew (L.)	V. 177–80, Africaine, w. in actn.; 183, pro. Cr.
Tullock, Andrew (L.)	VI. 6, in actn. Cuxhaven.
Tupman, George (L.)	IV. 306, Meleager, cutting out exped.
Tupper, Cary (L.)	I. 212, Victory, k. in actn. Bastia.
Tupper, Charles (L.)...	I. 87, in actn. Toulon.
Turner, Abraham (Mr.-Mt.)	III. 432, Africa, w. Trafalgar.
Turner, John (L.)	III. 105, Hannibal, w. Algesiras.
Turner, Joseph (C.) ...	I. 304, Tisiphone (F.S.), convoy escort.
Turner, Robert (Mid.)	IV. 248, Halifax, Hampton Rds., U.S.
Turner, William (S.)...	V. 250, Alacrity, w. in actn.

INDEX TO NAVAL OFFICERS 165

Turquand, Wm. James (L.)	II. 162, Canada, in actn. pro. Cr. III. 4, C. Railleur; 5-6, capture of Pallas; 477, Hound, wrkd. Shetland, drnd.
Twysden, Thomas (C.)	I. 439, Pylades, wrkd. Shetland. II. 154, Révolutionnaire, crsg. Channel; 399, capts. Bordelais (priv.).
Tyler, Charles (P.C.)...	I. 284, Diadem; 290, actn. off Genoa; 297, off Hyères. II. 289, Warrior, Keith's Flt. off Cadiz; 469, App. III. 47, Copenhagen; 384, Tonnant; 410-12, w. Trafalgar. Vl. 262, V.A. Com. at the Cape of Good Hope.
Tynmore, Jas. (M.L.)	III. 432, Africa, w. Trafalgar.
Tyrason, Don Miguel (C.) *Sp.*	II. 60-1, w. in actn. Cadiz.
Tyrrel, Edward (L.-Com.)	I. 433, Advice, wrkd. Honduras, crew saved.
Ulick, Geo. (Mr.) *U.S.*	VI. 232, in actn. Chandeleur Isles.
Ullock, Thomas (Pr.)	VI. 27-8, Apollo, w. cutting out exped.
Umfreville, John Brand (C.)	VI. 231, Childers, in actn. New Orleans.
Undrell, John (L.)......	IV. 328, Blossom, cutting out exped.
Uniacke, James (M.L.)	VI. 234, w. in actn. Malheureux Isles.
Uniacke, Robert (Mid.)	VI. 234, w. in actn. Malheureux Isles.
Unshank, Richard (B.)	V. 239, Amphion, k. in actn. off Lissa.
Upton, Clotworthy (P.-C.)	IV. 201, Sibylle, crsg. Great Belt; 372, capts. Espiègle. VI. 158, Junon, crsg. off Cape Sable; 200, crsg. off Marblehead, U.S.
Uriarte, Don Francisco (Cmde.) *Sp.*	III. 386, Sp. Santissima Trinidad; 428, captd. at Trafalgar; 457, destd.
Urmston, George Constantine (L.)	VI. 84, Marlborough, cutting out exped.
Urtesabel, Don Manuel (C.) *Sp.*	II. 110, Sp. Santa Cecilia destd. at Trinidad to prevent capture.
Usherwood, Wm. (L.)	V. 266-7, Sabine, cutting out exped.
Ussher, Thomas (act. L.)	I. 397-8, Pelican, in actn. IV. 132-3, L.Com. Colpoys, cutting out exped., pro. Cr.; 337-8, C. Redwing, actn. with Sp. gbts. V. 337, Hyacinth, in actn. off Spain. VI. 17-19, Undaunted, Medn.; 35, Adriatic; 121, conveys Napoleon to Elba.
Val, William De (C.) *Du.*	IV. 163-4, Du. Batavia captd. by Greyhound.
Valdés, Don Cayetano (C.) *Sp.*	III. 386, Sp. Neptuno; 434-7, Trafalgar.
Vale, Stephen (Mr.) ...	VI. 119, Bacchante, Adriatic.
Valentine, David (Mr.-Mt.)	I. 119, Thames, w. in actn.
Valentine, George (B.)	VI. 288, Infernal (bomb.), w. Algiers.
Valin, — (L.) *F.*	V. 17, Niemen, in actn.
Valk, — (C.) *Du.*	I. 416, Du. Bellona captd. at the Cape of Good Hope.
Valkenburg, — (C.) *Du.*	I. 415, Du. Van Tromp captd. at the Cape of Good Hope.
Vallack, Richd. Glyn (L.)	IV. 354, Seahorse, in actn.
Valle, De (A.) *Por.* ...	I. 262, Por. Sq. with Howe's Channel Flt.
Vallego, Don Gonzales (C.) *Sp.*	II. 59, St. Vincent, dismissed.
Vallentes, — (C.) *F.* ...	III. 256, Mozambique (priv.) cut out by the bts. of Emerald.
Valliant, Paul H. (Mid.)	I. 87, in actn. Toulon.
Vandangel, — (C.) *F.*	I. 141, Révolutionnaire, Brest Flt.
Vandeput, — (V.A.)...	I. 354, St. Albans, Sq. in the Tagus.
Vanderhart, Willem Augustus (C.) *Du.*	VI. 279, Du. Amstel, Algiers.
Vander-Veld, Gillet (C.) *Du.*	V. 43-4, Du. Zephyr captd. by Diana.

Vansittart, Henry (Mid.)	I. 78, Victory, w. in actn. Toulon. III. 121, C. Abergavenny, Port Royal, W. Indies. VI. 133, gun trials of Eurotas.
Vanstabel, — (Cmde.) F.	I. 60, Tigre, Brest Flt.; 66, in actn.; 68, Brest; 140, pro. R.A.; 142-3, 147, Sq. crsg.; 188-91, 259-61, Brest Flt.
Vashon, James (P.C.)	I. 227, St. Albans, crsg. Channel. II. 285, Neptune, Bridport's Sq. off Brest; 297, Medn. Flt.
Vashon, James G. (L.)	II. 374, Sibylle, in actn. V. 357, C. Thalia, convoy escort W. Indies.
Vassall, Nathaniel (L.)	II. 196, Vanguard, w. the Nile.
Vaughan, Henry (L.)...	I. 199, Russel, 1st June, pro. Cr. IV. 456, C. Imogène, fndrd. Leeward Isles, crew saved.
Vaughan, John T. (1st cl. Vol.)	VI. 136, Eurotas, k. in actn.
Veal, John (Mid.)	V. 126, Thames, cutting out exped.
Vega, François (L. Com.) F.	I. 371, Utile captd. by Southampton.
Vence, Jean Gaspar (R.A.) F.	I. 262-4, Sq. convoy escort Belleisle.
Venour, William (C.)...	III. 490, Calypso, fndrd. Jamica, drnd.
Verdoorn, — (C.) Du.	II. 76-9, Du. Delft captd. at Camperdown.
Vernon, Frederick (L.)	V. 40, Implacable, in actn. Baltic. VI. 11, C. Challenger; 11, 16, Medn. Sq. St. Sebastian.
Vesconte, Henry Le (L. Com.)	III. 68, Mallard, actn. off Etaples.
Vesconte, James Le (M.L.)	III. 406, Royal Sovereign, w. Trafalgar.
Vesconte, Philip Le (Mid.)	III. 55, Monarch, w. Copenhagen.
Vesey, Francis (C.) ...	II. 378, Amaranthe capts. F. Vengeur (priv.).
Vesey, Matthew (B.)...	V. 41, Bellerophon, w. in actn.
Veyer, — Le (C.) F....	IV. 116, Impétueux destd. by Br. Sq.
Victor, George (M.L.)	V. 255, Unité, cutting out exped.
Victor, John Geo. (Mid.)	III. 275, Maidstone, w. cutting out exped.
Vidal, — (C.) F.	IV. 271-2, Revanche (priv.), in actn. with Curieux.
Vieugna, — (C.) Neap.	IV. 123, Neap. Minerva, off Gaeta, Italy.
Vigney, De (C.) F. ...	I. 45, Hébé captd. by Rainbow.
Vignot, Jean François (C.) F.	I. 141, Montagne, Brest Flt.
Villamil, Don F. (C.) Sp.	II. 254, Sp. Pomona, actn. with Lion.
Villaret-Joyeuse, Louis Thomas (Cmde.) F.	I. 60, Trajan, Brest Flt.; 136, R.A. Côte d'Or, Com. at Toulon; 141, Montagne; 142-4, Flt. crsg.; 148-9, 153-5-8-9, 29th May; 160-2, 166, 181-4, 187-90-3, 1st June; 195, V.A.; 259, Com. Brest Flt.; 261, crsg.; 264, 268-70, Brest; 271-3-6, actn. off Isle Groix. II. 3, superseded. III. 163, Com. St. Domingo exped.; 247-8, 348, Gvr. of Martinique. IV. 80, A., Gvr. of Martinique. V. 70-2, capture of Martinique; 73, dismissed.
Villavicencio, Don Augustine (C.) Sp.	II. 59, St. Vincent, dismissed.
Villavicencio, Don Rafaël (C.) Sp.	III. 342, Sp. Firme, F. Sp. Flt. Toulon.
Villegris, Guil. Jean Noël La (C.) F.	I. 141, Achille, Brest Flt. III. 334, Mont Blanc, Toulon Flt.; 386, pro. Cmde.; 434, Trafalgar.
Villemadrin, C. E. L'Hospitalier (C.) F.	III. 334, Swiftsure, Toulon Flt.; 386, 413-15, Trafalgar. IV. 11, received by Napoleon.
Villeneuve, Alexandre Ducrest (C.) F.	II. 178, Justice, the Nile; 269, Décade captd. by Magnanime and consort. VI. 122-3, Alcmène captd. by Venerable and consort.

INDEX TO NAVAL OFFICERS 167

Villeneuve, P. C. J. Bap. Silv. (Cmde.) *F.*	I. 295, Toulon Rds.; 349, R.A. Formidable, F. Sp. Flt. Toulon; 351, Medn. II. 3–4, 23, Brest; 168–9, Malta exped.; 178, Aboukir Bay, Guillaume Tell; 193–4–99, the Nile; 212, blockaded in Malta; 445, capture of Malta. III. 216, invas. flotilla; 242–3, Bucentaure, Com. Toulon Flt.; 308–9, Ferrol; 311, off Brest; 328–30–1, Ferrol; 332, Cadiz; 334, Toulon; 336–9, Toulon; 340, Carthagena; 341–2, Cadiz Bay; 343, Martinique; 344–5–8–50–5, crsg. W. Indies; 363–5–76, 377–9, Calder's actn.; 384–5, Cadiz; 386–90, 394–6–9, 401, Trafalgar; 427, captd.; 464, Villeneuve's line of battle; 496, App. IV. 1, superseded; 11, d. at Paris; 63–72–3, 78–9, 85, comments on Villeneuve's Flt.
Villeneuve, — (L.) *F.*	V. 242, Favourite, in actn. off Lissa.
Villogomez, Don Diego (C.) *Sp.*	II. 413, Sp. Amfitrite, Sq. crsg. W. Indies.
Vincent, Bernard (L.-Com.) *F.*	V. 47–8, Seine destd. at Guadaloupe.
Vincent, Richard Budd (C.)	IV. 13–15-16, Arrow captd. by Incorruptible; 17, pro. P.C.; 456, App.
Vine, Geo. Ballard (L.)	IV. 185, Orpheus, cutting out exped.
Vine, Henry Loveday (M.L.)	IV. 438, Aigle, w. Scheldt exped.
Violett, James (L.Com.)	IV. 474, Raposa destd. at Carthagena.
Violette, Pierre François (C.) *F.*	IV. 48, Magnanime, Rochefort Sq.; 444, F. Majestueux, Toulon Flt. V. 315, R.A. Toulon.
Vitré, John Dennis De (L.Com.)	II. 132, Biter, crsg. off Ostende.
Vrignaud, Joseph Marie (C.) *F.*	III. 209, Marengo, Pondicherry; 250, Linois' Sq., actn. with E.I.C. ships. IV. 131, captd. by London, w. in actn.
Vyvian, William (M.L.)	III. 119, Melpomène, w. cutting out exped.
Vyvyan, Abel (C.) *E.I.C.*	II. 89, E.I.C. Canton, repulse of Sercey's F. Sq.
Wainwright, John (P.C.)	V. 66, Chiffonne, in actn. Persian Gulf. VI. 175, Tonnant, Chesapeake Bay; 180, capture of Washington.
Wakefield, Arthur (Mid.)	VI. 178, Hebrus, in actn. Bladensburg.
Wakeham, C. (Mid.)...	VI. 374, w. Navarino.
Walcott, John Edward (P.C.)	VI. 270–4, Tyne, in actn. Cuba.
Waldeck, — (C.) *Du.*	II. 343, Du. Guelderland blockaded in the Texel.
Waldegrave, Granville George (P.C.)	V. 125, Thames, crsg. off Naples; 127, cutting out exped.; 209–10, Volontaire, in actn. off Toulon. VI. 17, cutting out exped. Medn.
,, Hon. Granville George	
Waldegrave, Hon. William (P.C.)	I. 72, Courageux, Flt. off Toulon.
Waldegrave, Hon. William (V.A.)	I. 342, Barfleur, recapture of Nemesis. II. 34, 38, 48, St. Vincent; 58, pro. to a colonial post.
Waldegrave, Hon. William (L.)	IV. 448, Ville de Paris, cutting out exped.
Waldegrave, Hon. William (1st cl. Vol.)	V. 239, Amphion, w. in actn. off Lissa. VI. 21–3, Mid. Bacchante, cutting out expeds.
Wales, Rchd. Walter (C.)	VI. 158–60, Epervier captd. by U.S. Peacock; 387, App.
Walker, Benjamin (C.)	V. 47, Rosamond capts. Papillon.
Walker, Harry (L.) ...	IV. 168–9, Galatea; 240–1, k. cutting out expeds.
Walker, Henry (L.) ...	VI. 288, Leander, w. Algiers.
Walker, James (P.C.)	II. 75–8, Monmouth, Camperdown. III. 46, Isis, Copenhagen; 186, Vanguard capts. Creole; 291, crsg. IV. 236, Bedford Sidney Smith's Sq. off the Tagus.
Walker, John (L.)	II. 394, Adamant, cutting out exped.
Walker, Robert (L.) ...	V. 199, capture of Banda Neira.
Walker, R. G. W. (M.L.)	II. 80, Powerful, w. Camperdown.

Walker, Wm. (L. Com.)	I. 326–8, Rose, actn. with F. privs.
Walker, William Hovenden (L.)	IV. 264, Confiance, cutting out exped.
Walker, — (B.)	IV. 75, Swift, cutting out exped.
Wall, — (Mid.)	III. 280, Galatea, k. cutting out exped.
Wallace, Sir James (P.C.)	I. 127, Monarch, Martinique exped.; 408, V.A. Romney Com. at Newfoundland.
Wallace, John (L.) ...	III. 424, 436, Téméraire, Trafalgar.
Waller, Edmund (L.)	III. 114, Superb, w. in actn.
Waller, John (P.C.) ...	II. 61, Emerald, Cadiz; 63, Nelson's Sq. at Teneriffe; 66, Santa Cruz.
Waller, John (L.)	IV. 221, 230, Thunderer, w. Dardanelles.
Waller, John (C.)	IV. 77–8, Serpent bts. cut out Sp. San Christovel Pano 461, fndrd. Jamaica, drnd.
Waller, John (Gunner)	VI. 26, Kingfisher, cutting out exped.
Waller, Thomas Moutray (P.C.)	II. 206, Emerald, E. Indies. III. 12, Cadiz Bay.
Waller, William (L.)	I. 392, Victorious, in actn.
Wallington, Chas. (Mid.)	IV. 100, Superb, w. Duckworth's actn.
Wallis, Henry (Quartermaster)	III. 139–41, Beaulieu, cutting out exped.
Wallis, James (C.)	II. 354–6, loss of Proserpine; 474, App. III. 185, Naiad, crsg. off Brest.
Wallis, Provo William Parry (L.)	VI. 65, Shannon capts. U.S. Chesapeake; 66, pro. Cr.
Walpole, William (L.)	V. 344, w. in actn. Languelia.
Walpole, Hon. Wm. (L.)	III. 183, Minerve, cutting out exped.
Walters, Peter (Mr. Mt.)	II. 196, Minotaur, k. the Nile.
Walton, Jacob (P.C.)...	V. 447, Amethyst, wrkd. Plymouth Sound.
Warburton, Benj. (L.)	III. 135, Speedy, cutting out exped.
Ward, Charles (Vol.)...	V. 105, Quebec, cutting out exped.
Ward, William (L.) ...	IV. 134–5, Pique, w. in actn.
Wardenburg, Johan. Fred. Chr. (C.) *Du.*	VI. 279, Du. Eendragt, Algiers.
Ware, William (A.B.)	IV. 252, Melampus, deserter.
Waring, Henry (P.C.)	III. 296, Serapis, capture of Surinam.
Waring, Henry (M.L.)	V. 16, Amethyst, w. in actn.
Waring, James (L.) ...	VI. 13, Royalist, w. in actn.
Warrand, Thomas (L.)	III. 27, Minotaur, cutting out exped. V. 324, L.Com. Sealark, capts. Ville-de-Caen; 325, pro. Cr.
Warre, Henry (P.C.)...	I. 328–9, Mermaid capts. Républicaine and Brutus.
Warren, Charles Gayton (L.)	II. 381, Alcmène, cutting out exped.
Warren, Frederick (P.C.)	IV. 473, Meleager, wrkd. Jamaica. V. 39, Melpomène, actn. with Da. gbts.
Warren, Sir John Borlase, Bart., K.B. (Cmde.)	I. 222–6, Flora, Sq. crsg., capture of F. frigates; 233–4, K.B., Sq. crsg. des. F. frigates; 259, Sq. off Brest; 271–8–9, Pomone, Quiberon exped.; 330–1, crsg.; 355–7, Sq. crsg. engages F. frigates; 381–3–4, des. F. Andromaque; 437, App. II. 31, 95, Sq. crsg. des. Calliope; 119, Pomone, sent home; 142, Canada, Sq. off Ireland; 143–6, 149–51, 162–3, capture of Hoche and consorts; 228–9, Sq. off France; 450, R.A. Renown; 451–2, Cadiz exped.; 453, 460, 466, App. III. 15–16, Sq. crsg. off the Penmarcks; 26–7, off Vigo; 72–6, Medn.; 78, Porto Ferrajo; 80–1, 97, Valetta. IV. 88, V.A. Foudroyant; 89, Madeira; 113–15, 129, Sq. crsg; 130, capture of Marengo; 459, App. VI. 82–3, A. San Domingo; 90–5, Com. in Chesapeake Bay; 168, recalled.
Warren, Robert (Mid.)	III. 139–40, Robust, k. cutting out exped.
Warren, Samuel (P.C.)	III. 356, Glory; 361–2, Calder's actn. IV. 279, Diadem, Monte Video exped. V. 303–9, Présidente, capture of Java.

INDEX TO NAVAL OFFICERS 169

Warren, William Smith (Mid.)	III. 417, Achille, w. Trafalgar.
Warren, — (Mr.Mt.)...	V. 250, Alacrity, k. in actn.
Warrington, Lewis (C.) U.S.	VI. 159–61, U.S. Peacock capts. Epervier; 258, 261, 265, crsg.; 266–9, capts. E.I.C. Nautilus.
Waterface, Wm. (L.)...	IV. 447, Tigre, cutting out exped.
Waters, John (A.B.) ...	VI. 64–5, U.S. Chesapeake, deserter, drnd.
Waters, John (Mid.) ...	II. 323, w. in actn. Acre.
Waters, John Levi (L.)	II. 197, Swiftsure, the Nile; 210, pro. Cr.
Watkins, Frederick (L.)	I. 310–12, Blanche, in actn.; 313, pro. Cr.; 333, C. Resource, capture of Grenada. III. 8, Néréide capts. F. Vengeance (priv.); 38–9, 290, capture of Curaçoa.
Watkins, — (L.)	V. 59, E.I.C. Wasp, capture of St. Paul's, Isle Bourbon; 66, E.I.C. Nautilus, Persian Gulf.
Watling, John Wyatt (L.)	V. 142–4, Sirius, capture of Isle Bourbon; 146–8, Isle de la Passe; 155–6, 163–5, 171, Grand Port.
Watson, Christopher (L.)	II. 88, Lancaster, Camperdown, pro. Cr.
Watson, Edward (L.)	IV. 244, Glatton, k. cutting out exped.
Watson, James (L.)...	III. 6, Harpy, in actn.; 477, L.Com. Mastiff, wrkd. Yarmouth.
Watson, James R. (C.)	II. 457, Trompeuse, wrkd. Kinsale.
Watson, J. W. (Mid.)	III. 431, Leviathan, w. Trafalgar. IV. 131, London, w. in actn.
Watson, Joshua Rowley (L.)	I. 241, capture of Martinique. IV. 201, C. Inflexible, Copenhagen. V. 92, Alfred, Sq. at Guadaloupe; 208, Implacable, Flt. off Toulon.
Watson, Robert (P.C.)	I. 324, Isis, Sq. crsg. Norway.
Watson, Wm. (Mr.Mt.)	III. 406, Royal Sovereign, w. Trafalgar,
Watson, William Henry (L.) U.S.	VI. 79–80–2, U.S. Argus captd. by Pelican.
Watson, — (L.Com.)...	I. 443, Shark captd. through mutiny of crew.
Watt, Geo.Thos. L. (L.)	VI. 57–60, Shannon, k. in actn. with U.S. Chesapeake.
Watt, John (Mid.)	V. 101, Surveillante, cutting out exped.
Watt, Thos. Alex. (Mid.)	III. 275, w. cutting out exped.
Watt, William (S.)	VI. 328, Arachne, Burmese War.
Watts, George Edward (L.)	IV. 204, Comus, in actn.; 244–5, cutting out exped., pro. Cr. VI. 169, C. Jasseur, Chesapeake Bay.
Watts, Robert (Mid.)...	II. 67, w. in actn. Santa Cruz.
Watts, Wm. (act.Mr.)	VI. 32–3, Wizard, w. in actn.
Watts, Wm. A. (A.B.)	VI. 270, Eliza, w. in actn.
Wauchope, Robert (L.)	V. 165, Magicienne; 171, Isle of France.
Wearing, Thos. (M.L.)	III. 429, Conqueror, w. Trafalgar.
Weatherhead, John (L.)	II. 67, Theseus, k. in actn. Santa Cruz.
Weatherston, Jas. (Mid.)	II. 196, Vanguard, w. the Nile.
Weaver, Thos. (M.L.)	III. 129, Phœbe, in actn.
Webb, Chas. (L.Com.)	II. 228, Marquis Cobourg (cutter) capts. F. Revanche (priv.).
Webb, Chas. Jas. (Mid.)	II. 330, Theseus burnt at Acre, k.
Webb, Edwd. (Mr.Mt.)	VI. 21–22, Weasel, cutting out exped.; 23, act. L.
Webley, William Henry (L.)	II. 197, Zealous, the Nile; 210 pro. Cr. IV. 200, C. Centaur, Copenhagen; 275, capture of Madeira; 298, Baltic Flt.; 301, actn. with Rus. Flt.
Webley, — (L.)	I. 217, Juno, Toulon Rds.
Webster, John (Mr.Mt.)	IV. 447–9, Cumberland, w. cutting out exped.
Webster, Robert (L.)	II. 81, Belliqueux, k. Camperdown.
Webster, William (Mr.)	I. 175, Defence, k. 1st June.
Webster, William (L.)	IV. 270, Renommée, cutting out exped.
Weeks, John (L.Com.)	V. 320–2, Growler, in actn.; 324, pro. Cr.
Weir, Henry (L.Com.)	IV. 466, Ferreter captd. by Da. gbts. V. 325–6, C. Calypso, actn. with Da. Sq.; 327, pro. P.C.
Weir, — (L.)	IV. 257, Spartan, k. cutting out exped.
Weiss, William (Mid.)	VI. 57, Otter, cutting out exped.; 149, act.L. Néréide; 153–9, Isle of France exped.
Weld, Richard (L.) ...	VI. 259, Leander and U.S. frigates.

Wells, George (L.) ...	VI. 40-1, Amelia, k. in actn.
Wells, Hy. (L.) *U.S.*	VI. 102, Canadian Lakes.
Wells, John (P.C.) ...	II. 75-9, Lancaster, Camperdown.
Wells, Martin (Mid.)	II. 196, Minotaur, w. the Nile.
Wells, Thomas (P.C.)	I. 222, Melampus, Warren's Sq. crsg. ; 297-8, Defence, actn. off Hyères. II. 285, Glory, Sq. off Brest ; 297, Medn. Flt.
Wells, Thomas (L.) ...	IV. 123, Juno, in actn. Italy ; 369, act.L.Com. Cruiser, actn. with Da. gbts., pro. Cr. V. 319, C. Phipps, actn. off Boulogne.
Welmoes, — (Mid.) *Da.*	III. 59-60, in actn. Copenhagen.
Welsh, Charles (C.) ...	V. 442, Dominica, fndrd. near Tortola, drnd.
Welsh, John (A.B.) ...	VI. 270, Eliza, w. in actn.
Welsh, Richard (C.) ...	V. 442, Bustler, wrkd. France.
Welsh, Thomas (L.) ...	VI. 81, Pelican, in actn.
Wemyss, Charles (P.C.)	III. 142, Unicorn, crsg. Quiberon Bay.
Wemyss, Francis (Mid.)	IV. 367, Euryalus, cutting out exped.
Wemyss, James (M.C.)	III. 414, Bellerophon, w. Trafalgar.
Wemyss, James (C.) ...	VI. 34, Pylades, in actn. Port D'Anzo, Adriatic.
Wesley, George Nepean (Mr.Mt.)	VI. 287, Impregnable, w. Algiers.
West, Edward (Mid.)	II. 442, Foudroyant, w. in actn.
West, Henry (Mr.Mt.)	III. 432, Africa, w. Trafalgar.
West, John (P.C.)	IV. 385, Excellent, in actn. Rosas Bay. V. 35, off Trieste ; 208, Sultan, Flt. off Toulon.
West, — (S.)	VI. 274, Tyne, cutting out exped.
Westcott, George Blagden (P.C.)	I. 139, Impregnable, Channel Flt. II. 171, Majestic, Nelson's Flt. off Cadiz ; 189-90, 196, k. the Nile.
Western, John (L.) ...	I. 98-9, Syren, k. in actn. Holland.
Western, Thomas (P.C.)	II. 387, Tamar capts. Républicaine ; 236, London, Sq. off the Tagus.
Westphal, George Augustus (Mid.)	III. 421-5, Victory, w. Trafalgar. VI. 85, L. Marlborough ; 87, w. in actn. Chesapeake Bay ; 95, Sceptre, Ocracoke exped., Chesapeake Bay.
Westphal, Philip (L.)...	VI. 97, Junon, in actn. Delaware Bay.
Westropp, Palms (M.L.)	III. 417, Achille, w. Trafalgar.
Wetherall, Frederick Augustus (C.)	V. 47-8, Observateur, actn. with F. frigates.
Whaley, Thomas (L.)	VI. 21-5, Weasel, w. cutting out exped.
Wharrie, George (Mid.)	III. 416, Colossus, w. Trafalgar.
Wheatland, Jas. (Mt.)	III. 20, cutting out exped. Dunkerque.
Wheeler, Thomas (Gunner)	V. 216, Hawk, cutting out exped.
Whimper, Wm. (Mid.)	III. 55, Edgar, w. Copenhagen.
Whinyates, Thos. (C.)	V. 389-90, Frolic captd. by U.S. Wasp ; 390-1, w. in actn.; 393, pro. P.C.
Whipple, Thos. (C.Ck.)	III. 425, Victory, k. Trafalgar.
Whiston, John (L.Com.)	II. 220, Constitution (cutter), capture of Minorca. IV. 260, Rebuff, crsg. off Cherbourg.
Whitby, Henry (P.C.)	IV. 146-7, Leander, Sq. off New York. V. 41, Cerberus, Apso Rds. Finland ; 120, crsg. off Trieste.
Whitby, John (L.)......	I. 199, Cæsar, 1st June, pro. Cr. ; 262, C. Royal Sovereign, Sq. off Ushant. III. 175, Belleisle, Medn.
White, Abraham Harcourt (L.)	IV. 318, Seagull, k. in actn.
White, Charles (C.) ...	I. 324, Vestal, crsg. Norway.
White, E. J. T. (Pr.)	VI. 377, Brisk, Navarino.
White, Fredk. (Mid.)	III. 432, Africa, w. Trafalgar.
White, George (Mid.)	VI. 270, Eliza, in actn.
White, Geo. Rbt. (Mid.)	VI. 233, Seahorse, cutting out exped.
White, John (A.B.) ...	VI. 270, Eliza, in actn.

INDEX TO NAVAL OFFICERS 171

White, John Chambers (C.)	I. 381–3, Sylph with consort des. Andromaque. II. 95–6, with Anson des. Calliope; 140, crsg.; 302, actn. Isle of Aix. III. 73, Renown, Warren's Sq. off Cadiz; 80, Porto Ferrajo; 175, Flt. off Toulon. IV. 89, 129, Foudroyant, Sq. crsg. VI. 121, Centaur, in the Gironde.
White, John Jervis (Mr.)	IV. 323, Tartar, cutting out exped.
White, Joseph (M.C.)	II. 122, Mars, k. in actn.
White, Martin (C.) ...	IV. 461, Manly captd. by Du. gbts.
White, Thomas (act.-L.Com.)	II. 100–1, Pelican des. in actn. Trompeur; 197, Audacious, the Nile; 210, pro. Cr.; 474, C. Mosquito, captd. by Sp frigates off Cuba. III. 322, La Flêche, invas. flotilla, Channel.
White, William A. (Mr.) U.S.	VI. 61, U.S. Chesapeake, k. in actn.
White, William Grove (Mid.)	VI. 234, w. in actn. Malheureux Isles.
Whitehead, John (Mr.-Mt.)	II. 268, Leander, in actn. with Généreux.
Whithurst, Wm. (Mid.)	I. 155, Invincible, w. 29th May.
Whitshed, James Hawkins (P.C.)	II. 34, Namur; 38, 43–8, St. Vincent; 293, pro. R.A. Queen Charlotte; 294, Barfleur, Medn.
Whittaker, John (M.L.)	I. 108, Nymphe, w. in actn.
Whitter, Tristram (L.)	I. 176, Culloden, w. 1st June; 300, w. in actn. off Hyères.
Whitynow, — (L.) U.S.	I. 110, F. Embuscade, taken prisoner by Br. Boston off New York.
Whyley, John (Mid.)...	I. 275, Colossus, w. in actn. off Isle Groix.
Whylock, James (M.L.)	IV. 327, Mercury, cutting out exped. V. 37–8, cutting out exped. VI. 35, Furieuse, cutting out exped.
Whyte, Edward (L.)...	V. 341, Victorious, in actn.
Wickland, Thomas (Gunner)	V. 72, Amaranthe, w. in actn.
Wiggerts, — (C.) Du.	II. 76–9, Du. Haerlem captd. at Camperdown.
Wilcocks, — (M.L.)...	V. 348, Menelaus, cutting out exped.
Wilde, Sydenham (Mid.)	VI. 343, Burmese War.
Wildey, Henry (L.-Com.)	IV. 403, Whiting, Basque Rds. actn.
Wiley, John (L.Com.)	II. 376, Sparrow, crsg. off Porto Rico.
Wilkes, John (Mid.)...	V. 37, Mercury, cutting out exped.
Wilkey, John (Mid.)...	V. 289, Astrea, w. in actn. off Madagascar.
Wilkie, James (L.) ...	V. 326, Dictator, in actn.
Wilkin, Wm. (M.L.)	V. 42, k. cutting out exped.
Wilkinson, Isaac (B.)	III. 406, Royal Sovereign, w. Trafalgar.
Wilkinson, James (L.)	VI. 305–335, Liffey, Burmese War.
Wilkinson, Philip (P.C.)	II. 302, Unicorn, in actn. Isle of Aix. III. 15, Warren's Sq. crsg.; 494, Hussar, wrkd. on the Saintes, Bay of Biscay.
Wilkinson, Richard (L.Com.)	III. 66, Greyhound (cutter), w. in actn. with invas. flotilla.
Wilkinson, Wm. (L.)	II. 195, Goliath, w. the Nile. III. 57, Elephant, Copenhagen; 64, pro. Cr.
Wilkinson, Wm. (Mid.)	V. 126, Thames, cutting out exped.
Wilks, Thomas (L.) ...	III. 54, Bellona, w. Copenhagen.
Willan, Richard (C.Ck.)	I. 323, Dido, w. in actn.
Willaumez, Etienne Joseph (C.) F.	IV. 48, Majestueux, Rochefort Sq. crsg.
Willaumez, Jean Baptiste Philibert (C.) F.	I. 387, Sercey's Sq. crsg.; 388, Isle of France. II. 237, Isle of France. III. 181–2, Poursuivante engages Hercule; 313, R.A. Foudroyant, invas. flotilla. IV. 88, Sq. crsg.; 90–3, chased by Duckworth's Sq.; 108–13, Sq. crsg. W. Indies; 114–15, engages Anson; 116–17, Brest; 189, Sq. crsg.; 391, Océan; 392–3, Sq. off Isle Groix; 395, blockaded in Basque Rds.; 400, recalled.
Willcox, James (Mid.)	IV. 100, Superb, w. Duckworth's actn.

Willes, Cornelius (L.)	IV. 271, Grasshopper, in actn. off Carthagena.
Willes, George Wickens (L.)	IV. 221, Active, in actn. Dardanelles. V. 29, Spartan, cutting out exped.; 117–18, actn. with F. frigates, pro. Cr.; 327, C. Leveret, crsg. Heligoland.
Willetts, Moses de (L.)	IV. 373, Recruit, w. in actn.
Williams, Charles (L.)	III. 257, Penguin, in actn.
Williams, Edward (L.)	III. 418, Victory; 443, Trafalgar; 464, pro. Cr.
Williams, George (C.)	III. 494, Fearless, wrkd. in Cawsand Bay.
Williams, Henry (Mid.)	V. 289, Astrea, w. in actn.
Williams, James D. (M.L.)	III. 105, Hannibal, k. Algesiras.
Williams, John (Mid.)	III. 55, Glatton, w. Copenhagen.
Williams, John (L.Com.)	III. 218, Active, actn. off Ostende.
Williams, John (Mr.)	III. 115, Venerable, k. in actn.
Williams, John (L.) ...	IV. 206, Fearless, w. Copenhagen.
Williams, Peter (L.-Com.)	V. 110–11, Entreprenante, actn. with F. privs.
Williams, Richard (L.-Com.)	III. 235, Admiral Mitchell (cutter), actn. off Ostende.
Williams, Robert (L.)	I. 376, Glatton, in actn. II. 58, Prince George, St. Vincent, pro. Cr.
Williams, Robt. (act.S.)	V. 37, Mercury, cutting out exped.
Williams, Thos. (P.C.)	I. 365–7, Unicorn capts. Tribune; 368, kntd. II. 10, crsg. Channel; 87–8, Endymion engages Du. Brutus.
,, Sir Thomas	
Williams, Wm. (Mid.)	VI. 374, w. Navarino.
Williams, Wm. Peere (P.C.)	I. 39, Flora capts. Nymphe.
Williams, Woodward (Mr.)	III. 265, Scorpion, w. cutting out exped.
Williams, Zachary (L.)	IV. 180, Caroline, k. in actn.
Williams, — (L.)	III. 66, in actn. with invas. flotilla.
Williams, — (L.)	IV. 257, Spartan, k. in actn.
Williams, — (L.)	V. 84, Euryalus, Toulon.
Williams, — (M.Col.)	VI. 94, in actn. Chesapeake Bay.
Williamson, George (Mid.)	IV. 37, Cambrian, cutting out exped.
Williamson, Jas. (Mid.)	III. 441, Defiance, k. Trafalgar.
Williamson, John (P.C.)	II. 75, Agincourt, Camperdown; 88–9, court-martialled, dismissed.
Williamson, Nathaniel (Mr.)	V. 26, Bonne Citoyenne, in actn.
Willison, Wm. (Mid.)	I. 300, Culloden, k. in actn. off Hyères.
Willmet, William (B.)	III. 402, Victory; 425, w. Trafalgar.
Willoughby, Nisbet Josiah (act.L.)	III. 205–6, Hercule, St. Domingo; 292, L.; 293–6, at Curaçoa. IV. 229, Royal George, w. Dardanelles. V. 57, C. Otter; 58–60, capture of St. Paul's, Isle Bourbon; 61, Néréide; 138–41, w.; 143-6-9-50, Isle of France; 151–5, Isle de la Passe; 157–8, 159, w.; 161-3-8-9, Grand Port; 170, Port Louis; 204, capture of the Isle of France; 445, App.
Willson, James (M.C.)	VI. 287, Leander, k. Algiers.
Wilmer, — (L.) U.S.	VI. 154, U.S. Essex, k. in actn.
Wilmot, David (L.) ...	II. 234, Seahorse, w. in actn.; 236, pro. Cr.; 320, C. Alliance, off Alexandria; 324–5, k. in actn. at Acre.
Wilmot, Henry (A.B.)	VI. 270, Eliza, k. in actn.
Wilson, Andrew (L.)...	V. 119, Alceste, cutting out exped.; 263, w. in actn.; 266, pro. Cr.
Wilson, George (P.C.)	I. 65, Bellona, Channel Flt.; 189, Sq. off Ushant; 331–2, crsg. W. Indies. II. 109–10, Harvey's Sq. at Trinidad.
Wilson, Hy. (C.)E.I.C.	III. 250, E.I.C. Warley, actn. with Linois' Sq. E. Indies.
Wilson, Hy. Smith (L.)	IV. 30, Unicorn, cutting out exped.
Wilson, Henry S. (C.)	II. 474, Deux Amis, wrkd. Isle of Wight.

INDEX TO NAVAL OFFICERS 173

Wilson, John (Mr.) ...	I. 290, Agamemnon, w. in actn. off Genoa.
Wilson, John (L.Com.)	IV. 447, Tuscan, Sq. in Rosas Bay.
Wilson, Thomas (B.)...	IV. 318, Seagull, w. in actn.
Wilson, Thomas Henry (L.)	I. 245, w. capture of Martinique. III. 15, L.Com. Lark, capts. Imprenable (priv.).
Wilson, Wm. (Mr.Mt.)	II. 389, Arrow, w. in actn.
Wilson, William (Mr.)	IV. 316, Childers, cutting out exped. VI. 13, Royalist, w. in actn.
Wilson, — (L.)	II. 407, Surprise, cutting out exped.
Wilson, — (M.L.)......	III. 137, Tigre, cutting out exped.
Winchester, William (Mid.)	III. 130, Cleopatra, k. cutting out exped.
Winder, Rev. E. (Chaplain)	VI. 374, w. Navarino.
Wingate, George T.(L.-Com.)	IV. 457, Biter, wrkd. near Calais.
Winne, John (L.Com.)	I. 140, Rattler (cutter), Channel Flt. 182, 1st June. II. 88, Monarch. Camperdown, pro. Cr.
Winsor, George (Mid.)	VI. 309-12-26-28, 346-9-51, Burmese War.
Winter, De (A.) *Du*....	II. 32, Du. Flt. in the Texel; 74-6-9, Du. Vryheid captd. at Camperdown; 82, w., d. ; 84-5, causes of defeat.
Winthrop, Robert (P.C.)	II. 456, Undaunted, wrkd. W. Indies; 345-7, Circe, Holland exped. III. 476, Stag, wrkd. in Vigo Bay.
Wintle, Robert Boughton (L.)	V. 391-2, Frolic, w. in actn.
Wise, Dacres Furlong (Mid.)	VI. 288, Granicus, w. Algiers.
Wise, Henry (Mid.) ...	IV. 447, Cumberland, cutting out exped.
Wise, William Furlong (P.C.)	IV. 243-4, Mediator, in actn. St. Domingo. VI. 278, Granicus; 284, Algiers; 291, made C.B.
Withers, Thomas (C.)	III. 494, Tartarus (bomb.), wrkd. off Margate.
Wixon, Joseph (Mr.Mt.)	II. 49, Blenheim, k. St. Vincent.
Wodehouse, Hon. Philip (P.C.)	III. 490, Resistance, wrkd. on Cape St. Vincent. IV. 123, Intrepid, Sq. at Palermo; 288, Strachan's Sq. Medn.; 445, Sq. actn. with Baudin's F. Sq. VI. 66, Commissioner at Halifax.
Woinowich, — (R.A.) *Rus.*	II. 305, Rus. Sq. at Ancona.
Wolfe, George (P.C.)	III. 275-6, Aigle des. Charente and Joie; 312, off Ushant. IV. 313-14, w. in actn. with F. frigates; 400, 421, Basque Rds. actn.; 438, Scheldt exped.
Wolley, Isaac (L.)......	I. 241, capture of Martinique; 249, w. in actn. Guadaloupe. IV. 200, C. Captain, Copenhagen; 275, capture of Madeira.
Wolley, Thomas (P.C.)	I. 412, Arethusa, capture of Grenada. II. 98, capts. F. Gaieté; 112, Porto Rico; 231-2, crsg. off the Seine, rescue of Sir Sidney Smith; 405, crsg. off Cape Ortugal. III. 142, capts. F. Invention (priv.). V. 173, mutiny of Africaine, Plymouth.
Wolrige, Ambrose A. R. (M.L.)	VI. 285, Queen Charlotte, Algiers.
Wolrige, Charles (L.)...	V. 220, Quebec, cutting out exped.
Wolrige, William (L.)	V. 245, Volage, actn. off Lissa, pro. Cr.
Wolseley, John Hood (Mid.)	VI. 287, Superb, w. Algiers.
Wolseley, William (P.C.)	I. 94, Lowestoffe, Linzee's Sq. at Corsica; 207-11, Impérieuse, Corsica. II. 285, Terrible, Bridport's Flt. off Brest.
Wood, George (L.-Com.)	III. 230, Adder, off Boulogne. IV. 368, C. Turbulent, captd. by Da. flotilla; 474, App.
Wood, Geo. (C.) *E.I.C.*	IV. 144, E.I.C. Charlton, in actn.; 308, Colombo.
Wood, James (Car.) ...	IV. 269, Herald, w. cutting out exped.

Wood, James Athol (C.)	II. 469, Garland, wrkd. off Madagascar. IV. 275-7, pro. P. Latona, capture of Curaçoa. V. 18, Captain, Sq. at Guadaloupe; 69, Martinique exped; 313-14, kntd., Pompée, crsg. VI. 2, Medn. Flt.
,, SirJamesAthol	
Wood, John (Mr.)	III. 105, Hannibal, w. Algesiras.
Wood, John (P.C.) ...	IV. 52-3, Phaëton, actn. with Sémillante.
Wood, John (2nd Mt.) E.I.C.	IV. 154, E.I.C. Warren Hastings, w. in actn.
Wood, William (Mid.)	V. 256, Active, cutting out exped.
Wood, — (B.)	II. 401, Echo, cutting out exped.
Woodford, John (L.)...	IV. 206, Cruiser, k. Copenhagen.
Woodin, John (L.)......	III. 409, Belleisle, k. Trafalgar.
Woodin, Wm. Henry (L.Com.)	VI. 201, Harmony (T.S.), Penobscot exped.
Woodley, John (P.C.)	I. 94, Alcide, Linzee's Sq. at Corsica; 207-14, Corsica. II. 456, Leda fndrd., drnd.
Woodman, Wm. Ingle (L.)	IV. 365, Laurel, in actn.
Woodriff, Daniel (P.C.)	IV. 46-9, Calcutta captd. by F. Sq.; 456, App.
Woodward, Samuel (Mid.)	V. 277, Little Belt, k. in actn.
Wooldridge, James (P.C.)	IV. 400, Mediator; 405, w. in actn.; 428, Basque Rds. V. 93-5, Rainbow, actn. with Néréide; 442, App.
Wooldridge, William (L.Com.)	II. 474, Fox, wrkd. in the Gulf of Mexico. III. 149, Pasley capts. Sp. Rosario (priv.); 150, pro. Cr.
Woollcombe, Edward (P.C.)	V. 69, Ulysses, capture of Martinique.
Woollcombe, John Charles (C.)	IV. 363-6, Laurel captd. by Canonnière; 473, App. VI. 16, Révolutionnaire, St. Sebastian.
Woolsey, Charles (L.)	III. 292, Blanche, cutting out exped.
Woolsey, Melancthon Thos. (L.Com.) U.S.	VI. 102, U.S. Oneida, Lake Ontario; 204, Canadian Lakes.
Woolsey, William (C.)	IV. 30, Papillon, Jamaica; 461, fndrd., drnd.
Wordsworth, John (C.) E.I.C.	III. 250, E.I.C. Earl Abergavenny, actn. with Linois' F. Sq. E. Indies.
Worsley, Miller (L.) ...	VI. 208-9, in actn. Canadian Lakes.
Worsley, Richard (L.)	I. 229-30, Carysfort, in actn. pro. Cr. IV. 275, C. Intrepid, capture of Madeira.
Worth, James Alexander (L.Com.)	II. 294, Telegraph, Medn.; 375, capts. Hirondelle (priv.). VI. 122-3, C. Venerable, capture of F. frigates.
Worthy, John Dewdney (Mr.Mt.)	V. 304, w. capture of Java.
Wrangel, Count (C.) Swd.	IV. 299, Swd. Adolph Frederic, Br. Swd. Flt. Oro Rds.
Wray, George (Mid.)	IV. 230, Canopus, w. Dardanelles.
Wray, Luke Hy. (L.)	IV. 156, Port Mahon, cutting out exped.
Wrench, Matthew (L.)	I. 87, Toulon. II. 462, C. Lacedemonian, captd. by the F. in the W. Indies.
Wrickson, Henry (Mr.-Mt.)	II. 96, Sylph, k. in actn.
Wright, Frederick Augustus (L.)	VI. 48-9, Peacock, in actn.
Wright, John (C.)	IV. 75, Swift, crsg. Honduras Bay.
Wright, John Westley (Mid.)	I. 360-1, Diamond, taken prisoner. II. 231, escapes; 321, L. Tigre; 324, w. at Acre; 447, capture of Malta. III. 218, C. Vincejo, captd. by F. gbts; 219, w. in actn.; 220, d. at Paris; 494, App.
Wright, Patrick (Mr.-Mt.)	V. 109, Phipps, in actn.
Wright, — (Mid.)	III. 85, k. in actn. Egypt.
Wright, — (C.) E.I.C.	III. 269-70, on board F. Psyché in actn. with Wilhelmina.
Writt,— (L.Com.) Da.	VI. 6, Da. Liebe captd. by Blazer.

INDEX TO NAVAL OFFICERS

Wulff, — (C.) *Da*.......	IV. 316–17, Da. Lougen, actn. with Childers.
Wyborn, John (L.)......	IV. 440, in actn. at Flushing, Scheldt exped.
Wybourn, Marmaduke (M.C.)	VI. 85, Marlborough, in actn. Chesapeake Bay.
Wyke, George (Mid.)...	VI. 328, 343, Burmese War.
Wyvill, Christopher (Mid.)	V. 126, Thames, cutting out exped.
Yarker, Robert (L.) ...	III. 16, Fisgard, cutting out exped.
Yates, Richard Augustus (L.)	V. 105, Quebec, cutting out exped.
Yaulden, Hy. (Mr.Mt.)	III. 55, Elephant, k. Copenhagen.
Yelland, John (L.)......	III. 57, Monarch, Camperdown; 64, pro. Cr.; 315, C. Fury (bomb.), invas. flotilla.
Yeo, George (Mid.) ...	V. 77, Confiance, capture of Cayenne.
Yeo, James Lucas (L.)	IV. 32–5, Loire, at Muros; 36, C. Confiance; 237, Lisbon; 264, off Portugal; 306-7, off the Tagus. V. 73-7,
,, Sir James Lucas...	capture of Cayenne; 351, kntd. Southampton; 352–4, capts. Améthyste; 364, Jamaica. VI. 104–109, 114, Canadian Lakes; 203, pro. Cmde.; 204–6-7, 221, Com. in the Canadian Lakes; 381, App.
Yeoman, Bernard(Mid.)	IV. 367, Euryalus, cutting out exped.
Yorke, Joseph Sydney (C.)	I. 115, Circe, capture of Réunion; 324, Stag, off Norway. II. 273, off Bordeaux; 300, Medn. V. 95, kntd., Christian VII., Basque Rds.; 96, bts. des. F. coasters.
,, Sir Joseph Sydney	
Young, Edward (Mid.)	VI. 33, Wizard, w. in actn.
Young, George (M.C.)	III. 66, w. in actn. with invas. flotilla.
Young, George Peter Martyn (S.)	V. 141, Néréide, Isle of France.
Young, James (P.C.)...	II. 402, Ethalion capts. Sp. Thetis. III. 75, Pique, crsg., chased by Ganteaume's Sq. IV. 201, Valiant, Copenhagen.
Young, John (Mid.) ...	III. 410, Mars, w. Trafalgar.
Young, Robt. (L.Com.)	III. 19, Ann (cutter), cutting out of the Désirée.
Young, William (P.C.)	I. 72, Fortitude, Medn. Flt; 207–11–14, Hood, off Corsica; 284–90, actn. off Genoa; 297, off Hyères. II. 27, R.A. Spithead mutiny. IV. 425, Gambier's court-martial. V. 207, Com. Sq. off the Scheldt.
Young, William (P.C.)	III. 81, Foudroyant, Egypt exped.
Young, Wm. (Mr.Mt.)	VI. 80, Pelican, k. in actn.
Young, William (M.-private)	VI. 59, Shannon, k. in actn.
Young, — (Mid.)	I. 87, k. in actn. Toulon.
Younge, De (C.) *Du.*	II. 343, Du Cerberus, Sq. blockaded in the Texel; 347–8, captd. by the Br.
Younghusband, George (C.)	III. 195, Osprey, crsg. off Trinidad; 257–8, engages Egyptienne (priv.).
Yule, John (L.)	II. 197, Alexander, the Nile; 210, pro. Cr.
Yule, John (L.)	III. 391, Victory; 418, 443, Trafalgar; 464, pro. Cr.
Zegers, — (C.) *Du.* ...	II. 76–9, Du. Devries captd. at Camperdown.
Zievogel, Pietrus (C.) *Du.*	VI. 279, Du. Diana; 283, Algiers.
Zoetmans, — (C.) *Du.*	I. 416, Du. Braave, Sq. captd. at the Cape of Good Hope.

PART III

MILITARY OFFICERS

Abercromby, Sir Ralph (L.G.) I. 410–12, capture of St. Lucie. II. 109–11, capture of Trinidad; 112, Porto Rico; 344–51, Holland exped.; 452, G. III. 68, 81, Egypt exped.; 86, k. in actn.
Abercromby, — (Maj.-G.) ...... V. 184–6, actn. of Ceylon and Vénus; 203, capture of the Isle of France.
Agnew, — (Maj.D.A.-G.) ...... I. 337, capture of Trincomalee.
Airey, George (L.Col.)............ III. 80–1, Porto Ferrajo.
Aldwinkle, — (L.) .... V. 145–9, Isle of France; 161, Grand Port, k. in actn.
Ali Pasha, — (G.) *Turk*............ II. 214, Corfu.
Allen, Charles (L.) .... V. 199, capture of Banda Neira.
Andréossi, — (G.) *F*............... II. 127, invas. flotilla; 334–6, Alexandria. III. 180, Amb.
Andrews, — (Ad.) .... VI. 144, k. in actn.
Appling, — (Maj.) *U.S.*......... VI. 207, Canadian Lakes.
Arcos, Dos Condé (Gvr.) *Sp*...... V. 421, St. Salvador.
Armstrong, — (G.) *U.S.*............ VI. 177, Secretary of War.
Auchmuty, Sir Samuel (Br.G.)... IV. 279–81, Buenos Ayres. V. 296, L.G.; 310, capture of Java.
Augereau, — (G.) *F*............... III. 216, invas. flotilla.

Backhouse, — (Br.G.)............ IV. 191, Maldonado; 279, Goretti, S. America.
Bacon, — (C.) .... I. 275, w. in actn. off Isle Groix.
Baird, Sir David (Maj.G.) ...... IV. 186–9, Cape of Good Hope exped.
Baird, — (Maj.G.) .... III. 91, Egypt exped.
Ballesteros, — (G.) *Sp*............ V. 27, San Andero, Spain.
Bandoola, Maha (G.) *Burmah*... VI. 315–33, Burmese War.
Barbot, — (Ad.) *F*. .... IV. 80–4, Dominique, W. Indies.
Barbutt, — (C.) .... I. 338, Ceylon.
Barclay, — (Col.) .... V. 368, New York.
Barnes, — (L.Col.) .... V. 72, Fort Royal, W. Indies.
Barrois, — (Col.) *F*............... V. 289, w. in actn. off Madagascar.
Barrow, Thos. (L.Col.)............ II. 280, Honduras.
Barry, A. (Maj.) .... V. 176, Isle Bourbon.
Basden, James (Maj.)............ VI. 331, Burmese War.
Batenburg, — (L.Col.) *Du*....... III. 298, Surinam.
Baudot, — (G.) *F*. .... III. 86, k. in actn. Egypt.
Baynes, — (L.) .... II. 65, Santa Cruz.
Baynes, Edward (Col.-Ad.G.)... VI. 105, Canadian Lakes.
Beauharnois, Eugène (A.D.C.)*F.* II. 318, Suez.
Beauvoisins, — (Col.) *F*. ...... II. 319, Egypt.
Beckwith, Geo. (L.G.)............ V. 70, capture of Martinique; 190, capture of Guadaloupe.
  ,,   Sir George ....
Bellegarde, — (G.) *F*............ I. 244, Martinique.
Belliard, — (G.) *F*. .... III. 88–90, Egypt.

INDEX TO MILITARY OFFICERS 177

Bentinck, Lord William (L.G.)	VI. 20, Palermo.
Beresford, — (Maj.G.)	IV. 189–91, S. America. VI. 120, Mar. Bordeaux.
Bernadotte, — (G.) *F.*	II. 168, Vienna.
Berthier, — (G.) *F.*	II. 334-6, Egypt. III. 203, W. Indies ; 332, Mar. Minister of Marine.
Bianca, Casa (G.) *F.*	I. 213, surrender of Calvi. II. 127, invas. flotilla.
Birch, Richard (C.)	VI. 305, Burmese War.
Bird, — (C.) *U.S.*	VI. 190, Baltimore.
Blackiston, — (L.)	V. 204, capture of Isle of France.
Blair, Thomas (L.Col.)	VI. 342, Burmese War.
Blake, — (Col.) *U.S.*	V. 422, Boston.
Blomefield, — (G.) *U.S.*	VI. 132-6, Canadian Lakes.
Bloomfield, — (Maj.G.)	IV. 210, Copenhagen, created Baronet.
Blunt, — (Col.)	III. 150, capture of St. Eustatia, W. Indies.
Boetzelaer, Count (G.) *Du.*	I. 99, Gvr. of Willemstadt.
Bogart, Van (Col.) *Du.*	IV. 434, Scheldt exped.
Bon, — (G.) *F.*	II. 168, Malta exped. ; 318–20, Egypt.
Borin, — (G.) *F.*	II. 6, Ireland exped.
Bouchard, — (G.) *Neap.*	II. 317, surrender of Civita-Vecchia.
Boucret, — (G.) *F.*	I. 280, Belleisle.
Boudet, — (G.) *F.*	III. 163, St. Domingo exped.
Bowyer, — (G.)	IV. 279, capture of St. Thomas, W. Indies.
Bradford, George (L.)	I. 252, St. Domingo.
Braithwaite, — (Col.)	I. 133, Pondicherry.
Breen Nie Wook (G.) (*Burmah*)	VI. 343, Burmese War.
Brisbane, — (Maj.G.)	VI. 214-19, Lake Champlain.
Brock, Isaac (Col.)	III. 43, Copenhagen exped.
Bron, — (G.) *F.*	III. 84, Egypt.
Brooke, — (Col.)	VI. 189-91, Baltimore exped.
Brown, Philip (L.)	V. 199, capture of Banda Neira.
Brown, — (Maj.)	I. 338, Malacca, E. Indies.
Bruce, — (Maj.G.)	I. 127-8, Barbadoes.
Brues, — (Maj.G.) *Du.*	IV. 434, Zealand, Holland.
Brune, — (G.) *F.*	II. 349-50, Holland exped.
Brush, Oliver (L.)	V. 301, capture of Java.
Buget, — (Br.G.) *F.*	II. 432, siege of Genoa.
Bulger, — (L.)	VI. 209, Canadian Lakes.
Buonaparte, Joseph (G.) *F.*	IV. 122-3, Italy.
Burr, — (Col.) *E.I.C.*	III. 151, surrender of Ternate, E. Indies.
Burrard, — (L.G.)	IV. 210, Copenhagen exped., created Baronet.
Burrowes, — (C.)	VI. 314-15, Burmese War.
Camin, — (Ad.G.) *F.*	II. 217, Egypt exped.
Campbell, Sir Archibald, K.C.B. (Maj.G.)	VI. 302-6-8-11-18, 356, Com. Burmese War exped.
Campbell, Duncan (C.)	I. 82, k. in actn. Toulon.
Campbell, John (C.)	VI. 309, 349, Burmese War.
Campbell, — (Col.)	III. 284, Vizagapatam, Bengal.
Carador, — (L.Col.)	VI. 374, w. Navarino.
Carles, — (Maj.) *F. Royalist*	I. 129–30, W. Indies.
Carteau, — (G.) *F.*	I. 75-7, Toulon ; 82, superseded.
Casalta, — (G.) *Corsican*	I. 348-9, Corsica.
Cathcart, Lord (L.G.)	IV. 201-7-10, Com. at Copenhagen ; 296, G. Baltic ; 464, App.
Cavalier, — (Brg.G.) *F.*	III. 89, Egypt exped.
Cavan, Earl of (Maj.G.)	II. 451, in actn. at Ferrol, Spain.
Cawdor, Lord (Col.)	II. 90, Wales, Militia called out.
Cercaro, Pignatelli (G.) *Neap.*	V. 260, Com. at Palinuro, Calabria.
Chabot, — (G.) *F.*	II. 214, Com. Ven. Isles in the Adriatic.
Championnet, — (G.) *F.*	II. 213, capture of Rome ; 303, capture of Naples.
Charette, — (G.) *F. Royalist*	I. 281, Isle Noirmoutier.

N

Chatham, Earl of (L.G.)	IV. 433-4-40-1-3, Com. Scheldt exped.
Chervet, — (C.) *F.*	IV. 124, Isle Capri, Italy.
Christie, — (L.)	III. 119, w. cutting out exped. Sénégal.
Christophe, — (Chief)	III. 164, St. Domingo.
Church, — (Brg.G.)	II. 115, Com. at Irois Fort, Carcasse Bay
Church, — (C.)	IV. 449, capture of the Isle of Ithaca.
Claparède, — (G.) *F.*	IV. 80-1, Dominique, W. Indies.
Clarke, Alured (G.)	I. 335, capture of the Cape of Good Hope
Clarke, Charles William (Maj.)...	IV. 449, capture of the Isle of Cerigo.
Clément, — (G.) *F.*	II. 304, w. in actn. at Brindisi.
Clermont, Prosper de (Col.) *F.*...	I. 133, surrender of Pondicherry.
Clerveaux, — (Chief)	III. 164, St. Domingo.
Clinton, — (Col.)	III. 150, capture of Funchal, Madeira.
Coffin, — (L.Col.)	VI. 19-20, capture of Ponza.
Colgard, Etienne (Col.) *F.*	V. 139, Isle of France.
Collot, — (G.) *F.*	I. 247, Guadaloupe.
Conolly, — (C.)	I. 84, in actn. at Toulon.
Coote, Eyre (Col.)	I. 245, capture of Martinique. II. 131, Maj.G. Ostende. III. 88-92, Egypt exped. IV. 434, L.G. Sir Eyre, Scheldt exped.
,, Sir Eyre	
Coote, — (Maj.)	VI. 222, Lake Champlain.
Cotton, Sir Willoughby (Brg.G.)	VI. 329-31-2-6-9, 342, 354, Burmese War.
Court, Henry (C.Maj.) *E.I.C.*...	V. 192, Amboyna, E. Indies.
Cradock, Hon. — (L.Col.)	VI. 377, Burmese War.
Craig, James (Maj.G.)	I. 334, Com. at the capture of the Cape of Good Hope. III. 346, G., 378, Naples. IV. 121, Com. at Messina, Italy; 123, retired, ill-health.
,, Sir James	
Crawfurd, — (Brg.G.)	IV. 281, Buenos Ayres.
Crétin. — (G.) *F.*	II. 334, k. in actn. Alexandria.
Croghan, — (Col.) *U.S.*	VI. 208, Canadian Lakes.
Cuyler, — (Maj.G.)	I. 127, Com. attack on Martinique.
Daendels, — (G.) *Du.*	II. 32, Texel; 346-9, Holland. V. 195, Com. at Java; 302, superseded by G. Jansens.
Daker, William Jones (L.)	V. 199, capture of Banda Neira.
Dalhousie, — (Col.)	III. 85, Egypt exped.
Dalrymple, Sir Hew (L.G.)	IV. 296, Com. Br. forces in Spain.
Daniel, — (C.)	I. 252, St. Domingo.
Danseville, — (Commandant) *F.*	I. 126, St. Pierre, Nova Scotia.
Dansey, — (L.Col.)	I. 130, 250, capture of Jérémie, Cape Nicolas Mole.
Darby, — (Maj.)	V. 259, Palinuro.
Daru, Count (A.D.C.) *F.*	III. 331, Intendant-G. at Boulogne; 496, App.
Davies, — (C.) (A.D.C.)	II. 368-9, k. in actn. on board Sibylle.
Davis, — (L.)	V. 149-50, w. at Isle de la Passe; 159, Grand Port.
Davoust, — (G.) *F.*	II. 446, surrender of Malta. III. 315, Mar.; 318-21-6, invas. flotilla, Ostende.
Dearborn, — (G.) *U.S.*	VI. 103, Canadian Lakes.
Decaen, — (G.) *F.*	III. 168-9, 207-8, 283, Gvr.G. of Pondicherry. IV. 20, Gvr. of the Isle of France; 356, 363-4, Isle of France. V. 57, 97, 156, 167-70, Gvr. of Isle of France; 204-5, surrender of the Isle of France.
Desaix, — (G.) *F.*	II. 168, Malta exped.; 342, Egypt; 445-6-7, Egypt.
Desbrusleys, — (G.) *F.*	V. 61-2, surrender of Isle Bourbon.
Dessalines, — (Chief)	III. 164, St. Domingo.
Destaing, — (G.) *F.*	III. 86, w. in actn. Alexandria.
Devaux, — (G.) *F.*	III. 97, Cadiz.
Devilliers, — (Col.) *F.*	IV. 265, captd. off Corfu.
Dickson, — (Maj.)	VI. 209, Canadian Lakes.
Donzelot, — (Ad.G.) *F.*	II. 339, Kosseïr Bay.
Douglas, — (Brg.G.) *U.S.*	VI. 190, in actn. Baltimore.
Douglas, — (C.)	I. 77, k. in actn. at Toulon.

INDEX TO MILITARY OFFICERS 179

Doyle, — (Maj.G.) .... I. 280, Com. Quiberon exped.
Doyle, — (Brg.G.) .... III. 89, Egypt exped.
Drinkwater, — (L.Col.) .... II. 35, on board Br. Minerve.
Drummond, — (L.Col.) .... I. 248, Guadaloupe. VI. 204, L.G. Canadian Lakes.
Dugommier, — (G.) F............. I. 82-3-9, Com. forces at Toulon, w. in actn.
Dumas, — (G.) F................... II. 168, Malta exped ; 449, Cairo.
Dumonceau, — (G.) F............. II. 349, Holland exped.
Dumuy, — (G.) F. .... II. 168, Malta exped.
Duncan, — (Maj.).................. I. 345, capture of Porto Ferrajo, Spain.
Dundas, — (Maj.G.)............... I. 81-3-4, Toulon ; 207-8-10, Corsica ; 246-7, capture of Guadaloupe. II. 117, mutiny at the Cape of Good Hope ; 390, Com. at the Cape of Good Hope.
Duqua, — (G.) F.................. II. 168, Malta exped.
During, — (Col.) *Du.* .... V. 200, capture of Banda Neira.
Duvivier, — (G.) F. .... II. 334, k. in actn. Alexandria.

Edwards, T. (Maj.) .... V. 144, w. at the capture of Isle Bourbon.
Elliot, Sir Gilbert (Viceroy) ...... I. 84, council of war at Toulon ; 212, 344, Viceroy of Corsica. II. 35, on board Br. Minerve.
Elliott, — (C.) .... V. 176-8, k. in actn. on board Africaine.
Elrington, R. (L.Col.) .... VI. 327, Burmese War.
Ernouf, — (G.) F...... .... III. 277, 349, Gvr. of Guadaloupe. IV. 83, Dominique. V. 53, 191, surrender of Guadaloupe.
Etienne, — (Brg.G.) F. .... III. 92, surrender of Marabou, Egypt.
Evans, Richard Lacy (Maj.)...... VI. 310, Burmese War.
Evans, Thomas (Maj.) .... VI. 312, Burmese War ; 353, App.

Ferrand, — (G.) F. .... III. 207, San Jago, St. Domingo ; 243, St. Domingo. IV. 79, 85-8, Com. at St. Domingo.
Ferrior, Charles (Maj.) .... VI. 323, Burmese War.
Fontaine, — (Ad.G.) F. .... II. 138, Ireland exped.
Forbes, — (Maj.G.) .... I. 412, St. Domingo.
Foubert, — (C.) F. .... V. 347, Spain.
Foulstone, — (L.).................. V. 143, capture of Isle Bourbon.
Fox, — (G.) .... III. 80, Com. in Spain.
Fraser, Hugh (Brg.G.) .... VI. 311, Burmese War.
Fraser, — (L.Col.) .... V. 142-3, capture of Isle Bourbon.
Fraser, — (Maj.) .... I. 338, capture of Batticaloe Fort, E. Indies.
Fraser, — (Maj.G.) .... IV. 232-3, Egypt exped.; 435, L.G. Scheldt exped.
Frazer, — (L.Col.) .... III. 118, Com. at Gorée ; 298, captd. by F. Sq.
Friant, — (G.) F. .... III. 83-5, in actn. Alexandria.
Frith, William (Maj.) .... IV. 342, Burmese War.
Frœlich, — (G.) *Austrian* ...... II. 305, Ancona.
Fugières, — (G.) F. .... II. 334, w. in actn. Alexandria.

Gall, — (C.) .... VI. 202, w. in actn. Penobscot exped.
Garden, S. J. (L.).................. VI. 113, k. Canadian Lakes.
Garnier, — (G.) F. .... I. 82, Toulon.
Gauthier, — (G.) F. .... II. 303, Tuscany.
Gentili, — (G.) *Corsican* .... I. 347, Corsica. II. 70, Corfu.
Ghisilieri, — (G.) *Austrian* ...... IV. 126, Cattaro, Dalmatia.
Gifflenga, Alexandre (Col.) *Ital.* V. 233, 240-2, on board F. Favourite, actn. off Lissa.
Gillespie, Robert Rollo (Col.) ... V. 295, 302-4, capture of Java.
Gillman, — (L.)..................... V. 297, capture of Java.
Girardon, — (Brg.G.) F. .... II. 316, Italy.
Godard, — (C.) F. .... II. 333, k. in actn. at Aboukir Fort.
Godwin, — (L.Col.) .... VI. 313, 347-56, Burmese War.
Gordon, Sir Charles (Col.) ...... I. 245, Com. at Sainte Lucie, Martinique.
Gordon, — (C.)..................... III. 80, Porto Ferrajo, Spain.

N 2

Gossett, — (Maj.) .... VI. 280-5, Algiers.
Goudin, — (G.) *F.* .... V. 348, Com. at Biendom, Spain.
Graham, — (Brg.G.).............. I. 250, Guadaloupe, W. Indies.
Graham, — (G.) .... VI. 16, Com. forces at St. Sebastian, Spain.
Green, Sir Charles (Maj.G.)...... III. 296, Com. at the capture of Surinam.
Grey, Sir Charles (L.G.) .... I. 99, Ostende ; 241, Com. at capture of Martinique ; 244-7-8-9, Guadaloupe.
Grinfield, — (L.G.) .... III. 203, Com. at the capture of Sainte Lucie, St. Domingo.
Grosvenor, — (L.G.) .... IV. 434, Scheldt exped.
Grouchy, — (G.) *F.* .... II. 6-9, Ireland exped.
Gutteri, Don Juan Antonio (Gvr.) *Sp.* II. 67, at Santa Cruz.

Hamilton, John (Col.) .... IV. 249, Norfolk, U.S.
Hampfield, — (Col.)............... I. 252, St. Domingo, W. Indies.
Hampton, — (Maj.G.) *U.S.* ... VI. 115, Canadian Lakes.
Harcourt, — (Brg.G.) .... V. 191, capture of Guadaloupe.
Hardy, — (G.) *F.* .... III. 163, F. exped. to St. Domingo.
Harris,— (L.G.) .... II. 421, Com. at the capture of Seringapatam.
Hassan Bey, — (G.) *Turk.* ...... II. 327-8, Acre ; 333, Aboukir.
Henderson, — (Maj.) .... V. 70, Martinique, W. Indies.
Hermann, — (G.) *Rus.* .... II. 349, Holland exped.
Hervilly, Comte de (G.) *F. Royalist.* I. 278, w. in actn. Quiberon.
Heyland, Henry J. (L.) .... V. 301, capture of Java.
Hilliers, Baraguay de (Brg.G.) *F.* II. 234, captd. on board Sensible.
Hislop, — (Maj.G.) .... V. 190, Guadaloupe ; 409, L.G., Gvr. of Bombay ; 419-20, on board Java in actn. with U.S. Constitution.
Hobart, Lord (G.).................. I. 337, Gvr.G. of Madras.
Hoche, — (G.) *F.*.................. II. 2, 32, Com. Ireland exped.
Hoghton, — (Brg.G.) .... V. 71, Martinique.
Hope, Sir John (L.G.) .... IV. 433-5, 440, Scheldt exped.
Hope, — (Brg.G.) .... III. 86, w. in actn. Egypt.
Hopkinson, Charles (L.Col.) ... VI. 319, Burmese War.
Hornblow, — (Transport) ...... VI. 322, Burmese War.
Horne, — (L.) .... V. 178, w. in actn. on board Africaine.
Hoste, George (C.) .... V. 118, in actn. on board Spartan.
Hotz, — (Col.) *Austrian* .... IV. 125, surrender of Gaeta.
Hughes, — (Brg.G.)............... III. 297, capture of Surinam.
Hull, — (G.) *U.S.* .... VI. 90, Chesapeake.
Humbert, — (G.) *F.*............... II. 6-12, Com. Ireland exped. ; 22, wrkd. ; 137-8, 164, Com. Ireland exped.
Hungerford, — (G.) .... VI. 172, Chesapeake Bay.
Huntly, Marquis of (L.G.) ...... IV. 434, Scheldt exped.
Hutchinson, John Hely (Maj.G.) III. 87-8, Com. in Egypt ; 90, L.G. ; 91-2, surrender of Alexandria ; 94, made K.B., created Peer.

Ibrahim Bey (G.) *Turk.* .... II. 320, Acre ; 340, Gaza, Egypt ; 470, App.
Italinski, — (Amb.) *Rus.*......... IV. 215, Constantinople.
Izard, — (G.) *U.S.* .... VI. 212, Canadian Lakes.

Jackson, — (Amb.) .... IV. 201, at Copenhagen. V. 173, Amb. to U.S.
Jackson, — (G.) *U.S.* .... VI. 235, Com. in actn. Pearl River, U.S.
Jamelle, — (G.) *F.* .... VI. 309, Com. at the surrender of Java.
James, — (L.) .... II. 109, drnd. in the loss of the Tribune.
Janssens, — (L.G.) *Du.* .... IV. 188, Com. at the Cape of Good Hope. V. 302, Gvr. of Java ; 303-4-9-10, surrender of Java.
John, Henry (L.Col.) .... VI. 201, Penobscot exped.

INDEX TO MILITARY OFFICERS 181

Joubert, — (G.) *F.*	II. 213, Com. at Turin.
Junot, — (G.) *F.*	IV. 236, Com. exped. to Spain; 238, Lisbon.
Kalkreuth, — (G.) *Prussian*	IV. 197, Dantzic.
Kay, — (L.)	V. 260, k. in actn. Palinuro.
Keating, Henry S. (L.Col.)	V. 58-9, 61, capture of St. Paul's, Isle Bourbon; 142-5, capture of Isle Bourbon; 171-5, L.Govr. Isle Bourbon.
Kellerman, — (G.) *F.*	I. 82, Toulon.
Kelly, M. (L.Col.)	VI. 309, Burmese War.
Kerr, Thomas (L.)	VI. 305, Burmese War.
Kerverseau, — (G.) *F.*	III. 163, F. exped. to St. Domingo; 207, St. Domingo.
Kléber (G.) *F.*	II. 168, Malta exped.; 175, w. in actn. Alexandria; 317, Cairo; 329, Acre; 335-9-41-2, Com. Egypt exped.; 445-6-7, Cairo; 448-9, k. in actn.; 471, App.
Knowles, — (L.)	V. 297, capture of Java.
Kolein Menghie (G.) (*Burmah*)	VI. 341, Burmese War.
Lacroix, — (Brg.G.) *F.*	III. 89, Egypt exped.
Lacuée, Gérard (A.D.C.) *F.*	III. 74, A.D.C. to Napoleon.
Lagrange, — (G.) *F.*	III. 88-9, Ramanieh, Egypt. IV. 79-80-2-3, at Dominique; 85, Isle of Aix.
Laharpe, — (G.) *F.*	I. 82, Toulon.
Lake, — (L.G.)	II. 138, F. invas. of Ireland.
Lannes, — (G.) *F.*	II. 320-8, Acre; 334-6, Egypt. III. 326, Mar. invas. flotilla.
Lanusse, — (G.) *F.*	III. 84-5, Egypt; 86, k. in the Battle of Canopus, Egypt.
Lapoype, — (G.) *F.*	I. 72, 82-4, Toulon. III. 205-6, St. Domingo.
Lariboissière, — (G.) *F.*	III. 321, invas. flotilla.
Lasey, — (G.) *Rus.*	IV. 121, Naples.
Laureil, — (Maj.)	II. 231, Trinidad.
Lauriston, — (G.) *F.*	III. 242, Com. St. Helena exped.; 334-9, 350, Com. at Fort Royal.
Lausser, Johan Rudolph (Gvr.) *Du.*	III. 38, surrender of Curaçoa.
Lavalette, — (A.D.C.) *F.*	II. 336, A.D.C. to Napoleon, Egypt.
Leclerc, — (G.) *F.*	III. 150, Com. in Portugal; 163-4, F. exped. to St. Domingo; 165, d.
Lefebvre, — (Mar.) *F.*	IV. 197, Dantzic.
Leith, Sir James (L.G.)	VI. 229, Com. at the Leeward Isles.
Lemoine, — (L.)	I. 82, k. in actn. Toulon.
Leturcq, — (G.) *F.*	II. 334, k. in actn. Aboukir.
Lindolm, — (Ad.G.) *Da.*	III. 53, Copenhagen.
Liniers, — (Col.) *F.*	IV. 190-1, Buenos Ayres; 281, G. Com. at Buenos Ayres.
Lloyd, — (L.Col.)	III. 91, at Suez, Com. exped. to Cairo.
Lockhart, — (L.Col.)	IV. 283, exped. to Gressie, Java.
Longa, — (G.) *Sp.*	V. 336, Castro, Spain.
Macbean, William (Brg.G.)	VI. 302-8, 346-7, Burmese War.
McCreagh, Michael, C.B. (Brg.G.)	VI. 302-7-13-27-9, 356, Burmese War.
McDowall, Robert (L.Col.)	VI. 338, Burmese War.
McDowall, — (C.)	I. 248, Guadaloupe.
Mack, — (G.) *Austrian*	II. 213, in actn. at Rome.
Mackenzie, — (Col.)	V. 301, capture of Java.
McLeod, — (L.Col.)	IV. 125, Catanzaro, Calabria.

Macleod, — (L.Col.)	V. 143, capture of Isle Bourbon.
Macomb, Alexander(Maj.G)U.S.	VI. 213-14-16-19, Lake Champlain; 221, G. Lake Champlain.
Maitland, Frederick (Col.)	II. 345, Holland exped.; 427, Maj.G. Morbihan exped. V. 19, capture of the Saintes Isles; 70-1, capture of Martinique; 259, L.G. Com. at Sicily.
Maitland, Hon. Thomas (Brg.G.)	II. 280, Com. at St. Domingo.
Maitland, — (Brg.G.)	III. 296-7, capture of Surinam. IV. 311, L.G. Com. at Colombo, Ceylon.
Mallet, John (L.Col.)	VI. 315, Burmese War.
Marmont, — (G.) *F.*	II. 317, Alexandria, 333-4-6, Egypt. III. 332, Com. army in Holland.
Marques, Manoel (L.Col.) *Por.*	V. 73-5, capture of Cayenne.
Masséna, — (G.) *F.*	II. 432-5-6, surrender of Genoa.
Maxwell, Charles William (Maj.)	V. 67-8, capture of Sénégal.
Méjan, — (Col.) *F.*	II. 309, Com. at St. Elmo, Naples; 315, Maj.G. surrender of St. Elmo.
Mélas, — (G.) *Austrian*	II. 431-2-6, siege and capture of Genoa.
Melstedt, — (Maj.) *Da.*	V. 224-5, k. at the capture of Anholt.
Melville, Robert (G.)	I. 36, inventor of carriage ordnance (1779). II. 424, carronades established.
Ménage, — (G.) *F.*	II. 139, Ireland exped.
Menou, Abdallah Jacques (G.) *F.*	II. 168, Malta exped.; 450, Com. at Cairo. III. 82-6-8, 92-3, Egypt.
Michelson, — (G.) *Rus.*	IV. 215, Moldavia.
Milbanke, — (L.)	II. 316, k. in actn. at St. Elmo.
Miles, — C.B. (Col.)	VI. 310, Burmese War; 356, App.
Miollis, — (G.) *F.*	II. 303, Leghorn.
Missit, — (Maj.)	IV. 232, Alexandria.
Mitchell, — (L.Col.)	VI. 204, Canadian Lakes.
Moine, Le (G.) *F.*	I. 279, Com. at Nantes.
Monge, — (G.) *F.*	II. 160, k. in actn. on board Immortalité.
Monnet, — (G.) *F.*	IV. 439, Com. at the surrender of Flushing.
Monnier, — (G.) *F.*	II. 305, Com. at the surrender of Ancona.
Monson, Hon. Charles (C.)	I. 338, Molletive, Ceylon.
Monteil, — (L.Col.) *F.*	I. 127, Com. at the capture of Isle Tobago, W. Indies, by the Br.
Moore, Sir John (Maj.G.)	II. 347, Holland exped. III. 86, w. in actn. Egypt. IV. 298, Com. forces Baltic exped.
Moreau, — (G.) *F.*	II. 296, Genoa.
Morgan, — (G.) *F.*	III. 182, taken prisoner on board Creole.
Morlett, — (L.)	V. 145-9, Isle of France exped.; 161, k. in actn.
Mortier, — (G.) *F.*	III. 180, Coërveden, Hanover; 230, invas. flotilla.
Motard, — (Ad.G.) *F.*	II. 198, w. in actn. at the Nile.
Mouktar, — (G.) *Turk.*	II. 214, actns. with F. in Albania.
Mourad Bey (G.) *Turk.*	II. 340, Com. in Upper Egypt.
Mouret, — (G.) *F.*	I. 77-82, Toulon.
Mouret, — (L.) *F.*	III. 280, Saintes Guadaloupe.
Mulgrave, Lord (Brg.G.)	I. 79, Toulon.
Murat, — (G.) *F.*	II. 320, Acre; 334-6, Egypt. III. 74-8, Medn. V. 115-19, Naples; 124-6, Scylla. VI. 117 Minister.
Murray, George (L.Col.)	IV. 208, Copenhagen.
Murray, — (L.Col.)	II. 448, Suez. III. 91, Egypt.
Murray, — (Col.)	VI. 115, Canadian Lakes. 215, Lake Champlain.
Murray, — (C.)	VI. 319, Burmese War.
Myers, — (G.)	III. 347, Com. at Antigua.
Negra, Bocca (C.) *Sp.*	II. 281, Sp. attack on Honduras.
Napier, — (L.Col.)	VI. 94, Hampton, Norfolk, U.S.

INDEX TO MILITARY OFFICERS 183

Napoleon Buonaparte (L.) *F.* ...	I. 79, Toulon, pro. Brg.G ; 82, G. ; 346-7, G. Leghorn, Italy. II. 124-6, England invas. exped. ; 127, Toulon ; 167-72-4, Egypt exped. ; 214-17, 251, 317, Egypt ; 321, capture of Jaffa ; 324-5, Syria ; 328, Acre ; 334, Cairo ; 335-40, escapes from Egypt ; 412, Paris ; 425-6, 1st Consul ; 436, Battle of Marengo ; 476, App. III. 64, invas. flotilla ; 68, 76, Tunis ; 95-6, intrigues agst. England ; 147-50-2, Treaty of Amiens ; 162-3-4, St. Domingo exped. ; 169, war renewed ; 214-15, Emperor ; 229, Boulogne ; 230-1, invas. flotilla ; 240, 308-11, 1st Consul ; 326-9-31, invas. flotilla ; 338-42-3-7-8, 352-4, 370-1-2-6-8, 384, instructions to Villeneuve's Flt. ; 461, Trafalgar. IV. 10-12, 25-6, 78, Austria ; 196-8-9, 211-12, Treaty of Tilsit ; 235-7, Portugal exped. ; 348, Constantinople ; 427-31, Scheldt ; 432, Antwerp. V. 79, Antwerp ; 211, projected capture of E. Indies ; 218-22, Boulogne ; 312, Moscow retreat ; 355, Milan decree. VI. 121, abdicates ; 226, escapes from Elba ; 227, sent to St. Helena ; 229, treaty of peace.
Needhall, — (L.)	V. 145-9, Isle of France ; 161, w. in actn.
Nemion Maha (G.) *Burmah* ...	VI. 339, k. in actn. Burmese War.
Ney, — (Mar.) *F.*..................	III. 325, invas. flotilla.
Nichol, — (L.Col.)	VI. 211, Canadian Lakes.
Nixon, — (C.)	V. 199, capture of Banda Neira.
Noailles, — (G.) *F.*	III. 204-6-7, Com. at St. Nicholas, St. Domingo.
Noguès, — (Brg.G.) *F.*	III. 203, Sainte Lucie, W. Indies.
Nugent, Count G. (*Austrian*) ...	VI. 32, blockade of Trieste.
Nugent, — (L.Col.)	I. 80, Toulon.
Nunn, — (Maj.)	IV. 81-4, w. in actn. Dominique.
O'Connell, — (C.)..................	IV. 81-4, in actn. Dominique.
O'Donoghue, — (L.Col.).........	VI. 331, Burmese War.
O'Hara, — (Maj.G.)	I. 81-2, Toulon ; 83, w. in actn. ; II. 397, G., Gvr. of Gibraltar.
O'Neil, Arthur (Field Mar.) *Sp.*	II. 281, Com. Sp. attack on Honduras.
O'Reilly, —(C.).....................	VI. 329, 354, Burmese War.
Ogilvie, — (Brg.G.)	I. 126, capture of St. Pierre, Newfoundland.
Oswald, John (Brg.G.)	IV. 449, capture of Cephalonia. V. 80, capture of St. Maura.
Ott, Baron de (G.) *Austrian* ...	II. 432-6, siege and capture of Genoa.
Paget, — (Col.)	II. 221, capture of Minorca.
Pakenham, Sir Edward (Maj.G.)	VI. 235, k. in actn. U.S.
Pakenham, Hon. — (L.Col.) ...	V. 71, capture of Martinique.
Paoli, — (G.) *Corsican*............	I. 94-6, Corsica ; 207-10-12, Corsica.
Paul-Louvertue (Chief)............	III. 164, St. Domingo.
Pearson, — (Maj.)	V. 71, capture of Martinique.
Pearson, — (L.)	II. 45-6, in actn. Cape St. Vincent.
Peiman, — (Maj.G.) *Da*.........	IV. 202-7-8-9, Com. at Copenhagen.
Pernetly, — (Col.) *F.*	II. 139, Ireland exped.
Petrona Bey (G.) *Turk.*	VI. 363, Navarino.
Phelipeaux, —(Col.) *F. Royalist*	II. 231, Rouen ; 321-4, Acre ; 325, k. in actn.
Phillips, — (C.).....................	V. 192, capture of Amboyna, E. Indies.
Picton, — (Col.)	II. 230, Com. at Trinidad.
Pignatelli, — (Prince) *Neap.* ...	I. 84, council of war at Toulon.
Pigot, — (Maj.Gen.)...............	II. 445, Com. at the capture of Malta.
Pinto, Joaquim Manoel(Maj.)*Por.*	V. 74, capture of Cayenne.

Piper, Hugh (C.)	VI. 316, Burmese War.
Porlier, — (G.) *Sp.*	V. 336, Santander.
Power, — (Maj.Gen.)	VI. 214, Lake Champlain.
Prescott, — (L.G.)	I. 245, Gvr. of Martinique; 250, surrender of Fort Matilda, Guadaloupe.
Prevost, George (Brg.G.)	IV. 80-3-4, Gvr. of Dominique. V. 70, L.G.
,, Sir George	Sir George, Com. at the capture of Martinique. VI. 101-4, 109-14, 206, Com. at the Canadian Lakes; 212-13-15-19, Com. at Lake Champlain; 221-37, d. at Lake Champlain.
Prevost, — (Brg.Maj.)	IV. 82, Dominique.
Proctor, — (Col.)	VI. 109, Com. Amherstburgh, Canadian Lakes.
Prophalow, Van (L.Col.) *Du*.	IV. 188, surrender of Cape Town.
Puisaye, Comte de (Col.) *F. Royalist*	I. 278, Quiberon exped.
Pulteney, Sir James (L.G.)	II. 450, Com. at the capture of Ferrol.
Rabie, — (Col.) *F.*	VI. 32, surrender of Trieste.
Rambeaud, — (G.) *F.*	II. 329, k. in actn. Acre.
Ramsay, — (Maj.)	II. 428, in actn. at Quiberon.
Read, — (Col.) *U.S.*	VI. 186, in actn. Chesapeake Bay.
Reed, — (Maj.)	VI. 286, Algiers.
Regnier, (G.) *F.*	II. 168, Malta exped.; 320, Syria exped. IV. 122, Italy; 124-5, Battle of Maida; 294, capture of Scylla.
Renier, — (Ad.G.) *F.*	II. 21, drnd. in the loss of Droits de l'Homme.
Revel,de,—(Chevalier)*F.Royalist*	I. 84, council of war at Toulon.
Rey, — (G.) *F.*	II. 138-9, Ireland exped. VI. 16, St. Sebastian.
Reydez (C.) *Da*.	V. 224-5, w. at the capture of Anholt.
Reynier, — (G.) *F.*	III. 93, Egypt exped.
Ricard, — (G.) *F.*	I. 245, capture of Martinique.
Robertson, — (L.)	VI. 85, in actn. Chesapeake Bay.
Robertson, — (L.Col.)	IV. 294, Scylla, Lower Calabria.
Robertson, — (Col.)	VI. 27, Isle Augusta, Adriatic.
Robinson, — (Maj.)	I. 130, capture of Jérémie, Cape Nicolas Mole.
Rochambeau, — (G.) *F.*	I. 128, Gvr. of Martinique; 240-3-4, surrender of Martinique; 413, Cape François. III. 163-5, F. exped. to St. Domingo; 204, surrender of Cape François.
Roche, — (Col.) *F.*	VI. 20, w. in actn. Pietra Nera, Calabria.
Rockman, — (L.) *F.*	V. 138-40, Jacolet, Isle of France.
Roize, — (G.) *F.*	III. 86-8, k. at the Battle of Canopus, Egypt.
Romana, Marquis de la (G.) *Sp.*	IV. 303, Com. Sp. forces in Denmark.
Romilly, — (C.)	VI. 92, in actn. Chesapeake Bay.
Rose, — (C.)	VI. 332, k. in actn. Burmese War.
Ross, David (C.)	VI. 331, Burmese War.
Ross, — (C.)	V. 186, w. in actn. on board Ceylon.
Ross, — (Maj.G.)	VI. 174, Com. at Chesapeake Bay; 176-9, Battle of Bladensburg; 189, k. in actn. at Baltimore.
Rosslyn, Earl of (Maj.G.)	IV. 205, Copenhagen; 434-40, L.G. Scheldt exped.
Rousseau, — (G.) *F.*	IV. 436, Cadzand, Holland.
Sahuguet, — (G.) *F.*	III. 68, Com. reinforcements for Egypt.
St. Cyr, — (G.) *F.*	III. 378, Com. at Naples, Italy.
St. Julien,— (Maj.G.) *Austrian.*	II. 432, blockading Savona.
St. Michel, Lacombe (G.) *F.*	I. 211, Bastia, Corsica.
St. Susaune, — (Col.) *F.*	V. 144, Isle Bourbon.
Sale, R. (Maj.)	VI. 316-29-34, Burmese War; 342, L.Col. Burmese War.
Sarrazin, — (Ad.G.) *F.*	II. 138, Ireland exped.
Scholten, Van (Col.) *Da*.	IV. 279, surrender of Isle St. Thomas.

INDEX TO MILITARY OFFICERS 185

Scott, — (C.)	I. 335, w. at the capture of the Cape of Good Hope.
Sebastiani, — (G.) F.	IV. 213-15, Constantinople; 226, Isle Prota, Dardanelles.
Sherbrooke, Sir John Coape (G.)	VI. 200, Com. Penobscot exped., U.S.
Silna Maha (G.) *Burmah*	VI. 326, Burmese War.
Sluysken, — (G.) *Du.*	I. 334, Com. at the Cape of Good Hope.
Smith, — (L.Col.)	V. 66, Persian Gulf.
Smith, — (L.Col.)	VI. 313, Burmese War.
Soliman, Aga (L.Col.) *Turk*	II. 329, Acre.
Sombreuil, — (G.) F. *Royalist*	I. 278, Quiberon exped.; 279, executed.
Sorbier, — (G.) F.	III. 321, invas. flotilla.
Soult, — (Mar.) F.	III. 230, Boulogne; 326, invas. flotilla.
Soworow, — (G.) *Rus.*	II. 307, Italy.
Spencer, — (Maj.)	I. 252, capture of St. Domingo.
Spencer, — (Col.)	III. 87-8, Rosetta, Egypt exped.
Stewart, Duncan (L.)	V. 193, capture of Amboyna.
Stewart, — (L.Col.)	II. 451, capture of Ferrol. III. 43-50, Col. Copenhagen.
Stewart, — (Maj.)	VI. 20-1, k. in actn. Pietra Nera, Calabria.
Stricker, — (G.) *U.S.*	VI. 190, Baltimore.
Stuart, Hon. Charles (L.G.)	I. 212, Com. Corsica exped. II. 220-3, G. capture of Minorca.
Stuart, James (Col.)	I. 336-8, capture of Trincomalee, Ceylon; 414, capture of Colombo, Ceylon.
Stuart, Sir John (G.)	IV. 123, Com. at Messina, Italy; 124-5, Battle of Maida.
Suchet, — (G.) F.	II. 437, recapture of Genoa.
Taylor, — (G.) *U.S.*	VI. 95, Chesapeake; 173, w. in actn. Kinsale, U.S.
Taylor, — (Maj.)	VI. 115, capts. U.S. gbts. Canadian Lakes.
Tehudy, — (Col.) *Swiss*	II. 315, St. Elmo, Naples.
Tellier, Le (L.) F.	I. 209, Corsica.
Tharreau, — (G.) F.	III. 77-8, Porto Ferrajo.
Thornton, — (Col.)	VI. 234, Chandeleur Isles.
Tidy, — (L.Col.) *D.A.G.*	VI. 336-7, Burmese War.
Timbrell, — (C.)	VI. 352, Burmese War.
Todd, — (C.)	V. 145-9, Isle of France.
Toussaint-L'Ouverture (Chief)	II. 280, siege of St. Domingo. III. 162, Com. at St. Domingo; 164, d. in France.
Trigge, — (L.G.)	II. 420-1, Com. at the capture of Surinam. III. 150, capture of St. Bartholomew, W. Indies.
Valdez, — (L.G.) *Sp.*	I. 80-4, council of war at Toulon.
Vandamme, — (G.) F.	II. 349, Holland exped.
Vaubois, — (G.) F.	II. 168, Malta exped.; 174, Gvr. of Malta; 211, 437-9, 444, blockade of Malta; 445, surrenders.
Vaux, — (G.) F.	II. 341, w. in actn. Egypt.
Verdier, — (G.) F.	II. 341, Egypt exped.
Vilettes, — (L.Col.)	I. 211, Corsica exped.
Villeneuve, — (L.)	II. 111, k. at the capture of Trinidad.
Vinache, — (L.) F.	II. 333, surrender of Aboukir Fort.
Wadsworth, — (Col.) *U.S.*	VI. 170, Chesapeake Bay.
Wahab, — (Maj.)	VI. 303-7, Burmese War; 347, App.
Wale, — (Brg.G.)	V. 191, capture of Guadaloupe.
Ward, — (L.Col.)	II. 131-3, in actn. Ostende.
Washington, George (G.) *U.S.*	II. 360, Minister (1799).
Watrin, — (G.) F.	II. 78-9-81, Com. blockade of Porto Ferrajo, Isle of Elba.

Welles, — (Brg.G.) *U.S.*	V. 422, Boston.
Wellesley, Sir Arthur (Maj.G.)	IV. 208, Copenhagen ; 296, L.G. Battle of Vimiera.
Wellington, Marquis of	VI. 11, 120, 212, G. Bayonne.
Wetherall, — (Maj.G.)	V. 296, capture of Java.
White, — (L.)	VI. 267, passenger on board Nautilus.
White, — (Brg.G.)	I. 251, Com. St. Domingo exped.
Whitelock, — (L.Col.)	I. 129, Jérémie, W. Indies. IV. 281, L.G. Com. Buenos Ayres exped.
Whyte, — (Maj.G.)	I. 409, Com. exped. to Du. Guayana, S. America.
Williamson, — (Maj.G.)	I. 129, L.Gvr. of Jamaica.
Wilson, Christopher (C.)	VI. 316, Burmese War.
Winder, — (G.) *U.S.*	VI. 176-7, Battle of Bladensburg ; 188-90, Baltimore.
Wood, — (Col.)	IV. 231, M.P. (1808), moves for Parliamentary inquiry in Duckworth's actn.
Wood, — (C.)	V. 417, A.D.C. on board Java, w. in actn.
Yates, Charles (L.)	V. 199, capture of Banda Neira. VI. 315, Maj. ; 317-19-24, Burmese War.
York, H.R.H. Duke of (G.)	I. 98-9, Com. Holland exped. ; 344-9-50, Holland exped.

INDEX TO NAVAL ACTIONS

PART IV

NAVAL ACTIONS

GENERAL ACTIONS—LINE OF BATTLE SHIPS—FRIGATES—BRIGS OR SLOOPS

GENERAL ACTIONS

Algesiras, III. 97–107. Algiers, IV. 278–91.——Basque Roads, IV. 395–429.—— Calder's actn., III. 356–75. Camperdown, II. 75–88. Copenhagen, III. 45–62; IV. 200–12.——Dance's actn., E.I.C., III. 249–54. Dardanelles, IV. 217–31. Duckworth's actn., IV. 95–107.——E.I.C. ships' actns., I. 220–1; V. 132–6.——Genoa, I. 285–94. Gut of Gibraltar, III. 113–17.——Hood's actns., IV. 175–7, 299–301.—— Isle Groix, I. 273–6.——Lissa, V. 234–45.——Madagascar, V. 285–94 May 28th to 1st June, I. 145–200.——Navarino VI. 364–80. Nile, II. 171–210.——St. Vincent, II. 34–60. Strachan's actn., IV. 1–13.——Trafalgar, III. 384–474.

LINE OF BATTLE SHIPS

Agamemnon (64) and Fr. frigates, I. 117–18. Arrogant (74) and Victorious (74), with Fr. Sq., I. 390–4.——Calcutta (54) captd. by Fr. Sq., IV. 47–50. Centurion (50), with Marengo (74) and consorts, III. 283–6.——Glatton (54) and Fr. frigates, I. 372–6. ——Hoche (74), Fr. captd. by Br. Sq., II. 142–51.——Jupiter (50) repulsed by Preneuse (40), II. 392–4.—— Leander (50) captd. by Généreux (74), II. 259–65. Leopard (50) and Chesapeake (36), IV. 250–6.——Mars (74) capts. Hercule (74), II. 120–4.—— Romney (50) capts. Sibylle (40), I. 231–2.——Victorious (74) capts. Rivoli (74), V. 338–41.

FRIGATES

Æolus (32) and Didon (40), IV. 56–7. Africaine (38), captd. by Iphigénie (40) and Astrée (36), V. 173–9; recaptd. 181. Ambuscade (32) captd. by Baïonnaise (28), II. 273–9. Amelia (38) and Aréthuse (40), VI. 36–42. Amethyst (36) capts. Thetis (40), IV. 376–9; capts. Niemen (40), V. 14–16. Astræa (32) capts. Gloire (36), I. 315–16. ——Blanche (32) capts. Pique (36), I. 309–12. Blanche (36) captd. by Topaze (40) and consorts, IV. 38–46. Blanche (38) capts. Guerrière (40), IV. 160–2. Bordelais (24) des. Curieux (18), III. 124. Boston (32) and Embuscade (36), I. 110–12.—— Caroline (36) capts. Du. Maria-Riggersbergen (36), IV. 179–80. Carysfort (28) capts. Castor (32), I. 228–9. Cerberus (32) and five Sp. frigates, II. 404–5. Cleopatra (32) captd. by Ville de Milan (40), IV. 20–3. Clyde (38) capts. Vestale (36), II. 384–5. U.S. Constellation (36) capts. Insurgente (36), II. 363–4. Crescent (36) capts. Réunion (36), I. 114–16.——Dædalus (32) capts. Prudente (36), II. 357. Dryad (36) capts. Eoserpine (40), I. 369–70.——Endymion (40) and U.S. President (44), VI. 240–3. Prurotas (38) and Clorinde (40), VI. 132–8.——Fisgard (38) capts. Immortalité (40), II. 160–1.——Guerrière (38) captd. by U.S. Constitution (44), V. 372–83.—— Hebrus (36) capts. Etoile (40), VI. 128–30. Horatio (38) and consorts capture Junon (40), V. 5–8. Hyæna (24) captd. by Concorde (40), I. 105–6. Hydra (38) des. Confiante (36), II. 133–5.——Indefatigable (44) capts. Virginie (40), I. 361–2; also with Amazon (36) des. Droits de l'Homme (74), II. 13–22.——Java (38) captd. by U.S. Constitution (44),

V. 409-16.   Junon (38) captd. by Renommée (40) and consorts, V. 47-9. ——Lively (32) capts. Tourterelle (28), I. 313-15.   Lowestoffe (32) and Dido (28) capture Minerve (40), I. 321-23.——Macedonian (38) captd. by U.S. United States (44), V. 394-400. Mermaid (32) and Loire (40), II. 154-6.   Minerve (38), capture of, III. 182-5.—— Nymphe (36) capts. Cléopâtre (36), I. 106-9.——Phœbe (36) capts. Africaine (40), III. 127-9 ; also with Cherub (26) capts. U.S. Essex (46), VI. 150-3.   Phœnix (36) capts. Didon (40), IV. 65-71.——San Fiorenzo (36) capts. Psyché (32), IV. 18-20; also capts. Piémontaise (40), 308-10.   Santa Margarita (36) recapts. Thames (32), I. 366.   Seahorse (38) capts. Turk. Badere-Zaffer (52), IV. 349-54.   Seine (38) capts. Vengeance (40), III. 23-6.   Shannon (38) capts. U.S. Chesapeake (36), VI. 50-66.   Sibylle (38) capts. Forte (40), II. 365-74.   Southampton (32) and Vestale (36), I. 325-6 ; capts. Améthyste (44), V. 352-3.   Spartan (38), with Cérès (40) and consorts, V. 114-17. —— Terpsichore (32) capts. Sp. Mahonesa (34), I. 398-400 ; also capts. Vestale (36), 402-6. Thames (32) and Uranie (40), I. 118-19.——Unicorn (36) capts. Tribune (36), I. 367-8.——Venus (32) and Sémillante (36), I. 103-4.——Warren Hastings, E.I.C., captd. by Piémontaise, IV. 149-52.   Wilhelmina (32) (en flûte) and Psyche (36), III. 267-71.

BRIGS OR SLOOPS

Alacrity (18) captd. by Abeille (24), V. 248-52.——Bonne Citoyenne (20) capts. Furieuse (20) (en flûte), V. 23-5.   Boxer (14) captd. by U.S. Enterprise (16), VI. 75-6. ——Carnation (18) captd. by Palinure (16), VI. 331-3.   Childers (14) and Da. Lougen (20), IV. 316-17.——Fairy (16) and Harpy (18) with Pallas (38), III. 3-4.   Frolic (18) captd. by U.S. Wasp (18), V. 389-92.——Halcyon (16) capts. Sp. Neptuno (14), IV. 185.——Little Belt (20) and U.S. President (44), V. 275-81.——Osprey (18) and Egyptienne (36), III. 257.——Peacock (18) destd. by U.S. Hornet (20), VI. 46-8. Pelican (18) beats off Médée (36), I. 396 ; capts. U.S. Argus (20), VI. 78-81.   Penguin (18) captd. by U.S. Hornet (20), VI. 261-4.   Pitt (12) capts. Superbe (14), IV. 181-3. ——Reindeer (18) captd. by U.S. Wasp (20), VI. 161-3.——Speedy (14) capts. Sp. Gamo (32), III. 133.   Sylph (18) and a Fr. frigate, III. 145-6.——Wizard (16) and Requin (16), IV. 338-41.   Wolverine (13) destd. by Blonde (30), III. 259-60.

www.ingramcontent.com/pod-product-compliance
Lightning Source LLC
Chambersburg PA
CBHW071003160426
43193CB00012B/1896